"PEOPLE LOVE ME! MY MEN THINK I'M JESUS CHRIST!"

John Gotti laughed at the law as he defeated the government in trial after trial.

He waved and smiled at the admiring crowds as he strode through the city like a king in his thousand-dollar suits.

But he did even more than that.

He killed and killed and killed again in his dramatic rise from being an obscure Queens gangster to head man in the nation's most powerful crime family.

He conducted affairs with beautiful women while posing as a model husband and father.

He survived savage attacks against his life to enjoy the sweet taste of bloody revenge.

He was the ultimate New York Untouchable—until the most determined government anticrime force ever assembled found the one weak spot in his impregnable armor, and brought him down in a fall that shook the entire underworld.

GOTTI
Rise and Fall

GOTTI
Rise and Fall

· ·

**Jerry Capeci
and Gene Mustain**

AN ONYX BOOK

ONYX
Published by the Penguin Group
Penguin Books USA Inc., 375 Hudson Street,
New York, New York 10014, U.S.A.
Penguin Books Ltd, 27 Wrights Lane,
London W8 5TZ, England
Penguin Books Australia Ltd, Ringwood,
Victoria, Australia
Penguin Books Canada Ltd, 10 Alcorn Avenue,
Toronto, Ontario, Canada M4V 3B2
Penguin Books (N.Z.) Ltd, 182-190 Wairau Road,
Auckland 10, New Zealand

Penguin Books Ltd, Registered Offices:
Harmondsworth, Middlesex, England

First published by Onyx, an imprint of Dutton Signet,
a division of Penguin Books USA Inc.

First Printing, June, 1996
10 9 8 7 6

For my mother, Anna Capeci,
who always did her best
for our family—and still does

For Doreen, forever and again

ACKNOWLEDGMENTS

We worked on this book for nine years—but were aware of it only for the last three. Nine years, though, is how long in different forums we've been reporting on and writing about John Gotti and the Gambino family of Cosa Nostra.

During that time, close to an entire forest fell to provide the paper consumed by various law enforcement agencies to compile reports and legal papers on Gotti and the Gambino family. We've studied all the public paper and a great deal of the secret.

More crucially, our story also rests on multiple interviews with many of its key characters. We even spoke with Gotti once, for forty minutes, in what was more chat than actual interview—we happened to find ourselves in a situation that neither party could do anything about and so we decided to be sociable.

Some of our formal interviewees would surprise readers, if we could disclose their identities. For obvious reasons, they asked to remain anonymous.

Most conversations in the book come from the interviews, and from transcripts of tape recordings made by secret wiretaps and listening devices, grand jury and trial testimony, and in some cases from still-secret law enforcement interviews of witnesses and others with knowledge of events.

A few of the conversations are based on what people recall being told. As we said in our two previous books, *Mob Star* and *Murder Machine,* memory is never completely perfect, so no nonfiction book can be. But once again, as we complete our gangster trilogy, we have tried to make this one as true as experience and judgment enable it to be.

Some people we can publicly thank for giving us their time and patience. They include people who were or who are in either of New York's two federal prosecutor offices—Patrick Cotter, Patrick Fitzgerald, Frances Fragos, John Gleeson, Douglas Grover, Karyn Kenney, Walter Mack, Andrew Maloney, Kenneth McCabe, Edward McDonald, Leonard Michaels, James Orenstein, Charles Rose, and Laura Ward—as well in the Federal Bureau of Investigation, particularly William Doran, James Fox, George Gabriel, Bruce Mouw, Arthur Ruffels, and Joseph Valiquette.

At the state law enforcement level, we thank Michael Cherkasky, Ellen Corcella, Barbara Jones, Mark Feldman, Eric Krause, Robert Morgenthau, Jeffrey Schlanger, and Eric Seidel.

Though sometimes they couldn't say much, we also appreciate courtesies shown us by defense lawyers Albert Aronne, Joseph Benfante, Judd Burstein, Benjamin Brafman, Anthony Cardinale, Charles Carnesi, Bruce Cutler, David DePetris, James DiPietro, Jack Eversoff, Alan Futerfas, Jay Goldberg, David Greenfield, Albert Krieger, James LaRossa, John Mitchell, Richard Rehbock, Michael Rosen, George Santangelo, Gerald Shargel, and Joel Winograd. We also thank Lewis Kasman and Carlo Vaccarezza, two friends of John Gotti's, for agreeing to speak on the record.

We want to tip our hat to some buddies in the journalism trade who made covering Gotti a lot of fun, on occasion—Pete Bowles, Bill Boyle, John Cappelli, Bruce Frankel, Charles Feldman, Enzo Ficile, Ed Frost, Pablo Guzman, Murray Kempton, Hap Hairston, Beth Holland, Patricia Hurtado, David Lewis, Michael Lipack, Arnold Lubash, David Martin, Fran McMorris, Phil Messing, John Miller, Mary Murphy, Jim Nolan, Juliet Papa, Karen Phillips, Ron Powers, Bill Reilly, Shelly Strickler, and Angela Troisi.

Two others that we spend an awful lot of time with, star reporters Ying Chan and Tom Robbins, bolstered us with their friendship—as did Dominick Marrano, Eliot Wald, and our literary agent, Faith Childs.

Lastly, we thank people who forfeited an awful lot of

time with us, the people we love the most and who will always be tops in our book—Barbara, Matthew, Jenna, and Craig Capeci, and Ms. Doreen Weisenhaus.

JC, GM
New York City

Prologue

People loved me. I coulda been fuckin' president if I wasn't having so much fun doin' what I was doin'. You think I'm kiddin'? What's that Bill Clinton got? A forty-three approval ratin' in the polls? Stop any two people on the fuckin' street, one of 'em would like me. That puts me seven points ahead right there.

What'd he ever do I didn't do? He smoked pot, dodged the draft, and poked girls he wasn't married to. Went to Cambridge? Where's that? Massachusetts someplace? I went to Green Haven. Takes *cajones*, that's "balls" to you, to go there.

I didn't even dodge the draft neither. Had this run-in with a cement mixer when I was a kid. Fucked up my feet. Woulda never passed the physical, if my juvenile sheet didn't already knock me out. I tried pot, but could never see what the big deal was. Me? Just give me a martini and I'm happy as a *cacumbero*—"cucumber" to you. Boodles, if you got it. Straight up. Dry as the desert.

Minchia! One of those sure would taste good about now.

People loved me all right. I got letters, I get letters. Thousands of 'em. From all over the fuckin' world. They love me in fuckin' England. Must be some Cockney connection. Here's one right here. I'm not makin' this up, these letters are for real, my lawyers got all the copies. Let's see—I gotta get my readin' glasses—it's from the Canadian Red Cross Society. I know that ain't England, and Canada don't count in no election, but hold on a minute, I'm just pickin' one out of the pile. Just an example of what I'm talkin' about.

It says, "Dear Mr. Gotti, since your unique talent is unquestionably worthy of celebrity status, we would be very grateful if you would consider making a special contribution of some special item that could be auctioned."

It goes on, some stupid charity event. I love that, "unique talent." But letters like that I don't bother answerin'.

But here's one that got to me. From a lady in Pennsylvania. "Dear Mr. Gotti," she says. "I am writing this letter to you to see if you would write a letter of encouragement to my aunt who is terminally ill with cancer. She and I both are great admirers of yours and if anyone knows about courage it's you."

Ain't that somethin'? It goes on.

"I know in my heart a note of best wishes from you would mean so much. God bless you and your family. I pray you'll be reunited with your family in the very near future."

That one, I asked one of my lawyers to write the poor sick lady a letter. Give her somethin' to smile about. I told her to "stay strong." Which is one of my favorite sayin's.

My men used to say I was like Jesus Christ. I'm not foolin'. They did. Right after I became boss, guy comes up to me, he says he always knew I was gonna be boss because, even when we were just kids on the corner, I had what it took. So now he says he's so proud of me because I'm bringing peace to the family and makin' everybody feel good. He says, "You're Jesus Christ."

Back in '87, when I beat this case a little girl prosecutor tried to fuck me up with, a real frame job, a guy comes running down the street. This was when the fuckin' Mets weren't no lay-down Sally team. The guy says, "Queens has two world champions. The Mets and John Gotti!"

I was on the cover of *Time. People. New York.* I don't know how many fuckin' others. I lose track. They wrote songs about me and played 'em on Howard fucking Stern. Fuckin' public television did a big show on me. It was right after one they did on Eleanor Roosevelt or maybe Winston Churchill, some famous fuck, I don't even remember.

They called me lots of names. Johnny Boy. Dapper Don. Teflon Don. Prince of Mulberry Street. Two with fuckin' "king" in it—King of the Volcano. King of Queens. Naturally, they also called me the Godfather. You gotta go read the book to understand them all, but just John suited me fine. People get famous, they only need one name. Cher. Madonna. Magic. Michael. John.

I did get pretty fuckin' famous. I couldn't go nowhere and not be recognized. Uptown. Downtown. Motown. Notown. Made my work harder sometimes, but what're ya gonna do? Run and hide? I told my men, "We ain't runnin' scared." I wasn't like this boss they call Chin, a Mustache Pete if you ask me. Walkin' around in his pajamas to make people think he's some loony tune. Not my style. People know what we are; people ain't stupid.

I used to go down to Florida, to this rich kid friend of mine Lewis Kasman's place. Lot of celebrities there. They'd all come by the pool and bother me. I was in a bar once, fuckin' prime minister of Canada came up to me one night—there we go with Canada again, but what the fuck, I'm tellin' you things that happened—he came up to me and just asked to shake my fuckin' hand. So I let 'im. Sophia Loren? Same thing. Eddie Murphy? Forget about it. I met so many people, I lose track. Have to write myself little notes.

One time, I moved right into a suite that that Dan Quayle just left. Could still smell his cologne, or maybe it was the fuckin' Secret Service agents'. You know how a dog can smell a man's fear? Well, I could always smell an agent. Same thing with rats—informers to you, I had like a fifth sense, or is that a sixth? I forget.

Back up in New York, I used to have a martini or two at my buddy Carlo Vaccarezza's place on the Upper East Side. Real nice joint. Anthony Quinn came over to my table. Mickey Rourke came over. I met one lady there, Lisa Gastineau, who'd knock your socks off. She did mine, have to tell ya. She was that football player's ex-wife, and a real nice lady too. Called me Papa Schultz, like a lot of ladies did, 'cause I was such a throwback, a regular Dutch Schultz, brainy and ballsy and spiffy too, you know what I'm sayin'?

Those were the days. My kid Junior got married, I threw him a fifty-thousand-dollar banquet at the Helmsley Palace. Fuckin' Cristal Rose at every table. One Christmas, I spent two hundred balloons, that's thousands, holding a little feast by the water, fancy catering hall over in Canarsie, that's in Brooklyn. Whole world was there, every good fellow in my family and other families too.

I came out of the Bronx. Didn't have two cents to rub together when I was born neither. When Vicky had our first kid, I had to beat the hospital out of the fuckin' bill. Couldn't pay for my kid. Kids. I love my five kids. One's gone, but I still count 'im. We still send him messages with little notices in the *Daily News* every year. Vicky and the other kids do.

Beautiful kid. Smart as a whip. It hurts to think about him, and I'm one of the last of the fuckin' tough guys.

I learned what it's about from a tough guy. I'm not talkin' Carlo Gambino, but Neil. Carlo knew some things—he's the one who got me to read up on Machiavelli in the joint—but Neil, now there was a man's man. He'd call a cocksucker a cocksucker. To his face. You wanna do something about it? Let's dance, motherfucker. Pardon my language, but I get excited.

Neil shoulda been our boss after Carlo, not Paul, who was a *cazzu,* a prick. Don't ask me who killed Paul. For all I know, the cops killed fuckin' Paul. I just don't wanna get into that now. I don't make no admissions, unless I'm being hit with a parking ticket, malicious mopery, somethin' like that. Otherwise, the fuckin' government just uses it against you forever. *Minchia!*

A lot of people got famous with me. My lawyer Bruce Cutler, for one. They put him in *GQ* in a bikini, but without me, he was just a weight lifter. Jerry Shargel, another lawyer. They put him in *The New Yorker,* said maybe he's the best criminal defense guy there is. Yeah, well, I knew Jerry when he was down on his luck and he came to me beggin' for work.

As famous as I was, I wasn't a selfish boss. I coulda been a billionaire if I wanted. A billionaire! Guys ask me, "How come you never built a mansion?" Well, two reasons. One, I couldn't show it, because, you know, on paper I was only making eighty, ninety balloons a year. Two, I didn't need it. What do I need a mansion for?

Once, when I was lecturin' Frankie about Sammy startin' up all these new companies—Frankie and Sammy were two big guys of mine—I told Frankie, "All I want is a ham sandwich, a nice ham sandwich."

I used to throw dollars around, I put a lot of bookmakers' kids through college. But Frankie knew the point I was makin'. All I wanted was to be what I became. How many people get to do that?

My biggest problem was that I came along later than I should have. We'd built ourselves up pretty big and this bunch of Little Lord Fauntleroys decided to chop us down a notch. Me, Sammy, and Frankie. They threw the kitchen sink at us, and we'd never have had such a hard time fightin' 'em off if so many fellows weren't bein' jackasses, shovin' shit up their nose, or puttin' needles in their arms, or gettin' caught sellin' it.

But I don't wanna get into that neither; that is a very sensitive subject for me, and you'll just have to find out why on your own.

Well, that's enough of that. Gotta go do my push-ups. Stay strong.

We asked John Gotti to write the introduction for this book. Through his lawyer, he declined. So we crawled into his mind and wrote it for him. Based on our nine years of listening to tape-recorded conversations in which he participated, and writing and reporting about the man, we are confident that if he had accepted, his introduction would have turned out very close to what you have just read. As he said, the letters quoted above are real.

CHAPTER 1

• • • • • • • • • • • • •

Cosa Nostra

Sammy's heart began pounding after he heard some deadly serious voice from downstairs call out his name. But it was a good kind of heartbeat, born of joy, not fear, and a glorious feeling washed over him. He had been to the wedding altar, and in the delivery room twice, but never in his thirty-two years had he felt such exhilaration.

Even so, he kept it bottled inside as he began descending the stairs. The men waiting in the basement regarded the ceremony that was about to take place as a solemn event, as did he. This was how they replenished themselves, how they sustained their peculiar tradition.

Through experience, and he believed perhaps even by nature, Sammy was unusually adept at acting one way while feeling another—and so when he reached the bottom, he seemed calm, resolute, dead-serious.

He quickly recognized the towering presence of Paul, and as his alert eyes narrowed in the flickering candlelight, he saw many men seated in silence around a table. Like him, all were dressed in funeral parlor suits. Sammy usually wore construction foreman-type clothes, but his boss had told him to "dress up," meaning dignified, a clear hint that the long-awaited day had finally come.

Sammy saw Paul sit down and motion him to sit in an empty chair next to his at the head of the table, and as he walked toward it, he felt as though he was outside his body, like he was watching himself in a sweet dream.

"Do you know why you are here?" Paul asked.

"No," Sammy lied. He knew enough about what was happening to know that a man in his situation was never to assume it actually was.

"Look around," Paul said. "Do you know these men?"

"Yes," Sammy replied, knowing that in this instance it was okay to acknowledge that he did, by face if not by rank.

"We are an honored society, a society of Cosa Nostra," Paul said, using the Italian words for "our thing." "We are about to induct you as a member of our family of Cosa Nostra."

Sammy nodded solemnly as a second wave of utter joy coursed through him. The life he had wanted since he was a teenager and Cosa Nostra was known on his streets as the Mafia was becoming his. He kept nodding yes as Paul asked questions—Was he loyal? Would he obey the rules of Cosa Nostra and put its interests above his interests, even his wife and children? And because Cosa Nostra did not recognize any government, did he promise never to cooperate with any authority but his Cosa Nostra superiors?

These were the tenets of a tradition that originated in the villages of feudal Sicily, when groups of families formed clans to resist the tyranny of foreign invaders. The clans became known as "mafias," individual members as "mafioso," or men of honor.

Over the ages, as they became the unelected arbiters of local disputes, mafia clans became as corrupt and rapacious as any foreign invader; crime became their profession, a way of life that descendants of the so-called men of honor began exporting to America's shores in the latter part of the nineteenth century.

By 1945, when Sammy was born, the clans had begun secretly referring to their way of life as Cosa Nostra, and they were embedded in the fabric of many American cities, especially New York City, a laboratory for crime and also Sammy's hometown.

Cosa Nostra was the most powerful authority in neighborhoods populated by immigrants from Sicily and southern Italy. It was especially true in Bensonhurst, the neighborhood that incubated Sammy; it was as if part of Palermo had been transplanted lock, stock, and fig tree to Brooklyn, the "broken land" of an old Dutch colony that became one of the five boroughs of New York City.

Sammy's father came from a village outside Palermo and became a hardworking legitimate businessman who built up a small dress factory after sneaking into New

York from Canada around 1920. One day at the factory, where fourteen-year-old Sammy helped out, two snarling men came in and told Sammy's fifty-seven-year-old father that he was going to have work-stopping union problems unless he paid them money.

"What're we gonna do? They're gonna hurt you," Sammy said to his father, Gerardo, after the men left.

"Don't say a word about this," his father replied. "I'll take care of it, I know a man."

Sammy was his father's only son—an older brother had died of disease when Sammy was young, as had an older sister—and the youngest of three surviving children. He was a smallish kid who fought at the drop of a dime to prove he was not weak or afraid.

He also already knew his way around Bensonhurst well enough to know where to get a gun, and he was secretly carrying one the next time the two extortionists arrived at his father's factory. He intended to shoot if they began hurting his father.

To his surprise, the men came in and kissed his father on the cheek. "Why didn't you tell me you were a friend of Sevito?" one of them said. "We're sorry we troubled you."

After the men left, Sammy's father said, "I know Sevito from the old country. I spoke to him. He is a man of honor, a mafioso. We are legitimate people, mafiosi are not. But what could I do? The police? The men would have come back. Sometimes we need the mafiosi to protect us. Do you understand?"

Sammy understood because as a younger boy he had noticed how adults spoke in respectful yet fearful whispers about certain men in the neighborhood who acted like they owned it. Sammy picked up on things faster than other kids, even though he had failed two grades and done miserably on tests—but that was because he was born with a learning disability that no one knew anything about. The frustration he had trying to read numbers and letters was another reason he clocked any kid who looked at him funny.

"Yeah, I understand, but you didn't have nothin' to worry about," Sammy cockily told his father, taking out the gun and waving it boastfully, thinking his old man

would be impressed—until his father began beating the
daylights out of him.

"Never take up the gun! It'll break your mother's
heart! It makes you one of them! Do you understand!"

Sammy took his punishment stoically; stoicism, like
physical toughness, was already a hallmark. Still, from
that day forward, he knew he possessed the will to kill, if
need be, and he knew what he wanted to become—a man
of honor, a mafioso, a member of whatever society it was
that produced such potent men as Sevito.

In time, Sammy's parents gave up trying to steer him
toward a legitimate life. By 1968, when he was twenty-
three years old, Sammy eagerly accepted when a man
who acted as though he owned part of Bensonhurst invited him into his little gang of would-be Cosa Nostra car
thieves, burglars, and armed robbers.

"You will never catch me in a lie," Thomas "Shorty"
Spero told his new recruit. "I will never lie to you."

Now in the basement nine years later, Sammy took an
oath that he would never lie to Paul.

Paul paused for a time, giving weight to this final question: "If I asked, would you kill for me?"

"Yes," Sammy replied, as coldly as he could.

During his nine-year apprenticeship under Shorty
Spero, and others, the boy who had been ready to shoot
the two men who tried to extort his father had proved
himself capable of murder—once, in 1970. The murder,
ordered by Shorty Spero, had made this day of initiation
nearly inevitable, for the victim was a friend of Sammy's
and a member of Shorty's gang, yet Sammy did the job
calmly, resolutely, and well. Such ability was a main condition of membership in Cosa Nostra.

Shorty told Sammy that murder was how a society like
theirs maintained its law and order. Cosa Nostra was like
an army; it had to have its own laws. Shorty's analogy
made sense to Sammy; by that time, he had served in the
United States Army for two years and believed strongly
in discipline and chain of command.

Paul grabbed Sammy's trigger finger and pinched it so
hard that blood spurted out. He then held the finger over
a holy card of some Roman Catholic saint as another man
set the card afire. Sammy stared at Paul so intently that
he failed to see what saint was pictured on the card, but

he later found out any saint would have sufficed; only the blood and the fire mattered.

"Honor the oath," Paul said, as the flame licked at Sammy's finger. "If you divulge any of the secrets of this society, your soul will burn like this saint."

Sammy stayed still as a stone, honoring the oath with his pain and believing in it like he believed in nothing else. In the culture of Bensonhurst, betrayal was worse than murder. Do most anything, but never "rat."

Paul, boss of the Gambino family of Cosa Nostra, flicked the card away and held out his arms like a pope. He was a six-foot-two, sixty-two-year-old man with an equine face who always told regular people he was just the son of a butcher, which, in addition to all else, he actually was.

Sammy's face was mostly a gray block of granite, except for the indented cheeks and dark, hooded eyes. He looked perpetually mournful, even when he permitted himself a slight contented smile, as he did now, embracing Paul and kissing him on both cheeks. He had to reach up to do it, because he was only five feet five; he was as hard and sturdy as a concrete-filled drum, however—that was why some people called him Sammy Bull.

Paul stepped back and motioned toward the other men there to witness the ceremony by which the family "made" new members. Paul had become the leader a year before, in 1976, when over the wishes and resentments of some he succeeded his cousin and brother-in-law, Carlo Gambino, who had died of a heart attack at seventy-four.

For Paul, it was like following Frank Sinatra to the stage because Carlo was so legendary. Despite a life in crime, he had spent only twenty-two months in jail, for bootlegging whisky when he was young. Carlo had become boss in 1957. Over the next nineteen years, because local cops and politicians were no match and national authorities like the Federal Bureau of Investigation cared little about Cosa Nostra, he was very successful. Building on everyday rackets such as gambling, prostitution, and loan-sharking, he orchestrated schemes that affected everyday city life and commerce in many ways, from monopolistic practices that added a few dollars to the cost of clothes and food to the bid-rigging, bribes, and physical threats that added thousands to the cost of unloading ships and building skyscrapers.

Paul's surname was Castellano, but the family, or borgata, would carry on as the Gambino family, out of respect for its long-time don, or lord, the great Carlo.

As Paul made the introductions, Sammy embraced and kissed each man at the table. First came two men who, with Paul, made up what Paul called the "administration" of the family—Aniello Dellacroce, the underboss, or second-in-command, and Joe N. Gallo, the consigliere, or in-house lawyer or adviser. Then came several capos, or caporegimes—captains; they commanded decinas, or crews of soldiers.

The captains came from all five boroughs of New York City—Brooklyn, Queens, Staten Island, the Bronx, and Manhattan. Many held important positions in businesses, unions, and trade groups in the sanitation, garment, construction, shipping, trucking, and food industries.

Many, such as Don Carlo's son Thomas, were fabulously rich. Tommy Gambino practically ran the city's garment center, where many of the nation's clothes were sewn.

The captains directly commanded about two hundred made men and ten times as many unmade "associates," men who had not passed muster and might never do so. Nevertheless, associates, like soldiers, were to give captains a slice of any illegally earned pie, which the capos, after taking their own cut, were obliged to give the administration. The sizes of the slices depended on ability and ambition. The system, adapted from Julius Caesar's ideas about army structure, was designed to protect the boss; in Carlo's case, for nineteen glorious years, it did.

The men stood and locked hands in a circle around the newest initiate to Caesar's system, Salvatore "Sammy Bull" Gravano.

"You are now a member of our family," Paul said.

Paul then led Sammy over to an elderly man that Sammy had worked for for the last few years, Salvatore "Toddo" Aurello. "This is the capo of your decina," Paul said. "You must obey your capo like you obey me."

Sammy nodded respectfully and kissed his capo; he had

been an associate in Toddo Aurello's crew since a quarrel with Shorty Spero's brother led Shorty to regretfully decide it was best for everyone that Sammy associate with someone else. While with Toddo Aurello, Sammy had built up his own little crew of associates and begun to make attention-getting sums of money; being an "earner" was another important condition of membership in Cosa Nostra.

Sammy sat down at the table beside Toddo Aurello and watched as other men were called downstairs and also inducted. Afterward, Paul listed some additional rules—a made man was referred to as "a friend of ours," and unmade man "a friend of mine." Made men were never to deal in drugs, violate another's wife or children, or raise their hands against each other. The penalty for such crimes was death.

Sammy was stirred by the nobility of Paul's words; he briefly imagined himself as some character in *The Godfather*. He immediately regretted such a trivial thought but could not deny that the movie had sent him and many friends gloriously floating out of theaters five years before.

Paul next revealed to Sammy and the others the identities of the boss, underboss, and consigliere—the administrations—of four other families in New York. The families' competing interests, Paul added, were sorted out by a "Commission" composed of bosses of each family—although at this particular moment in time, one family's Commission privileges had been suspended; too many of its members had broken the Cosa Nostra rule against drug dealing.

The Commission wrote the laws of Cosa Nostra, and families wishing to "make" a new member had to get Commission approval. In former years, bosses of Cosa Nostra families in other cities had sat on the Commission, but these families had declined or gone their own way, and now all power resided in New York City, known in Cosa Nostra as "the volcano" because it was prone to violent eruption.

"You are now part of the brotherhood," Paul Castellano said after all the inductees had taken the oath.

Sammy felt as though he had been given the keys to some secret kingdom, and he had.

That was in 1977. Sammy Gravano always said that

day in a basement in the borough of Brooklyn was the proudest day in his life, and he meant it, even eight years later, in 1985, when he and nine others in the Gambino family murdered Paul Castellano.

CHAPTER 2

•••••••••••••

Johnny Boy

One of the other murderers of Paul Castellano was destined to become a household name: John Gotti. In 1985, however, he was just a local underworld phenomenon, a champion of Cosa Nostra's oldest traditions who looked thoroughly modern. He was a man of many such contradictions, and he had bullied and manipulated his way into a prominent but precarious position—acting capo of a decina in Queens that was in hot water with Paul.

"Johnny Boy" was made in 1977, the same year as Sammy Bull but in a later ceremony. Over eight years, in different crews in markedly different ways, each rose to prominence. They were not friends so much as acquaintances who saw each other at weddings, wakes, and funerals. They never committed a crime together until they committed the crime of their lives.

Gotti portrayed himself as a true believer of Cosa Nostra's rules, yet many of his most loyal followers dealt heroin, a drug that undermined New York City as much as the families themselves. He was clever, but crude; vain, but insecure. He enjoyed glittery nightclubs, but went home to a suburban-like house in Queens and a homespun wife addicted to soap operas. He was iron-willed, but weak; bold, but reckless to the point of stupidity. He claimed a sixth sense for "rats," but for eighteen years a close friend was an FBI informer. He felt grief, but was remorseless. He said he feared no man, yet he was afraid to fly.

In 1985, the year of his pact with Sammy Gravano, he was forty-five years old, five years Sammy's senior. The old ladies in his neighborhood in Queens said he looked like a movie star. With his silvery, swept-back hair and

customary tan, expensive clothes and stout, confident
bearing, he was physically striking—and with his wit and
mischievous smile, he could be charming.

But when the smile faded, his face suggested too much
villainy for a typical leading man's. A deep scar above
his right lip suggested knives in a back alley; then there
were his pronounced widow's peak, his eyebrows cocked
at dubious angles, and his prominent nose, stern jawline,
and dark, deep-set eyes. At rest, it was a secretive face,
devoid of much emotion except contempt, as if the chip
on his shoulder had ascended there.

The villainy emerged in stories he told about himself.
Over the years, many of these were captured on tape by
secret law enforcement listening devices; almost from the
outset of his Cosa Nostra career, Gotti was always saying
things he should not have, in places where he should have
known better. He often embroidered his stories—but in
ways that made the self-portrait all the more revealing.

In one story he boisterously recounted for his crew
how, in a fight with a man he later learned was a cop, he
broke the cop's legs, ankles, and jaw—and then told them
how he delighted in humiliating his vanquished opponent.

"I told him, 'You want to play anymore? You want to
play, you cocksucker?' I opened his mouth with my finger and put the gun in. 'You want to play anymore?' He
couldn't talk, he was crying like a baby."

A transcript of these overheard homages would fill a
dugout at Yankee Stadium, which was three or four Joe
DiMaggio fly balls from where he was born in the Bronx
in the autumn of 1940, as one of thirteen children and the
third of seven brothers, but he was the son named John
Joseph Gotti Jr. by his mother because he so resembled
his father, a normally broke day laborer.

After Gotti Jr. became infamous, and supposedly nonfiction books and articles were written about him, he was
amazed to see how some writers embroidered his father's
story. They portrayed Gotti Sr. as a Neapolitan immigrant
who scraped a few dollars together and sailed steerage
class to America.

Once, after they met, Gotti expressed his amazement to
Sammy Gravano. "These fuckin' bums that write books,
they're worse than us. My fuckin' father was born in New

Jersey. He ain't never been in Italy his whole fuckin' life. My mother neither."

Gotti's paternal grandparents were the ones who had sailed steerage class to America; they came from a village near Naples, an area populated in the sixth century by Teutonic marauders known as the Goti. His father met his mother, Fannie, after fleeing a dirt-poor Depression-era life in rural New Jersey and crossing the Hudson River to look for work in New York City.

What galled Gotti Jr. even more about the portrayals of his father was that they always insisted Gotti Sr. was an especially hardworking man.

"The guy never worked a fuckin' day in his life," Gotti Jr. complained to Sammy. "He was a rolling stone; he never provided for the family. He never did nothin'. He never earned nothin'. And we never had nothin'."

Gotti's bitterly exaggerated tirade betrayed where the chip on his shoulder came from. At various times Gotti Sr. did work, but at irregular jobs for menial wages that always made his one pleasure in life, gambling, an extremely high-risk diversion. He never won enough or made enough to provide much of anything for his and Fannie's thirteen children, who were born over sixteen years' time; because of poor medical care, two died in infancy.

John Gotti Jr.'s childhood was an endurance test of poverty, the gloom of early death, and four noisy tenement rooms crowded with bawling, brawling children and parents fraught with stress.

It was not surprising that he hit the streets soon as he could and took to them a fierce, in-your-face attitude that impressed and intimidated boys who were older and bigger. When Johnny Boy clocked kids, it was out of anger as much as desire to show he was not weak or afraid.

He learned about the Cosa Nostra way of life the same way most Italian–American boys who were not sons of mafiosi did, by watching the rhythms of the streets, overhearing adult whispers, and hanging around older boys—including his lumberjack-like brother Peter, who was two years older.

The largest colony of Italian Americans in the country was huddled together in northeast Manhattan, which was a long fly ball from the Gotti tenement in the South

Bronx. It was on the streets of Italian Harlem, as the neighborhood was known, that Gotti saw his first mafiosi, and what sights they were for a bitter boy like him. Seemingly, they had everything—money, power, respect—while he, definitely, had nothing.

When Gotti was ten, the father he disparaged did scrape a few bucks together and took his brood to Brooklyn, to a rented house in a neighborhood known as Sheepshead Bay. He might have turned out differently if they had been able to stay, because it was a tranquil community by the Atlantic Ocean where second-generation Italian Americans were moving into the mainstream of society; the mafiosi had less sway there. But after a year the house was sold to a developer, and the family moved to a working-class neighborhood in central Brooklyn known as East New York, where the Cosa Nostra drumbeat thumped as loudly as in Bensonhurst.

East New York was a Wild West cattle town. Streets teemed with betting parlors, bars, and storefronts selling hijacked goods. With the acquiescence of cops, mafiosi operated in plain view. Though he lived in a New Jersey mansion, the master of this ragged universe was a vicious Cosa Nostra boss, Albert Anastasia; a talented, less vicious "earner" of his was Carlo Gambino.

Anastasia's cattle town was the worst place for a boy with anger in his heart and holes in his pockets, and by age twelve Gotti was caught up in the street-level action as a member of a miniature borgata of fleet-footed and foul-mouthed boys who ran errands for the mafiosi. His older brother Peter was a member; brother Richard, two years younger, soon would be.

He stayed in school, but not for more than a few days at a time; his teachers barely minded his absences—because he was a "discipline problem" and a "bully," according to their remarks in his school records. The records also showed that on an IQ test he scored 110, or in the average range of intelligence—a score later inflated by myth makers in Gotti's circle to 140, or near-genius.

Gotti's parents cared little about his school attendance too, even as he began sporting unexplained pocket change and a tattoo of a serpent on his right shoulder; their horizons were limited to the next day's struggle, and if a

cocky child like Johnny Boy could make it on his own a
little early, fine.

His first brush with the law came in 1954, his four-
teenth year, but it only made him more cocky, figura-
tively and literally. A portable cement mixer he and some
pals were trying to steal off a job site for some mafioso
with a construction company tipped over and crushed the
toes of his feet; cops believed him when he said they
were just kids horsing around.

He was laid up in a hospital all summer with his injuries, which he always blamed for his small feet—at least,
they were small for someone who would grow to five feet
nine and 180 pounds. The injuries also caused him to develop a distinctive lope, a way of bouncing off the balls
of his feet just before his toes hit the ground and shot
spikes of pain to his brain. It seemed like a strut a teenager like him might adopt just for public use, but he strutted in private too.

At age sixteen, soon as the law allowed, he quit school
for good to run full time with a teenage street gang and
Cosa Nostra farm team called the Fulton-Rockaway
Boys, after an intersection that crisscrossed their turf. Unlike most teenage gangs of the era, the Boys were concerned about more than their turf. They stole cars, dealt
in stolen merchandise, ripped off stores, mugged drunks
stumbling out of betting parlors.

Gotti flourished in the gang and was soon a leader. He
might have possessed only average intelligence, but it put
him ahead of most of his peers, including brothers Peter
and Richard, who also joined the gang. The biggest differences between Gotti and other gang members, however, were his violent temper and his overbearing attitude,
which caused boys of weaker disposition to fall into line.
He also was physically strong and always ready to back
up his cement-mixer swagger with his fists.

Some of the boys who fell into line would hang on to
Gotti's coattails all their lives. One of the first was
Angelo Ruggiero, who was East New York born and
bred. Whereas Gotti was well built and striking, Angelo
was pudgy and had a bulldog face. He was a fidgety, talk-
ative chain-smoker the others called Quack-Quack, because he was always squawking about something.

Angelo was of at least average intelligence too and

tough, but hardly as dynamic and dashing as young Gotti, who began to spend the proceeds of his Fulton-Rockaway scores on garish but carefully coordinated outfits—the start of the former hand-me-down boy's clotheshorse reputation. As they grew older, Angelo began telephoning Gotti almost every morning, until he became a kind of appointments secretary.

Another who fell in line behind Gotti was Wilfred Johnson, a hulking amateur boxer with a face to prove it. "Wilfred" was far too formal a name in East New York, so he became known as Willie Boy. His father was an American Indian. Many of Willie Boy's early fights took place outside the ring, when kids shouted mock war whoops and called him a half-breed. Willie Boy was fiercely proud of his father, an ironworker who risked his life walking the "high-steel" of Manhattan skyscraper projects, and bitter about the teasing he took from the all-Italian boys.

Gotti committed one of his early violent crimes with Willie Boy, after a local mafioso asked them to administer a beating to some miscreant of the volcano. They found the man in the office of a used-car lot that doubled as a front for a stolen-car ring. The ring happened to be under investigation by the police—and this was how John Joseph Gotti Jr. was captured on law enforcement tape for the first time: the police had planted a listening device in the office.

The cops monitoring the bug heard the sounds of cloth ripping and fists smashing into flesh and bone.

Worried that the man might be killed, a quick-thinking cop telephoned the fire department and reported a fire at the used-car lot. The approaching sirens caused Gotti and Willie Boy to back off and run away, and the firemen found a naked, bleeding man who refused to say anything. Without a complaining witness, police could not make a case against Johnny Boy and Willie Boy.

Gotti slid out of many cases while making his now-inevitable transition from Fulton-Rockaway Boy to Cosa Nostra associate. He was arrested for minor crimes five times from 1957 to 1961 but never spent a day behind bars. The charges were always dismissed or plea-bargained into probation. As a result, he had a hard time taking seriously a system that was so easy to beat.

His hardest problems with the system involved the woman he impregnated on some passionate night in August 1960, when he was two months shy of his twentieth birthday. The woman's name was Victoria DiGiorgio. She was seventeen, and pretty, petite, and half Jewish on her father's side. Her parents had divorced when Vicky was two, and she later took her stepdad's name.

The child of this union was born in April 1961, and its parents did not marry until March 1962. Vicky always said it was because she wanted to live with a man before marrying him, but the truth was more complicated. She was as feisty as he was hot-fused, and they were always fighting.

The marriage was called off many times, and even after they tied the knot, they separated many times. Although she eventually accepted it, Vicky was against the criminal road her husband was taking—and angry that he spent so much of his time hanging out in bars and so much of their money on a nascent addiction to betting on dice, cards, and sporting events.

Stormy as the relationship was, they had two more children, but after he was arrested four more times, and actually spent a few months in jail in 1966, Vicky applied for public welfare and took him to family court a couple of times for nonsupport.

By that time, Gotti was a full-fledged but hardly prosperous associate of an East New York crew. His fortunes began to change, and his relationship with Vicky began to settle down after the elderly captain of the crew, Carmine Fatico, aghast that large numbers of blacks and Puerto Ricans were migrating into East New York, moved his storefront headquarters to a white working-class neighborhood in Queens known as Ozone Park.

As a field of plunder, Ozone Park was an astute choice because it was next to John F. Kennedy International Airport. Hundreds of trucks carrying goods in and out of the airport rumbled along the streets of Ozone Park every day. Hundreds of airport workers lived there; they were a ready source of tips about which trucks carried what, especially if they fell into debt to the bookmaking and loansharking operation that the crew established in the

honky-tonks of Ozone Park and surrounding neighborhoods. In 1966 Gotti began making a nice living as a hijacker.

So did other young criminals who followed him to
Queens. In addition to Willie Boy, the group now included yet another Gotti brother, Gene, who was six years
younger, and a younger brother of Angelo Ruggiero's
named Salvatore. Gene did not fall in line behind his
overbearing brother as easily as Peter and Richard did,
because he was closest to him in temperament, if not in
appearance, size, and intelligence.

Gene was with John and Angelo when they all picked
up their first hijacking charge in 1968—and their first
ticket to prison. Impersonating truckers, they drove a
rented U-Haul truck right into an airport cargo area and
loaded it up with women's dresses. Unfortunately for
them, the FBI had mounted one of its occasional crack-
downs on airport thefts, and agents were watching the
whole thing.

The federal case led to a separate state hijacking case
against John and Angelo after the police showed their
photographs to witnesses of a similar caper at the airport.
While on bail, they were involved in yet another hijacking that led to a second federal case in 1969, after they
had already been incarcerated at the United States penitentiary in Lewisburg, Pennsylvania.

John and Angelo were away for nearly three years, but
they caught two lucky breaks: Prosecutors abandoned the
second federal case after a judge ruled that some evidence
was illegally obtained. Then, in the state case, their lawyer, Michael Coiro, sweet-talked a judge in the famously
friendly Queens courthouse into a deal permitting them to
plead guilty and to regard their time in Lewisburg as the
penalty. Over the years, Michael Coiro, who had come
recommended by Carmine Fatico, would frequently demonstrate an agile touch with the authorities in Queens and
would become closer to John and Angelo than a lawyer
ever should have.

John Gotti began to flourish after he left prison in 1972
and rejoined the Ozone Park crew, which was headquar-
tered in a plain storefront known as the Bergin Hunt and
Fish Club, "Bergin" being a misspelled salute to a street
in the old East New York stomping ground. It was mainly

a crew of associates when Gotti returned; most of the "made" men had either died or grown feeble. Carlo Gambino, who succeeded the former King of Brooklyn, Albert Anastasia, as boss, had not made any new soldiers since 1957, partly because he was afraid of mistakenly initiating a drug dealer into the family.

In the Gambino family, the Ozone Park crew was valued but not highly regarded. Its young hotheads could be counted on to perform the violent acts occasionally necessary, but in the main they were a humdrum brew of legbreakers, hijackers, thieves, bookmakers, and loan sharks with not much talent for the more sophisticated scams that interested Carlo.

In such a crew, just as in the Fulton-Rockaway Boys, Johnny Boy Gotti simply brought more intelligence, bearing, and willpower to the table. His timing also was impeccable. A few months after Gotti left prison, Carmine Fatico, the decina's elderly captain, was indicted on loansharking charges; he stopped coming to the Bergin and named thirty-two-year-old Gotti his "representante," his eyes and ears on the street.

For all his parole officer knew, Gotti worked for Vicky's stepfather, who had built up a successful construction company. Vicky wished it were true that her husband worked for her father, but she accommodated herself to the former's criminal ways and focused on her children; she had given birth to a fourth child before he went to prison and had another, the last, after he came home.

"I don't know what he does," she would tell a detective who came to her home some years later. "All I know is, he provides."

As Fatico's eyes and ears, Gotti saw his status soar. He also met a man who filled the gap in his life left by his stressed-out father, a man he grew to idolize and imitate—Aniello Dellacroce, underboss of the Gambino family.

Dellacroce, whose first name was Americanized to Neil, was Carlo's bad cop. He was fierce, violent, foulmouthed, and clever, and Carlo relied on him when a mix of treachery and trickery was needed to settle some contentious matter. Once, as a young gunman for Albert

Anastasia, he adopted the guise of a Catholic priest—
Father Timothy O'Neill—while carrying out a murder.

In 1972 he was fifty-nine years old. FBI agents thought
he was the boss of the family that Anastasia had once
headed; a year earlier, a United States Senate committee
probing organized crime issued a report calling Dellacroce "the most powerful boss in New York."

The faulty intelligence was a product of Neil
Dellacroce's high visibility. Unlike Carlo, who kept as far
out of the public eye as possible, Neil lorded over the Little Italy neighborhood of Manhattan in a public way. His
base was the Ravenite Social Club, which was both an
unofficial city hall and a popular gathering place for
gangsters from his own and other families.

The Ravenite was just a two-room storefront on the
ground level of a red-brick tenement on Mulberry Street,
a boisterous canyon in the heart of Little Italy. Charles
"Lucky" Luciano—an early architect of Cosa Nostra—
had hung out there some forty years before. And now
John Gotti began hanging out there once every week,
usually on Saturdays—the day Neil required him to bring
messages from Fatico and cash from the crew's operations.

Neil, and thus Gotti, were not overconcerned about law
enforcement surveillance because the people of the neighborhood alerted Neil as soon as any unfamiliar cars or
people were spotted near the club. Neil, who had spent
only a year in jail despite his life in crime, had won their
loyalty by giving solace and money to those in need, and
he had also gained their respect by being the always
fierce, occasionally just arbiter of local disputes.

Neil took an early shine to Gotti and invited him to
witness some of these arbitrations, which Gotti enjoyed
recalling for the boys back at the Bergin Hunt and Fish—
where he always referred to Neil as "a man, a man's
man." In the corrupted machismo of Cosa Nostra, that
was the highest accolade, incorporating notions of loyalty
to friends; strength of heart, mind, and body; charisma;
leadership; and, most of all, criminal daring and know-
how.

The man's man was unfaithful to his wife—he was the
father of two out-of-wedlock daughters whom he
supported—but the Cosa Nostra rule about women did

not require fidelity; it only forbade a made man from cov-
eting another's wife or daughter. Someday Gotti would
invoke a highly technical interpretation of that rule to justify his own infidelity; as his treatment of Vicky during
the early years showed, he believed women were pleasur-
able but burdensome.

One of Neil's arbitrations arose out of a dispute between two fathers whose teenage boys had fought over a
girl; one of the boys had pulled a gun and wounded the
other. The shooter's father was summoned and forced to
apologize to the other boy's family, pay the medical
costs, and explain why his son was armed.

"Where did that idiot son of yours get this gun that he
carries around in the street shootin' people?" demanded
Neil.

"I don't remember."

"If I come across the fuckin' table and take your
fuckin' eyes out, would ya remember?"

"Now, well, yes, it was in a drawer in my house."

Gotti already was inclined to it, but the angry menace
and exaggerated threats of the leadership style he developed as he moved up in Cosa Nostra were echoes of
Neil's style.

Like Gotti, Neil was a gambler who bet large sums on
dice, cards, horses, and ball teams. And it was a weekend
of gambling at a Puerto Rican resort that led, in 1972, to
another prison term for Neil—and another burst in status
for his young protégé.

The Internal Revenue Service discovered that while
Neil was in Puerto Rico, he lost more in three days of
gambling than he claimed in income for an entire year.
After a quick trial, he was convicted and sentenced to a
year; he faced five more afterward, however, because
earlier he had refused to testify before a grand jury despite a grant of immunity.

With Carmine Fatico still lying low and Neil Dellacroce in prison, John Gotti began reporting directly to
Carlo Gambino—a highly unusual privilege for a soldier,
much less an associate, but Carlo, who valued Neil's
opinion, had no doubt been told by Neil that Johnny Boy
was a man, a man's man.

In 1973, three years shy of his death, Carlo was
seventy-one years old. He had more money than he knew

what to do with and a heart condition that made climbing stairs a chore. But he had no intention of retiring. Traditionally, a Cosa Nostra boss serves as long as he wishes, even if he is in prison, and Carlo was an arch traditionalist. Although he owned an estate on Long Island, he spent much of his time in Brooklyn, in a plain apartment in Sheepshead Bay, which is where Gotti began seeing him—at a time when *The Godfather* was still filling theaters.

Later in life, Gotti growled on a hidden listening device that Carlo was a "rat motherfucker, a back-door motherfucker" because Carlo never promoted him. But at the outset, Gotti was completely in awe of Carlo, who in his anecdotage was prone to lectures that made him sound like a character in a movie.

All the young men Carlo met got the same lecture; it was about the qualities a man must have to defeat his enemies; and it always featured the same parable: "You have to be like a lion and a fox. The lion scares away the wolves. The fox recognizes traps. If you are a lion and a fox, nothing will defeat you."

Gotti did not recognize Carlo's words as unoriginal. Only later, in a prison library, did he learn that Carlo was borrowing from Niccolò Machiavelli, the sixteenth-century Florentine politician and philosopher. As he read, he could understand why. Carlo had found a justification for his life in Machiavelli's *The Prince:* Whatever a ruler must do to hold on to the power, he must do.

Eventually Gotti also would begin borrowing parables from Machiavelli. At the time, he just thought Carlo was the wisest man he had ever met; when he got into a bar fight and was arrested for disorderly conduct, he gave his name as "John DeCarlo."

After a meeting with Don Carlo, Gotti would return to the Bergin Hunt and Fish Club in Ozone Park with his chest out and his head high. He took great pleasure in passing along Carlo's orders.

"Carlo says some trucks we can't hit because they got an in with other families," he announced one day. "He says we can't get involved in no counterfeitin', or nothin' with stocks and bonds."

Most of the crew had no idea what stocks and bonds were, but Carlo had banned stock-and-bond fraud and counterfeiting because these were federal crimes, and Carlo feared and respected federal crime fighters more than he did the New York City Police Department.

Carlo had also told Gotti to reemphasize the ban on drug dealing. This was a problem for the Ozone Park crew. Peter Gotti was dealing cocaine. Salvatore Ruggiero was dealing heroin; so was Willie Boy, and so was a new associate of the crew whom Gotti had more or less adopted in prison—Anthony Rampino, a lanky, cadaverous-looking hood with a budding personal heroin problem.

"If you're dealin', you're fuckin' playin' with fire, and if you get caught, you're fuckin' dead," Gotti said.

Few took him seriously, not then, and not after any of his anti-drug speeches over the years. Too many people close to him were drug dealers. But the boys at the Bergin understood that as the acting caporegime, Gotti had to spout the official line. As the acting caporegime, entitled to tribute from below, he also did not have to risk "playin' with fire" in order to make a living.

Carlo also banned one more crime—the kidnapping of other criminals for ransom, a crime then in vogue with some renegade and foolish denizens of the volcano. Carlo was personally upset about this trend because in January 1973, a nephew of his—kidnapped seven months earlier—was found shot to death, even though a hundred-thousand-dollar ransom had been paid.

The family had launched an effort to identify the kidnappers so that the inevitable revenge could be taken. Neil had already told Gotti that the Bergin crew would do the avenging.

The assignment was another personal honor, and in May 1973—when the kidnappers' leader was identified as an Irish-American hoodlum named James McBratney—Gotti got the chance to fulfill it and "make his bones," that is, commit his first murder.

Impersonating cops, Gotti and two associates found McBratney in a bar and tried to drag him away. The victim put up a fight and was shot to death—in full view of several witnesses.

Two months later, two witnesses picked two of the killers out of a police photo array. One was Gotti's chainsmoking, coattailing pal Angelo Ruggiero, now the father of a son named John, and the other was a Bergin nobody, who was murdered shortly after he and Angelo were arrested and released on bail. Many cops concluded that Gotti and Angelo killed the man to eliminate the chance of his making a deal for himself and testifying against them.

The NYPD had no idea who the third killer of McBratney was but the FBI did—thanks to Willie Boy Johnson, who had become a secret informer, an occupation as perilous as working high steel without a net. Willie Boy, code-named Source Wahoo by the FBI, had begun talking seven years earlier, after Fatico reneged on a promise to help Willie Boy's wife and children when Willie Boy had to go away to prison for a few months.

By that time, Willie Boy also knew he would never become a made man because he was part Indian. He would continue to commit crimes with Italian–American gangsters all his life, because he was a criminal and they ruled the volcano; but he made them pay for their bias—while making a few dollars for himself by selling information to the FBI as the highly prized Source Wahoo.

Willie Boy told the FBI that he had overheard Gotti bragging about the McBratney murder, and the FBI passed it on to the NYPD. When Gotti learned the police were looking for him, he left Vicky and his five children for a series of Queens hideouts. He eluded cops for nearly a year, until the spring of 1974, when Willie Boy gave the FBI another tip and Gotti was arrested in a Queens bar while talking to Anthony Rampino, his Lewisburg prison buddy.

Rampino's nickname was Roach, because he was not the most pleasant-looking man, but he introduced himself to other people, including Willie Boy, as "John's man." And, judging by the boasts that John's man made, Gotti— even while on the lam in a murder case—was thinking big thoughts.

"Johnny Boy and us, we're gonna take it all over someday," Rampino told another Bergin hanger-on who recalled the boast for the FBI years later. Rampino said his man had endeared himself to Carlo and was already close to Neil, who was growing old.

Carlo retained Roy M. Cohn, the Machiavellian boy wonder of the Army-McCarthy hearings, to represent

Gotti, who was freed on bail secured by the deed to Vicky's parents' house. Knowing their outlaw son-in-law was likely headed to prison again, they wanted to make her as comfortable as possible, so they also put up the money for her first real home—a pretty eight-room Cape Cod style house in Howard Beach, a middle-class community just south of Ozone Park. Until now, she and John had resided in a series of increasingly better—but crowded—apartments.

Roy Cohn had become one of New York's top lawyer-fixers. It took nearly a year, but he plea-bargained the McBratney case all the way down to attempted manslaughter. Gotti and Angelo got away with murder and would have to serve only two years in state prison—less time than they had served for hijacking seven thousand dollars' worth of women's clothes in 1968.

Gotti was sent to a prison eighty miles north of Queens; there he would be reunited with a friend who had in the meantime lost an armed-robbery case, a man who was one of his early partners in crime—the underworld trapeze artist Willie Boy Johnson.

Late in 1976, while John Gotti was in prison and reading up on Machiavelli, Carlo Gambino, who was a lion and a fox but not invincible, suffered another heart attack.

While on his deathbed, Carlo made a decision that led to a fault line beneath the surface of his family—a fissure that was not apparent in the exhilarating atmosphere of Sammy Gravano's induction ceremony, held only a few months later.

Carlo told his capos that they must choose Paul Castellano, his cousin and brother-in-law, as his successor. By tradition, a new boss was chosen in a vote of the capos, most of whom favored Neil Dellacroce, the underboss, now sixty-three and due out of prison soon on the tax case that had gotten him in trouble in 1972. Most of the capos thought Neil was a "man's man."

Paul, a caporegime, was not as admired. He was aloof by nature, and his ties to Carlo made him more so. Believing that people resented him, he never forged many relationships outside an inner circle. With Carlo's corrupt influence, he had built upon his father's butcher shop and become a multimillionaire in the meatpacking business; his soldiers, mainly an aging group of loan sharks and bookmakers in Brooklyn, were not nearly as well off, but they were still expected to grease Paul's palms, even in an off week. In the family, Paul was regarded as selfish and cheap.

Despite all of this, the capos obeyed Carlo's deathbed command and elected Paul boss. Paul could have chosen his own underboss, but in a move that belied the shaky ground he felt beneath his feet, he asked Neil to stay on as underboss and gave him near autonomy over crews more involved with "blue-collar" crimes, such as the crew of hijackers at the Bergin Hunt and Fish Club in Ozone Park.

Paul would focus on the family's "white-collar" crews, the ones more involved in construction bid rigging and labor union racketeering, like the crew in Bensonhurst that included Sammy Gravano. Paul resorted to violence when it served his purposes, but he disdained men who made their money in violent crimes.

Cosa Nostra tradition—the boss was above challenge— was enough to prevent a rupture, but the fault line widened in the early years of Paul's reign. At the outset, he held court in a Bensonhurst social club, but he was unnerved by the cops and FBI agents who sat in cars across the street and snapped photographs of the club's patrons. Before long, he retreated to his million-dollar house on a Staten Island hilltop; the house was known as the White House because it resembled the real one. Meanwhile, Neil left prison and resumed a high-profile life in Little Italy, confident that his supportive neighbors made it impossible for cops and agents to conduct much meaningful surveillance.

Inevitably, the Gambino family evolved into two families—the Paul branch and the Neil branch. Paul avoided the Ravenite and rarely ventured into the other clubs in which capos in both branches oversaw schemes and hustles. Anyone who had to see Paul had to request an audience, and because of this, soldiers began referring to him, mockingly and behind his back, as "the Pope."

Right after his election, however, Paul did lift the ban on new soldiers that Carlo had imposed. The ceremony in which Sammy was "made" was one of several that took place early in Paul's reign. In one of the others, Gene Gotti, much to brother John's consternation, got his "button," before John did, but Gene had earned it by running the Bergin without major problems while John was away.

The other Gotti brothers, Peter and Richard, did not pass muster with Paul or Neil because they were not earners. Peter was a small-time cocaine dealer and Richard a part-time thief; they actually worked at legitimate jobs now and then. Angelo's younger brother Salvatore was not made either, but he was making so much money dealing heroin—hundreds of thousands in the previous three years—that he no longer had any Cosa Nostra ambition.

In 1977 John and Angelo were made shortly after they got out of state prison. A pal of theirs from Fulton-Rockaway days, John Carneglia, a hijacker like them who had gone into the car theft and auto-salvage business in Queens, also was made, but two more friends were not. Anthony Rampino was deemed just not to have enough on the ball. Willie Boy Johnson, on the other hand, had plenty on the ball; he had done everything right, except that he was sired by a Native American father.

Gotti, Angelo, and Carneglia took the same oath as Sammy Bull Gravano, the same vow of fealty requiring them always to obey the boss and never to raise hands against one another, never to violate another's wife or children, and never to deal drugs.

In time, they would break all of these rules.

CHAPTER 3

• • • • • • • • • • • • •

Sammy Bull

The first time Sammy Gravano was caught committing a crime, he cried. In 1953, at age eight, while walking to Public School 186 in Bensonhurst, he had adopted the routine of stopping at a corner store and admitting two duty-free cupcakes to his lunch bag while pretending to browse. Finally, the store's owner paid attention to the little kid who came in but rarely bought anything. He caught Sammy red-handed.

"Please don't tell my father," Sammy bawled. "Please. I'll never do it again."

The boy's fear of his father seemed so real, the owner gave Sammy a pass. "All right, all right, kid, but don't do it again. Here, take the damn cupcakes and get on to school."

Sammy was doing poorly at school, and that was partly why he began stealing—to prove to himself he was good at something. He felt as smart if not smarter than other kids because he noticed things on the street that they walked right by. But in school he did so badly on tests that everyone treated him like the class idiot.

An explanation for this paradox came later. At the time, few teachers knew anything about dyslexia, a learning disability that caused Sammy's eyes to transpose letters and numbers.

The undiagnosed and tortured little boy also stole to prove his bravery. He was small compared with other kids his age and was usually the first to scream "Give up" when neighborhood friends played a game called "piling on." Yelling "give up" while at the bottom of the pile was the sensible thing, but his playmates did not let him off the hook so easily: "Sammy is a pussy. Sammy is a pussy."

In his mind, crime proved otherwise. He grew more criminal with age, particularly after he was "left back" and required to repeat fourth grade. Humiliated, he fought anyone who looked at him funny. His behavior mystified his parents, Gerardo and Katarina, but they never knew anything about dyslexia either.

Sammy, unlike many other Bensonhurst kids, had a lot going for him at home. He got a lot of attention because only a sister five years older remained there, and his father made a good living operating a small dress factory that he had acquired, good enough to provide the family a comfortable three-story house with a stand of Sicilian figs in the backyard. Even so, Sammy carried on like some deprived boy from the other side of the tracks.

His parents tried various remedies, including corporal punishment, but a good licking from his father never changed him for long. While not especially religious themselves, they also tried to put the fear of God in him by requiring him to attend mass at Our Lady of Guadaloupe Roman Catholic Church every Sunday. But the mandatory attendance bred hostility, and then contempt, after his parents arranged for his Confirmation and first Holy Communion to fall on the same convenient day through an extra large donation to the collection plate.

The point of no return arrived when Sammy was fourteen. He failed eighth grade at McKinley Junior High School and was sent to a special school, a holding pen really, for students deemed incapable of learning. Somehow he lasted a year, but then some classmate waved a Bible in his face and Sammy punched the kid out. The authorities sent Sammy home and told his parents not to bother sending him back. It was the end of his formal education.

He began running with a little gang of dropouts known as the Rampers, who bullied kids in soda shops by the elevated West End subway tracks linking Bensonhurst to Coney Island amusements. He also began working at his father's garment factory, and though he had already felt Cosa Nostra vibrations on the streets, that was where he got his first firsthand look—when the two goons tried to extort his father and his father sought help from a man from the old country named Sevito, even as Sammy was out getting a gun and, at age fourteen, planning to shoot his father's tormentors.

Because of Sevito, the gun was unnecessary, but Sammy got his worst licking yet and the first of many fruitless lectures from his father about "that life"—which was code for "Cosa Nostra."

"Never get involved with that life! You respect it, but stay away! That life is not for you. We're decent people."

Sammy would only nod his insincere assent. He had difficulty comprehending why his father was so virtuous when the world was so obviously corrupt and unfair.

One of Sammy's responsibilities at the dress factory was the payroll. Everyone was paid in cash, and after his father withdrew the money from a local bank, Sammy's job was to place the proper amount in a brown envelope for each of a dozen workers. One week he had five hundred dollars left over.

"Hey, Pop," he said, "I messed up, or we just beat the bank for five hundred smackeroos."

Gerardo Gravano and his son then checked all the envelopes and found that everyone had been paid what they were owed.

"That's two-fifty each for us!" Sammy shouted.

"No, no," Gerardo said. "We've gotta take it back. The bank lady made a mistake. She's gonna be short, lose her job."

Sammy protested, but his father slapped him in the head, then went alone to the bank and returned the money.

The bank was so appreciative that two ranking officers later came to the Gravano house to personally compliment Gerardo on his honesty. After they left, Sammy smarted off about a reward meaning more than words, and his father smacked him again.

At age sixteen, on his way toward Cosa Nostra, Sammy began courting serious trouble. Gang fights. Joyrides. Larceny. Car theft. Burglary. And, finally, armed robbery. Of course, to him, his behavior was serious only when he was caught, which was not often, and even then his parents did not always know—while he was not good with numbers or letters, he told stories that his frustrated parents would at least entertain, if not believe.

One time, when he was still sixteen, he learned that the

police wanted him for an armed robbery. Afraid he was finally going to jail, he took off and wound up in Tijuana, Mexico, where local cops grabbed him on a warrant and held him for several roach-infested days, until his parents bailed him out.

As a juvenile, he got a break on the jam back home, then went on his punky way. Finally, after three more years of cheap crimes, he was arrested for throwing a punch at a cop and brought before a judge, this time as an adult. The judge gave him one last break: plead guilty, enlist in the Army, do not go to jail.

Sammy told his lawyer he'd take jail over the Army, but the lawyer said: "Don't be stupid. Take the deal, then just don't go. Nothin' will happen. The judge can't make the Army take you."

A few weeks later, Sammy wanted to shoot his lawyer when a letter came ordering him to report for a preinduction physical. After passing it, he and many others were told by some sergeant that because of a national emergency most would be sworn in that day.

It was 1964. A military buildup was under way for the Vietnam War, but that wasn't why Sammy began to sweat; he had met a girl, Lorraine. The infatuation was just now getting interesting.

"Not me, sir, gotta go home," he told the sergeant.

"Try it, and you're goin' straight to jail, pal."

From the induction center, Sammy telephoned his mother Katarina—she was still there for him, despite everything.

"You won't believe what's goin' on here. They're gonna keep me. They're keepin' everyone. Even cripples!"

"Salvatore, put someone in charge on the line."

"Sorry, ma'am," the sergeant drolled, as Sammy eavesdropped. "That's how it is, this is the law, these are the rules. He'll probably be going to Fort Jackson, that's in South Carolina."

"Minchia!" Sammy screamed, using an Italian word indicating great and profane dismay. "South Carolina! I'm from Brooklyn, that's New York. I can't go to South Carolina!"

That night, without saying good-bye to Lorraine, Sammy was compelled to leave for South Carolina. Over the next two years he went to various posts, but never South Vietnam. He actually grew to like the Army; it had a system for everything, rules for every situation, and a simple, sensible chain of command.

Unfortunately for many, he did not make a career out of the Army. He served only two years and was honorably discharged.

By 1966, when Sammy came home to Brooklyn, his parents—not that they could have swayed him from crime any more than before—had sold the dress factory, retired, and moved to Long Island. He went back to his old ways, although he did periodically work on various construction jobs with his sister Frances's husband, Edward Garafola, who also was Cosa Nostra–bound.

It seemed to Sammy that everyone in Bensonhurst was "mobbed up," connected somehow to someone connected to what his father had called the Mafia. Part of it was the company Sammy and Eddie Garafolo kept—young criminals like themselves—but Cosa Nostra, though starting to lose its hold, still was a dominant influence in Bensonhurst in the 1960s; young criminals learned early that if they wanted to go on living, they'd better get mobbed up.

Sammy mobbed up first, in 1968. His entrée was a punk-buddy, Thomas Spero, whose uncle by the same name was associated with the Colombo family. The uncle, known as Shorty, invited Sammy into his little crew of would-be burglars and armed robbers with an avuncular speech about how he would never lie.

Though he continued working in construction off and on with his brother-in-law for a few more years, Sammy became a professional criminal. He was involved in countless robberies and burglaries until, in 1970, Shorty gave him a contract to kill a criminal who had double-crossed Shorty. At least that's what Shorty said; later Sammy would learn that the motive was so venal—a friend of Shorty's simply had designs on the victim's wife and wanted her to be a widow—that, had he known, he might have refused to do it; but at the time he thought he was being tested and so he leapt over the line separating mere criminals from cold-blooded murderers.

The murder was how he came to the attention of

higher-ups in the Colombo family—just as in Queens a young criminal named John Gotti was getting noticed by Gambino leaders. Shorty Spero's boss, a caporegime named Carmine Persico, asked to meet the kid who so cleanly put two shots into his first victim's head.

"So you think you're a tough guy?" Carmine asked.

"I got *cajones,* I do what I'm told," Sammy said.

Sammy was becoming a tough guy, physically and emotionally. He boxed in a local gym and lifted weights, and while still only five feet five, he was strong—"like a bull," someone said—and so nobody piled on Sammy Bull anymore. His success as a criminal, and his ability to murder without remorse, pushed his inferiority about his still unexplained performance in class into a forgotten corner of his mind. In addition, he had become, of all things, an uncommonly good chess player; he picked it up during idle moments in social clubs. It was like the Army—systematic, with rules for every situation, and the pieces had identifiable rank and power.

He became a stickler for rules, and he had little patience with people who broke the rules he set for customers of the loan-sharking "book" that he began to build with his armed-robbery proceeds. One time, in a bar, one of his customers told Sammy he did not have to pay on time, or at all, because he was connected to Joseph Colombo himself, boss of Carmine Persico and the Colombo family.

"Okay, chief, can we talk outside a bit?" Sammy said.

"Sure, but you ain't gettin' paid."

Outside, Sammy got right to the point and fractured the man's jaw. People came out of the bar, and one of the man's friends pulled Sammy off and gave him the money he was owed.

The next day Carmine Persico telephoned Shorty Spero and said Joseph Colombo wanted to see Sammy. Shorty told his protégé to show the boss respect but speak the truth.

So Sammy told Colombo: "I'm sorry if I hurt the guy, but he answered me wrong, and he was usin' your name to beat me. He owes and he has to pay, those are the rules."

Colombo was impressed. "*Minchia,* you're a tough guy, aren't you? You got a bad fuckin' temper, too. But if you got a problem in the future, talk to Shorty or Carmine before you go off like a wild man."

About that time, Sammy fell in love for the second and last time in his life—Lorraine had drifted toward someone else while he was in the Army—when he met a woman from the neighborhood named Debra Scibetta. Like Vicky Gotti, Debra was feisty but homespun. Sammy would later boast to friends that she was also loyal "like a wolf" because she was the kind to "mate once and die."

Unlike Vicky, Debra knew what she was getting into, falling in love with a criminal; her uncle was a gangster and had spent ten years in jail. Unlike Vicky's husband, however, Sammy stopped hanging out in bars and social clubs once he got married; he did not gamble either, so the impact of "the life" on the marriage was minimal. The couple would have two children; their names, Karen and Gerard, were Sammy's attempt to make some amends with his parents, Katarina and Gerardo.

In 1972, a year after the marriage, Sammy became the center of a tug of wills that changed the direction of his Cosa Nostra career. Carmine Persico suggested to Shorty that it was time for Sammy to move up and work directly for him. This infuriated not Shorty but Shorty's brother—father of Thomas Spero, the young friend of Sammy's who had led him to Shorty four years before.

Shorty's brother wanted his son to move up, not Sammy. This led to a couple of angry meetings involving all concerned. Finally, Shorty decided to nip ill-will in the bud, so he told Sammy: "My brother's a shit, but blood. If he don't get what he wants, and you jump ahead of little Tommy, we'll never be done dealin' with it. But you deserve to move up, so I have decided little Tommy will go with Carmine and I am releasin' you."

"Releasin' me? I've worked so hard."

"I am releasin' you to our friend Toddo," Shorty replied, using a nickname Sammy recognized as that of Salvatore Aurello, a caporegime in the Gambino family.

Sammy protested, but Shorty kept saying what an honor it would be to be associated with a man like Salvatore "Toddo" Aurello, who was revered in Bensonhurst the way Sevito once was.

"He's with Carlo, who's like Carmine, but bigger. It's

good. It's squared with Carmine. Everything's been worked out."

Sammy's future had been decided for him, but that was the way it was in Cosa Nostra. Those were the rules, and he obeyed them. At age twenty-seven, Sammy Bull went to work for Toddo.

Where Shorty was a Cosa Nostra pawn, Toddo was a bishop, and like Neil Dellacroce with John Gotti, he gathered Sammy under his wing and over the years lectured him about the virtue of playing all the pieces and looking beyond the next move.

Toddo tapped into Sammy's construction know-how and used him in his crew's union schemes, a role requiring frequent meetings. Once, in a scene that could have been filmed and spliced into *The Godfather,* Sammy visited Toddo in the old man's backyard. Toddo was dressed in black and waring a wool fedora despite the sun. He was sitting in an old beach chair and smoking a cigar, talking about his fig trees and spraying his tomato plants with a hose, when his wife announced another visitor.

The visitor was another associate, who told Toddo he needed to speak about a problem he was having with some other man.

"Excuse me," Sammy said. "I'll be goin' now."

"No, no, Sammy, stay," Toddo said to him, and then to the other man, "You can talk in front of Sammy."

The visitor described his problem with the other man, which was money, then left.

"So, Sammy, what should I do in this situation?"

"I'd send a couple guys with bats and break the other guy's fuckin' legs."

"Good, I'm glad you answered that way because it shows what I thought. One, you got *cajones.* Two, you're stupid. But the two is part of being young. I'm gonna send for the other guy, and you come here tomorrow, same time."

Sammy did as ordered, and the other man told a story that was the opposite of the first man's story.

"What now, Sammy?"

"I guess I'd have to investigate more. This guy sounded real sincere. But so did the other guy."

"Good, maybe you learn a lesson now? If you ever get in a position like mine, you gotta listen with both ears, and some place between the two stories is the truth. If you ever make a decision after only one guy talks to you, you won't last long."

Naturally, Toddo became as important in Sammy Gravano's life as Neil Dellacroce did in John Gotti's. And that's why, in 1977, after Carlo died, it was the proudest, most glorious day of Sammy Bull's life when in a basement den in Bensonhurst, Paul inducted him into the Gambino family—as one of the men below, Sammy's sponsor, Toddo Aurello, beamed with approval.

The Aurello decina in Bensonhurst was one Paul tended to on a hands-on basis. Before moving into his plush mansion on Staten Island, Paul had spent most of his life in Bensonhurst; his father's butcher shop, which with Carlo's help he had spun into a meatpacking empire, was still there. The crew made its money in labor and construction rackets, the things that interested him most.

Sammy did not learn about the fault line beneath the surface of the family until he got into the swing of made-man things and Gambino veterans explained how some crews were "Neil crews" while some, like his, were "Paul crews." Toddo downplayed the notion, but only out of loyalty to Paul, Sammy soon concluded. The schism bothered him; it mocked the noble words of Paul's speech.

One veteran who acquainted Sammy with the subtleties of the landscape was Frank DeCicco, a Staten Island capo also active in construction and labor rackets. He was a rugged-looking man—a block of granite like Sammy, only bigger, with a large swirl of jet-black hair falling in waves to the middle of his forehead. Toddo had described him as tough and cagey—boss material—and Sammy quickly learned that DeCicco was one of the few in Paul's wing who fraternized with the Neil wing.

As they became friends, DeCicco invited Sammy to accompany him to the Ravenite to play pinochle with Neil, or to the Bergin to shoot dice in a gambling parlor above the club that Gotti set up for men who enjoyed it as much as he and DeCicco did. Sometimes Sammy would stop at the Ravenite, but never the Bergin because he was neither a gambler nor a night owl.

Sammy did not meet Gotti until 1978, when at a social

club in Bensonhurst DeCicco's father pulled him aside
and said, "I want you to meet a guy, a friend of mine, an
up-and-comer."

Sammy spoke to Gotti about nothing for a while. He
was mildly impressed, but Gotti was too boisterous in
speech, manner, and clothes for his taste. Like Toddo,
Sammy believed the best Cosa Nostra style was low-key,
and as far as clothes were concerned, he felt overdressed
in a sports jacket; he almost always wore simple
clothes—jeans, T-shirt, leather jacket.

Sammy and Gotti chatted at wakes, weddings, and
Christmas parties, but that was it. Beyond events like
these, Sammy rarely socialized. He preferred working,
and under Toddo's influence he worked hard and rose in
stature as Gotti rose under Neil.

With cash from his loan-sharking book and his shakedowns of unions and companies, Sammy formed his own
construction company. He bought hidden interests in restaurants, nightclubs, and bars, including a Bensonhurst
bar-restaurant known as Tali's, to which many men, including friends from his teen period, gravitated and
formed the nucleus of a crew within the Aurello crew.

One of those friends from the early days was Louis
Milito, whom Sammy sponsored when Paul agreed to
"open the books" again and make more soldiers. Sammy
also sponsored his brother-in-law, Edward Garafola. The
new inductees would become two of Sammy's staunchest
allies and business partners.

While Sammy was becoming better known for his ability as an earner, the steeliness that made Carmine Persico
and Joseph Colombo take notice remained a hallmark. In
1977, the year Sammy was made, Paul took notice and
sent him on his second murder mission.

Sammy did not even know Victim No. 2's name, or the
motive, but the "piece of work" went as smoothly as his
first in 1970.

In 1978, the man who told Sammy never to pick up the
gun, his father, Gerardo, quietly passed away on Long Island. Sammy's mother would live five more years, but
she might have died right then if she had known what a
stone-hearted Cosa Nostra stalwart, what a stickler for
rules, Sammy had become; that same year he helped murder Debra Gravano's brother, Nicholas Scibetta.

The murder came after Scibetta, a low-achieving associate of another crew, fell victim to a contagion that
swept through young gangster ranks in the 1970s with
more velocity than in the larger society—cocaine. His
disease distorted his vision and made him believe that his
relationship with his powerful brother-in-law made him
powerful.

The more degenerate Nicky Scibetta became, the more
cocaine he bought and sold for personal use, the more he
fell under a cloud; when drug-paranoid Paul heard multiple whispers from soldiers in his and other families that
Nicky was giving off "rat" signals, he did what Carlo
would have done: He ordered Nicky killed.

He gave the contract to the complaining soldiers and
told them not to tell Sammy. But out of respect for
Sammy, they went "off the record"—as the practice of
sharing secret information in Cosa Nostra was known—
and did tell him.

Sammy was trapped; if he complained to Paul, he
would be betraying the friends who had tipped him—to
save someone he had never liked and had warned many
times—just because the man was his brother-in-law. The
familial tie was paltry reason, in Sammy's stern book,
and so he stood knowingly by while his Victim No. 3—
legally, mere knowledge made Sammy culpable—was
silenced.

Sammy spoke about his inaction with the brother-in-
law that he liked, Eddie Garafola. "Nicky's uncle did ten
years rather than rat, so Nicky knew the rules. What the
fuck was I supposed to do?"

"You put up a squawk, who knows what shit happens
to you. Nicky sure as shit ain't worth dyin' for."

"There's that, but the guy was warned. We can't have
guys runnin' around with coke comin' out their nostrils."

Nicky Scibetta's nostrils were never found. As Sammy
stood by and did nothing, the actual killers took the body
away, then dismembered it and scattered the pieces—an
unusual technique in Cosa Nostra, except in an emerging
decina of Studio 54 cocaine addicts led by a former
butcher's apprentice, Roy DeMeo.

Eventually, the DeMeo crew would be brought to justice by a thigh that a homeless man found in a dumpster,
but the hand and arm of Scibetta that were found and

identified by a ring on a finger brought no justice. They were just buried, in a closed coffin.

Sammy attended the wake and funeral with Debra and mourned Nicky with the other relatives. Of course, he never told her he was partly responsible for her brother's murder. How could he? Debra knew only generally about "the life." Even for her, it would be hard to understand how Cosa Nostra rules were more important than family relationships.

In this situation, deceit was better than truth, and Sammy's ability to carry off such deceit made him feel the same way he felt when he was inducted—that by nature he was unusually adept at feeling one way while acting another. It was as though nature had compensated him for what he at long last had learned about himself: dyslexia. His son Gerard had it too, but teachers and doctors knew enough about it now and put kids in special schools, not holding pens.

In 1980, with close buddy Louis Milito, Sammy sent Victim No. 4 to the cemetery. It was another contract from Paul, and in Sammy's mind it was his most important murder to date because it showed how much Paul had come to trust him. The victim was a capo in Philadelphia who ran afoul of the local Cosa Nostra boss, who asked Paul to do him a service during the victim's night-on-the-town visit to New York.

Victims became blank slates to Sammy; they meant nothing, were nothing. And, in 1981, when the Philadelphia boss sought another favor from Paul, Victim No. 5 was dispatched, after a road trip Sammy took to the City of Brotherly Love.

While a stickler for rules himself, Sammy was beginning to understand that Cosa Nostra was intrinsically unruly; with men in pursuit of dishonest money, how could it be otherwise? The higher he climbed in his and Paul's wing of the family, the more he saw that rules didn't occur in a vacuum; very often situations arose in which decisions had to be made about greater and lesser rules.

It happened all the time in Sammy's own little crew, and he tried to respond judiciously, as he was taught by Toddo—who was beginning to slow down and turn some duties over to Sammy. While less dogmatic, Sammy remained highly intolerant of people who broke such a basic rule as Thou shalt not steal from the family.

In 1981 he caught a business partner, a soldier in another decina, cooking the books of a family-run drywall construction firm; the attempted swindle was so infuriating that he flew off the handle and broke a rule loftily cited by Paul when Sammy was made: A made man shall not raise hands against another.

"Don't try robbin' us because you won't enjoy the money!" he screamed at Louis DiBono, a chubby, jolly soldier of some status because he was an earner and as knowledgeable about construction as Sammy. "Or you're whacked!"

Sammy felt justified because he had caught DiBono hiding the borgata's true share of a windfall made when, with Sammy's backdoor help, he got away with nonunion labor on a union job.

DiBono, however, put Sammy's neck on the chopping block by running to his captain and saying he had been not only falsely accused but threatened by a made man; his capo complained to Paul and asked him for permission to kill Sammy.

Now Paul had to enter the vacuum and make a decision about greater and lesser rules. He ordered DeCicco to bring Sammy to a "sitdown" with the administration—Paul, Neil, and consigliere Joe N. Gallo, the family's elderly, white-haired "adviser," or lawyer, who was another holdover from Carlo's era.

As an aloof leader, Paul was unaware that DeCicco was now a close friend of Sammy's. And so he never knew that DeCicco—just before Sammy's first sitdown with the family leadership—pulled Sammy aside and offered a dangerous bit of off-the-record advice.

"DiBono will come up with a story that'll make it hard to say he was cheatin'. So when they ask if you made the threat, just deny it. It's your fuckin' word against his."

Sammy was amazed and disheartened that at the top of the family such games were played. "No, Frankie," he said, "I'm not gonna run away from it. I don't care what the rat says."

DiBono did deny, during the sitdown in Paul's mansion on Staten Island, and the paperwork on the deal in question was now plausible enough to make Sammy's ac-

cusations unclear. Paul then cast dubious eyes upon
Sammy.

"I did threaten Louie," Sammy responded, in his low,
steely way. "I ain't never done that to a friend of ours.
But this guy is a scumbag. He's a cheat, a liar and he was
robbin' us."

"Maybe you thought so, but even if you did, you can't
raise hands against a friend of ours," Paul said. "Only I
can do that."

Sammy stared into Paul's eyes. "He was robbin' the
family. Let me kill him now. I'll kill him now, right at
this table."

For its fire and fury, the remark was impressive, but
not the obedient one Paul wanted to hear, and he stared
his displeasure at Sammy until Neil Dellacroce spoke.

"Maybe Sammy did wrong. He should've taken this to
his capo, we all know that. But his motives were good.
That's what we want, good motives. So I think the best
thing here is, he and Louie, they shake hands and we
chalk up a misunderstanding."

With that remark, the sitdown dissolved into face-
saving on everyone's part, and Sammy arrived at a new
understanding about who the real, if not official, power in
the Gambino family was.

Paul officially concluded the sitdown by ordering
Sammy and DiBono to terminate their business relationship, shake hands, and vow not to raise them against one
another again—a promise that each made then but that
would be difficult to keep as time rolled by.

"Neil," DeCicco later commented to Sammy,
"would've made a great fuckin' boss. He knows this life
of ours better than Paul, but what're we gonna do?"

"Nothin'. Paul's boss. Way it is. Cosa Nostra."

To Sammy's surprise, Paul drew him closer after the
sitdown. On occasion, Paul even invited him to the White
House for small chats with DeCicco and others—
invitations that John Gotti never got. Paul welcomed
Gotti to Staten Island when Gotti had some money-
stuffed envelope in hand, but not to shoot the breeze.

Shooting the breeze once with Paul, Sammy was astounded to hear him muse that a murder contract ought to
be let on Joseph Bonanno, founder of the Cosa Nostra
family bearing his name, who had recently retired to Ar-

izona and authorized a sanitized book about his life as a boy in Sicily and as a man in the volcano.

"Our whole thing is, never rat, and here this guy writes a book that puts us all in one big conspiracy," Paul said. "Carlo would die 'cause he never trusted Joe Banannas anyway."

"A boss bein' a rat, not a good example, that's for sure, but that family's time has come and gone," Sammy said, trying to honor the principle while minimizing the damage. "They get no respect in the street.'

By musing about murdering another boss, Paul was admitting Sammy to his inner circle. Sammy was flattered but the more time he spent there, the less Paul enthralled him. Paul seemed trapped in a situation of his own making—he was the boss of only half a family, and that made him both resentful and insecure.

Once at a Christmas party at Paul's house, Sammy said he was leaving to pay his respects to Neil, who was holding his own Christmas party at the Ravenite in Little Italy.

"Where're you goin'?" Paul demanded. "You're on our side!"

The naked partisanship was another mockery of Paul's noble induction speech. "He looked at me like I had five fuckin' heads," Sammy later told DeCicco. "What's his fuckin' problem? We're supposed to one family. What does he mean, 'our side'?"

By 1982, anyone who knew their way around the volcano knew Sammy Gravano was not anyone to trifle with. Frank Fiala thought he knew his way around, but he was wrong and so he became Victim No. 6; the murder boosted Sammy's reputation—and his personal finances.

Fiala was a Czech immigrant who landed in New York in 1969 at age twenty-four without money or English-language skills; by 1982, he was a playboy cocaine dealer who had acquired several million dollars, two airplanes, a helicopter, a Rolls-Royce, and the machine-tool company that gave him his first American job.

Sammy and two partners now secretly owned a nightclub, the Plaza Suite disco, in a neighborhood known as Gravesend, directly east of Bensonhurst. Fiala lived nearby and patronized the Plaza Suite, where he gave

women all the cocaine they could sniff if they agreed to
go home with him later.

Fiala was so pleased with his reception at the club that
he asked a club manager who worked for Sammy if he
could rent it out for one evening, to throw himself a party
marking the thirteenth anniversary of his arrival in the
land of opportunity.

Sammy said forget about it. But later he agreed to meet
Fiala, after Fiala insisted so strongly to club employees
that Sammy took notice.

"I love this place. I want a big party. We'll advertise it
on the radio. We'll give a big door prize—a yacht, a car,
a plane, what do I care?" Fiala said.

"It's not for rent," Sammy said. "It's not worth it to us.
It'll be bad for our regular customers."

Fiala kept insisting, Sammy kept resisting, until Fiala
made an offer that piqued Sammy's greed meter.

"Okay, I guarantee you, you'll win the door prize."

Over the next few weeks, while making his party plans,
the cocaine dealer became fixated on the Plaza Suite
disco. He told Sammy he had to buy it and would pay a
million dollars. Sammy thought Fiala had begun using
too much of his own product; the property and building,
in Gravesend terms, were worth about a hundred fifty
thousand dollars—which was a cheap home in the
suburbs, by New York terms.

Still, the Plaza Suite was a steady source of "skim"—
cash income that could be hidden from the Internal Revenue Service—so Sammy turned Fiala down.

To keep an eye on things, Sammy also ordered about
twenty of his associates to attend Fiala's party, at which
the stoned guest of honor gave a teary-eyed speech about
his penniless arrival in America. Everyone applauded,
and then Fiala—in a bizarre cocaine frenzy—took out a
razor and soap and shaved himself bald.

Later in the evening, one of Sammy's men noticed that
Fiala was taking an attaché case from table to table, opening it and displaying a submachine gun. Guns were
against house policy, and Sammy's men confiscated it.
One of them telephoned Sammy and said he better drop
by, because Fiala was getting out of control.

"I want my gun back," Fiala slobbered when Sammy
approached him.

"You can have it, but this party's over. Get everybody out."

Too intoxicated to protest, Fiala left. He was back in a few days, however, with another offer to buy the Plaza Suite for the same wildly inflated one million dollars. The disco had become a toy he had to have, like his planes, helicopter, and Rolls.

Sammy balked again, but Eddie Garafola urged him to sell. "That's four or five times what it's worth. Sell it!"

Reluctantly, Sammy agreed to discuss the offer. Reluctance turned to enthusiasm when Fiala agreed to pay three-quarters of the million-dollar purchase price under the table, in cash—meaning tax-free. Fiala was a bozo, but the deal was a bonanza.

Some phony papers were drawn up by lawyers for both sides, and the deal was set for closing on Monday, June 28, 1982. Fiala signed checks for the bogus price, but he had trouble getting the under-the-table cash together because of money-laundering laws requiring banks to make a paper trail of cash transactions of more than ten thousand dollars. Sammy got him out of this jam by arranging for Fiala to deposit a certified check into a dummy account provided by a friend who owned an armored-car company.

Cocaine-induced delusion was the only explanation for what happened next. On the Friday night before the official closing, Fiala walked into the Plaza Suite with his attaché case and two Doberman pinschers and told the employees he was now the owner and was taking over an office Sammy kept at the club. One employee contacted Sammy, who collected Garafola and went to see Fiala.

They found him, as advertised, in Sammy's office, seated at Sammy's desk, with the two Dobermans standing sentry. Sammy was about to tell Fiala off when Fiala reached in a desk drawer and pulled out his submachine gun, then invited them to sit down.

Sammy's knees buckled a bit. He saw Garafola turn white. He thought they would be shot in the back if they tried to run for the door. The only option was to sit and play whatever contest Fiala had in mind—which was eating crow.

"You know, one time, some Colombians gave me some business problems. They were tough people, but I took

care of them. Wiped them all out. Did I ever tell you what
I always say, 'Greaseballs ain't pimples on a Colombian's
ass'?"

"Never heard that one," Sammy smiled.

"I am a nice guy, Sammy. I am going to bring in people from all over the world and make this a first-class
place. So don't be angry at me that I just wanted to get
goin' a little early."

"No, no problem. You'll get the deed on Monday."

"I figured you'd see it that way."

"There's no need for guns and dogs here," Sammy
said. "It's ridiculous. We have a great deal here, and everybody's happy."

Fiala put down the submachine gun and invited Sammy
and Garafola to visit his club anytime. They all shook
hands, and the brothers-in-law—astounded by Fiala's gall
and stupidity—left.

"That motherfucker goes tonight," Sammy told
Garafola outside the club. "He's gone."

And that night Fiala was history. He was shot in both
eyes by a ski-masked team of Sammy's men, outside the
club in front of a dozen people waiting on line to get in,
as Sammy and Garafola watched from across the street. It
took police twelve hours to coax the Dobermans out of
Sammy's office—the only headway they ever made on
the case. Not that it mattered much in terms of justice in
the volcano; Frank Fiala had indeed murdered two rival
cocaine dealers—and their children.

In a few weeks Sammy returned the phony purchase
price to lawyers for Fiala. He kept the nearly three-
quarters of a million dollars under-the-table money deposited into the dummy account he had arranged with the
friend who owned the armored-car company. He also kept
the Plaza Suite disco—and bought a nice big house on
Staten Island and a lovely horse farm in New Jersey.

By 1983, at age thirty-eight, Sammy was one of the
most powerful and wealthy men in the borgata. In addition to all his other interests, he and Louie Milito secretly controlled one of the city's largest steel-erection
companies. In practical terms, because Toddo was virtually retired, Sammy was boss of the Aurello decina.
Though Paul did not promote him to capo, or acting capo,

he treated him as such and counted on him to keep the far-flung parts of his own construction empire in order.

Paul also kept Sammy apprised of matters in other crews. One day he told Sammy he had given DeCicco a contract to murder Roy DeMeo, the former butcher's apprentice who had become a soldier and leader of a band of Studio 54 cocaine addicts known for disposing of murder victims by dismemberment.

Like so many others, DeMeo had broken Paul's no-drug-dealing policy and was the target of a federal grand jury investigation. Paul feared that the investigation might lead to him because, as boss, he had been accepting tributes from DeMeo since 1976. DeMeo had begun behaving erratically as the investigation heated up, and Paul was afraid that he might become a "rat."

"Here's a guy who was making a fortune stealing cars," Paul said. "Roy's guys were shippin' a hundred cars a week overseas at five thousand a pop. He didn't need to be a drug dealer."

"Nobody does, there's enough money out there without drugs. Roy had a lot on the ball, he don't need to deal."

"But sometimes I think there are more of them in this family than guys like me and you. It's a shame."

Just when Sammy thought Paul was leading up to asking him to help DeCicco execute the hit, Paul displayed a newspaper clipping showing that DeCicco had already accomplished the mission. DeMeo's body had been found in the trunk of a car.

"I know you knew 'im, but is this okay with ya?" Paul asked.

"If you're not mad, I'm not," Sammy Bull said.

CHAPTER 4

• • • • • • • • • • • • •

King of Queens

From 1977 to 1983, as Sammy rose in the Paul wing of
the family, Gotti rose in the Neil wing. Because he was
flamboyant, and closer to Neil than Sammy was to Paul,
Gotti's rise was louder and faster. He lacked Sammy's ex-
pertise in construction and unions, however, and never
personally ran companies. He got by on bread-and-butter
rackets—bookmaking, loan-sharking—but was always
scrambling to pay his own gambling debts and support
his family, including a young son who caused much grief,
for Gotti and others. As in his Fulton-Rockaway Boys
era, he dominated men around him. But none who toiled
in his long shadow dared complain—except to the FBI.

He left prison in 1977 after completing his two-year
hitch in the James McBratney revenge-murder case. After
Paul inducted him into the family and gave him his "button" as his sponsor, Neil, stood by, Gotti reclaimed the
seat brother Gene had kept warm at the Bergin Hunt and
Fish Club in Queens and moved into aging caporegime
Carmine Fatico's former office.

Fatico was in a legally induced slumber. He had beaten
two loan-sharking cases but lost a hijacking case and was
waiting to be sentenced. Lawyer-fixer Roy Cohn, who
had gotten Gotti and Angelo such a sweet deal in the
McBratney case, was representing Fatico and trying to
persuade a judge that his sixty-seven-year-old client was
a candidate for probation, not prison.

The argument required model-citizen behavior from
Fatico because probation officers were writing a report
for the judge, so Fatico rarely even left his house on Long
Island anymore.

With Fatico so far on the sidelines, it rankled Gotti that

officially he was still only a fill-in. To his ears, his title—
"acting capo"—sounded bogus. In his mind, the three
years he had filled in for Fatico before prison—not to
mention the reason that he went to prison—entitled him
to not only his button but official caporegime status as
well.

Willie Boy Johnson was still in prison on his armed-
robbery case, but the FBI knew about Gotti's displeasure
because it had developed another quisling in the Bergin
crew, William Battista. Like Willie Boy, Billy Battista
was not a made man, but in his case it was because he
had lost his zest for the life; a former hijacker, now at age
fifty he wanted only to work in the crew's bookmaking
operation. He began talking to the FBI because he was a
family man and afraid of jail, and he thought a friendship
with the FBI might help if the operation were ever
busted.

After Battista, or any informant, met with an agent, the
agent prepared a written account for the bureau's files.
These still-secret memos show that Battista, who was
thirteen years older than Gotti, took him with a very large
grain of salt.

Early on, Battista said Gotti wanted official capo status
so badly he hoped Fatico got prison, not probation; that
way Paul would have less reason to deny him. "Source
spoke to John, and he's actually hoping that Fatico gets
jail time," an FBI agent wrote after a rendezvous with
Battista, whose code name was Source BQ, after the
FBI's Brooklyn-Queens field office.

Gotti took his grievance to Neil, but Neil was a Cosa
Nostra traditionalist who understood Paul's reluctance to
promote such a newly made man to caporegime. Besides,
Neil pointed out, a rising star in the Toddo Aurello crew
in Brooklyn was in the same fix.

At this stage, Gotti knew Paul in the way a tenant
knows an absentee landlord, someone entitled by owner-
ship to rent that was picked up by someone else. But
Paul's refusal to promote Gotti widened the fault line in
the Gambino family, as far as Gotti and the Bergin Hunt
and Fish Club were concerned.

"Paul's the boss, but we're with Neil," Gotti told James
Cardinali, a young robber who hung his hat at the Bergin.
"Paul has nothin' to do with us."

As acting captain, however, Gotti began to make a lot
more money. He was now entitled to tributes from anyone
who wanted to hang his hat at the Bergin—and dozens of
young gangsters like James Cardinali flocked there when
Johnny Boy came marching home. He also was entitled to
a weekly share of the Bergin's bookmaking operation; the
amount depended on the weekly take, of course, but
bookmaking operations—like legal gambling casinos—
rarely lose money, because the house controls the odds.

He put some cash into his own loan-shark book, which
produced more cash, since underground bankers like him
and Sammy charged usurious interest. And—not that it
mattered much, comparatively—he also began receiving
several thousand dollars a year as a no-show salesman for
another friend from childhood, who had turned a rinky-
dink operation into one of the city's biggest plumbing and
heating construction companies. The job gave Gotti the
appearance of employment for the purpose of income tax
returns.

Later on, after Gotti's supposed employment became a
public issue, city officials quizzed Gotti's friend about the
purported job. The friend, Anthony Gurino, said Gotti
drove around the city looking for construction projects
the company might bid on. "What John does is point out
locations," Gurino said shamelessly.

The money suddenly available to the acting capo
fueled his fondness for gambling, and when Gotti bet, he
always bet heavily. Once, he won two hundred twenty-
five thousand dollars on the Brooklyn number, an illegal
version of a state lottery, but lost it in two addicted days
of craps. A fifty-thousand-dollar win in a weekend of bets
on professional or college sports contests was not
unusual—and neither was such a loss.

When the losses came in streaks, as they frequently
did, he borrowed from other loan sharks and kept making
so-called dime bets, a thousand dollars, several days and
nights a week, at thoroughbred and harness racing tracks
near his and Vicky's new home in Howard Beach—
adjacent to Ozone Park but more upscale.

He often used his influence to wangle better terms on
his debts, but he did pay. That was part of his degeneracy,
putting himself in debt, then scrambling to come up with
the money.

"How much? Dime?" one of his bookmakers, unknow- ingly talking on a wiretapped telephone at the Bergin, asked Gotti in 1979.

"Yeah, what the fuck," came the reply. "I'll get myself really in fuckin' jeopardy."

The Bergin telephone—actually a pay telephone in a store next door—was wiretapped by NYPD cops investi- gating the crew's bookmaking. A few associates would be arrested on minor charges, but the investigation never touched Gotti or his top aides.

His top aides were Angelo, who had a similar ghost job with Anthony Gurino and had also moved his family into Howard Beach; Gene, who was on the payroll of another company and had moved to Long Island; John Carneglia, whose auto-salvage yard was making enough money on stolen cars that he required no phony job, and Anthony Rampino, whose physical features had now led to the nickname Roach and whose wife made his "legit" money.

Later, after prison, Willie Boy moved into the inner cir- cle, and Gotti used him and Rampino to collect his loan- shark payments. A menacing look from either the FBI's Source Wahoo or Roach was usually enough to encourage debtors to pay on a timely basis.

Gotti relied on brothers Peter and Richard to a much lesser extent, but he kept them involved. He appointed Peter caretaker of the Bergin and Richard manager of a companion club around the corner, the Our Friends Social Club.

Angelo never had to worry about throwing brother Salvatore a few dollars; Salvatore was now a millionaire— thanks to heroin—but also a fugitive, to avoid arrest in a tax case related to his dealing. While "in the wind," he had continued to deal, and some of his money was hidden in companies controlled by their mutual plumber friend from childhood, Anthony Gurino.

The Bergin telephone wiretap and a listening device planted during a later investigation showed that Gotti dominated his men the way Neil Dellacroce dominated Little Italy fathers who tried to lie about where their sons obtained firearms. As an associate learned after failing to return a Gotti telephone call promptly, it was hard to get a word in edgewise with volcanic John.

"Hi, buddy," the man said when he finally got back to Gotti.

"Buddy, my fuckin' balls! What, I got to reach out for you three days in a-fuckin' advance!"

"Pal, my wife just called me."

"You know, let me tell you something'! I need an example! Don't let you be the fuckin' example! Do you understand me?"

"Listen, John . . ."

"Listen, I called your fuckin' house five times yesterday; now . . . if you're going to disregard my motherfuckin' phone calls, I'll blow you and that fuckin' house up!"

"I never disregard anything you . . ."

"This is not a fuckin' game . . . my time is valuable . . . if I ever hear anybody else calls you and you respond within five days, I'll fuckin' kill you . . . !"

Gotti demanded that his main men make regular appearances at the Bergin; it angered him when anyone was away for more than a day or two at a time. They were expected to attend a group meal held on Wednesday night and afterward to play cards until the sun rose. As the drinks flowed, Gotti would ramble about almost any topic and make pronouncements about his personal philosophy.

"I never lie to any man because I don't fear anyone," he would say. "The only time you lie is when you're afraid."

From 1979 on, Gotti had every reason to believe that every time he spoke inside the Bergin, someone in law enforcement was eavesdropping. But it did not always stop him from joking and talking in a way that could cause legal trouble.

"Your partner was here the other day askin' me to shoot him in the head, and I would've if he didn't tell me in a taped joint," he said in the Bergin one day, to a nightclub owner who was behind on a hundred-thousand-dollar loan.

"You deserve to get hit, but the reason why you ain't . . . is because I gave my word that if you come up here to straighten it out, you wouldn't be killed, but that is gonna be off if you don't come up with it."

"Johnny, you're the best," the man replied.

In another echo of Neil, Gotti made the Bergin an unofficial city hall of Ozone Park, a community of mainly blue-collar people descended from Italian, Irish, and Polish immigrants. Culturally, they were almost as insular as the people of Little Italy—and as contemptuous of the real city hall, which was in culturally distant Manhattan and run for rich people by bureaucrats.

The club was on 101st Avenue, main street, and Gotti told his men to patronize their small-merchant neighbors' shops. He went to Manhattan to buy the exquisite double-breasted suits and floral silk ties he now wore, but he got his hair trimmed and his nails polished on 101st Avenue. He contributed to community events and helped underwrite the annual Fourth of July celebration.

"It's amazin' when we walk down the streets," John's "man" Anthony Rampino told a friend. "It's like he's King of Queens."

Gotti still got in the trenches with his troops, however, especially when it helped Neil—who was indicted again in 1979 and charged with being the money man in a Florida loan-sharking operation managed by an associate in the family's Florida crew. Everyone figured that Neil, a friendly-looking old man when need be would beat the case if he did not have to sit in front of a jury with a younger, more-rough-and-guilty-looking associate.

Gotti, Angelo, Willie Boy, and Rampino flew to Florida; it was one of the few times Gotti had flown, and, as before he did not like it; in time, he would refuse to fly and would travel to his regular Florida vacations by car or train. He was not afraid to fly, he explained to Willie Boy; he just did not like putting his life in anyone else's hands, such as a pilot's.

In Miami Beach, Neil's loan-sharking associate exited the Tropicana Hotel one day and disappeared. Whatever happened to him was likely brutal, because his body was never found.

Willie Boy did not tell the FBI about the trip; once back at the Bergin with a tan, he told James Cardinali, the young robber who hung out there, that he, Gotti, and the others had gone to Florida for "a piece of work."

One year later, senior citizen Neil, alone at the defense table, beat the case. A year after that, Gene Gotti was overheard on a wiretap of Angelo's telephone saying the crew had committed eight murders for the family—

which, at the time, was twice the number that Sammy Gravano had.

Meanwhile, within earshot of the bug at the Bergin, brother John exclaimed: "We're the toughest fuckin' guys in the fuckin' world!" He was talking about another situation, but the remark captured the esprit de corps of the Bergin Hunt and Fish crew.

In 1980 the leader of the tough guys experienced grief for the first time, the kind of grief that his victims' relatives no doubt had known well. One of his five children, a twelve-year-old boy named Frank, a promising student and athlete, was killed when he took a ride on a friend's motorized minibike and was struck by a car.

Frank was a couple of blocks from home when a car driven by John Favara—a backyard neighbor of the Gotti family whose own son played with the Gotti children—turned a corner. Favara was momentarily blinded by the low sun of a late-winter day; he did not see the boy on the minibike dart into the street from behind the far side of a dumpster parked by a house under renovation.

John and Vicky Gotti dressed only in black for many months to come. Vicky was especially grief-stricken; she had acquiesced and let John have his separate world, but her children were her world. She refused to accept a NYPD finding that John Favara, a service manager for a furniture store, was not at fault; Vicky cried to friends that he had to have been drinking or speeding.

Two days after the accident, a woman anonymously telephoned the local police precinct and said: "The driver of the car that killed Frank Gotti will be eliminated."

That same day, Favara found a printed death threat in his mailbox. Over the next several weeks, a woman who seemed to be disguising her voice called his house with another death threat; the word "murderer" was spray-painted on his car, and a funeral card and photograph of Frank Gotti were left in his mailbox.

Finally, three months later, Vicky Gotti attacked Favara with a baseball bat. He was hospitalized, but rather than press charges, he decided, he ought to move out of Howard beach.

Two months later, two days before he was to complete the sale of his home and move to Long Island, three men approached Favara as he left his job. They clubbed him on the head with a two-by-four and threw him into a van, which disappeared down a nearby highway—as did he, forever.

One of the three men stayed and drove Favara's car away; most people familiar with the case believe that Favara and his car were compacted into a small package of steel and bones at John Carneglia's auto-salvage yard.

Trying to assist the police investigation of Favara's disappearance, FBI agents contacted their informants. Willie Boy Johnson said he knew nothing, not even gossip—probably because he, and Rampino, were involved. Source BQ, however, said Gotti had not planned to seek revenge against Favara but that Vicky was so distraught he finally did. Battista added, accurately, that the body would not be found and that Gotti had driven to Florida with Vicky to give himself "a solid alibi."

Detectives from Nassau County, where Favara was abducted, later visited Vicky at home. She cordially invited them into her living room, which featured a shrinelike memorial to her son.

"I don't know what happened to him," she said about Favara. "I'm not sorry if something did. He never sent me a condolence card. He never apologized. He never even got his car fixed."

Nassau County detective Gary Schriffen asked if her husband was home and what he did for a living.

"I don't know where he is, and I don't know what he does. I'm an old-fashioned woman. All I know is, he provides."

The detectives knew where Gotti was; they found him at the Bergin. He was still wearing all black, and he joked to them that they should watch what they said, because the Bergin was bugged.

When the discussion got around to John Favara, Gotti sounded very much like his wife. "I don't know what happened. I'm not sorry if somethin' did. He killed my kid."

In a few months, when Frank would have turned thirteen, and on each of his subsequent birthdays, Vicky placed in memoriam notices in the *Daily News,* "New York's Hometown Paper." So would three of their four other children, after they were married and each named their firstborn son Frank. The messages were always poignant and tenderly crafted—as if they were from people incapable of deliberately causing grief in anyone else's home.

"Missing the smile that warmed our hearts," said one from Frank's parents. "Missing you each day we're apart. Sleep in peace, sweet prince, until we meet again."

Over the next months, the Bergin boss gambled more heavily. He lost so much that Billy Battista told the FBI he did not understand how Gotti afforded the upper-middle-class lifestyle he provided Vicky and their remaining children—one of whom, a son named John, attended the same private military prep school that Carlo Gambino's privileged son Tommy had.

As a key man in the Bergin book, Battista knew about Gotti's big losses. While Gotti bet with other books—no point in winning his own money—Battista was in contact with other bookmakers, who often "lay off" some action to each other to avoid the heavy losses that occur when a long-shot underdog in some heavily wagered event pulls an upset.

Paul also learned about Gotti's binge bets and complained to Neil, but Neil—who liked the action too—pointed out that Gotti always paid up and that despite how strange a therapy it seemed, gambling was Johnny Boy's way of putting grief behind him.

Still, Gotti's gambling made Paul question his fitness for leadership. With typical Sicilian bias for people of Neapolitan origin, Paul already had a low opinion of Gotti's fitness. Like his ancestors, he thought Neapolitans were brash, garish, unreliable, too emotional. And so, even after Roy Cohn got Carmine Fatico a probation deal instead of prison and Carmine went into full retirement, Paul refused to promote Gotti beyond acting capo.

Of course, Gotti questioned Paul's fitness. Paul had ridden brother-in-law Carlo's coattails to power and then retreated to Staten Island to run the family with a small clique of capos and soldiers. He was weak and insecure; he wasn't "a man's man."

Indirectly, Neil sometimes bolstered Gotti's low regard. As a Cosa Nostra traditionalist, Neil believed that the boss had to be obeyed once the boss made up his mind.

But because he was so powerful in his own right, and used to outrank Paul, he spoke his mind in front of Paul without fear—something Sammy learned when Neil took over the sitdown involving Sammy's accusations against Louis DiBono, his former drywall partner.

Once, in a meeting at Paul's attended by Neil, Gotti, and consigliere Joe N. Gallo, Paul complained that a soldier in another family had gone to Neil about a problem, not him.

"Hey, stick this fuckin' job up your ass!" Neil screamed at Paul. "And make me a soldier. Every time a guy likes me, he's a motherfucker?"

"Wait a minute, Neil," said Gallo, a holdover from Carlo's time who silently respected Neil more than Paul. "You can't talk to Paul like ..."

"Shut the fuck up!" Neil shot back. "Every fuckin' time a guy likes me, he's a cocksucker, he's done something wrong!"

Confronted with his underboss's anger, Paul mouthed a weak reply meant to show that his job was full of grief too. "Well, then, if you don't want your job, I don't want my job."

To Neil's protégé, Gotti, Paul sounded like he was whining. A Cosa Nostra boss was supposed to be strong, like Carlo, like Neil, like a lion. Later, Gotti told Sammy, "Fuckin' Paul, you oughta seen it, he was actin' like a fuckin' faggot!"

Meanwhile, back at the Bergin, the bookmaker Billy Battista continued to be mystified about where Gotti was getting the cash to cover his gambling losses and support his family. He told the FBI that some crew associates were talking among themselves about setting up their own scores—because Gotti wasn't arranging any.

Finally, in 1981, Source BQ began to hear and see evidence that offered an explanation for Gotti's cash; he told the FBI he believed that Gotti was now playing with fire—dealing drugs.

He became suspicious when a Bergin habitué told him that Gotti and Angelo Ruggiero always had rolls of quarters on them because they were talking with Angelo's fugitive brother, Salvatore, the heroin dealer, from an ever-changing series of pay telephones.

Then Battista saw Mark Reiter, a known heroin dealer

with connections to the heroin market in Harlem, at the Bergin for closed-door meetings with Gotti and Angelo. Once Salvatore himself even slipped into town under the name Stephen Terri for a secret meeting with Gotti and Angelo.

The evidence mounted even as Gotti continued to warn crew associates that they played with fire if they dealt drugs.

"If I ever catch anybody sellin' drugs, I'll kill them. I'm not gonna let no one embarrass me and I'll make an example out of the first one I catch," he told the young robber who hung out at the Bergin, James Cardinali.

The warnings, however, sounded as hollow as they did in the early 1970s, when Gotti assembled the Bergin crew and delivered an anti-drug message from Carlo—at a time when everyone knew his brother Peter was dealing cocaine and Rampino was dealing heroin.

Despite his posturing, Gotti never punished anyone who dealt drugs. Even Cardinali—the subject of a direct, personal warning, who was so low-ranking it would have cost Gotti nothing to make an example—was never punished when he began dealing both heroin and cocaine so openly that Bergin regulars such as Willie Boy knew and had told the FBI about it.

Source BQ, Battista, told the FBI that Gotti was pretending to toe the Cosa Nostra line re-enunciated by Paul and that Gotti would limit his exposure in heroin to investor and let the men he trusted most—Angelo, Gene, Willie Boy, Carneglia—do the dirty work on the condition that they never, ever, mention his name.

Neither the FBI nor the NYPD—or even Paul, for that matter—would ever find evidence that proved Battista's premise. But it was a very sound premise.

Battista's heroin-dealing suspicions arose as the FBI and the Justice Department laid plans for a major crackdown on Cosa Nostra. Under founding director J. Edgar Hoover, who never even conceded the existence of Cosa Nostra, only five FBI agents in New York were assigned to organized-crime, or OC, cases. The bureau had committed dozens more agents to the battle since his death in 1972, but without much result.

In 1979, however, bureau bosses in New York reorganized the OC section into distinct squads, one for each of the five families; then, after Ronald Reagan was elected, Congress gave the Justice Department more money for agents and prosecutors and eased legal restrictions on electronic surveillance. In one speech, Reagan urged an attack on "the evil enemy within."

Accordingly, late in 1981, a thirteen-member squad of agents in New York, known as the "Gambino squad," launched an electronic assault against Angelo Ruggiero. It targeted him because he had told Willie Boy that his home telephone in Howard Beach was "safe," and Source Wahoo had passed the remark on.

If Angelo was bragging that his telephone was safe, he was probably using it to discuss illegal business. In an affidavit listing Angelo, and John and Gene Gotti, as the main targets of the investigation, the Gambino squad asked a federal judge for permission to wiretap Angelo's home telephone. The request was granted and quickly accomplished. Angelo had not done anything special to secure his phone; his boast was just more of the chatter for which he was known.

While "up" on Angelo's telephone, the Gambino squad learned what a degenerate gambler Gotti had become. On November 11, 1981, a Sunday two days after the wiretap, Angelo telephoned Gotti to ask how the professional football games Gotti had bet on that day were going. In reply, each "dime" Gotti mentioned represented a one-thousand-dollar wager.

"I bet the Buffalo Bills six dimes, they're gettin' killed, ten-nothin'. I bet New England for six dimes, I'm gettin' killed with New England. I bet six dimes on Chicago, they're losin'. I bet three dimes on Kansas City. They're winnin', but maybe they'll lose too, these motherfuckers."

Angelo then asked Gotti which teams he had bet on in games to be played later in the day.

"The Washington Redskins. I bet them for six dimes. Maybe they'll lose too."

Angelo tried to steer the conversation elsewhere, but Gotti only wanted to talk about the jeopardy he was facing.

"We're gettin' killed, that's more important! I'm stuck almost thirty dimes here and nowhere to fucking go!"

Angelo tried again. He told Gotti a story that ended with a remark about a man loyal to his brother "all his life."

"Ah, Christ on the fuckin' cross! Right now I'd give up my fuckin' life just to have fuckin' Buffalo win one!"

The following Sunday, when Angelo tracked Gotti down at a bar that was a center of the Bergin bookmaking operation, Gotti was in a worse mood, and his comments showed that his personal financial situation was as tenuous as Battista suspected.

"Did you hang yourself yet?" Angelo asked as Gotti came on the pay telephone at the Cozy Corner Bar. This time they used "dollar" as a synonym for a thousand dollars.

"Forget about it. If I tell you what I lost, you won't believe it."

"I could believe it."

"Forget about it. I got killed. Forget about it. I lost fifty-three dollars. You know the last time I lost fifty-three dollars?"

"I know all about it."

"On my son's grave, I ain't got fifty-three cents."

Three days after that conversation, the ears of Gambino squad agents perked up when Angelo, on the phone with Gene Gotti, said the word "babania"—which in the volcano meant heroin.

Angelo's reference to heroin and the informant reports from Source BQ persuaded a federal judge to allow the Gambino squad to tighten the electronic surveillance noose around Angelo. Early in 1982, after Angelo moved out of Howard Beach and into a new home in Cedarhurst, Long Island, so did three FBI listening devices, which agents posing as construction workers planted in his basement den, kitchen, and dining room.

The agents also increased physical surveillance of Angelo, and sometimes they let Angelo know they were around, to see what discussion it might provoke on the wiretaps and bugs. Angelo was agitated by the surveillance, and at one point he moaned—within earshot of Source Wahoo—that he was going to get even with one of the surveillants, Special Agent Don McCormick.

The threat provoked the first meeting between the Gambino squad boss and the Ozone Park crew boss. The

Gambino squad boss was an FBI agent out of central casting, Bruce Mouw. He was tall, slim, and as wholesome-looking as a midshipman in dress whites, which the thirty-eight-year-old Iowa native had once been.

With McCormick, Mouw knocked on the Gotti home in Howard Beach—the first in the neighborhood with a satellite TV antenna and the only one with an outdoor video surveillance system and a large Neapolitan mastiff named Charlie, who was kept in a pen beside the door to the house that the family used.

The security was for John's sake, the satellite antenna for Vicky's. She liked television, particularly soap operas, and she normally had several sets in the house on at once as she cleaned up. Because John did not permit strangers—even maids, since they might be agents planting bugs—she did her own housework, behind curtains always fully drawn to the world outside.

Her bedroom was always last because her husband was such a night animal and late sleeper—normally he slept until around eleven in the morning, sometimes later, when Angelo telephoned to remind him of the day's agenda.

Mouw and McCormick came earlier in hopes of annoying Gotti, but Vicky, answering their knock, surprised them by politely saying her husband was up and would be right down.

Gotti always bragged to his crew that he never gave the time of day to cops and agents—no matter how innocuous the inquiry. But these were fatuous boasts; most of the time, he was perfectly civil to cops and agents, as he was when he greeted Mouw and McCormick.

"What can I do for you?" he smiled. When Gotti chose to smile, the normally stern, unfriendly lines of his face did soften, and it was a winning, mischievous smile.

Mouw introduced himself and McCormick and went straight to the point. "Tell your pal Angelo to knock off the threatening talk, or somebody's going to pay."

"Ah, Angelo, he'd never say nothin' like that."

"He did, and we don't like our guys being threatened."

"Must be a mistake somewhere. I'll talk to him."

* * *

With Angelo's phones tapped and his house bugged, the FBI investigation gathered steam. Gotti seemed to sense the growing peril. He told Angelo, "Get in your car and come see me" when Angelo wanted to talk. He told Mark Reiter, the heroin dealer at the Bergin, to stop hanging around. Reiter, however, remained in Howard Beach, where he moved into Angelo's mother's house.

Agents up on Angelo's telephone overheard his daughter say a "Mark" had left a package. Agents in Florida learned that a Salvatore Ruggiero courier had departed for New York with thirteen kilos of heroin. New Jersey agents surveilled Angelo and John Carneglia as the pair met with two dealers from Canada.

And, back in New York, Gambino squad agents overheard Gene Gotti tell Angelo the only reason the "Pope" was against drugs was that Paul "never had to struggle for a quarter in his life."

As these clues piled up, Paul put some bite in his bark about drugs, after two soldiers accused another of dealing heroin. To get his message across further to people he suspected needed to hear it most, Paul decided that John Gotti would do the biting.

In April 1982, he summoned Gotti to Staten Island and gave him a contract to kill Peter "Little Pete" Tambone, who had been made, or "straightened out," in Carlo's time. Gotti obviously told Angelo about this, because Angelo was soon quoting Paul and Gotti while talking with a visitor to his bugged house.

"John, we got a bad problem with Little Pete," Paul told Gotti, according to Angelo "You know anybody that's straightened out who moves babania gets killed."

"'Yeah, I know, Paul, but Little Pete? He's a grandfather."

"Too bad. He knew the rules."

Gotti said okay, then collected Angelo and went straight to Neil and asked him to intercede on the sixty-two-year-old Tambone's behalf. Only in the Gambino family, with its built-in fault line, would soldiers so casually run to the underboss and ask to talk the boss out of something they did not want.

It never came out on the bugs, but the intensity with which Gotti and Angelo fought for Little Pete—who was not a member of the Bergin crew—suggested to the agents that Tambone might have been caught selling heroin purchased from Angelo. Conversations between Angelo and others—but never Gotti—did show they were worried about the precedent-setting effect of Tambone's murder on their futures, but with Neil, they made it seem that they were objecting only because Tambone was old and likable.

"What kind of family are we? Killin' Pete?" Gotti said. "No drugs, John."

"*Minchia,* Pete ain't no drug dealer. He was makin' for his family. I never saw Paul turn away a dirty dollar."

Neil spoke to Paul and persuaded him to put Tambone's fate up to the Commission, the Cosa Nostra board of directors. After weeks of negotiations that showed how corrupting the drug virus was, the Commission—composed of only four bosses now that a fifth had been banned because too many of his soldiers dealt drugs—held a vote on whether Tambone should live.

The result was a two-two deadlock. Paul, joined by Vincent Gigante, a former boxer nicknamed Chin who was the Genovese family boss, voted for the death penalty. Two other bosses—who were not as prosperous as Paul and Chin—voted for a conditional pardon. Without a majority, Paul relented, and allowed Tambone to live.

Angelo gave Tambone the news and the penalty that would be imposed instead: He could not engage in family business for six months; he would have to apologize to Paul and pretend he never handled heroin, only the money for the deal; and he would have to endure what Angelo described as "a riot act from John."

"But that'll be just a formality," Angelo added.

The Tambone crisis ended just as another began. On May 6, 1982, Salvatore Ruggiero—who had been hiding out for six years in Florida, Ohio, and Pennsylvania—hired a private plane at an airport near his latest hideout in New Jersey and flew south to Florida with his wife and two pilots. He intended to look over some investment property and wrap another heroin deal.

Over the Atlantic Ocean, off the coast of southern Georgia, two malfunctioning alarms in the cockpit of the Lear jet sounded high-pitched warnings, which caused one of the pilots to make an unnecessary adjustment in his descent pattern toward Orlando International Airport.

The plane spun out of control and plunged to the sea until it struck water nose first at shattering speed, killing all aboard if they had not already died of fright.

The company that leased the plane notified a drug-dealing friend of Salvatore's who had rented planes with him before. The friend telephoned Angelo, and Angelo, Gene, and Carneglia dashed to Salvatore's New Jersey hideout and took away all the papers, valuables, and heroin they could find.

Two days later, Michael Coiro, the trusty lawyer for Angelo and the Gotti brothers since their days as airport hijackers, came up from semiretirement in Florida to help Angelo sort out the complicated tangle of his brother's assets.

Coiro was at Angelo's bugged house when Sammy's friend Frank DeCicco, the capo who kept a foot in both branches of the family, stopped by to pay his respects.

"Gene found the heroin," Coiro told DeCicco, referring to the search of Salvatore's hideout.

John Gotti paid his respects at a church memorial service for Salvatore that drew hundreds of hoodlums. He and the victim, as boys in East New York, had been caught in a stolen car, and now John would never be caught in an airplane again.

"That ain't no way to die," he told DeCicco. "When I go, let it be in the street, like a man."

Back in Angelo's house, agents monitoring the bugs overheard Angelo utter a similar sentiment—it was hard to accept Salvatore's death because he was found in so many "fuckin' pieces."

"If he would've been shot in the head and found in the streets, that's part of our life, I could accept it," he added.

Coiro stayed in New York for several weeks to help Angelo out, but he also dug himself a grave, because while Angelo was trying to untangle his brother's hidden interests in property and companies, he was also trying to sell Salvatore's heroin.

"If I get some money, will you hold it?" Angelo asked Coiro, a slim man with a raspy voice and curly salt-and-pepper hair.

"Yeah," Coiro said, breaching the lawyer-client line.

"Nobody is to know but us," Gene interjected. "You're

not our lawyer, you're one of us as far as we're concerned."

"I know it, Gene, and I feel that way too."

At one point, Coiro recalled for Angelo and Gene how Gene's brother John had scolded him for not visiting right away when he first arrived in New York to help Angelo.

"So I said, 'John, I was over there at Angelo's, where I thought I had to be, doin' what I had to do. I didn't know you were unaware of what was going on.' "

The sarcastic tone of Gene's pointed reply to Coiro's story bolstered the soundness of Billy Battista's premise about John, because it strongly implied that John knew what was going on: "You believe he's unaware of all this, huh?"

"I figured he knew about it, Genie."

For several more months, the bugs in Angelo's house picked up dozens of highly incriminating conversations. "There's a lot of profit in heroin!" Angelo exclaimed one day, after Salvatore's heroin was sold, and after Gene and Carneglia flew to Florida and bought more from one of Salvatore's suppliers.

John Gotti was not overheard on the bugs in Angelo's house. As acting capo, he never went to soldiers' homes. Bruce Mouw and the Gambino squad kept hoping he would, but he never did—and finally they decided to lower the boom on the others.

On August 8, 1983, Angelo, Gene, Carneglia, Reiter, Michael Coiro, and several more go-betweens and errand boys were arrested and accused of dealing multiple kilos of heroin. Willie Boy, who was involved, skated free. As the person who told the FBI about Angelo's "safe" phone and the layout of Angelo's home, he had reason to suspect the house was "hot" and had avoided it.

Battista, unaware that Willie Boy also was a double agent, told the FBI he was surprised that Willie Boy was not arrested. "I know Willie Boy is dealin' with Mark Reiter," Battista told his contact agent. "Everybody knows it."

With the Peter Tambone controversy not far in the past, the arrests put immediate stress on the Gambino fault line.

Years later, Mouw and others said the day the arrests came down was the day Paul really died. Undeniably, the pot did begin to boil that day, but the main ingredients were still lacking.

CHAPTER 5

•••••••••••••

The Fist

The heroin-dealing arrests of Angelo, Gene, and Carneglia—key men in the Gotti crew of the Neil wing—were an assault on Paul's credibility and foreshadowed a showdown. But the lay of the land would change, and his position would be weaker than he knew when he finally chose to assert his authority and discipline the crew. In the meantime, the newly reinvigorated FBI and other law enforcement agencies sharply increased the pressure on the "evil enemy within," and Paul, Neil, and Gotti soon confronted urgent, freedom-threatening legal problems of their own.

Especially Paul. As agents and prosecutors began to target Cosa Nostra bosses—under a newly appreciated racketeering law that made bosses as vulnerable to prosecution as the lowliest member of a "criminal enterprise" such as a Mafia family—the insulation that Carlo had enjoyed evaporated, and Paul began to suffer the consequences of being his cousin, brother-in-law, and successor.

He would be indicted twice and warned that a third case was on the way. His troubles made him more aloof—and more antagonistic, even toward men who had served loyally. He began breaking rules, causing the soft ground beneath him to shift further. In minds beside John Gotti's, the heroin scandal in the Gotti crew would take a backseat to Paul's problems—and Paul's behavior.

At the drama's outset, Angelo and the others appeared to be in a worse spot than Peter Tambone a couple months before. Little Pete had merely been accused of dealing by other soldiers, but the Gotti men had been arrested by FBI agents. In Carlo's time, and supposedly

Paul's, an arrest on heroin charges was a capital crime, punishable immediately.

But the Tambone situation had shown that Paul's time was not the same as Carlo's. One of the five families had lost its right to vote on the Commission because of drug dealing, and even when Paul took Neil's advice and left Tambone's fate up to Commission bosses in good repute, only the hard-nosed former boxer, Vincent "Chin" Gigante of the Genovese family, had supported him—creating the impotent spectacle of a two-two deadlock.

Against that backdrop, Paul had to confront the challenge to his authority and credibility on his own, without the Commission. Obviously the new situation was more complex than that of the fading old soldier Tambone, or even that of Roy DeMeo, the ex-butcher's-apprentice-turned-drug-dealer whom Paul had contracted DeCicco to kill eights months earlier, before DeMeo was even arrested.

The new situation involved an entire crew, but it wasn't just any crew. The Gotti crew did in Neil's wing what Sammy and DeCicco did in Paul's— carry out contracts efficiently—and Paul had to consider the consequences of taking it on. Moreover, Angelo was John Gotti's oldest friend; Gene was a brother; even Carneglia was special, because he was a top earner.

Paul instantly knew that this was one of those situations in which it was especially true that rules do not occur in a vacuum; he could not eliminate core members of the Gotti crew without a response from the hotheaded Neapolitan, and maybe even Neil—despite Neil's consistent support of the drug ban.

Still, he had to react somehow. How could he expect anyone to obey him if he allowed egregious offenses to go unpunished? How could he enforce any rules if he overlooked a main rule—one handed down, as he was, by Carlo?

With a nonviolent response his most realistic option, Paul mulled over several ideas, such as "busting" Gotti down to soldier and reassigning his men to other crews on the grounds that Gotti could not control his—but while he mulled Angelo concocted a cover story that he and Gotti asked Neil to carry to Paul.

The story was that the heroin case would never amount

to much. Angelo and the others happened to be bugged as they tried to sort out the finances of Angelo's brother Salvatore, whose affairs might have involved drugs, but Salvatore was not a soldier or even an associate, so Paul had no authority over him.

In any case, Neil told Paul, the truth would emerge soon enough—in Angelo's and the others' own words, because the case was based on tape-recorded evidence. So why not wait until the government prosecutors, as required in pretrial proceedings, began turning over copies of the tapes to defense lawyers?

As his own overheard words on a different bug later showed, Neil did not believe that Angelo and the others were just mopping up Salvatore's affairs—but he intervened to protect their acting capo and his protégé, Gotti.

As Gotti saw Neil as the father his wished he'd had, Neil saw Gotti as the son he had wanted. Gotti was everything that Neil's real son, Armond, was not—loyal, reliable, strong. To Neil's bitter dismay, his twenty-eight-year-old blood son had caught the cocaine virus and was becoming another Nicholas Scibetta, a punk who traded on connections. The fierce old gangster was boss of Little Italy but not of his own son—no matter how much he yelled.

"I never wanted to put shit up my nose or arm," Gotti would say, when Neil complained about Armond. "A martini or two, all the blast I want. That other shit—not natural."

At the time, Neil and Gotti had another reason for man-to-man talks; Gotti had become infatuated with Neil's out-of-wedlock daughter, Shannon Grillo, wife of a yet-unmade Gambino associate. Neil loved Shannon, and had provided for her, but it pained him to see his would-be son risking the same mistakes he had made, and he told Gotti to stay away from her.

Even so, as someone who had cheated on his wife, it was as hard for Neil to keep Gotti away from Shannon as it was to keep Armond from cocaine. Shannon was young, blond and far livelier than the now permanently mournful Vicky Gotti—and Gotti dated her openly. Shannon's marriage was dubious enough that her husband, who extorted nightclub owners on Manhattan's Upper East Side for a living, really didn't care. Ernie Grillo was another example of a gangster getting his kicks from cocaine lately.

Gotti enjoyed taking Shannon to restaurants that they saw touted in *New York,* a slick magazine that Vicky would never read. She called Gotti "Papa Schultz"—after Dutch Schultz, the heavily romanced gangster-about-town of an earlier New York. He got a kick out of the nickname, and other gangster girlfriends they met around town began calling him that too.

Gambino squad agents learned about the affair and followed the couple to the Terrace Restaurant at Columbia University in Manhattan one night. They considered taking surveillance photos and showing them to Gotti, to see if the threat of exposure might make him an informer, but they decided that as a gambler he would call their play and take his losses if he had to.

While unable to reach Armond or Gotti, Neil did get Paul to delay a reaction to the Angelo situation until Paul was able to personally review the tapes. His real plan was to keep delaying Paul until inaction took over, the best solution for everyone. His initial intervention did give Paul a dignified reason to do nothing but tell Gotti to turn over the tapes to him, once prosecutors turned them over to defense lawyers.

Several delays in the pretrial stages of the case delayed the government's production of the tapes and played into Neil's strategy. Then, early in 1984, Paul began to face more serious problems than what to do about the heroin arrests.

The investigation of Roy DeMeo that Paul had feared would lead to him did lead to him—even with DeMeo dead. Paul was indicted on charges that as DeMeo's ultimate boss, he profited from a ten-year-long rampage by DeMeo and several frenzied associates that included murder for hire, drug dealing, an international car-theft operation, child pornography, and prostitution.

DeMeo's operational boss was a caporegime who was loyal to Paul, but prosecutors had a witness set to testify that when DeMeo's capo was not around, he took money from DeMeo straight to Paul. Under the Racketeer-Influenced and Corrupt Organizations Act, the law that prosecutors were starting to use against the families, that made Paul—as the boss of the "criminal enterprise" known as the Gambino family—almost as guilty as DeMeo.

After his arrest, Paul was released on bail; under RICO, as the racketeering and conspiracy law was commonly known, he faced life in prison if convicted at trial.

The case against Paul made Gotti believe he might skate free of the Angelo situation and even succeed Paul—according to Willie Boy Johnson. After a clandestine meeting with Willie Boy, an FBI agent put a memo in the Source Wahoo file that said Gotti and the Ozone Park crew were "contemplating their rise to power" and "gloating in the troubles that have recently befallen" Paul.

That same year, Paul learned that the troubles befalling him were certain to grow much worse. The FBI's Gambino squad had been pursuing more than Angelo and the heroin case. The squad had used remarks captured in Angelo's house—comments about the Commission and the Tambone matter—to establish the probable cause it needed to get judicial permission to secretly break into Paul's mansion and install a bug there. In the last year, that bug had recorded many damaging conversations between Paul and others.

Paul's lawyers told him he was vulnerable to two more RICO cases—one aimed at bosses on the Commission and a second aimed at the Gambino administration, which prosecutors referred to as the "hierarchy." In both, as in the DeMeo case, sixty-nine-year-old Paul faced the prospect of spending his last days in prison.

Despite everything, however, Paul remained acutely interested in making money. And because he blamed many of his problems on the weakness and stupidity of his soldiers, he looked elsewhere for partners when business opportunities came along—particularly to the Genovese family, whose boss, Chin Gigante, had been the only one to support him in the Commission vote on Tambone and who shared Paul's dim view of flamboyant gangsters like Gotti.

Chin was an exceptionally low-profile boss. For many years, his personal family—including a brother who was an activist Roman Catholic priest in the Bronx—had insisted that the ex-fighter was a punch-drunk old man; why else would he shuffle around the streets of Little Italy in his bathrobe and dockworker's hat, mumbling to himself?

One reason would be to give himself an established senility defense in case some prosecutor—as one ultimately would—tried to bring a case against him. So far, the act had fooled the FBI, which believed another man was the Genovese boss. But Gigante was the boss, though such a secretive one that he forbade his soldiers to speak his name to anyone. Instead, they referred to the boss of the city's second-largest family by rubbing their chins.

Paul and Chin had known each other for almost thirty years; they admired each other. When Paul, even as his legal troubles grew, decided to form a new construction company, he made Chin and a couple of Genovese stand-ins his partners.

In a business context it was a small development. But in a Gambino family context, it was large, especially in the minds of the stalwarts of the family's construction-based schemes, Sammy Gravano and Frank DeCicco—once they began seeing Chin's stand-ins steering business to Genovese-connected firms.

"I understand Paul doin' somethin' with the Chin, but not if it hurts people in our family," Sammy complained to DeCicco.

"Paul's for himself," DeCicco replied "He likes being boss 'cause of the money, but he fuckin' hates the job."

Sammy and DeCicco's grumbling must have made its way back to Paul, according to what Louis Milito, Sammy's partner in a steel-erection company, later told DeCicco.

Milito was at Paul's mansion on Staten Island, waiting to go into a meeting, when he overheard Paul tell a top aide that no one had any right to complain about his business dealings.

"It's none of their fuckin' business," Paul said to Thomas Bilotti, his favorite caporegime, who also served as his driver. "We got guys who don't tell half of what they're up to, so why should I care what they think?"

"Some of these companies were with Frankie and Sammy."

"I don't care if Sammy or Frankie or anyone else minds."

"Then there's Deebee," replied Bilotti, using the nickname of Robert DiBernardo, an influential soldier and also an oddity in that he belonged to no crew but instead reported directly to Paul about an International Brotherhood of Teamsters local he controlled. "Deebee's always talking and making things worse than they are."

"I don't care about Deebee either. He gets plenty too."

When DeCicco told him what Milito overheard, Sammy took it as the rant of a perturbed old man—not a threat. But he began feeling differently after a Gambino capo involved in a dispute with a Genovese capo was murdered and Paul acknowledged that he gave Chin permission to eliminate the Gambino man.

"Incredible! You don't let people in another family kill a captain in our family!" Sammy said later to DeCicco, the only person he trusted with such complaints. "Two guys have a beef, sit 'em down, work it out. But don't give up your own. Where we goin' here? Ain't we a Cosa Nostra?"

"Not since Carlo's dead, is what some people say."

"This is worse than lettin' Neil have his own crews! At least Neil's with us!"

Normally stoic Sammy was prone to agitation these days. He had begun taking anabolic steroids, a "miracle" drug that many professional athletes were using, to increase musculature and speed. The boxing workout begun years before were now part of his morning ritual, and at age thirty-eight in 1983, he began a doctor-prescribed steroid program recommended by professional boxers and trainers at Gleason's Gym in Brooklyn. He stopped after several months because his foot speed failed to improve.

The steroids, however, added more bulk to his already bulky five-foot-five body. "Bull" became an even more apt nickname, but the patient had wild mood swings—mellow one moment, hot-tempered the next—and while in a hot temper, he put two more notches on his murder belt. Victims No. 7 and 8 were eliminated so fast they never even got to tell anyone what gangland rules they broke.

By summer 1984, Paul's demand for copies of the tapes from the FBI's Angelo investigation—the proof of whether Angelo and the others were drug dealers or were just mopping up for Salvatore—was still on the table. Prosecutors had given copies to Angelo's defense lawyers, but Angelo invented a reason why they could not be given to Paul: The tapes were full of embarrassing personal details about his home life and contained some joking remarks about others that might be misinterpreted.

Once again, Neil ran interference with Paul. This time, he was a particularly effective—and sympathetic—conciliator. He had been stricken by cancer and was undergoing chemotherapy. He was going to die soon, and now did not seem to be the time to issue an ultimatum for the tapes. Once again, Paul had a dignified reason to back off.

Gotti, protégé and would-be son, assumed many of the seventy-one-year-old Neil's duties. Gotti was still romancing Shannon Grillo, but Neil did not ask about this anymore, and Gotti did not offer. The night life of Papa Schultz was not as important as the day life. At age forty-four, while still an acting capo, Gotti became de facto leader of the Neil wing.

Such prestige, and Paul's failure to bring the dispute over Angelo's tapes to a head, made Gotti feel and act like a boss; many people, sensing change in the air, treated him as one.

When one of his two daughters got married, he hosted a *Godfather*-like reception for a thousand guests. Thirty tables were designated for the bride's father's acquaintances, and one by one, each came to his table to pay homage as the singer Connie Francis sang love songs and comedian George Kirby told jokes.

Even at other people's wedding receptions, even one in the Paul wing, Gotti became the star attraction, a role that he relished—as another overheard conversation on the Bergin bug showed.

"Hey, Bobby," Gotti said to one of many men in the club that day, "Whose wedding was that this weekend we went to?"

"Ah, Frankie DeCicco's son."

"Whose wedding did it look like it was?"

"Yours."

"How many people come and bother me until what

time in the morning? They had to put a chair next to
me."

"Three o'clock. Three-fifteen."

"Every good fellow and every non-good fellow," Gotti
said, distinguishing between made and unmade men,
"came and bothered me. My brother Pete said he clocked
seventy-five guys. I say he undersold me. I'd say there
was more than seventy-five guys who came and talked to
me."

The show of respect for Gotti—and his friendly discussions with DeCicco, father of the bridegroom, and another guest, Sammy—would not have been as effusive if
Paul had been at the reception, but Paul, citing the press
of other business, had sent regrets.

Despite his rising stature, Gotti still behaved like a
common thug. That summer, after a burly mechanic kept
leaning on his car's horn to protest being stalled in traffic
behind a car double-parked outside the Cozy Corner Bar,
a center of the Bergin bookmaking operation, Gotti
punched him in the face.

The mechanic, who repaired refrigerated meat lockers
for a living, called the police, and Gotti was arrested for
the first time in a decade, then jailed and released on bail.
It was a cheap case that few people paid any attention to
at the time.

Gotti reacted to business challenges the same way.
Early in 1985, he was caught on another hidden listening
device, this one a body wire worn by an informer trying
to work his way out of a heroin case unrelated to
Angelo's. The informer went to the Bergin with a bookmaker reporting in to Gotti that some strangers had
opened a competing operation in Gotti territory, near the
Cozy Corner Bar. The bookmaker had warned the men to
shut down, but they refused because they had a "sponsor"
just as important as Gotti.

"Forget about that," Gotti said, after being briefed. "I
got four thousand guys. I'll send 'em in from every
neighborhood."

The bookmaker said he wasn't sure who the men's
sponsor was. but Gotti forbade a competing game under
any conditions. "I don't give a fuck who they come up
with. I'll tell you right now, I need the exercise. They're
not gonna play nothin'."

At the time, Gotti had learned he might be facing a federal RICO case too. Unlike the cases against Paul and the cases beginning to fall against other bosses and cops in other families, the one against him was being assembled by an assistant United States attorney in Brooklyn—not the FBI squads and prosecutors specifically assigned to bring Cosa Nostra down.

Assistant U.S. attorney Diana Giacalone had grown up in Queens and walked past the Bergin Hunt and Fish on her way to parochial school. She learned about Gotti while trying a minor case involving two armed robbers remotely linked to the Bergin.

Investigating Gotti, Giacalone learned about Neil, and even though he was likely to die before a trial, he became a target too. So did Neil's wayward son, Armond, who managed to keep an eye on a few things for Neil in Little Italy, such as which vendors could participate in local festivals. Giacalone also was zeroing in on several of Gotti's men at the Bergin, including his brother Gene, Carneglia, and Rampino.

As a rank chauvinist, Gotti had a hard time taking a woman prosecutor seriously. "I guarantee you no girl is ever gonna put us in jail," he bayed to Rampino. "We'll make her cry, we'll buy her jury. Whatever the fuck it takes, but, guaranteed, she'll never put us in jail."

Early in March 1985, a story whose object it was to enhance the importance of Giacalone's case, was leaked to the *Daily News*. It was the first time Gotti's name had appeared in print since the McBratney case twelve years before—and the first time ever in one of the city's big papers, a fact worth noting, given the media explosion to come in just a short while.

More important, the story contained a big error—but one that served Gotti's interests and made him begin to appreciate the value of media manipulation. The story correctly noted Paul's legal problems—which did now include one of the two additional cases his lawyers had warned about, the Commission case—but it added that "law enforcement sources" believed Gotti was now the acting boss of the Gambino family.

Because Paul was so aloof, Gotti knew that many soldiers in both wings would take the story literally. It made him even more resolved to defy Paul on the Angelo tapes, should Paul demand them after Neil died.

"I bet fuckin' Paul gagged when he read the fuckin' *News!*" Gotti said to Rampino. "That *cazzu,* he's gotta hate it. 'Cause he knows I already got a thousand guys that love me."

A few weeks later, Neil, Gotti, Armond, Gene, Carneglia, Willie Boy, Rampino, and a few others were indicted under the RICO law and accused of crimes ranging from murder to loan-sharking. If convicted, they all faced twenty or more years in prison—essentially career-ending penalties.

Neil was arraigned and granted bail during a special hearing at his home. The others were arraigned and granted bail normally, all but Willie Boy. In her investigation, Giacalone discovered to her amazement that Willie Boy, a killer and leg-breaker for Gotti and Neil the last eighteen years, was the high-wire actor in the Gotti crew—the FBI's Source Wahoo.

Trying to strengthen her case, she included him in the indictment—a decision that for legal reasons meant his informer role would have to be disclosed to his codefendants. She hoped that prospect would make Willie Boy fear for his life and decide to switch sides—become a cooperating witness and testify against the others. She met with him privately before the bail hearing and warned him of her plans.

But Willie Boy said he would never testify and begged her to reconsider: "I'll be killed. My family will be slaughtered."

What Giacalone said in reply was merely legal mumbo jumbo to Willie Boy. He felt betrayed; so did his FBI handlers. They felt that he was so valuable she should have left him out of her case. But during her investigation Giacalone had feuded with the Gambino squad and with prosecutors especially assigned, unlike her, to Cosa Nostra cases. They had given her no favors, and so she gave them none.

Giacalone urged Willie Boy at least to ask the judge in the case to place him in protective custody, but Willie Boy said he would risk life on the streets rather than trust the government again. And even before Gotti told him all would be forgiven as long as he remained at the defense table as a codefendant and refused to testify for the government, Source Wahoo ended all contact with the FBI.

"I'm gonna give you a pass, and I give you my word no one will bother you," Gotti told Willie Boy. "After we win this case, you won't be able to be in the life again. But you'll get a job, you'll have your family, and you'll be all right."

Meanwhile, Billy Battista informed the FBI that Gotti was startled to learn about Willie Boy and thought the FBI was up to some trick; the East New York pals had committed so many crimes together that Gotti could not conceive of Willie Boy being a "rat."

In a few months, however, the FBI's memos about Willie Boy were turned over to defense lawyers, and Gotti read them and saw how much Willie Boy had provided to the FBI—crucial tips such as the location of Gotti's hideout when the police were seeking to arrest him for the revenge killing of James McBratney.

As Gotti later told Sammy, the FBI memos also revealed how much Willie Boy edited himself. "There're some bodies he could have told 'em about, it could've been a lot fuckin' worse."

Although Gotti was not specific, he was no doubt referring to, among others, the murders of a loan-sharking codefendant of Neil's in Florida—and of his backyard neighbor, John Favara.

Willie Boy also never put Gotti in the middle of a heroin deal, but he had good reason to keep quiet about drugs. Just as Battista always said, Willie Boy was a part-time heroin dealer.

A few months later, after Battista learned from a friendly FBI agent that Giacalone was going to throw him into her case as an unindicted coconspirator and reveal his identity in the same turn of the screw, he collected his wife and fled the state; he was not seen again, not by anyone at the Bergin, anyway.

By then, Willie Boy was in jail. After he refused to make a deal and be a cooperating witness, Giacalone got a judge to deny him bail and consign him to protective custody—despite Willie Boy's vehement protests that he'd rather take his chances on the street. The FBI was furious at the turn of events and deprived of its sources inside the Gotti crew.

In the spring of 1985, Paul was seventy years old. The trial in the first of his cases, the one accusing him of profiting from Roy DeMeo's operations, was to begin soon; but even if he won, he still faced trial in the Commission case, and if he won that, the still-evolving case aimed at the Gambino hierarchy—him, Neil, and consigliere Joe N. Gallo—would by then be waiting for him.

The dispute over Angelo's tapes was still unresolved, but a few excerpts had appeared in pretrial legal papers submitted by prosecutors in the Commission case, and these told Paul that the Gambino squad had also overheard busybody Angelo talking about Peter Tambone and the Commission with unauthorized parties.

"Angelo and them know we got this rule," Paul told Sammy one day. "Made guys aren't supposed to talk about the Commission with guys who aren't made, and that's what this loudmouth did."

"A lot of rules gettin' broke lately, Paul," replied Sammy, confident that Paul would not detect his irony. "Ain't right."

Once again, Paul asked for Angelo's tapes, but again, Neil encouraged delay—now because Angelo's lawyers were challenging the tapes on many different legal grounds, and there was a good chance a judge might dismiss the case, making everything moot. It was a weak excuse, founded on high improbability, but Paul's will to force a showdown while Neil was alive was as weak as before.

Indeed, early that summer, Paul went out of his way to make Neil feel good about the situation he would soon leave behind. He told Neil that if it turned out Gotti was not personally involved in heroin, he would, despite his misgivings, make Gotti one of three "acting street bosses" who would run the family should Paul lose the DeMeo trial and be imprisoned.

The other two acting street bosses would be Paul's favorite capo, Tommy Bilotti, and Carlo's son, Tommy Gambino. They, like Gotti, would still take their orders from Paul, however. Under a Cosa Nostra tradition that he intended to invoke, a boss had a right to stay in power until he died, even if imprisoned.

Paul even summoned Gotti to Staten Island to explain the arrangement. "I'm gonna set it up so you and the two Tommies run things for me if I'm in the can," he said. "I'm tryin' to create a peaceful transition here."

"If it's okay with them, it's okay with me," Gotti said.

Back in Ozone Park, however, Gotti spat on Paul's proposal: Bilotti was a gofer; Gambino was just Carlo's rich son; and, in any case, the borgata could not have three acting bosses.

"We're just a token here, we're gonna end up with nothin'," he told Angelo and others. "We've been here before; this puttin' people in temporary actin' positions is bullshit."

As later events made clear, Paul was not deeply committed to the plan. It was really more about pleasing someone he had always felt very insecure about. And while his announcement did please Neil, it also sealed Paul's fate—because it made Gotti decide that it was now time to be a lion and a fox, time to make his move and murder Paul Castellano.

Gotti was not the type to actually quote from the pages of Niccolò Machiavelli, but he often said that Machiavelli had said all there was to say about human nature and boasted that he had read all of the consigliere-like philosopher's writings—including *The Prince,* in which Machiavelli said that a prince must sometimes act outside traditional codes because sometimes great actions by individuals are needed to give old institutions new vigor.

"We weren't gonna be lay-down Sallies" was how Gotti later described his decision. "We were makin' a Cosa Nostra again."

He dispatched Angelo to float trial balloons beyond Ozone Park. Angelo went first to Sammy and said he had good reason to believe that as soon as Neil died, Paul would try to kill him. It was the kind of lie that betrayal makes necessary; in truth, Angelo and Gotti believed that when Paul finally chose to discipline the crew, he would not consider violence a viable option.

So Angelo told Sammy, "Paul ain't leavin' me no

choice. This is off the record, but if I decided to whack him, you with me?"

"Is John with ya?"

"You think I'd be here if he ain't?"

"Is John with ya?"

"He's in on it. He sent me."

Sammy Bull, now off steroids, begged off a firm commitment. Paul's behavior for the last two years—granting Gigante permission to kill a Gambino capo, steering business to a personal company at the expense of family-connected companies—was not enough to make him want to kill Paul, an act of Cosa Nostra treason that had occurred only once in his lifetime, in 1957, when the Gambino boss, Albert Anastasia, was slain in a barbershop.

Sammy said he had to think it over. He wanted time to consider the chessboard, especially the position of the DeCicco piece. "Let me speak to Frankie and some others," he said, "see how it feels to them."

"I think Frankie will go along, and so will Deebee," Angelo replied, referring in the second instance to Robert DiBernardo, the influential soldier-at-large who reported directly to Paul about the Teamsters local he controlled.

By agreeing to test the water himself, Sammy signaled his belief that Paul was simply too unloved to win a showdown with the Gotti crew. If Paul intended to kill Angelo, he would have to kill Gotti, and if he did that, the Bergin crew would mount a devastating war of revenge—and not many soldiers Sammy knew were eager to fight and die for Paul.

Angelo's approach backed Sammy against a wall of pride and ambition. Gotti had respected him by allowing Angelo to impart such dangerous information; it was a sign that Gotti wanted to build a unified family, and if he succeeded, all who sided with him would benefit.

Sammy told Angelo he would let him know soon. The Fist, as the plotters eventually called themselves (because they became five strong and used a clenched-fist salute to greet one another) began to take shape.

At the time of Angelo's approach, Sammy was confronting a legal problem of his own. It was a small one next to the cases facing Paul, Neil, Gotti, and the others:

He and Eddie Garafola faced a couple of years in prison after being accused of failing to pay income taxes on the windfall they had made in 1982, when the deluded Frank Fiala attempted to buy the Plaza Suite disco.

The police got nowhere investigating Fiala's murder, but a federal prosecutor in Brooklyn had traced to Sammy the nearly three-quarters of a million dollars in under-the-table cash that Fiala paid Sammy only days before he was killed—for prematurely taking over Sammy's office at the disco and making such foolhardy remarks as "greaseballs ain't pimples on a Colombian's ass."

After a lawyer in the deal was hauled before a grand jury that was investigating the transaction, Sammy and Eddie began preparing their defense by reporting the money to the IRS and paying the taxes, but the late payment looked as fishy as it was, and they were indicted and arrested. Sammy, who had not been arrested since his Shorty Spero era, was released on bail secured by his Staten Island home—the one partially bought with Fiala money.

The trial was held in August 1985. Sammy was represented by a rising talent of the criminal defense bar, Gerald Shargel, a tall, bearded protégé of Michael Coiro's; many prosecutors and FBI agents loathed Shargel because they thought that he, like Coiro, was too enamored of his clients' power and money.

Indeed, at the time Shargel would have been preparing to defend a lesser codefendant of Paul's in the DeMeo case if a judge had not ruled that Shargel was a "house counsel" to the DeMeo crew—after a DeMeo turncoat testified in a pretrial hearing that DeMeo once gave Shargel a hundred thousand dollars cash in a paper bag to represent crew members on various charges.

Jerry Shargel was highly recommended to Sammy by one of Paul's attorneys. He worked the courtroom the way a good chess player uses all the pieces and looks beyond the next move; after a weeklong trial, Sammy and Garafola were found not guilty.

Shargel persuaded the jury that another lawyer involved in the crooked deal with Fiala was actually being truthful when he testified that he told Sammy and Eddie not to report the income until a year later, for some cockamamie tax reason.

A few years in prison on a tax conviction would have given Sammy a reason to watch the Gambino family revolution from the sidelines. But he was too ambitious for that, and so he began sounding out others even as he prepared for and stood trial.

DeCicco signed on, mainly for the same reasons as Sammy—but also because he had felt slighted when Angelo told him that Paul had proposed making Tommy Bilotti an acting street boss. DeCicco had cultivated popularity in both wings and felt that he would have been a much more symbolically apt choice if Paul was serious about making a peaceful transition.

He also felt that he and Sammy were the keys to the plot. "I don't believe John would be doin' this," he told Sammy, "if you and me weren't goin' along; he wouldn't make a move without us."

"I don't know about that, but comin' forward like this, lettin' us know, that took balls."

"*Minchia,* anybody can kill. But that don't mean they can be boss. That's what we're lookin' at here, John as boss. I don't know if he's the best we got."

"He's actin' like a boss here. By comin' forward like this, he controls the situation. We follow or we lose."

Robert "Deebee" DiBernardo also threw in. Like Sammy, he was only a soldier, but he was more influential and wealthy than most capos. He virtually ran a Teamsters local that provided drivers for all major construction sites in the city, and he was well aware of how much business Paul had steered either to himself or to companies linked to Chin Gigante's Genovese family. As a man who reported directly to Paul, he had status—and so his defection boosted the confidence of the others, who began to use him to ferry messages back and forth.

The plotters were all in their forties. Hoping that a respected elderly capo's support might lessen the chance of a retaliatory war, they called on Joseph Armone, a sixty-seven-year-old friend of Neil's known to resent Paul's cushy ride up the ladder. While Paul had spent only a year in prison—when he was young, for contempt of court—Armone had spent almost half his life there. He was a childhood acquaintance of Lucky Luciano, an early architect of Cosa Nostra in New York. Paul was no Lucky, and Armone signed on too.

Given the Angelo-tapes dispute, the plotters decided that Angelo should not be a major player—it was better for the revolution if it seemed to be only about Paul's leadership. In the minds of the men from Paul's wing, leadership was the issue, not drug dealing.

Regarding drug dealing, they believed Paul was a hypocrite; they never knew him to turn down tributes from men he suspected of drug dealing, such men as Roy DeMeo, as long as the money was offered under some other pretense. The drug ban was really a rule against getting caught—the only reason the Angelo situation had gotten out of hand.

"Forget about Roy DeMeo," Sammy said to DeCicco, in the rush of justification preceding Paul's demise. "I know for a fact that fuckin' Louis DiBono's capo is a big dealer."

"He just pretends he makes it on that food business of his."

"And he'll give Paul the keys to a Mercedes and say he had a good year, that's it. Everybody's happy."

With Angelo out for appearance's sake, the plot consisted of five men—Gotti, Sammy, Armone, DeCicco, Deebee—each a symbolic finger of the clenched-fist salute they used to show their solidarity.

Members of the Fist contacted influential men in three other Cosa Nostra families—Luchese, Colombo, and Bonanno—and asked for support if "something happened" to Paul. They approached men they regarded as the next generation of leaders, because most of the current leaders had fallen victim to the RICO sword and were awaiting trial and facing life in prison without parole. For obvious reasons, Paul's friend Chin Gigante was not contacted.

Gotti and Angelo told Neil the same thing that Angelo told Sammy—they had reason to believe Paul intended to try to kill them, once he finally decided to act.

That was the gist of conversations captured on a recently installed listening device in Neil's home. Neil was fading fast, but he was still a target in the Gambino hierarchy case, and so he had not been spared a break-in by an FBI black-bag squad, which planted the bug in his bedroom—where, except for trips to his doctors, he was spending his final days.

This bug showed Neil was weary of telling lies and looking for a way to end the crisis without bloodshed. "I've been tellin' Paul, Angelo can't give you the tapes because his family is on there,' " he said after Gotti and Angelo came to visit. "I've been trying to make you get away with these tapes, but Jesus Christ Almighty, I can't stop the guy from always bringing it up. Unless I tell the guy, 'Why don't you go fuck yourself?' "

Late in the summer of 1985, after the tapes were made public in a pretrial proceeding in Angelo's case, one of Paul's lawyers got copies of them—and heard the truths on them.

But Paul did nothing, out of deference to Neil, as the plot against him hardened and he finally began standing trial in the DeMeo case. Then, on December 2, 1985, Neil died, in a hospital, under his old Catholic priest alias, Timothy O'Neill. Afraid of surveillance, Paul boycotted the wake—an incredible breach of family etiquette regardless of his fears.

Instead, liberated by Neil's death to do what he pleased, he summoned the caporegimes and announced that he was going to close the Ravenite and assign John Gotti and soldiers in what he pointedly referred to as the Fatico crew to other decinas. In other words, he was demoting Neil's protégé and eliminating the Bergin crew.

"From what I read on those tapes of Angelo's, the government has a good case there, and that isn't going to be much of a crew anyway," Paul said, as Gotti silently seethed.

Just as Neil predicted, and Gotti and Angelo suspected, Paul was not going to risk ruin by violent action, but his proposals were more than enough to agitate the hair trigger controlling the plot in place against him—and Paul added more provocation. He said that Tommy Bilotti would succeed Neil as underboss and that he was shelving his earlier idea of a triumvirate of acting bosses.

Piling untimely moves one upon another, he also noted that one of that morning's newspapers had suggested that Neil was a longtime secret informer for the FBI.

"There's a rumor out that Neil was a rat," he said, unable to control his jealousy even now, even though the article was just disinformation that some law enforcement

source had fed some writer trying to enliven Neil's obituary notice.

As DeCicco and Tommy Gambino tried to calm him,
Gotti flew into a rage. "Whoever said that, I'll throw 'em
off a fuckin' building!"

"Where there's smoke, there's fire," Paul replied, in-
sulting the memory of a man's man and ensuring that in
two weeks more, the Fist would finally come smashing
down.

CHAPTER 6

• • • • • • • • • • • • •

Sparks

The assassins gathered in a park by the East River as the purple gloom of a wintry twilight fell across the city. It was December 16, 1985. Christmas displays were twinkling on in the windows of a giant public housing project overlooking the park. Twenty blocks north along the curving East River Drive, many tens of thousands of office workers were exiting the great mountain range of skyscrapers in midtown Manhattan.

Four of the ten men, the designated shooters, wore identical tan trench coats and cossack-like fur hats. The outfits were meant to confuse potential witnesses and cause recollection of coats and hats but not faces. The other six men, backup shooters and getaway drivers, were dressed for anonymity.

John Gotti had given everyone their assignments the night before, in a meeting at a storefront in Bensonhurst that Sammy used for his construction businesses. But now as they huddled in the park, with its barren trees and the East River's treacherous currents rushing past, Gotti—with Sammy at his side—went over the details one final time.

In a few minutes the team would be leaving for the ambush site—a street outside an elegant midtown restaurant. Although they had made the correct assumption, some of the assassins did not officially know who it was that they had been summoned to kill; it was for their benefit that Gotti said: "It's Paul's who's gettin' popped. So this gotta go right. We ain't allowed no misses."

The assassins were all soldiers or associates loyal to the Gotti wing, including Angelo Ruggiero and two others stamping their feet against the cold, John Carneglia and Anthony Rampino.

"Whoever else's there has to go, probably be Tommy," Gotti added, meaning Paul's loyalist and driver, Thomas Bilotti. But Bilotti—Paul's newly named underboss—was almost as important a target as Paul. To increase the odds of his agenda, a family takeover without a fight, Gotti had to eliminate Bilotti too.

Gotti turned to the designated shooters. In unintentional but revealing fashion, he had selected four drug dealers as the triggermen; they included two men under indictment with Angelo in the heroin case—Carneglia and Edward Lino, a Bonanno associate who wasn't facing as many serious charges as Carneglia and the rest, since he had not been caught uttering too many incriminating words at Angelo's house.

"Once you make a move, don't leave until they're dead. If you don't get 'em there, we lose. We're all gonna be dead."

As Gotti spoke, Angelo dragged on a Marlboro and fidgeted with one of the team's walkie-talkies. "These fuckers gotta be the same channel," he said to no one.

Sammy stood beside Gotti, calm, resolute, deadserious. He hardly said a word, beyond reminding the shooters of the lethal certainty of "head shots."

A few days before, right after revealing his plans to break up the Gotti crew, Paul had handed the Fist this opportunity by scheduling a dinner meeting with five captains, including Tommy Gambino, Carlo's son, and James Failla, an elder loyalist from Carlo's era. Fatefully, he also invited a capo he believed was loyal—Frank DeCicco, who quickly alerted Gotti and Sammy.

Now DeCicco was already en route to the restaurant; after the ambush, he was to discourage reprisal and encourage unity by telling the other capos they need not fear for their own lives.

The restaurant, Sparks Steak House, was on East Forty-sixth Street between Second and Third Avenues, in midtown, one of the most pedestrian-congested areas in the world. The anonymity and bustle of midtown, however, made East Forty-sixth an ideal stage for surprise, particularly at a going-home hour.

"Sparks, 5 p.m.," read an entry in Paul's diary, which

also contained reminders about meetings with his defense lawyers in the DeMeo trial, which was in recess for the holidays.

That week, Sparks had been rated the city's top steakhouse by *New York* magazine, and it was popular with businessmen, and diplomats and spies from the United Nations complex two blocks east. The year before, it also had been the topic of a tirade by Paul, in which the doomed millionaire moaned in the presence of the FBI bug then in his mansion that Sparks's management had not given him anything on the house during previous visits—despite his influence in the union that represented Sparks's employees.

"Ya know who's busy makin' a fortune?" Paul said to two union fixers. "Fuckin' Sparks. What those guys do is good for a hundred grand a week. Me, I don't get five cents when I go in there. They don't even buy you a drink."

The plan was to shoot Paul and Bilotti as they pulled up beside Sparks and the two stone lions on the sidewalk—strong lions, but not wise like foxes to traps—and turned over their car, as they inevitably would, to a parking attendant.

Carneglia, Eddie Lino, and the other two designated shooters would pair off and approach from either side of the car. Rampino, a backup shooter, would loiter across the street, in the unlikely event that the victims escaped the fusillade. Angelo and two other backups would position themselves toward the Second Avenue side of East Forty-sixth, where two getaway cars would be waiting.

Gotti and Sammy Gravano would be watching the hit from a car on the Third Avenue side of East Forty-sixth Street, with Sammy ready to jump out and begin firing a .357 Magnum if the victims somehow managed to evade the shooters and Rampino, and flee toward Third Avenue.

It was an excellent plan—the targets boxed in, a kill zone worthy of a military-style ambush. Later, people were surprised that Gene Gotti was not on the team. But as in the Army, the borgatas had a rule against sending brothers into combat together.

"Let's go," John Gotti said as the run-through in the park ended. "Don't fuckin' forget, whoever's with Paul has to go too. If fuckin' somethin' goes wrong, and we miss 'em goin' in, we go into the restaurant and take the motherfuckers there."

Until now, Sammy had given assassins last-minute reminders. But Gotti had taken command and Sammy was comfortable taking a backseat. He had what his ego required—he had been chosen to be alongside as the Fist arrived at the point of no return.

After DeCicco expressed reservations early in the plot, Sammy also had dwelled on the question of whether Gotti was the right person to lead the Gambino family. Gotti was overbearing, flashy, temperamental; and because he had spent so much time in jail, he lacked the hands-on know-how of men his age, men like DeCicco—and even Sammy, who was five years younger.

Still, underneath Gotti's bluster, Sammy thought he saw a man of Cosa Nostra, a man of daring if not know-how—especially after DeCicco said, as the plot thickened, that they had no choice but to support Gotti.

"I could be John's underboss, but he could never be mine," DeCicco had said. "His ego couldn't handle it; if I was boss, we'd just have the same problems again."

Sammy accommodated himself to Gotti's ego too, for his own good and the good of the family—the equation he felt he always tried to make, despite how difficult it sometimes was.

Anticipating vengeance from Paul loyalists, Sammy had moved with two other men, pistols, and ammo into the basement apartment of an associate on Staten Island. Gotti had mulled over similar plans but was gambling they wouldn't be necessary.

"Sammy," Gotti said on the way to Sparks, "nobody'll give a fuck about this *cazzu*—not enough to fuck with us, you watch."

"I don't know, John. Killin' a boss."

"Paul ain't a real boss. Never was."

With Gotti at the wheel, they departed the park in a black Lincoln with tinted windows. The shooters and backups left in the getaway cars. With Frank DeCicco already at Sparks, only two members of the Fist were absent—Joseph Armone, the aging capo recruited for post-assassination politics, and soldier-at-large Robert DiBernardo, the Teamsters fixer. Armone was too infirm to be on the street in an ambush; Deebee was young but not a shooter, and so he had been told to take a trip to Florida.

The drive uptown took ten minutes. Recalling it a few years later, Gotti told Sammy that Paul was to blame for what was to happen because he resented strength and talked behind people's backs and was so jealous of Neil that he was afraid to let Neil be a good underboss.

"He wasn't half the man Neil was. He never understood Neil was happy bein' underboss. He should've blown the guy, but he was geloso. He wasn't a man. If you're a tough guy, he hated you. And any time he could knock you, he knocked you."

Sammy recalled the story of being at a Christmas party at Paul's and how Paul upbraided him when he said he was leaving to attend a Christmas party at Neil's, and then Gotti said how much he hated going to Paul's mansion.

"Every time I went there on a Saturday, I hated it. I hated the fuckin' world, because whoever was there before me, as soon as they left, he cursed them out. You know when you leave, he's gonna say it about you."

In the end, Gotti said, Paul just did not know "the life." He was "a fuckin' fish on the desert, a fish outta water."

In midtown, after circling the block once, Gotti and Sammy pulled into a parking space that opened on the northwest corner of Third Avenue and East Forty-sixth, a one-way eastbound street. The vantage point was ideal; they could look across Third at the entrance to Sparks, which was only a few doors east of the southeast corner of East Forty-sixth and Third.

From inside the Lincoln, Sammy saw backup shooter Rampino lurking by an office-supply store directly across from Sparks and, amid the hubbub of pedestrians, a mailman emptying a box at the corner. Furtively, he clicked on one of the team's walkie-talkies and notified the others where he and Gotti were parked.

In the next instant, a nearly identical black Lincoln pulled alongside the parked Lincoln with Gotti and Sammy and stopped for a red light; when Sammy glanced to his right, he was startled to see Paul, and Tommy Bilotti, who was at the wheel of the second Lincoln and reaching for something in the glove compartment.

"Holy fuck," Sammy whispered, like he had just witnessed a supernatural event. He briefly felt like he had at his induction, like he was floating in a dream, but the adrenaline pouring into his stomach jolted him alert.

He turned toward Gotti and flicked his head back, to point Gotti to what he had seen, but the light changed and Victims No. 9 and 10 on Sammy's murder ledger moved off.

Sammy whispered again into his walkie-talkie: "Paul and Tommy are coming through the intersection now."

It was an advantageous heads-up for the designated shooters. They could stop strolling back and forth in their long tan coats and fur hats, trying to become part of the swelling crowds of Christmas rush-hour shoppers, and get ready to kill.

The killing began as soon as Bilotti drove across Third Avenue and stopped in front of Sparks. He and Paul never had a chance. The two shooters assigned to Paul fired six bullets into his head as he stepped out of the car on the curb side.

The gun of one shooter assigned to Bilotti jammed, but the other's did not, so Bilotti was shot as he, frozen in surprise, saw Paul shot. Carneglia, assigned to Paul, saw the gunman on the other team unable to fire; calmly, he walked around the front of the car and fired be-sure shots into Bilotti's head.

Pedestrians began scrambling every which way. When the light on East Forty-sixth changed, impatient drivers carried Gotti and Sammy inconspicuously through the intersection, across Third, right alongside the bodies, then past the shooters high-tailing it east to Second Avenue and the getaway cars.

Some later wondered whether it was foolish for them to have risked being seen on the street or hemmed in by stalled traffic. But at the time their faces were not well known. And if somehow they had gotten trapped on the block and cops sought to question them, they had a simple explanation; They were on their way to a dinner meeting with Paul.

Unimpeded, Gotti cruised down the block, then turned south on Second Avenue and melted into the anonymity and bustle of midtown before anyone thought to dial 911.

Sammy tuned the Lincoln's radio to 1010 WINS, an all-news station. "Maybe there'll be a bulletin," he said.

"They better make it an obituary!" Gotti said, slapping the wheel of the car. "Those fucks are gone! What a piece of work!"

"Everybody did okay. How it's supposed to go."

Gotti guided his Lincoln down to Thirty-fourth Street, over to East River Drive and down to the entrance to the Brooklyn-Battery Tunnel at the tip of Manhattan, then through the tunnel to Sammy's construction company office in Brooklyn.

Meanwhile, hearing gunshots inside Sparks, DeCicco and two capos hastened to leave. Outside, they saw Paul's car and the bodies and hurried away. One of the capos, James Failla, the elder loyalist who practically ran the city's private sanitation industry, began to shake.

"I could've been in that car with Paul," he said to DeCicco. "They were gonna give me a lift."

"But you weren't, and you don't have another thing to worry about. Let's just keep on walkin' out of here."

Down the block they ran into Tommy Gambino, Paul's nephew; a few minutes late for his dinner meeting with Paul, he was walking toward Sparks, vaguely aware of some commotion ahead.

DeCicco motioned him to turn around, then fell in beside him. Gambino was a man of boarding schools and country clubs who was worth a hundred million dollars; he was likely one of the few men in the family who had not been required to "make his bones"—commit a murder—before his induction.

"Your uncle's been shot," DeCicco said.

"Is he dead?"

"He is, so's Tommy."

"Jesus, what's going on?"

"Don't worry, everyone else is okay. Got to your car and leave. We'll be in touch."

DeCicco went to his car and drove to Bensonhurst to meet Gotti and Sammy at Sammy's construction office. There, before DeCicco reported on his conversations with Failla and Gambino, everyone embraced and kissed each other on the cheeks.

"I told them no one else is gonna get hurt," DeCicco said.

"Good, they got the fuckin' message right there," Gotti replied, still pumped with excitement.

"But we could get hurt, we could all be dead in six months."

"You worry more than Sammy! I'm tellin' you, no one fuckin' liked Paul except maybe his nephew, but that's blood and Tommy ain't gonna give us problems. We did everybody a favor!"

"We could have a massive war with Jimmy Brown and them," DeCicco said, referring to James Failla by his nickname.

"Forget about it, Jimmy Brown's an old *cazzu* too! We ain't runnin' scared of him!"

"We just took out the boss," Sammy said. "But I'm ready. We're ready. We gotta be."

"We'll all nose around tomorrow and see what's what," Gotti said, calming down. "But we didn't come this far to be lay-down Sallys now."

Back on East Forty-sixth Street, the shooters had slipped away east toward Second Avenue and hopped into the getaway cars.

A public relations executive leaving his office had taken a long look at the most deliberate shooter, Carneglia, the one who calmly strode around the front of the car and fired into Bilotti after finishing with Paul. A delivery man for a photo finisher got a good glance at one of the backups, Rampino, whose sunken eyes and acne scars made for a hard-to-forget face.

A retired cop walking on Third Avenue toward East Forty-seventh Street when the gunfire began had followed the shooters toward Second. But they were in the getaway cars and gone when he reached the corner and dialed 911.

One of the witnesses did not recall any fur hats. One said the tan trench coats were dark. The two who were not former cops were not eager to talk about the faces they had seen, and the ex-cop had not seen any faces.

In the heart of midtown during a Christmas rush hour, the Fist had boldly executed what looked to be a perfect crime.

The double murder was the biggest gangland story since 1957, when Carlo's predecessor, Albert Anastasia, had been assassinated; the city's noisy media went after it with almost the same gusto as a mayoral murder. The court files of several pending Cosa Nostra cases contained a few references to intrigues in the Gambino family. The information was vague and confusing, but enough to feed an inky avalanche that lasted several days.

Even the most causal readers and viewers were introduced to the name John Gotti, who was identified in most of the stories as the probable culprit. Overnight, he became more of a public figure than Paul or Neil had ever been.

In one widely distributed remark, Remo Franceschini, boss of an NYPD detective squad in Queens, cast the murders as a grab for power and flatly predicted, "Gotti will emerge as the head of the other capos."

High-minded outrage kept the avalanche going. "The decent citizens of this country are demeaned in the eyes of the world if brazen cold-blooded murders can be perpetrated on a street in New York," said federal court of appeals judge Irving J. Kaufman, chairman of the president's Commission on Organized Crime.

"The waste of a human life is shocking, no matter who it is," added United States district court judge Kevin Duffy, who was presiding over the DeMeo case, as he adjourned it for three weeks to weigh motions from Paul's codefendants for a mistrial (they were eventually denied).

Reporters who tried to contact Gotti at his home in Howard Beach were told he was not available. A lawyer who had recently begun representing Gotti, however, said his client had declined a request from the FBI to submit to a voluntary interview because he knew "nothing about the murders." Such unequivocal denials would eventually become almost a full-time occupation for the lawyer, Bruce Cutler, a loquacious former prosecutor with a likable and shamelessly outrageous style.

Without much detail to go on, many reporters wrote stories that emphasized how young Gotti was compared with the other Cosa Nostra bosses and went on about his style, looks, and penchant for showy double-breasted suits. Thus, words such as "youthful," "dashing," and "dapper" became part of his early public image.

Paul was buried a few days later in Brooklyn, where he had been born to Sicilian immigrants seventy years before. Citing the life Paul had lived, the local Catholic bishop denied him a funeral mass. Only personal family members attended his wake, because by that time the transfer of power in his Cosa Nostra family had begun, and even ardent loyalists were afraid that an act of respect might be seen as portending an act of vengeance.

The transfer of power had begun two days after the murders when—even as detectives continued to canvass offices along East Forty-sixth Street and Third Avenue for witnesses—almost all of the borgata's capos gathered for a tense meeting at a restaurant owned by Sammy and others twelve blocks north on Third.

Technically, the meeting was convened by the only surviving member of the Gambino administration, the seventy-five-year-old in-house adviser, consigliere Joe N. Gallo. But Gotti was telling him what to do. One captain about as old as Gallo failed to show; he had checked into a hospital for treatment of a sudden nerve disorder. Another, Tommy Gambino, was given an excused absence.

"I sent a message to Tommy that it was okay for him not to come," Gotti told Sammy. "I told him what happened with Paul was business, but with him being Paul's nephew, it would be a little awkward for him here. Tommy's a sweetheart. We want him to know we got nothing against him."

Gotti intended to take over no matter what happened at the meeting, but he preferred an "election" by the caporegimes—and so before the meeting he had sent old-time capo Joseph Armone, recruited into the plot for just such a purpose, to Gallo and others with a simple message: Gotti was taking over, and the family risked a horrible war if anyone resisted.

Gallo, a Carlo holdover who had never regarded Paul too highly, got the message. He had not managed to achieve the distinction of never having been charged with a crime by taking chances, and so now he did not risk offending Gotti by asking any questions about the murders. In the winter of his life, he was happy just to be well enough to be alive during a critical time.

In that vein, before the meeting Gallo explained to Gotti and the other conspirators the Cosa Nostra rules that apply when the rule that a boss cannot be killed without approval from the four other Commission bosses is broken. The Fist had contacted only acting bosses in only three of the four families—and then only on an "off-the-record" basis, meaning, in Cosa Nostraspeak, that the contacts were never made.

"You cannot ever tell the truth about this," Gallo advised. "The Commission has a rule, you must have its permission to take a boss down. You broke that rule. You can't ever admit that to anyone. Sooner or later, you'll have to come up with a story about what happened, but you can't ever admit it."

Against that wonderland backdrop, the meeting—held around a conference table in the restaurant's basement—began. Most of the captains had brought bodyguards, but the bodyguards had been told to remain upstairs—by Sammy and Angelo, the only soldiers in the room; they made it clear that they were armed and as Gallo spoke they stood behind the table like a stony palace guard.

It was all the takeover evidence the capos needed, but the seating—Gotti on one side of Gallo, DeCicco on the other—provided more.

"It's terrible, what's happened," Gallo began. "But we don't know who killed Paul, we're investigatin'. Nobody feels worse for Paul's and Tommy's families than me. But we're a family too and we have to stay strong. So that's why we called you here."

None of the captains believed him, of course. But the armed sentries and seating arrangements made reassurance more important than truth. Nobody had any questions about the murders; Gallo, speaking for Gotti, gave them the only answers they wanted.

"Everyone in this room is gonna be all right. Nobody is in trouble. Nobody is gonna get hurt. We don't want nobody carrying guns or overreactin' to anything."

The election could have been accomplished right there, but Gotti had already decided to give anyone who wanted to challenge him an interval of opportunity, so Gallo announced that after a few more days of investigation, he would call another meeting, at which Paul's successor would be chosen.

In the meantime, this was to be a private Gambino matter. "We don't want no discussion about this outside the family. We don't want nobody getting involved in our business. We will elect our own boss."

Still, Gotti felt compelled to say something to the other Cosa Nostra families, to pay some deference to the tradition of cooperation and communication—and so over the next couple of days, Angelo and Sammy were dispatched to give the other families the same messages Gallo had given the Gambino capos, plus one more: With so many cops and FBI agents investigating the murders, now was not the time for loose talk.

Three families—Luchese, Bonanno, and Colombo—responded positively. Paul's crazy-like-a-fox friend, Genovese boss Chin Gigante, was more quarrelsome—and not just because the murder of his construction partner meant that he was likely to lose money. He sent a return message saying that while he accepted the situation "for now," a Commission rule had been broken; someday, someone would have to pay.

"Chin's just blowin' smoke," Gotti told Sammy. "He's too smart to mess with us."

"He'd get others to do it."

"We gonna be all right. As long as we keep denyin', nobody's got proof of nothing."

Still denyin', John Joseph Gotti Jr. was elected boss of the nation's biggest Cosa Nostra family when the caporegimes convened a second time, just before New Year's Day, 1986.

Gotti was scheduled to stand trial in two cases in the next couple of months; one, the case in Queens state court arising from a street fracas with a refrigeration mechanic over a double-parked car in 1984, was more embarrassing than worrisome; in the other, Diana Giacalone's RICO case in Brooklyn, he faced forty years in prison with little chance of parole until he had served twenty-five years—a de facto life sentence, if he was convicted, since he was now forty-five years old. But no one with a vote dared cite that albatross as a liability.

Frank DeCicco—who had said that while he could be Gotti's underboss, Gotti could never be his—nominated Gotti. With the deck so stacked, the other capos followed suit and gave their own seconding speeches. Without having to fire another shot, or duck one, the King of Queens became king of the volcano.

CHAPTER 7
• • • • • • • • • • • • •
Central Casting

The media deluge after the Sparks murders was really just prologue. Early in 1986, Gotti would become a media phenomenon. Pretrial matters in one of the two cases pending against him—the worrisome federal case in Brooklyn—and many surprise turns in the pretrial and trial of the assault case in Queens yielded day after day of legend-making headlines that catapulted him into the city's consciousness in a way that no single gangster had become part of any city's consiousness since Al Capone exited Brooklyn to run rampant in Chicago half a century before.

Outside the public eye, Gotti began putting his imprint on the borgata. Loyalists would be rewarded, neutralists won over, doubters dealt with. His confidence and defiance—despite his legal problems and those of so many in his and the other families—were breathtaking.

"The law's gonna be tough with us, okay?" he told a group of loyalists at the Bergin one day, soon after taking over. The group now included Eddie Lino, a minor defendant in the heroin case and one of the designated shooters at Sparks.

"But if I can get a year run without being interrupted, get a year, I'm gonna put this thing together where they could never break it, never destroy it, even if we die."

"It's a helluva legacy to leave," one of the man replied.

"We got some fuckin' nice thing," Gotti hummed, "if we just be careful."

The Gotti explosion in the media was partly simple timing. If pretrial matters requiring him to appear in court had come later, not in the wake of Sparks, fewer reporters would have come to see the alleged new boss of the

Gambino family in person. But the early coverage had tickled the media fancy, and Gotti drew to courthouses not just the regular beat reporters but fashion writers, gossip columnists, and feature specialists.

What they got was a gangster right out of central casting, a man who looked, talked, and walked like a gangster. They got the silvery hair, the double-breasted suit with matching pocket hanky, the camel overcoat, the pinky ring, the voice of gravel and sandpaper, and the strut—seemingly practiced but really the result of his adolescent encounter with a cement mixer.

To the media's delight—beginning on January 13, with his first post-Sparks public appearance, a pretrial hearing in the RICO case in Brooklyn brought by Diane Giacalone—Gotti brought even more to the role: charm, wit, and supreme confidence.

"I'm the boss of my family," he coyly said, setting up his own punch line after reporters cornered him outside and asked if he was the new boss of the Gambino family—"my wife and kids."

For reporters used to the nastiness of gangsters fleeing courthouses with coats over their heads, his style was unique. But only a year before, when the *Daily News* had falsely described him as "acting boss" of the entire Gambino family, Gotti had learned how the media could be a useful tool.

The usefulness in that case was the message of power left with the lower echelons of the family. Now, the media could be useful in leaving a message of likability with the masses—out of which would come the jurors who would someday sit in judgment of him. So, like a savvy politician cast in a sudden ill light, he tried to give the media something to work with—a smile, a quip, anything to help reporters fashion stories that might favorably affect the public's perception.

That it was not a politician acting like this, but a Mafia gangster, only fueled the journalistic throng that moved him in a rolling wave of bodies and shouted questions to the courthouse exit after the pretrial hearing ended.

"We don't know nothing ourselves," he said when a question about whether the Sparks murders had elevated him to the throne invited another opportunistic reply. "We hear it from the same place you get it. We get it from the FBI."

The throng reached the exit as a late-arriving female reporter was trying to get inside and catch up with the story.

"I was brought up to hold the door open for ladies," Gotti said with a mischievous wink—"girl" reporters were not the same as "girl" prosecutors—as he clutched the door with one hand and flamboyantly ushered her inside with the other.

Outside, Gotti made his way to a black Cadillac waiting at the curb. As a bodyguard opened a rear door, he turned and gave a friendly wave, then sped off.

It was a marvelous performance—contrived yet natural, like that of a regular talk-show guest who has learned that it matters less what is said than how it is said. In the media coverage that followed, Gotti got four stars.

He was presented as a gangster, but not as an unlikable or evil man. As in the stories following Sparks, the substance of him—the violence, the treachery, the overbearing ego—was not yet part of the available record, and so he came off as a swashbuckling rogue. One headline writer called him "Dapper Don," two words emphasizing style and inviting legend-making.

The gushing in the media rankled the city's law enforcement establishment, especially a small group of investigators who had secretly been privy to many of Gotti's conversations, including the one in which he bragged to his men how he had once beaten a cop to a pulp and then made him beg for mercy.

These investigators worked for the New York State Organized Crime Task Force; the year before, they had planted a bug in the wall of a storefront next to the Bergin. It was installed after Gotti was indicted in the Giacalone RICO case, so none of the conversations it recorded could be used against him when that trial, due to start in three months, began.

The task force, a minor player in Cosa Nostra prosecutions, was trying to build its own case against Gotti; it began when a minor hood, arrested for heroin, negotiated his way out of jail by bragging, untruthfully, that he was a made man who could infiltrate the Bergin crew.

For six months, investigators eavesdropped on conversations that revealed more about Gotti's personality than about crimes, and so the bug was deactivated in October 1985. Two months later, however, the Sparks murders encouraged a judge to secretly authorize the investigators to turn it back on.

One of the early conversations captured by the reactivated bug featured Gotti lecturing his eldest son, John A. Gotti, about the peril of indiscreet talk on telephones; it also showed that he was grooming him to follow in his footsteps. Young Gotti, nicknamed Junior, was a graduate of the private La Salle Military Academy, alma mater of Carlo Gambino's son, Tommy.

The conversation began with Gotti complaining that he had been told that one of Junior's friends had referred to him by name in a telephone conversation.

"I'm gonna give him a kick in the fuckin' ass," Gotti told his son. "The fuckin' guy uses my name on the fuckin' phone!"

"You serious?" Junior replied, trying to tell his dad he already knew how serious a breach this was. "The guy's so full of shit it ain't funny."

"You tell 'em, next time don't be mentioning no fuckin' names on the fuckin' phone or I'll put him in the fuckin' hospital. And before you do anything or before he does any fuckin' thing, you tell me first. There're reasons why I don't want people to go bothering people on the fuckin' phone."

Junior was twenty-two years old and president of the newly formed Samson Trucking Company—off to a flying start because of Sparks coconspirator Robert DiBernardo's control of a Teamsters local, which put the arm on contractors to toss jobs to Junior.

Junior chose "Samson" as his company name because he was a bodybuilding addict, and though short-haired, he was strong. He looked more like his mother than his father, more half-Jewish like she was, but he was an ill-tempered chip off the Gotti block. Like his father, he was currently under indictment for assault—the result of a bar brawl in which he slugged an off-duty cop. His father had been unable to get him out of that jam, since the victim was a cop, but in 1983 his father had paid a detective in Queens ten thousand dollars to keep Junior's name out of a case in which Junior and his nightlife pals got into another bar brawl and someone was fatally stabbed.

Just as Gotti's rise to power meant a successful trucking company for Junior, it meant good things for the men who helped Gotti take power. Gotti made DeCicco his underboss and promoted Angelo to caporegime of the Bergin crew; Sammy also was elevated to capo, replacing mentor Toddo Aurello in title now as well as fact. Toddo, who hadn't done much but water his tomato plants the last couple of years, made the transition painless by telling Sammy, after Sparks, that he would recommend it to Gotti.

"It's your time now," said Toddo, who never asked if Sammy was involved in the murders. "Just remember, you can't always believe the first story you hear."

Elderly caporegime Joseph Armone was rewarded too, with an infusion of new young earners to help him line his trousers. Joe N. Gallo was reappointed consigliere—a reward that meant more to him than it did to Gotti, who kept him in the job only to make other old-timers such as Sparks dinner guest James Failla feel better about the future.

The only member of the Fist who did not see an immediate benefit was DiBernardo. "But Deebee's already a wealthy guy," Angelo explained to Sammy. "He's richer than any of us and he did it without even havin' a crew. He's good where he's at."

"He's always been in a funny spot, reportin' just to Paul."

"And now he reports to John. John loves him."

As his lecture to Junior showed, Gotti became more paranoid about eavesdropping at the Bergin and elsewhere. Having seen Angelo, Gene, Carneglia, and Paul talk their way into so much trouble, Gotti—whenever possible—began discussing serious topics outdoors, in so-called "walk-talks"; indoors, he ran tap water, turned on radios, spoke in code. Still, on occasion, the reactivated state bug at the Bergin Hunt and Fish Club overheard bits and pieces of conversations that showed him coming to grips with power and making others do the same.

Early in January, before he had grasped how much Gotti's view of himself had changed, Angelo brought his old friend and new boss a problem involving a loan-shark customer.

"I don't deal with this anymore," Gotti said irritably, adding that Angelo should have known that such a trivial problem was beneath him now.

In that same vein, Gotti also told Angelo what he planned to tell soldiers who violated protocol and sought to bring him a business deal without going through a captain—or "skipper"—first.

"I'll tell them, 'Listen, your skipper will keep me up to date, you keep your skipper up to date.' I can't socialize with these guys. I can't bring myself down. I'm a boss, you know what I mean? I gotta isolate myself a little bit."

In symbolic moves, Gotti also tried to remind fence-sitters what a money-grubbing boss Paul sometimes had been. He told an elderly capo in the old Paul wing that he would not accept any "tribute" from him. Even though it was well known that the capo wasn't making money and was dipping into his retirement savings to stay on Paul's good side, Paul had continued to take tributes.

Gotti also devised a new formula for payoffs that a contractor had been making to Paul and Bilotti and would now be making to him, so that soldiers actually involved in the dirty work of making the contractor see the wisdom of paying off got bigger shares.

These bones to the troops hardly mattered. Plenty of money was headed Gotti's way as was evident in another exchange with Angelo in which he spoke of a pending deal with some contractor: "He's won a deal, he's supposed to get a job. Three and a half million in contracts, a hundred and ninety-five thousand dollars in kickbacks, or more. He says it all goes to Johnny Gotti!"

On another day, a man came to see Gotti with a story about two men in another family who had stolen millions by playing a shell game with gasoline-wholesaling companies; by transferring custody of the gas from one phony company to another, they were able to evade responsibility for state and federal taxes.

"Twenty-eight cents a gallon you can steal," the man said. "I'm talkin' about twenty, thirty million gallons a month."

Gotti whistled as his mind whirled, and he calculated that even at two cents per gallon on thirty million gallons, "that's six hundred thousand dollars!" He told the man to find a way to cut him in on the scheme.

He did not get excited about every deal. One day, a visitor urged him to enter the recording industry by providing venture capital for an album by a new artist. The visitor even brought along a sample tape, but Gotti was lukewarm. New singers were risky investments, and the industry was too dishonest.

"They change two or three sounds, they make their own record, and you get fucked," he said.

Early on, Gotti also made sure that his men and others knew that he would be quick to use force when matters displeased him. Thus, in Brooklyn, a new restaurant owned by a man who was having second thoughts about doing business with Gambino soldiers was torched. In Manhattan, a carpenters union leader who ordered goons to trash a Gambino-connected restaurant being built with nonunion labor was given four warning bullets in the buttocks and legs.

Holding court at the Bergin, Gotti told his men he did not believe in giving many warnings to people who caused problems because people should know better. "People ain't stupid, they know what we are," he said.

Sammy Gravano was never overheard on the bug hidden in the wall of the storefront next to the Bergin. No one ever saw him in the retinues that accompanied Gotti to courthouses. He was more powerful than ever, but he stayed in the shadows.

While known in Cosa Nostra, Sammy was what he seemed to his law-abiding Staten Island neighbors to be—an industrious construction-company owner. He worked hard at maintaining the pretense; in his mind, Cosa Nostra meant being undercover, living a secret life, the way Toddo Aurello always had.

When he saw Gotti, it was usually at out-of-the-way Italian restaurants in Brooklyn or Queens. Sometimes they met at Neil's old club in Little Italy, the Ravenite; Paul had threatened to close it, but it remained open and was managed by an elderly soldier who lived with his wife in an apartment two floors above.

"When we beat this girl in Brooklyn, I might set up

shop down here," Gotti told Sammy at the Ravenite one day.

"There's some symbolism there."

"Paul, he'd roll over, but Neil, he'd love it."

While Gotti and DeCicco ran the family, Sammy tended to his construction businesses, his bars and restaurants, and his crew. Sometimes his bosses used him to deliver messages or shore up relations with what Gotti had called "the other side," decinas and soldiers that still identified more with Paul than Gotti.

Gotti put a couple of suspected malcontents into Sammy's crew, the message being, Shape up or be shipped out. People knew that Sammy did not suffer malcontents or troublemakers for very long. In fact, shortly after his promotion to capo, Sammy made a blank slate out of a crew associate who had caught the cocaine virus.

Sammy had committed too many crimes with Nicholas Mormando to have his freedom hinge on a man who might say or do anything to get to the next high, particularly one so wired one day that he told Sammy he was starting his own crew. Mormando—Victim No. 11 on Sammy's list—was duped into getting into the front seat of a car in which another associate, Joseph Paruta, was already sitting in the backseat with a pistol.

Paruta looked older than he was, which was sixty, and he was known as "Old Man Joe." He had been hanging around the Gravano crew for many years. He ran errands mainly, but he also was a secret weapon—"my Luca Braza," Sammy had boasted to Gotti, referring to the retarded-henchman character in *The Godfather.*

One of the malcontents was an old friend of Sammy's from early Bensonhurst days, Louie Milito. Sammy had sponsored him into the family and they had committed murders for Paul in the 1970s; they were still financial partners through the steel-erection company they controlled.

But Milito had misread the pre-Sparks terrain and aligned with the other side. He was the one who had overheard Paul tell Bilotti he did not care if DeCicco, Sammy, or anyone was upset by his business dealings with the Genovese family. Thinking that DeCicco and Sammy were destined to be old news, Milito promptly began a loan-sharking book with Bilotti and avoided his old friends.

DeCicco wanted to kill Milito, but Sammy was willing to grant him the mistake of saddling up with Bilotti, the man he guessed would succeed Paul someday.

"Let me talk to him," he told DeCicco. "I'll tell him we know he betrayed us and why. I'll tell him he has to stay on Staten Island and mind his own business. He can't expand."

DeCicco relented and Milito lived, for the time being.

Thomas Bilotti's older brother, Joseph, was also assigned to Sammy's crew and also advised to lay low.

"The administration has told me to tell you that you won't be killed," Sammy told "Joey." "You're all right. What happened wasn't about you. You're still a friend of ours, you'll be with me, but we want you to stay on Staten Island and mind your own business. If you need anything, come to me."

Sammy curled back one side of his own leather jacket to show Joey Bilotti he was carrying a pistol; the gesture was more reassuring than threatening because if Joey had not been all right, he would already have been dead.

In another administration message, Sammy told Joey to turn over to the family any money of his brother's that stemmed from companies or schemes owned or controlled by the family. He spoke without apology or sympathy because this was a long-standing practice of Cosa Nostra; the same ritual demand was made of relatives of all soldiers who died, violently or not.

"We don't want anything that's his personally. You make sure that gets to his relatives, but we want what's ours."

Sammy later told DeCicco about his talk with Joey Bilotti. "I like Joey, he understands. He knows he has no reason to fear us. He understands the life."

No one at Gleason's Gym in Brooklyn, where Sammy went most mornings to work out, knew of his secret life. A few suspected he was a mobbed-up contractor, but none knew he was such a big-time gangster. He was just a small, tough, unusually competitive guy trying to stay in shape by boxing men twenty years younger.

"What happened to you?" Gotti asked one day, when

Sammy showed up at a meeting with puffy eyes and swollen jaw.

"I been to the gym."

"Are you fuckin' nuts? You're forty fuckin' years old!"

"You ought to see the other guy."

Sometimes he sparred with professional boxers who trained at Gleason's. Once he landed such a solid punch to the head of heavyweight contender Renaldo Snipes that Snipes vowed that he would not go easy on Sammy in the next round just because he was six inches shorter and fifty pounds lighter.

"Nah, that's enough for me," Sammy said, giving up for the first time in a very long time, but with a smile.

Sammy's trainer at Gleason's was Teddy Atlas, a student of Cus D'Amato, who guided many boxers to world titles. For four years, before leaving D'Amato's boxing mecca in the Catskill Mountains to start his own career, Atlas had trained a young thug from Brooklyn named Mike Tyson, an eventual heavyweight champ whom D'Amato more or less adopted out of reform school.

Teddy Atlas told Sammy that one of Cus D'Amato's theories was that all boxers feel fear when they enter the ring, so the key to winning is controlling fear.

"I don't have any fear, I enjoy boxing," Sammy said.

"You have it, everybody has it, and you have to control it, make it work for you. You gotta face your insecurities."

The only insecurity Sammy felt was that, at age forty, he grew tired more quickly, but Atlas said even that was something he could learn to overcome—through hypnosis.

Sammy tried it three times. "You're throwin' lefts, rights, you're not gettin' tired," the hypnotist would incantate, after waving a shiny object back and forth and telling Sammy to close his eyes. "Now your right arm will raise."

But the right arm never raised merely on command. The third time, to see if being more relaxed made a difference, Sammy saw the hypnotist after a few martinis—but, still, nothing.

The hypnotist finally threw down his shiny object. "I'm sorry. With some people, it just doesn't work. They just fight too much. They won't go under."

Even if Gotti had been so inclined, it would have been impossible for him to stay as far in the shadows as Sammy did. Gotti was facing two public trials. The first, which began in March 1986, stemmed from an incident nearly eighteen months in the past.

Romual Piecyk was a big, gruff, hotheaded man whose car one day was blocked by a double-parked car outside the Cozy Corner Bar in Maspeth, a working-class community east of Ozone Park.

"Get that fuckin' car out of the street," he yelled in the general direction of two men talking on the sidewalk.

"Just hold it," replied one of the men, John Gotti.

The thirty-five-year-old Piecyk, a refrigeration mechanic, was six feet two, two hundred pounds. As a younger man, he had been arrested for public drunkenness, assault, and possession of a weapon. He had settled down now, and his wife was pregnant, but he still thought of himself as a tough guy.

He bolted out of his car toward Gotti and the other man, one of Gotti's gambling friends, but bolted right back as soon as they slapped him in the face a few times. The other man even dipped into Piecyk's shirt pocket (he had just cashed his paycheck) and took three hundred and twenty-five dollars—a surcharge for being bothered.

Gotti and the other man left Piecyk humiliated in the street and went into the Cozy Corner. Piecyk called the police, who escorted him into the restaurant, where he identified the well-dressed men who had slapped him.

"Okay, you two are under arrest," one of the cops said.

"Do you know who I am?" Gotti replied.

"Step out," said the officer, who did not.

"*Minchia,* let me talk to this guy."

The cop refused and Gotti was led away in handcuffs like a low-rent mugger, then booked and released on bail. Later, when higher-ranking authorities in the Queens district attorney's office asked Piecyk if he wanted to go forward with the case, they were less than forthright.

"Do you know who this punk Gotti is?" was all one asked.

"I don't care!" Piecyk shouted.

"Are you willing to testify?"

"Of course I am!"

In a few days, Piecyk went before a grand jury, and

Gotti and his friend were indicted for felony assault and theft.

Now, in March 1986, the case was set for trial. Usually such a case would never have reached a New York court-room; it would have been plea-bargained down to a mis-demeanor, or dismissed altogether, because it was one side's word against the other's. In this case Piecyk was at least partially to blame because of his belligerent manner at the scene.

But the Queens district attorney refused to make a deal—and forgo the chance to portray the alleged new boss of the Gambino family as a thug while getting some headlines to boot.

In the Sparks aftermath, however, Piecyk had read and heard that Gotti was not just a well-dressed "punk." That alone would have accounted for his feet of clay as the time for him to testify against Gotti drew near. But his telephone also began ringing at all hours, and the brakes on his van were slashed. On his way to and from work, he noticed bulky men following him.

Gotti did not permit his men to take more direct action. The case was too hot. But he also was confident that Piecyk would get the message: People were not stupid, they knew what he was.

Indeed, the intimidation began having its intended ef-fects. Piecyk stopped taking calls from Queens officials getting ready for trial. He went into hiding. In a letter he wrote to his wife, released later, he sought to explain why: "The media printed that [Gotti] was next in line for godfather," he wrote. "Naturally, my idea of pursuing this matter dropped."

In his letter, Piecyk complained bitterly about the way he was deceived at the time of the arrest. "I feel I have been lied to by the laws that are supposed to protect us. I have been a pawn in the power game between the gov-ernment and the mob. . . . I can't and will not live the rest of my life in fear."

Three weeks before trial, Piecyk talked with a *Daily News* reporter. He now denied that he had received ha-rassing telephone calls or that the brakes on his van had been slashed. He did say he would appear at the trial—but on Gotti's side.

"I'm not going to go against Mr. Gotti. I'm going in his behalf. I don't want to hurt Mr. Gotti."

The interview ignited another round of stories that ran to the eve of trial. The spotlight became too much for Piecyk. An acquaintance said the poor man, whose refrigeration repairman's job took him into large freezers used to store animal carcasses, began having nightmares in which he was the carcass on a hook.

The day before he was to testify, Piecyk checked himself into a hospital and made plans to flee to Pennsylvania and avoid going to court for either side. Someone tipped off detectives in Queens, however, and he was arrested, taken into custody, and told he had no choice but to testify.

Understandably, Gotti strutted into court like the game was already over. He was accompanied by the same attorney who was defending him in Giacalone's federal RICO case in Brooklyn—Bruce Cutler, the loquacious former prosecutor who had handled Gotti's no-comments and denials after the Sparks murders.

Cutler had begun representing Gotti the year before, when Gotti was just an acting capo. After becoming boss, Gotti could have dismissed Cutler—who was relatively new to defense work—and taken his pick of the city's talented criminal defense bar.

But Gotti stayed with Cutler, who in the meantime had won a murder case for a young Ozone Park punk with a performance that wowed the punk's acquaintances in the Bergin Hunt and Fish Club.

"Stay with Brucie," Angelo advised. "He's good. He breaks the judge's balls."

The thirty-eight-year-old lawyer's courtroom style mirrored Gotti's personal style—hyperbolic, swaggering, sarcastic, yet charming when he wanted to be. He had an actor's ability to turn rage on and off, to drip contempt for hostile witnesses, and to radiate belief in a client's innocence.

"This crime is beneath John," Cutler cooed to reporters.

What he told the jury was equally coy. Piecyk was drunk and picked the fight, he said during his opening statement. Gotti only intervened to help the man he was talking to when Piecyk ran at them like a madman. Gotti was concerned because he knew his companion, a man of slight build, had a heart condition.

At the defense table Gotti seemed respectful and, when Piecyk was finally brought to the stand, deeply pained, as if some terrible miscarriage of justice was about to happen.

One was, but not the one Gotti was trying to imply.

Piecyk was wearing dark glasses, and he began chewing on his nails as the prosecutor's questioning brought him ever closer to the heart of the case. Finally, assistant district attorney Kirke Bartley asked if the men who "punched and smacked" him were in the courtroom.

"I don't see them now," he replied, without looking up.

Bartley asked Piecyk to try looking around the courtroom.

Piecyk looked left, right, up, down, and then, briefly, at the defense table.

"I do not," he said.

Bartley tried it another way. Did Piecyk recall how the men who assaulted him were dressed?

"To be perfectly honest, it was so long ago, I don't remember. I don't remember who slapped me. I have no recollection of what the two men looked like or how they were dressed."

I FORGOTTI! a memorable *New York Post* headline screamed the next day as the judge in the case dismissed the charges.

With his mischievous smile, Gotti exited the courthouse through the now customary media horde, which would be reassembling in two weeks' time for the opening of the trial of the federal case in Brooklyn. "The confusion has all been cleared up," he said.

One case down, and one to go—by hook or by crook.

The media coverage of his court cases made Gotti a highly recognizable figure, and he relished the attention and deference now accorded him when he and an inner circle of pals patronized some restaurant or nightclub— the glitzier, the better.

The in-crowd sometimes included DeCicco, but never Sammy—and rarely Angelo, Gene, or Carneglia. Under the terms of their bail in the heroin case, they were not supposed to "consort with criminals"; the trial in that

case had been delayed many times, first because of diffi-
cult pretrial legal issues, now because two defendants,
Gene and Carneglia, were about to go on trial in the
Giacalone case with Gene's brother.

The inner circle included men, mostly bachelors, who
liked to eat, drink, gamble, and throw money around as
much as Gotti did. Some were friends before he took
over, some he drew into his orbit afterward—men like
Eddie Lino, a Sparks shooter and minor defendant in the
heroin case who was a friend of Angelo's first.

Lino, a Bonanno family associate, ran a school bus
company but made most of his money in heroin and
cocaine—and when Gotti induced him to switch allegiance and gave him a Gambino family "button," it was
more proof that Gotti had always spoken with forked
tongue on the drug issue.

The nocturnal-carousing group also included Joe Watts,
an unusual example, because he was neither made nor Italian, which automatically prevented him from ever getting a button. He was a friend of Sammy's and DeCicco's
first, and even Paul's, because he was yet another gangster from Staten Island practiced in the art of making
money in the construction industry. Like Deebee, he also
was wealthy, which he liked to demonstrate by picking up
the nearest restaurant tab; he became a friend of Gotti's
after Sammy coaxed him into serving as a backup shooter
and getaway driver on East Forty-sixth Street.

Sometimes, Lino or Watts and other members of the in-
group would be distracted elsewhere, but one never was.
Starting in 1985, after his promotion to capo, Jack
D'Amico was always at Gotti's elbow during a social
event. He was from New Jersey, but he worked and
played in Manhattan. He was a great player—witty, salt-
and-pepper swarthy, debonair—and fond of his newfound
job in the glow of the limelight, minding the boss on a
night out.

On some evenings, the group began with dinner at
some nice Italian restaurant in Brooklyn recommended by
the man Gotti had chosen as his top bodyguard, Barthol-
omew "Bobby" Boriello, who resided in Sammy's old
neighborhood, Bensonhurst. Boriello was a friendly giant;
like Eddie Lino, he had been an associate of the Bonanno
family, whose Commission privileges had been taken

away because of drug dealing. Like Lino, he welcomed the dawn of the Gotti era in the Gambino family.

After Brooklyn, and before convening at some night-club like Regine's or Club A on the high-priced Ease Side of Manhattan, the group would stop for a pick-me-up at one of the boss's favorite spots—Da Noi, a plush, velvety restaurant with a Don Juan aura. It was operated by Carlo Vaccarezza, a velvety Italian immigrant whom Gotti had met and befriended a few years before, when Gotti was bouncing around New York without being recognized.

Gotti and Vaccarezza got along well partly because both were self-made men. Vaccarezza landed in Miami as a steward on a cruise line, made his way to New York, became manager of a corporate cafeteria, and then went into the restaurant business with a prominent professional baseball player, Rusty Staub.

That's where Gotti and Vaccarezza met, at Rusty Staub's, a popular steakhouse in midtown. Before break-ing away to start Da Noi, Vaccarezza was arrested in a big loan-sharking case, but he beat it and, to celebrate, bought a powerful speedboat that he christened *Not Guilty.* He shipped it to Florida, and he and Gotti—during Gotti's regular Florida holidays—grew closer while hang-ing out on *Not Guilty.*

Da Noi—"to us"—was also on Manhattan's East Side, one of the wealthiest neighborhoods in the country. It drew many well-off patrons, including actor Anthony Quinn, who had portrayed gangsters in a hundred films. Vaccarezza introduced Quinn to Gotti and sent a bottle of Cristal Rose champagne over to a table that they shared for a while.

"I grew up in a tough neighborhood," Quinn told Gotti, in an oblique reference to the Willie Boy Johnson situa-tion, which the media had recently revisited, "a place where people lied, stole, and cheated. But one thing we never did was betray each other."

"It was the same where I grew up," Gotti said gravely.

Of course, in the case of both men, it was the cham-pagne talking; quite obviously Gotti had just betrayed Paul.

It was not the first time Gotti had been in the company of a celebrity actor. Years before, when Gotti was still just boss of the Bergin, actor Jon Voight came out to

Ozone Park to soak up some atmosphere for a role he was considering. Nor would it be the last; after Gotti took over, actor Mickey Rourke sought him out for similar inspiration.

When Gotti was out on the town, Jack D'Amico, Eddie Lino, Joe Watts, Bobby Boriello, and whoever else might be along that night kept an eye on the environs and guarded the approach to Gotti's table. Backslappers and celebrity hounds were kept at bay until D'Amico and the others felt they were harmless and not armed with cameras.

They were particularly careful about female fans. In one of the few concessions he made to his notoriety, Gotti became more discreet about being seen in public with women other than his wife. As marred as it was to people who knew, he valued his reputation as a faithful, devoted husband. Naturally, he also did not want to upset Vicky—the only person who ever got angry at him in public.

Gotti was still seeing Neil's daughter Shannon Grillo, but not as openly. Still, he was so well known now that it was hard to keep the relationship secret. The FBI learned that he and Shannon were still an item when a former cop, now security chief of the Barbizon Hotel in Manhattan, contacted the FBI after seeing Gotti on television and said agents might be interested in a small fracas that had taken place at the hotel recently.

Two men had tried to rent a room without signing the hotel register. A clerk insisted they had to sign, and after several minutes of argument, John Gotti—accompanied by Shannon—came into the lobby and angrily told the men to stop being stupid and just sign a name, any name.

"It don't fuckin' matter," Gotti said. "Make it man in the moon, who gives a shit?"

"Will that be cash, sir?" the clerk smiled.

"Give this nice fella his money," Gotti told one of his unimaginative errand boys.

Papa Schultz and Shannon then went to their room.

The FBI hardly minded if Gotti was having an affair with Neil's married daughter. It had already decided it would do no good to try and blackmail him with photographs because he would never become an informer. But agents were always in the market for Gotti information, so two of them went to the Barbizon, and the clerk identified the two men with Gotti that night as men the agents knew to be occasional bodyguards.

Checking the register, they determined the night in question to be December 9, 1985—seven nights after Neil died. A made man was not supposed to violate another man's wife or children, but in the minds of some it looked as if Gotti was managing to do both with the same woman.

In one of the few times he felt compelled to speak about the situation, Gotti offered a tortured explanation. "It's not really a violation," he told Sammy. "Sandy's a great girl, but she's not the daughter of Neil's wife. And that bum husband of hers, that Ernie, he's not made. He's even lucky he's alive."

Gotti rarely took Vicky to the same nightclubs he and his men patronized. Vicky did not enjoy the scene. He did, however, bring her when he visited with one of his more unlikely social friends, Lewis Kasman, a fast-talking young businessman.

Kasman's family had made a fortune in Manhattan's garment district—first in a company that manufactured women's clothes under a label popular in the 1960s, Ship & Shore, and later in other firms that made clothing accessories.

They met in 1978 at a party at the house of Michael Coiro, the lawyer who represented the Gotti brothers and Angelo on their hijacking cases and who was now under indictment with Angelo and Gene in the heroin case—because he was overheard on the Angelo bugs agreeing to hold their heroin-bought assets.

At that time Coiro was living well in Merrick, Long Island. Kasman, twenty-two years old, lived next door in a million-dollar home. He was smart, glib, and solicitous, a young man on the make—a "nice Jewish boy," he always told Gotti—who was capable of making old ladies and suspicious men feel at ease.

Gotti and Kasman became further acquainted at Belmont Park, a horse-racing track just on the other side of the Queens border with Long Island and home of the Belmont Stakes, a Triple Crown event. Kasman was not a gambler, but he enjoyed the atmosphere in the track's clubhouse, where a high-rolling crowd of lawyers, politicians, and gangsters like Gotti urged the ponies home.

Before joining his family's garment empire, Kasman worked for Long Island lawyers and politicians. At age twenty-one, he was a secretary for the top elected official in Nassau County; later, he was a clerk in the law office of Armand D'Amato, a state legislator whose brother Alfonse was elected to the United States Senate in 1980.

After a few months, Armand D'Amato asked Kasman to manage the business of one of his clients, a man facing indictment for padding his payroll with ghost employees. Kasman thus became the impresario of a restaurant and four Long Island discos, but he remained active in politics and worked in the campaigns of both Armand and Alfonse. In 1980, he escorted the D'Amato brothers' mother to a Ronald Reagan fundraiser at the Waldorf-Astoria Hotel in Manhattan.

"I took Mama D'Amato to the Waldorf," Kasman later recalled to Gotti, as they spoke about the different upbringings they had. "The Secret Service had to check me out."

"They didn't check very far!"

Kasman knew of Gotti's world but never asked questions.

"I have no knowledge of that side of his life," he said to friends in his suburban Jewish world who warned him that it was dangerous to know such a man. "And I don't care. We just happen to like each other. We just enjoy each other's company. He knows I don't need him and he doesn't need me."

Kasman was needy emotionally, though. He also told friends that he and Gotti, eighteen years his senior, really grew close after Gotti's son Frank was killed and after Kasman's dad died. It struck many in Gotti's world as wishful thinking, but after those deaths, Kasman began telling people he was "John Gotti's adopted son."

After Kasman married, left politics, and took his place in his family's garment center businesses, and after Gotti became boss, Gotti and Vicky were guests at barbecues by the tennis court and pool of a new three-million-dollar home Kasman purchased in the posh suburb of Woodbury.

The exquisite surroundings would cause Gotti to reflect on the deprivation of his childhood, and Kasman to say that it had turned out not to matter.

"Forget opportunity, there were some days there wasn't enough food on the table," Gotti said one day.

"I know it was a terrible way to live, John, but look how you've pulled yourself up. You've got cars, a nice house. Your kids are fine, a lot of people love you. I've been around a lot of impressive people. Harvard-trained. But you put them all to shame."

CHAPTER 8

• • • • • • • • • • • •

Chin Music

By April of 1986, Gotti was riding high. His strong-arm win in the Romual Piecyk case made him more confident that somehow his bigger legal problem, the RICO case, could also be won—if not by intimidating witnesses, then by bribing a juror, just two of the tricks he intended to play if he got the chance. While he was a believer in the value of a positive media image, he could hardly count on image alone to sway a jury. But, in a good sign for a gambler, the case was set for trial on April 7—in Courtroom 11 of the United States courthouse in Brooklyn.

He also believed that the Fist had managed the ideal coup—a total takeover, with no loss of its blood. He knew "the other side"—people in the old Paul wing—felt isolated and resentful, but nothing had happened since Sparks to alter his opinion that no one cared enough about Paul to strike back.

With loyalists like DeCicco, Angelo, Armone, Sammy, Deebee, and others around, he felt that his grip on the borgata was secure. With people like Kasman idolizing him, and D'Amico and his nightlife crew squiring him around like a movie star, he felt loved.

One astounding excerpt from the Bergin bug, in which he recalled for an associate some devotional comments that some unidentified capo made, showed how loved Gotti was feeling.

The capo, Gotti recalled, began by saying how he always knew Gotti would be boss someday and how happy that made him. "He says, 'John, I always knew, when you was young even. Someday here, you're gonna be boss. I'm so proud. I swear on my Jesus Christ.' Then he told me, 'You're Jesus Christ,' you know?"

Given such adulation, it was not surprising that Gotti remained sure that eventually the other side would forget and forgive Paul, and fall into line. Without seeming overeager, he tried to encourage the process.

After first requiring each of the capos to visit him at the Bergin in January and February, he began paying goodwill trips to their clubs in March and April. He told DeCicco he would not make the mistake Paul made—be lulled into a false sense of security by assuming that mere position guaranteed loyalty.

"That's what he allowed himself to be tricked into, Frankie," he told his underboss, during a discussion about family unity at the Bergin.

The comment turned out to be one of the most ironic of many John Gotti ironies captured on tape through the years because at the time a plot to kill Gotti and his underboss by lulling them into a false sense of security was gathering momentum.

Gotti was set up for delusion. Until Sparks, he was just an acting caporegime who had never sat in on a Commission meeting, and so he failed to appreciate that his realm was larger than the Gambino family and that in the current disarray of Cosa Nostra, Chin Gigante was the hidebound keeper of the realm.

After Sparks, in response to the messages Gotti had sent to the other families telling them that the Gambino family was at peace and solving its own problems, Chin had sent one back—someday, someone would have to pay for Paul. That message had fallen on the same ears that believed Paul was so ill-loved that no one cared. But Chin cared, and so did two capos from the other side.

One was the elderly James Failla, who controlled the city's private sanitation industry and was in Sparks that night waiting for Paul. The other was Daniel Marino, a trucking-company owner who had supervised trade-show shakedowns for Paul at the city's exhibition centers; he was the same age as Gotti, forty-six.

Gigante, still shuffling around Little Italy in his pajamas to make the FBI think he was crazy, set the plot in motion right after Paul was buried. As the only boss who was not in hot water or facing trial in the Commission case—prosecutors had wrongly accused someone else of being the Genovese boss—Chin became a Commission of one and decided to punish the men who broke the Commission rule that a boss cannot be killed without other bosses' approval.

He also intended to play kingmaker. After Gotti and DeCicco were dead, he would step in and urge the Gambino capos to elect Failla, who had been a friend as long as Paul was, as their new boss. Failla, at his urging, would then choose Marino, the nephew of another friend, as his underboss. As was his custom, Chin communicated his intentions through an emissary.

"Gotti cannot get away with this," the emissary told the two Gambino capos, quoting Chin. "If bosses die like this, Cosa Nostra is dead. Might as well pick a boss off the street."

Failla and Marino thought Gotti was as bad for the Gambino family as Chin thought he was for Cosa Nostra—too flashy, reckless, and inexperienced, a hotheaded hijacker in a double-breasted suit. But they were disinclined to challenge him themselves, because of the Bergin crew's reputation for violence.

"Don't worry," the emissary said. "You won't have anything to do with it. People outside your borgata will be used. You'll have clean hands."

Failla and Marion agreed to go along. All the plot required them to do was to say nothing, act normal, and bide their time—and so it was easy for them, when they visited Gotti at the Bergin, to contribute to his false sense of security.

"Jimmy Brown's a smart old fuck," Gotti said to Sammy one day, using Failla's nickname. "He and Danny Boy ain't gonna be no problem. They're with us a hundred percent."

With Failla and Marino aboard, all that remained was for Chin to pick the time, place, and method, and those plans were well under way by April Fool's Day, a week before Gotti began standing trial in Brooklyn.

Legally, Gotti faced a daunting challenge. The RICO law under which he and other gangsters had been charged was a powerful prosecutorial weapon—available since 1970 but not widely used until Ronald Reagan and the Congress turned the Justice Department loose on Cosa Nostra in 1981.

Its focus was entities, not individuals, families rather than soldiers. Until RICO, federal law mainly saw individuals committing criminal acts; it did not see organizations whose individuals committed crimes on behalf of the organizations.

RICO introduced two new concepts: "criminal enterprise" and "pattern of racketeering." A criminal enterprise was any group "associated in fact" whose members committed crimes for group purposes. A racketeering pattern was two or more violations of state and federal laws regarding murder, kidnapping, hijacking, extortion, fraud, and twenty-seven other crimes.

The penalty for a RICO conviction—up to twenty years in prison for each count—was much more severe than most of those provided under the state and federal laws covering the crimes that a prosecutor could allege as part of the pattern of racketeering.

Another RICO provision was especially ominous to defendants like Gotti. It permitted prosecutors to charge crimes for which a defendant had already been convicted and punished in state court—on the theory that the enterprise nature of the crime had gone unpunished.

In Gotti's case, the provision gave the government a huge head start. In 1975 he was convicted of attempted manslaughter for the botched revenge murder of James McBratney. In 1973 he was convicted twice of hijacking. Because the RICO case against him was filed in 1985, all three convictions fit into the fifteen-year period over which crimes could be linked as part of the same pattern of racketeering.

As a result, Diane Giacalone, the prosecutor who defied the FBI and developed the case against Gotti virtually on her own as an assistant United States attorney for the Eastern District of New York, was halfway home. All she had to do was prove to the jury that the crimes were committed on behalf of an illegal criminal enterprise, the Bergin crew of the Gambino family.

And to make matters worse for Gotti, one of the case's original defendants had already pleaded guilty and, in doing so, admitted that the Bergin crew of the Gambino family existed and that he belonged to it. His plea was now part of the evidence against Gotti and the six remaining codefendants—who included his brother Gene, John

Carneglia, Anthony Rampino, and the now-unmasked Willie Boy Johnson, who had been in protective custody for more than a year.

The plea was an especially bitter pill for Gotti to swallow because the man who made it—and violated the fundamental Cosa Nostra principle of noncooperation with state authority—was Armond Dellacroce, son of Neil. But after his father died, thirty-year-old Armond had slipped deeper into a cocaine-and-alcohol problem and become a basket case.

He told his lawyer to quietly arrange a guilty plea because he did not feel up to standing trial, however. It turned out that he was not just running away from the trial. He failed to show for his sentencing and thus became a fugitive. A few months later his body was found in a hotel room; he had drunk himself to death.

Armond's plea upset Gotti more than his death did; realizing that the plea would be used against him, Gotti issued an edict: No matter how good a deal a prosecutor might offer, no member of the Gambino family could ever admit in a plea agreement that it existed.

"No more fuckin' deals like that, that's over," he later said to Sammy, while drawing a parallel to recent history. "The government will use it in every fuckin' case. It's like with Paul, we don't admit nothin', it never happened."

Because he had so much to lose, after coming so far, Gotti intended to win by almost whatever means necessary, and Armond's guilty plea lent a sense of urgency to the Piecyk-type tactics Gotti began employing a few days before the start of trial.

He ordered two men from the Bergin to intimidate a witness scheduled to testify about one of the three murder charges in the case, the killing of an off-duty court bailiff—allegedly by the codefendant who exhibited such fiery cool outside Sparks, John Carneglia. It was the only murder in the case with "jury appeal"; the other two involved mobsters, McBratney and the loan shark that Gotti and his men murdered in Florida for Neil.

Posing as cops, a Gotti ploy dating back to the McBratney era, the men went to what they thought was the witness's home, but he had moved. Later that week, however, while the witness was driving along an expressway, they pulled alongside his vehicle and shouted that they wanted to talk to him about a murder.

The witness sped away and lost his pursuers in traffic. But he reported the incident to Giacalone, who then learned that probably the same men had visited the man's former home. Well aware of events in the Piecyk case, she had developed a contingency plan should similar events begin to take place in her case.

When the trial began on April 7, she complained about the two incidents to the presiding judge and warned that if there were any more, she would resort to a weapon available to her under a recently passed law. The law allowed her to seek to revoke Gotti's bail and send him to prison, if she could prove that while free on bail he had continued to engage in the illegal business of the Gambino enterprise.

Hearing these echos of the Piecyk case, the media made the incidents and Giacalone's warning into a story that threatened to run through the usually unnewsworthy days of jury selection, a complicated matter in any Cosa Nostra case, but more so now with the so-called Dapper Don.

After a fourth day of stories, Gotti's newly prominent and newly defense-minded lawyer, Bruce Cutler, complained to the judge that a "carnival atmosphere" had taken hold.

"They're making my client into a monster!" he exclaimed, alleging that the media had created an impression that "anyone who looks at Mr. Gotti disappears and is afraid" and that a "crescendo of hysteria" had created the idea that "my client is somehow a wild man."

By the end of the first week, after questioning potential jurors, United States district court judge Eugene Nickerson had found none whose ability to be impartial was unaffected by the media coverage of Gotti, Sparks, and the Piecyk case.

Judge Nickerson had forecast a two-month trial, but he of course was as unaware as John Gotti of how badly Chin Gigante wanted to avenge the unauthorized murder of a Commission boss; over the weekend, the judge's forecast and the search for untainted jurors went up in smoke.

* * *

The first strike in what became Chin Gigante's secret war against John Gotti came on a Sunday morning in Bensonhurst. It was an elaborately planned ambush made possible by Gotti's decision to pay goodwill visits to the other side.

Gotti and DeCicco were scheduled to meet at Jimmy Brown Failla's social club, fraternize for a while with Failla, Danny Marino, and others, then drive together in DeCicco's car to Manhattan to meet other family members at the Ravenite.

Sammy Gravano also was scheduled to be at Failla's club, known as the Veterans and Friends, but Chin had decreed a simple equation for Sparks: a boss and an underboss had been killed, and so only a boss and an underboss would be killed now. Then the slate would be clean.

As Chin's emissary had promised Failla and Marino, only people outside the Gambino family were involved in the ambush. The leader was a Luchese family capo, Anthony Casso, whom Chin had grown to trust after Casso accompanied his boss to a couple of Commission meetings. In the Luchese family, Casso was as accomplished in murder as Gotti and Sammy were in the Gambino.

Chin and Casso decided that to accomplish the goal of killing only Gotti and DeCicco, a simple Sparks-style ambush wouldn't do. With so many men from different corners of the family at the Veterans and Friends Club, it might provoke a tremendous shoot-out.

But when DeCicco told Failla that he and Gotti intended to meet at the club, then drive together to Manhattan, he gave the plotters an idea: a remote-control car bomb. From there, Casso assembled the details. Once Gotti and DeCicco were in the club, a "planter" would sneak under DeCicco's car and affix the bomb to the undercarriage; then, from some distance away, a "lookout" would wait until Gotti and DeCicco got in the car; the lookout would signal the "button" man, who would be waiting even farther away—with his finger on the bomb's remote-controlled detonator.

Casso himself didn't even have to be on the scene—and no one who was there would have any firsthand idea of whom to blame.

The only problem with the plan was that the planter, the lookout, and the button were already in place and never told that Gotti had changed his mind that morning and had telephoned the Veterans and Friends to tell DeCicco to meet him in "New York"—which was how they referred to both Manhattan and Little Italy.

"John just called," DeCicco told Sammy inside the club. "We're gonna meet him down in New York. We'll take my car."

At that point, a soldier asked DeCicco for the business card of a lawyer DeCicco had promised to recommend. But DeCicco had left the business card in the glove compartment of his car.

"Want me to get it?" Sammy asked.

"Nah, you'll never find the fuckin' thing. I'll get it."

DeCicco and the soldier, a gray-haired man of about Gotti's age and build, left the club and walked toward DeCicco's car, which was parked across the street in front of an automobile dealership.

From a couple of hundred feet away, the lookout thought he saw Gotti and DeCicco. He waited until one of them, DeCicco, opened the car door and sat on the front seat. Then, he waved toward the button man, who was another couple of hundred feet away.

The explosion sent shards of metal ripping through DeCicco and flung the soldier, still half outside the car, into the air.

Sammy and several others raced out of the club, pulled the badly mangled and unconscious DeCicco out of the now-burning car, and put him by the soldier, who was conscious but badly wounded.

"Get a fuckin' ambulance!" Sammy screamed.

A cop happened to drive by seconds later in a police van, and Sammy and the others put both victims inside. The soldier survived, but DeCicco died en route to Victory Memorial Hospital.

Remembering how prepared for war he had been in the immediate wake of Sparks and thinking how foolish it was for him, DeCicco, and Gotti to have let their guard down, Sammy went back inside the Veterans and Friends. In the tangle of his emotions, he made nothing of the fact that Failla and Marino had not come outside.

"I don't know what the fuck this is about, but I'm

goin' over to my office and wait to hear from John," he told Failla.

"Cops are gonna be crawlin' all over," Failla said. "Call me if you need me. I'll be home."

"No fuckin' use stayin' here," Marino said. "I'll be home, too. Keep me posted."

After they left, Eddie Garafola said to Sammy, "What fuckin' good are they gonna do at home?"

"Wimps, what the fuck do I know? You go meet John. Tell him I'm gettin' guns ready and waitin' to hear from him."

After Garafola described the demise of DeCicco, Gotti drove to Bensonhurst and cruised past the still-smoldering car, then went to the Bergin and telephoned Sammy to meet him.

Sammy arrived just as someone asked Gotti how he felt.

"I was doing good 'til a couple hours ago. The bomb was fuckin' something. The car was bombed like they put gasoline on it. You gotta see the car, you wouldn't believe the car."

"I saw it, John," Sammy said, "I pulled Frankie out."

"I heard, Sammy. I heard it was too late."

"Who the fuck did it?"

"I don't know, fuckin' cops? Who .he fuck knows?"

"Chin?"

"Nah, he wouldn't use fuckin' bombs, he'd want ya to know. It's some renegade element. Maybe Bilotti's relatives."

No matter who was responsible, Gotti added, now was a time for showing unity and strength, and so he would order the capos to order everyone in the family to attend DeCicco's wake. "Who the fuck did it, they got to know we ain't afraid. They wanna play some more, let 'em fuckin' try some more. We gotta be strong against people who are strong."

The response impressed Sammy. Whatever his faults, John Gotti was strong. He might be reckless, but he was fearless, and that's what the situation born of the Fist demanded.

"You're right, John, you're right," Sammy said.

Almost every member of the family, including Failla and Marino, did attend the wake, as did even an emissary from

Chin. Twenty-five years before, at another family wake, young Danny Marino and other hotheads fractured the skull of an FBI agent taking photographs outside the wake of a family member, but this time he and everyone else ignored the agents, cops, and reporters who surveilled DeCicco's wake.

He and Failla were more interested in what Chin's emissary whispered into their ears: "There'll be another time."

The next morning, Frank DeCicco was laid to rest in the same cemetery as the man he had helped betray, Paul.

Over the next several days, Gotti advanced several other motives and theories and ordered Sammy to investigate. Gotti never said anything to Sammy indicating that he suspected Chin was involved. One reason was that years before, Neil had told Gotti that the Commission had adopted a rule against car bombs as a means of assassination because it exposed passersby to harm. The bigger reason was that he felt Chin was like Paul—all bark, no bite.

Sammy never found any evidence linking the bomb to anyone, and soon the bigger question became, Who would replace DeCicco?

By virtue of the risks they had taken, all surviving members of the Fist—Armone, Sammy, Deebee—were candidates. But the only man who launched a campaign was Angelo Ruggiero, who had been excised out of the conspiracy for appearance's sake. He was facing a practical life sentence, too, once his heroin case finally went to trial, but to him—as similar peril was to Gotti—that was beside the point.

"I want it," he told Sammy outside the Bergin. "I fuckin' deserve it. I know this life. I've been in it all my fuckin' life, payin' my dues."

"It's John's call," Sammy replied diplomatically; but as a friend of DeCicco's, it irked him that Angelo, whose résumé ran from hijacking to drug dealing to murder, thought he was up to filling DeCicco's shoes.

In Sammy's mind, Angelo was clearly inappropriate on other grounds. It was not something he could point out to him without causing trouble, but the more cases the government had filed against Cosa Nostra, the more evident it had become that Angelo, more than any other individual, had caused the most damage.

The damage went beyond the Gambino family. While his home and telephone were secretly wired, Angelo had discussed more than heroin. He talked about Cosa Nostra structure, history, and politics—giving the FBI the probable cause it needed to ask a judge for permission to plant bugs in Paul's and Neil's houses. And now Angelo tapes, Paul tapes, and Neil tapes were being used in Cosa Nostra cases all over New York—a universe more than a city, and so big that the fight against Cosa Nostra was being carried on in many politically distinct, jealously guarded jurisdictions.

The tapes also would be used in a case coming down the pike—the Gambino hierarchy case; with Paul and Neil gone, the word from family lawyers responding to subpoenas from the government was that the main targets seemed to be Joseph Armone, Joe N. Gallo, and a few capos, including Angelo, but not Sammy—whom the FBI knew about but hadn't yet targeted. For legal reasons related to the Giacalone case, Gotti also was getting a pass.

Even so, enough trouble was in store, and here was Angelo, saying he deserved to be underboss. But Sammy continued to be diplomatic as pudgy Angelo lit up another Marlboro. "Whatever John says is good with me, you know that," he said.

Back in court for the Giacalone case twenty-four hours after the bombing, Bruce Cutler asked Judge Nickerson to delay the trial until the latest media storm ran its course. He said stories implying that "some of Mr. Gotti's friends might have had complicity or involvement" in the bombing had "shattered" his client's presumption of innocence.

Nickerson drolly denied the motion. Because of pretrial delays related to Neil's illness and demise, the case was already way behind schedule, and he wanted to press ahead and select a jury despite the out-of-court headlines.

Over a two-week period, Nickerson interviewed more than two hundred candidates for the pool of potential jurors from which the jury would be chosen. But the bombing had cast a long shadow over the courtroom;

Nickerson found only nine people who said they could judge the evidence fairly.

Many others trembled when they, one by one, came into court to be questioned and walked by the defense table, at which were seated, in addition to Gotti, the gangster from central casting, six of the most dangerous-looking men in New York—three from the Bergin crew, two from another crew in Neil's wing, and Willie Boy Johnson.

Of the Bergin bunch, the scariest was Anthony Rampino, a backup shooter at Sparks; with his dark, deep-set eyes, hollow cheeks, and acne scars, Rampino looked half-dead. And since he was now a heroin addict, he was like a zombie most of the time.

Gene Gotti lacked the dangerously handsome features that made his brother so imposing, but with his beady eyes and half-cocked sneer, he looked as though he had taken part in some of the eight murders he once said the crew had committed for Paul. John Carneglia, dark, powerfully built, and perpetually scowling, was as menacing as a snake ready to strike.

Willie Boy, the beefy ex-boxer and ex–Source Wahoo, arrived at the courthouse each day in a prison van from the Metropolitan Correctional Center in Manhattan. He had been housed there in a witness-security unit for more than a year, after refusing to cave in to Giacalone's pressure and testify against the others.

Just when the DeCicco publicity died down, disaster struck Judge Nickerson's jury-screening process. The prospect of being chosen to deliver verdicts on such defendants caused the nine people that Nickerson had so far chosen for the jury pool to violate his order not to talk about the case.

When Nickerson found out that they had, he dismissed them and threw in the towel, saying on April 28 that because of all the publicity, he was delaying the trial until August.

Gotti, playing victim for the media, predicted that the judge would blame him. "I'll get banged around with this," he said.

It was Diane Giacalone, however, who came after him—and she used a real victim, Romual Piecyk, to get him.

Saying that the delay heightened the chance of further

witness intimidation, she filed a motion seeking revocation of Gotti's bail and requesting that he be detained in prison while the case was abeyed.

Hearings were held in early May. Under the same new law she had threatened to use earlier, a defendant could be detained if there was a strong likelihood that he had continued to engage in crimes, such as intimidating a witness, while on bail.

In the case of Romual Piecyk, the evidence was far beyond strong. The cops in that case took the stand to tell how the brakes on Piecyk's van had been slashed and how he had made, then retracted, complaints that "Gotti's people" followed him and made harassing telephone calls at odd hours. An agent also testified that an informant told him that several Gotti crew members had bragged of giving Piecyk "a kick in the ass."

Putting his own spin on it, Bruce Cutler argued that Piecyk had frightened himself into silence, after reading about Gotti's "violent and impulsive" reputation. The testimony from the stand was just "regurgitation of newspaper articles."

Judge Nickerson sided with Giacalone. "Gotti had a clear motive to prevent Piecyk from testifying and the boldness to accomplish that end," he said in a written opinion issued on May 13; he gave Gotti six days to tidy up his affairs before surrendering to the United States Marshals Service.

It was enough time for one last desperate move; lo and behold, the now-famous refrigeration mechanic, Romual Piecyk, contacted Cutler and signed an affidavit in which he said: "At no time was I ever warned, threatened, coerced or in any way persuaded not to testify against John Gotti, or anyone else."

Citing the friendly affidavit, Cutler filed a motion asking for another go in court. But no one had believed poor Piecyk when he tried to retract his charges that "Gotti's people" threatened him, and no one believed him now; what was believed was that he had been given another kick in the ass.

"The motion is denied," Nickerson said.

Cutler quickly appealed to a higher federal court, which declined to intervene, and the game was finally up.

Gotti now confronted the real possibility of never leaving prison again. The trial was not scheduled to start
again until August; for the same reasons that he was being imprisoned, he would not be granted bail while it was
held. If found guilty, he was vulnerable to a forty-year
sentence and was not likely to be freed to await the outcome of an appeal.

"John's ready for whatever happens," his brother Richard told reporters who trekked to Ozone Park for reaction.
"He's a man."

In a few days, disappointed agents for the state Organized Crime Task Force also traveled to Ozone Park, to
shut down their eavesdropping "plant" near the Bergin
Hunt and Fish Club. With the target of their investigation
going to prison, the agents no longer had legal authority
to listen in on conversations.

While their bug had yielded little direct evidence, it
had pointed investigators down some promising paths. As
with Willie Boy Johnson and Billy Battista, Diane
Giacalone had shut down a valuable vein of information.
Unknowingly, of course, she also mooted Chin's plan to
collect the other half of the price he was charging for
Paul's murder.

Meanwhile, Gotti made plans to run the family from
prison. When Paul was making such plans, and proposed
that a trio of men carry out his orders, Gotti had been
scornful. But now it seemed like a good idea, and Gotti
informed Angelo Ruggiero, Joseph Armone, and Sammy
Gravano that they would be in "charge of the street"
while he was away. Much to Angelo's chagrin, he said he
would appoint an underboss later.

On the day of his surrender, May 19, Gotti showed up
at the courthouse wearing a tan safari suit. Outside, as reporters and TV cameras recorded the scene, he slipped
out of a pair of tan loafers and into shoes fit for prison,
Reebok sneakers.

"Let's go," he beamed at his brother Peter, as he
strolled inside. "We're ready for Freddy."

"Freddy" was the undertaker in an old comic strip,
Smilin' Jack, and "ready for Freddy" was an old Brooklyn expression for being ready for anything, even an undertaker. The media loved the line and there were smiles

all around. Even headed off to prison, possibly for life, the Dapper Don whistled past the graveyard.

His wit in the face of adversity was now a hallmark. It made him seem less dangerous. But even while he was behind bars, he would send someone to the undertaker.

CHAPTER 9

• • • • • • • • • • • • •

Tying In

DeCicco's murder and Gotti's jailing pushed Sammy out of the place where he felt most comfortable—the shadows. Six months before, he was a soldier. Now, at age forty-one, he and two men he knew only casually—Angelo and Armone—were in day-to-day command of the family. Events were moving too fast, but one of the Sparks rules, one of Sammy's, was that there would be no turning back. He would need to remind himself of this as events moved even faster, sometimes treacherously.

Gotti was incarcerated in a nine-by-twelve-foot steel-and-concrete cell at the Metropolitan Correctional Center (MCC) in lower Manhattan, a modern high-rise prison that from a distance could be mistaken for a cheap apartment tower. It was the same prison where, in a segregated section for prisoners whose lives were thought to be in danger, Willie Boy Johnson was being held.

The prison was in the same stand of buildings that contained the state and federal courts in Manhattan and the headquarters of the NYPD and the FBI—all just a short stroll south of the Ravenite Social Club in Little Italy and just a short drive east of Sammy's office in Brooklyn.

Practically speaking, however, Gotti might as well have been in Cedar Rapids—at least in Sammy's view. He and Gotti could not speak on the telephone, because the MCC phones were monitored. And Gotti's visitor privileges, limited by MCC rules, included only his lawyers, personal family members like Gene, and his oldest friend, Angelo.

Angelo's access to Gotti—visits were not monitored—gave him an edge over Sammy and Armone, and it would quickly cause problems, for them and for the other surviving member of the Fist, soldier-at-large Robert DiBernardo.

By bribing its president, Deebee controlled Local 282 of the International Brotherhood of Teamsters; its members drove the trucks that delivered concrete and supplies to the city's major construction projects. He had the power to make or break contractors by either granting union favors or causing union problems at job sites.

For instance, a contractor saved money on a job if Local 282 waived a contractual provision requiring that a Teamster foreman be on hand at all jobs—with no work to do other than stop nonunion drivers from coming onto the site. If, on the other hand, Local 282 enforced that featherbedding rule and others like it, it could drive a contractor out of business.

Such make-or-break power was an endless source of graft and the linchpin of Deebee's former importance to Paul. With Deebee in union control, Paul could steer projects to firms willing to pay bribes for relaxed rules. He could influence which companies bid on jobs and steer the big jobs to firms controlled by him.

Deebee also used the union to pass around no-show jobs, an important service to anyone whose real job was Cosa Nostra but nevertheless had to display to the Internal Revenue Service some source of income. So far as the IRS knew, both of the late Gambino underbosses, Bilotti and DeCicco, were just foremen for Local 282 when they were murdered.

The union made Deebee a wealthy man. He invested his money in a loan-shark book and companies involved in the production and marketing of X-rated films and magazines. Despite the rough-and-tumble world he inhabited, he was not personally violent; he was like Tommy Gambino, Carlo's gentlemanly son, a businessman with gangster ties, who lived with his wife and children in a nice Long Island suburb and belonged to a country club.

Over the last few years, because of their mutual fields of plunder, Sammy and Deebee had been meeting at least once a week at Sammy's office in Bensonhurst. They were opposites, but still friends, and Sammy was flattered when Deebee casually suggested, after Gotti was jailed, that Sammy should be the next underboss.

"I don't know about that," replied Sammy, still adjusting to the idea of being an acting street boss. "I'm just helping mind the store until John figures out what he wants. I'm good where I'm at. I'm makin' money, I got a good crew."

"You got the brains and the balls for it," Deebee said.

"There's others too. Angelo for one. He's hot for it."

"John loves ya. You know what he told me before he went into the can? He said he wishes he had five Sammys out there."

"I don't need it, Deebee. Angelo seems to."

"I don't know about Angelo. There's the heroin thing. But what's he done? He was always borrowin' off me. Still owes me. Him and John both. They got big lawyer bills."

Sammy never mentioned the conversation to anyone; Deebee must have, and soon, because when Sammy saw Angelo in a few days, Angelo was furious.

"Is it true Deebee was talkin' you up for underboss?"

"He mentioned it, but it was just talk."

"John will make his decision for that spot. It ain't Deebee's place to talk about it. It's fuckin' subversive."

"Subversive? With John? If Deebee was subversive, we'd be dead and Paul'd be alive."

"Yeah, well, all I can say is, John ain't gonna like it."

Sammy wanted to say there was no reason to tell Gotti about such chatter, but he didn't; it would only give Angelo more reason to argue to Gotti that there was something to it, and that maybe Sammy was subversive too.

"Ange, just don't paint it the wrong way."

Sammy never learned exactly what Angelo told Gotti, but it was obviously bad, because the next time he saw Angelo, Angelo said: "John's sent an order that we gotta kill Deebee. It's because Deebee's been talkin' behind his back."

Sammy was briefly speechless, then sputtered, "He didn't mean nothin'! He was just talkin'. And it ain't talkin' behind John's back for him to bullshit about underboss."

"No, it's worse, Sammy. John heard Deebee was sayin' John don't know enough to be a boss. Deebee was sayin' someone like fuckin' asshole Jimmy Brown'd be a better boss."

"I don't believe it. You got to reach out to John, and ask him to hold up on it until we can discuss it."

"No, this has gotta be done. John is steamin'."

"Where're we goin' here? Deebee ain't dangerous. Maybe he talked, Deebee's just a talker, that's why he's so good."

Angelo, however, said Gotti had already picked out a place and a plan.

"But Deebee don't even have a crew. He ain't a shooter! He ain't no threat!"

"John wants you in on it."

Sammy fell silent, realizing now that his own loyalty had been put on the line—whether by Angelo or Gotti he could not be sure—but it didn't matter, the result was the same. For the first time, he felt doubt about the wisdom of joining the Fist. He already felt isolated by DeCicco's death, and now Gotti was planning to eliminate the only plotter left who, besides him, came from the Paul wing.

Angelo said the plan called for Sammy and others to lure Deebee to the home of the mother of a Bergin soldier. "It'll be a meeting about construction and you'll be sittin' there when he comes down to the basement, and who's ever behind 'im will pop him in the head. The old lady won't be there."

"I'm against this, Ange," Sammy said, knowing that what he felt was no longer important. "It ain't somethin' we gotta do, but John's the boss."

"John'll feel good, knowing you're in his corner a hundred percent."

"He never had no reason to doubt it. It's the same with Deebee. But John's the boss."

Angelo contacted Sammy a few days later. "We can't get that guy's mom's place. But John says we have to do it right away. So he wants you to take care of it."

It occurred to Sammy that Deebee was about to be murdered only because Angelo, and maybe Gotti, owed him money and wanted to erase the debt—but the thought quickly passed. He could not afford such thoughts now, or any hesitation.

"If it's gotta be done right away," he said, "I can do it right in my office. Deebee comes by a couple times a week. I'll set it up right there."

"Good, set it up and let me know what you need."

Early the evening of June 5, 1986, only seventeen days after Gotti was jailed at the MCC, Deebee arrived at Sammy's office and was told by one of Sammy's men that Sammy and some crew members were drinking coffee in a room one floor below.

The others included Sammy's Luca Braza, Joseph Paruta, the not-so-elderly "Old Man Joe." After Deebee came downstairs, Old Man Joe rose to get him some coffee. Paruta had been ill lately, but as always he was feeling well enough to kill. He walked to a cabinet, retrieved a silencer-equipped .38-caliber revolver from a secret compartment, walked back, and shot Sammy's Victim No. 12 in the back of the head, twice.

Sammy and others stashed Deebee's body in an adjacent room because it was still too busy on the street to take the body out. Angelo, who had agreed to supervise the job later in the night, sat out the actual hit. He waited in the parking lot of the Nebraska Diner in Coney Island until Sammy reported in a little while later.

"It's done," Sammy said, without any emotion. "His car's out front. Here're the keys. You gotta get rid of it, too."

"We got plans for that."

Sammy drove to where he normally met with his crew, Tali's, a bar and restaurant he owned near his old childhood home. Later that night, Angelo arrived; he was accompanied by Carneglia, who, unlike Gotti, was free on bail in the delayed Giacalone case, and several others—including two who seemed so young that Sammy assumed they were teenagers who worked for Carneglia at his scrapyard.

The disposal party also included a man nearly sixty years old—Frank LoCascio, a captain from the Bronx whom Sammy barely knew. LoCascio's decina was one of those that used to report to Neil, and one of his drug-dealing crew members had served as one of the four designated shooters outside Sparks. Still, since he was now getting personally involved in Deebee's murder, Sammy concluded that LoCascio also must have been made to feel that it was necessary to show his loyalty to Gotti.

Sammy accompanied the group back to his office and helped carry Deebee's body up from the basement and outside, where it was placed in the trunk of a car and driven away by LoCascio.

Deebee's body was never found. His new Mercedes was never found either. Carneglia, an expert at chopping up cars as well as at be-sure shots, and the young men with him drove it away.

Having shown his loyalty, Sammy was now compelled to show lack of remorse. Gotti, through Angelo, ordered him to meet with Deebee's business contacts and inventory the dead man's assets.

This was a far easier chore. As Sammy had shown with his brother-in-law Nicky Scibetta, remorse was a useless emotion once the deed was done, and so he contacted Deebee's business associates. He told them Deebee was missing and that he was trying to get to the bottom of it, then gave a speech much like the one he had given Tommy Bilotti's brother, Joey.

"We don't want nothin' Deebee's family ought to get, but anything he did in our name, we want to know about," he told one of Deebee's partners in the X-rated film-and-magazine business. "Any illegitimate things, those belong to us."

"It ain't easy, tellin' the difference," the man replied.

"Any questions, you send me a message."

He also met with the corrupt president of Teamsters Local 282, Bobby Sasso. "From here on in, you report directly to me. You can't meet with nobody in our family or people in other families without my permission."

Having no choice in the matter, Sasso nodded his agreement.

"From now on, when you and me meet, it'll be in some hotel room at fuckin' three in the morning. Understand? Also, I don't want your face at any more family weddings or funerals. It used to be we expected you to show your respect, but that's off now. We gotta be careful now. Cops all over the place. Got it?"

Sammy and Sasso did begin meeting at three in the morning, at a hot-sheet motel in Brooklyn. In a situation that was about as perverse as life in the borgata got, Sammy—who didn't even know his friend Deebee's final resting place—became the Cosa Nostra boss of Local 282.

Throwing in some more perversity—as though he was

having fun confounding things—Gotti, a few days later, stiffed childhood pal Angelo and named Joseph Armone underboss.

This decision renewed Sammy's confidence in Gotti. Putting the best face on Deebee's murder—that it was really about his alleged subversiveness, not the fact that Angelo and maybe Gotti owed him loan-shark money—Sammy thought it was still an incredibly temperamental and vicious act for Gotti to order it based on inherently suspect stories that Angelo brought him.

But in promoting Armone, Gotti was showing sound judgment. As unaware as Gotti that it was already too late to worry about the loyalty of capos like James Failla and Daniel Marino, Sammy felt that sixty-eight-year-old Armone would make the other side feel more comfortable about the future under Gotti.

Joe Piney, as Armone was known—because as a boy he began in crime by stealing Christmas trees—also was the right choice for relations with other families, which loathed even the sound of Angelo's voice—which was being heard in court cases around the city, because of his tapes.

The one liability Joe Piney had, legal trouble, was the same one Angelo and so many others, except Sammy, had. He was about to be indicted in the long-anticipated Gambino hierarchy case, again partly thanks to Angelo's tapes. Indeed, in June 1986, only days after Gotti's decision, Joe Piney was indicted, along with consigliere Joe N. Gallo, Angelo, and several others.

As expected, because of legal reasons related to the Diane Giacalone case, Gotti got a pass. The court papers did refer to him as a coconspirator, but only anonymously, because federal lawyers did not want to give Gotti lawyer Bruce Cutler another reason to cry about prejudicial publicity once the Giacalone case was reconvened in Brooklyn—where the hierarchy case would also be tried, but by the Cosa Nostra specialists in her office.

All but one defendant in the hierarchy case made bail; much to his anger and others' joy, Angelo Ruggiero was the one who did not. The reason was that he lost his temper during the bail hearing and shook his finger menacingly when a prosecutor argued against bail because

Angelo was now a defendant in two major cases, the new one plus the heroin case.

"This is like fuckin' Russia," Angelo wailed, as he was led away to the MCC, but not to the same wing as Gotti.

As underboss, Joe Piney Armone—a frail man with horn-rim glasses and a perpetual grimace who looked every bit of sixty-eight—was in charge of the street. But under his bail terms, he was told not to "consort" with criminals, and so his ability to meet with the troops became severely limited.

"It's a fuckin' crime, they put you in prison before they fuckin' convict you," he complained to Sammy. "We'll use one of my guys for messages, but you'll be the one out front."

Talk about events moving too fast! Eight months down the road from Sparks, every member of the Fist but Sammy was dead, in prison, or headed there. On a practical level, Sammy Gravano became the de facto acting boss of the Gambino family.

Much to his dismay, the *Daily News*—just as it had a year before with Gotti—gave Sammy an inaugural half-page splash in its Sunday editions on July 25, 1986. Having no recent photograph to decorate its story, which described him as "the family's up-and-comer," the *News* published a photograph of Sammy from his early twenties, when he wore his hair long and looked like a young hood standing on line to get into the *Godfather*.

The story ended his low profile at Gleason's Gym and gave his sparring partners second thoughts about throwing big punches.

One of the first messages Joe Piney sent Sammy was that they ought to do something to provide their imprisoned boss a little extra income—and it was in pursuit of this goal that Sammy made peace with an old enemy, Louie DiBono.

DiBono was the soldier-contractor he had threatened to kill several years before, when he caught DiBono attempting to cheat the family out of its share of a windfall made on a nonunion drywall construction job. The threat prompted the sitdown at Paul's mansion in which Neil intervened on Sammy's behalf.

"Why don't you get somethin' up with Louie?"

Armone said in the message. "Make it so John gets a piece of each job."

At first, Sammy didn't want anything to do with DiBono, but on reflection he realized that under the changed circumstances, DiBono would be eager to do anything he wanted.

"What's past is past," he told DiBono, after calling him to a meeting and explaining what the new underboss wanted on behalf of the boss. "We've got a new slate here, and we're just looking to do something for John."

"However I can help, you know that," DiBono replied. "I know you was just doing what you thought was right last time. You just read the records wrong, but that was my fault. I was keeping bad records."

"Bad records, right. Well, this time, we're gonna set up a company the legit way, with lawyers and everything. Me and you will get fifty-fifty on paper, but I split my fifty with John, but that's between him and me."

"Of course."

"I'll give you some men, and whatever help you need with the unions. But you run it all. I don't have the fuckin' time."

Gotti, naturally, liked the arrangement and sent Sammy a message via his brother Gene that it augured well for family unity that Sammy and DiBono could bury the hatchet so easily.

Gene also brought another message—John wanted Sammy and Frank LoCascio to visit each crew and give pep talks: John wasn't worried about the future, so they shouldn't be.

"John's bothered that guys are gonna get down, what with him in the can, and me and Angelo and Joe Piney and everybody fucked up with these fuckin' cases," Gene said. "So you and Frankie, he likes Frankie, he wants you two to tie in with people and keep everybody strong. Only made guys."

Sammy didn't have to be told that a tie-in, as an official crew meeting was called, was for made men only. He had attended a few tie-ins under Toddo Aurello, and they were as ritualistic as an induction ceremony. They began with the men seated around a table, "tying in" by holding hands. When they tied in, capos and soldiers became equals, no matter differences in wealth and ability, and reaffirmed their loyalty to their boss and to the idealized notions of Cosa Nostra.

Over the next several months, virtually every crew in the family—including the crews of James Failla and Danny Marino—tied in under such secret arrangements that even the FBI never learned about them. Only crews in Florida and Connecticut did not meet, and in time Sammy intended to get to them too.

Sometimes Sammy and LoCascio asked other capos to join them, to underline the overall theme of unity. The presence of multiple capos added weight to the moment, but it also helped to break the ice; many times for Sammy, less often for the veteran LoCascio, they were meeting men they had never met before.

That Sammy did not know soldiers in his own family was not surprising. Many soldiers operated businesses or held positions in unions and trade groups that required little interaction with anyone but their own captains. Sammy knew other soldiers only by their nicknames, and if there was no business reason to know the real name, he did not want to. Although hardly a shield against prosecution, nicknames made it harder for authorities who might be eavesdropping on conversations to figure out who was who.

Holding hands with LoCascio, assorted other capos, and the soldiers of a decina, Sammy gave a little speech—which during one tie-in went like this:

"We are a committee sent by our boss, John Gotti. He asked us to tell you to stay strong and unified. We are a Cosa Nostra. If we remain strong, no one can hurt us. We live by the rules of Cosa Nostra. You cannot ever go against Cosa Nostra; that means you can never make no admission about the family, in any shape or form. We can never raise our hands against one another."

Struck by the irony of his last remark, Sammy was unable to remind the men that they were not supposed to deal in drugs—or act on amorous feelings for another made man's wife or children.

Still, with his belief in rules and rituals, he enjoyed the tie-ins immensely. They could never have the same effect as his induction ceremony, when he was so naive about the fraternity he was joining—but they did wash away, if only briefly, the grime of everyday reality and the memory of such tawdry moments as the murder of Deebee.

In the tie-ins, Sammy became better acquainted with Frank LoCascio. It was hard, however, because LoCascio barely spoke, unless spoken to. He had been a made man even before Carlo was boss, and he carried himself with the manner of someone who'd seen it all, liked little of it, but accepted that he was doomed to endure it. With his spectacles, slightly hunched shoulders, and graying hair, he did call to mind a grumpy old municipal clerk, instead of a capo in command of a loan-sharking and bookmaking operation in the Bronx who still helped dispose of bodies.

"This was a good idea John had," Sammy told LoCascio after leaving one tie-in.

"John's an old-timer at heart," said LoCascio. "Like me."

In between tie-ins, Sammy got some bad news about an old-timer, Joseph Paruta—whose ill health at the time of Deebee's murder was diagnosed as cancer.

Sammy loved Old Man Joe, who had been around the Aurello crew before Sammy was. He possessed little talent, beyond the one that Aurello and then Sammy exploited at crucial times, but he was fanatically loyal. Still, because he was limited, no one ever proposed that he become a made man—a lifelong snub that Sammy moved to undo when Paruta fell ill and took to his deathbed.

In normal times, the Commission controlled who became a made man by requiring each family to submit lists of proposed members to the others for approval. Nowadays, however, because of the government crackdown, the Commission was not meeting.

So, to give Old Man Joe his button, Sammy—after getting Gotti's approval through Gene—made a list with only Paruta's name on it and submitted it to acting bosses and underbosses in the other four families.

"We gotta do this for Joe," Sammy said to one. "He's dead soon, so it don't matter. But he deserves it."

After no one objected, Sammy tried to make initiation day special. He asked LoCascio and several other capos, including Jimmy Brown Failla and Danny Marino, to attend the ceremony. All did, though most had never met Paruta.

When the delegation arrived at Paruta's house, his wife escorted them into his bedroom, then left and closed the door.

"What's up, Sammy?" Paruta said. His cancer was spreading fast, and he was in tremendous pain, despite the morphine shots his wife was administering. "Who're these bums?"

Everyone laughed. "These are friends of mine," Sammy said solemnly. "And we're here to make you a friend of ours."

Sammy felt a vaguely familiar rush of exhilaration as he saw that Paruta, despite the morphine, instantly realized the significance of his words. Friend of ours.

Paruta's eyes began to moisten when Sammy took his trigger finger and held it over a holy card of some saint. Under the circumstances, there was no need for fire or blood.

"We are an honored society, a society of Cosa Nostra," Sammy began.

He tried to recall the words and rules of his own induction ceremony nine years before, right down to when Paul asked him, as he now asked Paruta, "If I asked, would you kill for me?"

"Yes," Paruta softly cried.

Sammy fought back his own tears, as did others in the room. The moment was so poignant, so pure, such a reaffirmation of the glory of Cosa Nostra. "Welcome to the brotherhood," Sammy said.

The next day, Paruta's wife telephoned Sammy. "He looks great. He says he feels like he's cured. But, you know, with the morphine, he's high as a kite."

One month later, Paruta himself telephoned and asked Sammy to visit. "I appreciate what you done for me," he said, once Sammy sat beside his bed. "I'm dyin' a friend of ours, but you gotta do me one more favor."

"Whatever you want, Joe, you know that."

"I want you to kill me."

"I can't do that!"

"You gotta. I can't take this pain anymore. Kill me. Just put a fuckin' pistol to my head."

"I can't, Joe, I love you!"

Paruta balled his fists. "*Minchia*, what's wrong with you? Fuckin' limp-wrist. Tough guy! Where's your fuckin' balls?"

It was all Paruta wanted to talk about during many more visits. Finally, Sammy sent a message to Gotti through Gene, asking for Gotti's approval to grant Paruta his last wish.

The jailed Gotti said no. It was too risky. How would Sammy get rid of the body? What would he tell Paruta's wife? After all he had done, it would be ridiculous for Sammy to get arrested for a mercy killing of one of his own men.

Paruta, however, would not let Sammy off the hook. "I did so much for you. Can't you do this for me?"

Finally, Sammy said yes. He sent word back to Gotti that he was going to disobey an order and kill Paruta. He was counting on Gotti to forgive, since he had obeyed the more important order involving Deebee.

Sammy, ready to commit his thirteenth murder, then visited Paruta. "Send your wife out tomorrow," he said. "Tell her to leave the back door open."

The next morning, after Sammy woke up ready to put a pillow over Paruta's head and shoot him behind an ear, his brother-in-law Eddie Garafola telephoned with some late-breaking news.

"I just heard they took the old man to the hospital," Garafola said. "He died on the way."

"Ain't that a pisser? He let me off the fuckin' hook."

Sammy thought that maybe all Old Man Joe really wanted was for Sammy to say yes. Then he could die, feeling that he really was a friend of ours.

CHAPTER 10

• • • • • • • • • • • • •

Mendacity

The Giacalone case resumed in Brooklyn on August 18, 1986. The storm that broke over the case in April, when Frank DeCicco was blown up, had drifted away, but the media's fascination with the so-called Dapper Don would be rekindled and would remain heated over the seven tortuous months it took for the trial to run its frequently incredible course.

Some say a trial is a search for truth, but Gotti and his codefendants were searching for only one thing, freedom. When the trial came to its stunning end, the truth of what happened would be locked away—and someone not on trial, Sammy Gravano, would hold the key.

The trial was a media circus, and an early, sorry sideshow featured Romual Piecyk in a press conference on the courthouse steps. "I was never threatened or harassed or intimidated by Mr. Gotti," he said, sounding less believable with each verb. "I honestly feel Mr. Gotti should be out on bail."

The early media coverage provoked a lawyer for one of the other six codefendants to complain to United States district court judge Eugene Nickerson that "this case against Gotti is the biggest media event since World War II."

After an FBI agent ignited another sideshow by testifying, in a different case in the same courthouse, that an informant told him that Gotti orchestrated the Sparks murders, another defense lawyer cried, "The government and the press have made John Gotti the most feared man in America today."

The defense's grumbling was two-faced, of course, because Gotti had begun trying to plant favorable notions in the media months before. In fact, Gotti gave one of the defense lawyers in the case permission to tell a magazine writer that he was not the one-dimensional thug his enemies in law enforcement claimed, and the proof was that while in the MCC Gotti read serious books, such as Machiavelli's *The Prince*.

Manipulation aside, the media's obsession with Gotti was remarkable. To illustrate a story on the Cosa Nostra crackdown, *Time* magazine employed Andy Warhol to draw Gotti for its cover. Most national news organizations, and many from abroad, assigned reporters to the trial, including two already working on a book about the Cosa Nostra man of the year's rise; the book would be called *Mob Star,* a title that Gotti came to like, despite his annoyance at the book's revelations, which included his overheard conversations on the Bergin bug.

The secretly taped conversations showed that the Bergin crew of the Gambino family existed, a burden that the prosecution had to meet in the trial, but because the Bergin bug was planted after Gotti and his codefendants were indicted, Diane Giacalone could not use the conversations to make her case.

Confronted again with the difficult job of finding jurors who were unaffected by the publicity and unafraid to serve without bias, Judge Nickerson decided that the identities of potential jurors would be kept secret and that the actual jurors, once chosen, would serve anonymously. Personal information—names, addresses, and occupations—would be locked away with the chief courthouse clerk, unavailable even to the judge.

These steps were designed to make potential jurors more honest and comfortable when the judge interviewed them. But they also gave Giacalone and coprosecutor John Gleeson some comfort. They made it harder for Gotti to affect the outcome by bribery or intimidation.

It took a month to pick a jury; therefore, the trial really did not start until September 16. According to who or what they looked like, the anonymous jurors—a mostly middle-brow, middle-class, middle-aged collection of unlikely peers of John Gotti—were immediately given nicknames by the defense team.

An overweight housewife became the Heavy Lady; a young, attractive Italian woman, the Girl. A round-faced

black man was Willie Mays. A studious-looking businessman, Larry King. And an ex-Marine, the D.I., for drill in-
structor.

Gotti arrived at the courthouse each day in an MCC
van. Thanks to brother Peter and son John, who were responsible for delivering freshly pressed clothes to the
prison each week—a different ensemble for each day—he
always looked like a robust trucking-company executive
new to riches, once his jailers took off the handcuffs he
was required to wear en route to court.

He was kept in a holding room until just before the
start of the day's session, and then, in a ritual repeated
every day, he bounced into the courtroom through a rear
door and accepted the hugs and kisses of codefendants on
bail. Most days, the audience included sundry soldiers,
hangers-on, and Cosa Nostra junkies, who stood when
Gotti entered, as if he were the judge.

Willie Boy Johnson, who came in the same van and
was kept in the same holding room, always trailed defer-
entially behind. He got handshakes, not kisses; to some,
it was still unclear how Gotti really felt abut the forcibly
retired Source Wahoo.

"Fuckin' rat," a soldier in the audience hissed one day,
after Willie Boy walked to the defense table and took his
seat, which was one away from Gotti's.

But Gotti had told codefendants to treat Willie Boy the
same, because he had redeemed himself by refusing to
cave in to Giacalone's pressure and become a government
witness against them. Willie Boy doubted whether all had
been forgiven, but he tried to act as if he believed it had.

"You believe that fuckin' rat bum?" he whispered to
Gotti at one point early in the trial, as some low-level
mobster—one of seven who had crossed paths with Gotti
that Giacalone would bring to the stand—testified for the
government.

"He's a rat and his nose is bigger than Pinocchio's."
Gotti replied, after overcoming his astonishment at Willie
Boy calling someone else a rat—the worst insult in Cosa
Nostra.

Seven defendants were on trial—Gotti, his brother
Gene, Willie Boy, John Carneglia, Anthony Rampino, and
two others from another crew that once reported to Neil
Dellacroce—but when it came to the defense's trial strat-

egy, only the elder Gotti's interests mattered. And now that he seemed deprived of a realistic chance to bribe or intimidate a juror, and because he could hardly be sure that his early wooing of the media had planted a favorable seed in some juror's mind, Gotti needed a courtroom strategy.

The one he decided on didn't require any prodding from his lawyers, although they all agreed with him. The strategy was to put Diane Giacalone on trial, to portray her as vindictive and ambitious, and to argue that her RICO case was unfair because it relied, in Gotti's example, on dusty convictions from his past.

The strategy was riskier than it seemed. In front of a jury, the soft-spoken, rail-thin Giacalone—who bore a passing resemblance to comedienne Lily Tomlin—seemed as vindictive and ambitious as the average Girl Scout. In manner and appearance, she was as proper and straight-laced as any thirty-six-year-old assistant United States attorney trained to keep the jury's eyes on the case, not the prosecutor.

In pretrial proceedings, however, with no jury present, Gotti and his lawyers had seen that Giacalone was a hard-nosed tough-talking competitor. They also learned about angry meetings she'd had with FBI agents over the Willie Boy situation and then with witnesses she had planned to use, then dropped.

The defense also knew that the case itself was almost entirely a product of Giacalone's initiative. Normally, major racketeering cases begin with an investigation by the FBI or another federal agency—but Giacalone began this case herself and almost single-handedly pushed it to indictment. In addition, in Brooklyn, Cosa Nostra cases were normally tried by prosecutors from a special squad known as the Eastern District Organized Crime Strike Force, a quasi-independent unit of the United States attorney's office for the Eastern District, which included Brooklyn.

Giacalone was not a member of the Eastern District Strike Force and had never tried a RICO case; she had tried one case involving a minor Cosa Nostra figure, but she lost it.

She began her investigation after Gotti's name came up in one of her earlier trials. In that one, two young Queens hoods accused of robbery were thought to have paid homage to Gotti, then acting captain of the Bergin crew, by giving him a hefty chunk of a multimillion-dollar score from an armored-car job.

The homage was incidental to the armored-car case, which Giacalone won, but it was an intriguing bit of information for an assistant U.S. attorney coming to grips with the potential and power of her job.

By opening a case on Gotti, Giacalone stepped on toes. But her immediate supervisor was married to her boss, the U.S. Attorney for the Eastern District, and most people believed that this was why she was permitted to proceed against Gotti over the objections of the Eastern District Strike Force and the FBI, both of which wanted to save Gotti for the Gambino hierarchy case indicted a couple months earlier, the one involving Joseph Armone, Joe N. Gallo, Angelo Ruggiero, and others.

Ambition, toughness, and political ability were traits that Gotti admired, but not in a woman, particularly one trying to put him in jail for forty years, meaning life. From the time Giacalone stood for her opening statement in a red power suit—and Gotti at the defense table snickered about "the lady in red"—Gotti, his codefendants, and their lawyers passed up no chance to try to bully, torment, and rattle her.

Gotti always led the charge, assisted by Bruce Cutler, the lawyer whose courtroom style mirrored Gotti's Cosa Nostra style. With their bull necks, broad shoulders, and barrel chests, Gotti and Cutler were physically similar, too. And over the months of pretrial, Cutler had begun showing a fancy for double-breasted suits and flashy ties with matching pocket squares.

After Giacalone's straightforward, federal-style opening statement, Cutler got up with a fury that stunned the jury to attention. In a career-making performance that was frequently bombastic and preposterous but always seemingly heartfelt, Cutler regained the confidence Gotti had shown in keeping him as his attorney even though after becoming boss Gotti could have had his pick of lawyers; that confidence had waned a little when Cutler could not stop Giacalone from revoking his bail.

Prowling the courtroom like the champion college wrestler that he once had been, Cutler strode to a blackboard where Giacalone had sketched a Gambino family tree, then erased it—"because it tells you about a secret underworld that doesn't exist!"

He derided Giacalone's "half-truths and lies!" He said she had targeted poor Gotti because she just didn't like him or his loyal friends, didn't like overhearing him on wiretaps cursing and making bets on horse races, didn't like him because he took such pride in his appearance!

"So when he sits there resplendent in his suit," Cutler beseeched, "it's not out of being bold! It is out of pride! That's what made this country great!"

Giacalone's case was a "fantasy," Cutler fumed as he wound up for a big finish. Her indictment "stunk," and "a fancy wine dressing called RICO" did not make it smell better! With most eyes in the courtroom locked on him, Cutler grabbed a copy of the indictment, and after lifting it in the air—"It still is rancid! It's still rotten! It still makes you retch and vomit!"—and shouting, "This is where it belongs!"—loudly slam-dunked it into a waste can.

Veins in his neck still throbbing, Cutler returned to the defense table as if he wanted to grapple for several more rounds. He had given a voice to a client's rage and shown belief in his innocence. Then and there, as Gotti reached to shake his hand, Bruce Cutler became Gotti's lawyer for good—just as Jerry Shargel had become Sammy's because of his work in the Frank Fiala tax case.

Soon Cutler would become a hot media property too, and he would say in interviews that if he had kids, John Gotti was a man's man he would want them to emulate.

The anger of Cutler's argument, with its bitter references to Giacalone, foreshadowed the defense strategy—which became a lot more personal as the trial progressed.

Cutler got one of Giacalone's witnesses to call her "a slut and a blow job." He got one of his witnesses—a bank robber she had planned to use but dumped after concluding that he was a liar—to say that during a pretrial interview Giacalone gave him her panties and told him to masturbate his prison frustrations away.

It was a base story, invented by Gotti and told by a man trying to make amends for once being in Giacalone's camp; but the get-Giacalone strategy called for throwing as much mud as possible and hoping it stuck in the minds of the Heavy Lady, Willie Mays, the D.I., and the other jurors.

Giacalone "really wanted to frame Mr. Gotti and the others," the bank robber testified.

Several times the jurors could hear Gotti mumbling at the defense table. The comments were calculated interruptions, meant to throw Giacalone off balance.

"She's trying to protect that murderer," he said about one of her witnesses. "She's the murderer, that mother."

Many times a frustrated Giacalone asked Judge Nickerson to send the jury out of the courtroom, so she could complain about the latest insult from the defense.

"It's not true, your honor," Gotti would say, like a schoolyard bully who knows the teacher did not hear him tormenting a classmate. "Those are all lies."

Nickerson warned Gotti and Cutler several times that they were flirting with a contempt citation, but he never pulled the trigger. At the trial dragged long past his two-month forecast, the sixty-seven-year-old judge grew plainly weary of the battle and eager for it to end without decisive action from him.

After one nasty moment in court, Giacalone told Nickerson that the defense had decided "it is advantageous to harass me" and "create a record that is absolutely false" in the "face of the most extraordinary harassment" ever seen in any court.

"Let's move on," the judge said, as if he could not bear any more distraction.

The emotional strain on Giacalone was enormous, and so was the physical strain; at the end of each day's battering in court, she had to spend several more hours preparing memos and briefs for the next or future days.

Even more pressure lay behind the scenes. Midway through the trial, she arrived home at her apartment and discovered evidence of an attempted break-in. Unsure of a connection to the trial, she nonetheless reported it to Andrew Maloney—who, after Gotti was indicted, had replaced Giacalone's boss and become the U.S. attorney for the Eastern District. Maloney reported it to the U.S. Marshals Service, the agency responsible for providing security to federal judges, prosecutors, and jurors.

The Marshals Service recommended around-the-clock security for Giacalone. But without proof that the attempted break-in was the work of the defendants, Giacalone told Maloney that the federal bodyguards were overreacting.

"Maybe they could just pass by now and then," she said.

But with the Marshals Service, it was either its way or no way. "Either we live with her, or we won't take responsibility," a Marshals supervisor told Maloney, a veteran New-York-born-and-bred lawyer who, earlier in his career, had grappled with the rigid ropes of federal bureaucracies as an assistant U.S. attorney in Manhattan.

With nothing more than an attempted break-in of unknown origin and purpose to go on, Maloney left it to Giacalone to decide. She decided that bodyguards would just be more pressure, and the Marshals Service disclaimed responsibility for her safety. At Maloney's request, the New York City Police Department made periodic checks of her apartment and her street, and no further attempted break-ins occurred.

Still, every time she came home at night, Giacalone looked over her shoulder—and wondered if the men she had looked at all day had taken the fight to her doorstep, and whether more Romual Piecyk–type stunts, or worse, were in store.

While Maloney was reasonably confident that Gotti, if he was behind the break-in, would not dare take the intimidation to another level, the thought still crossed his mind. While not extremely demonstrative, Maloney was instinctively protective. He was the father of six children, and while in the Army, he had commanded a unit of the Rangers, the most select, all-volunteer troops the Army has. While he was good-natured—most people called him "Andy"—he also was instinctively combative; in the early 1950s, he was a welterweight boxing champion at the U.S. Military Academy at West Point.

Even now, at age fifty-five, protective and combative Andy Maloney—still almost as trim as in his West Point days—would have enjoyed taking the Dapper Don out behind a woodshed for a private meeting about the get-Giacalone tactics. Limited to a legal battlefield, Maloney decided to lift his troop's morale in another way. Not long after the break-in at her apartment, Maloney told

Giacalone that once the trial was over, she would be his new chief of special prosecutions, a prestige job.

In the first five months of the trial, in other federal courtrooms in Brooklyn and Manhattan, prosecutors using Angelo tapes, Paul tapes, Neil tapes, and other evidence won all their cases against the hierarchies of the other families, as well as the Commission case—in which Paul would have been a defendant, had he lived. In Washington and New York, government officials were proclaiming that "the enemy within" was on the way out.

Gotti never seemed concerned that this federal tidal wave would sweep him away to a life behind bars. Anytime anyone he did not recognize, but suspected of being important, came into court, he made a point during the first available recess of putting his optimism on display.

Such was the case one day when he noticed in the last row of the spectator section a physically imposing young man whose serious bearing, conservative suit, and neatly clipped hair and mustache could mean only one thing—FBI agent.

"Hey, you," Gotti said, after courtroom spectators had filed into the hallway to smoke and talk. "Who would you be?"

George Gabriel, age twenty-nine, smiled back. Fulfilling a childhood dream, he had joined the FBI six years before but only recently had been assigned to OC, the organized-crime section, specifically the Gambino squad.

He was in the courtroom to take his first in-person look at Gotti. He had seen enough televised Gotti and heard enough from others to know that Gotti liked teasing encounters with agents, much as Gotti had been overheard boasting on wiretaps that he never gave agents the time of day.

Adopting his own teasing manner, Gabriel slowly unlimbered his six-foot-four, two-hundred-twenty-five-pound frame and rose to his feet. He looked to his left, then his right, then pointed at himself and said, "Who, me?"

"Yeah. Who're you?"

Gabriel identified himself and, letting Gotti know he had a reason for being in court, said he worked for Bruce Mouw, a name he knew would stick in Gotti's craw;

Mouw was the Gambino squad boss who, years back, had gone to Gotti's house to tell him to tell Angelo to stop making threats against FBI agents.

Gotti narrowed his eyes. "You tell Mouw that I am gonna be home soon. Guaranteed. This little broad ain't got a case."

"I'll tell him. And tell you what, if you're home soon, I'll be there to congratulate you."

Many times, during other recesses, Gotti gave the same I'll-be-home-soon message to reporters.

"They got no case," he said at one point, pointing toward Giacalone and her trial assistant, John Gleeson, a relatively inexperienced but promising young prosecutor. "If my kids ever lied as much as these guys, they'd have no dinner."

During another recess on another day, when asked whether he thought a witness had been truthful, Gotti showed that Niccolò Machiavelli had chased him to a dictionary on occasion.

"Mendacity," he said. "The word for today is 'mendacity.' It's the art of being mendacious."

The reporters loved these smart-alecky encounters. Gotti lived up to the devil-may-care notices they wrote.

On yet another day, when a defense lawyer rushed into the courtroom during a recess and announced that he had just been informed by his office that each of the three bosses convicted in the Commission case had just received one-hundred-year sentences, Gotti dismissed the news as unimportant.

"Got nothing to do with us. We're walkin' out of here."

As the Giacalone case wound down, another fight between the lawyers took place. This time, it was between Cutler and the new kid on the block—John Gleeson, who had left a safe but unexciting job on Wall Street for a lower-paid job and a heady chance to become a trial lawyer at a young age.

With his tortoiseshell eyeglasses, subdued suits, and low-key manner, the thirty-three-year-old Gleeson was a perfect federal stereotype. In this, his first big case, he also had exhibited a fine legal mind and verbal agility. Because her relations with the FBI were strained, Giacalone had asked Gleeson to oversee what little FBI presence there was in the case—the start of what became a long and fruitful relationship between the Jesuit-trained Gleeson and the Gambino squad.

During the early part of the trial, before the attacks on Giacalone drained him of goodwill, Gleeson had managed a polite accord with Gotti. During breaks, they chatted about innocuous subjects; as someone to talk with, Gleeson appreciated Gotti much more than Cutler.

The Gleeson-Cutler confrontation began when the defense tried to subpoena the job records of Gleeson's wife, a nurse, in a wildly implausible quest for evidence that she had helped the government get prescription drugs for a witness. It escalated when Cutler, in a bullying cross-examination of the doctor who prescribed the drugs, kept interrupting the doctor's answers.

"I object to Mr. Cutler's manner, which is peculiarly offensive," Gleeson told the judge.

"It isn't really helpful," Nickerson told Cutler.

"I am doing the best I can, your honor," Cutler protested. "I am not a doctor."

In an instant of anger that summed up his frustrations with the case and the treatment of Giacalone, Gleeson left his Wall Street manners behind and said, "He is not a lawyer either."

For Cutler, it was hard not to take the words personally, for they struck at his insecurity. Cutler did not possess the same fine legal mind as Gleeson; he was smart, but not acute, when it came to tiny principles. When he was on a case, the briefs, the motions, the fine points, were left to others; Cutler was a performer, a clever three-card monte player.

The next day they clashed again when Gleeson told the judge at a sidebar that he believed that Cutler had encouraged a witness to lie. If true, it was a crime that could have cost Cutler his right to practice law if he were ever formally accused and convicted. He never would be, but the witness was eventually accused of lying and would plead guilty.

"Don't worry about that fuckin' punk," Gotti whispered to Cutler, after Cutler registered a protest against Gleeson's inference with Judge Nickerson and returned to his seat. "We're walkin' the fuck out of here, I can feel it."

When the time for closing arguments finally came, fatigue became Giacalone's new enemy. Rail-thin when the trial had started seven months before, she seemed emaciated now, as she stood to address the jury. In a valiant effort to link the dots strewn across eighteen thousand pages of trial transcript, she spoke for five brutal hours. Her voice was weak and raspy, and she frequently misidentified witnesses.

Watching from an aisle seat in the spectator section, Andy Maloney was worried that she might not make it to the end—but she did. As Gotti sat at the defense table alternately bemused and indignant, Giacalone called the Bergin crew a "frightening reality" whose members "exercised their power without regard to the law or human life."

"The trial was not neat," she added, "it was not a careful little package. The evidence wasn't perfect. The truth is not like that. The truth has ragged edges."

It was a ragged summation, but heroic and truthful.

In another three-card monte display of showmanship, Cutler adopted a different tone for his final argument. For the first time he turned his voltage down, speaking in a soft, mournful voice, like a man on his deathbed asking that his cousin and brother-in-law succeed him as boss of the company.

"You want to get John Gotti? Get some evidence on him. You want to bring him to trial some other place, go ahead and do so. Find that he did something wrong. Find a witness. Do it the right way."

Slowly, he paced by the jury box and glanced balefully at the prosecution table. "The government is people. It's my government, it's John Gotti's government, it's your government. But it's people; people do things wrong. You are the only shield we have against abuse of power, against tyranny."

The jury deliberated for a week. Most onlookers were certain of a guilty verdict. The defense had put up a ferocious battle, but the RICO law was a powerful weapon. The jury had not heard the Bergin tapes, but much other evidence showed that the Bergin crew of the Gambino family existed and was a criminal enterprise. And despite efforts to depict Gotti's prior convictions as isolated acts of youth, evidence showed that all three were related to his enterprise membership; under RICO, only two were necessary.

Codefendants on bail paced the hallways, but Gotti and Willie Boy spent most of the week in a locked room. Willie Boy's fortunes had sunk even lower. At the Metropolitan Correctional Center, he forgot that telephone calls placed by MCC inmates from a collect-calls-only telephone were monitored, and he had been taped discussing a small heroin deal with his son. It was going to cost him some more time in prison, no matter what.

Each time the jury wanted to review some pieces of evidence, Gotti and Willie Boy were brought back into court, where Gotti continued to display an astounding level of confidence.

"We're walkin' out of here," he mouthed to reporters, while pointing at the prosecution table. "They didn't put on a case."

On a Friday the 13th, in March of 1987, shortly after lunch, the jury informed Judge Nickerson that it had reached a verdict on both counts of the indictment, conspiracy and racketeering. It took half an hour for the participants to assemble in the big marble and mahogany room. Beaming like a father of the bride, Gotti strode in through a rear door and accepted the ritual kisses and hugs of the codefendants.

Andy Maloney came down from his office to watch from his aisle seat in the spectator section. Recently, despite all the precautions taken to safeguard the jury, he had begun to wonder whether its integrity had been breached. His suspicion was based on a memo that Bruce Mouw had put on his desk a few weeks before; it said that an informant had told the Gambino squad that Gotti somehow had gotten a "hook" into the jury.

Maloney had not shared the memo with Giacalone and Gleeson, or Judge Nickerson; in doing so, he would have risked an immediate mistrial, and without anything more concrete than the word of a single, uncorroborated informant, that seemed too high a price to pay. He remained unsure how much credence the memo deserved until, in court, he saw Gotti acting like the father of the bride, kissing and embracing his men.

"He looks too damn cool," he whispered to an aide

seated next to him. "I have thirty years in this game and I've seen a lot of tough guys begin to sweat about now."

With a look of utter relief, Judge Nickerson pounded his gavel, ordered all to their seats, and told his bailiff to bring in the jury. The courtroom grew absolutely still as the jurors, their eyes down, filed in; all the fury and farce of the previous months were being funneled into one heart-stopping moment.

Reading from a form, Nickerson's clerk, William Walsh, asked "Larry King," the jury foreperson: "Count one, the conspiracy count, how do you find John Gotti, guilty or not guilty?"

"Not guilty."

A collective gasp rose from the audience. But Gotti showed no emotion; he had ordered everyone at his table to remain calm until both verdicts for each defendant were announced.

But he began smiling ever so mischievously as the clerk and the foreperson worked their way through Gene Gotti, Carneglia, Willie Boy, Rampino, and the rest—all not guilty.

Without waiting to hear the verdicts on the second count, Maloney exited the courtroom in disgust. His predecessor as U.S. attorney had given Giacalone permission to proceed against Gotti over the protests of the Eastern District Strike Force and the FBI. But Maloney had reviewed her case and thought it was solid. Something in the courtroom smelled rotten, and he was now sure the odor was coming from the jury box.

It went the same way on the second count, not-guilties up and down the line, and then the rejoicing began. Gotti threw a clenched fist in the air, then gleefully punched Cutler in the shoulder. After ten months in jail, he was going home.

"Justice!" someone in the audience screamed, as at the prosecution table, shell-shocked Diane Giacalone and John Gleeson—who, despite all, had been confident they had won—struggled to appear impassive.

Gotti turned toward the jurors and began clapping; his men and lawyers joined in, followed by Cosa Nostra loyalists in the audience, and suddenly the courtroom became like a Broadway theater at curtain call. Most of the jurors seemed embarrassed by the ovation; most looked down, or to the judge; one, the ex-Marine known as D.I., fidgeted in his seat as if he were a target on a live firing range.

The D.I. could not flee the courtroom soon enough. The clapping made him anxious because Gotti's applause was really only for him. He was the reason Gotti was so confident: Almost six months before, after he was chosen to serve on the jury, George Pape, a middle-aged suburbanite with a drinking problem, offered to sell himself. Gotti, through Sammy, bought him for sixty thousand dollars. The case was fixed from the get-go. Gotti had gone ahead with the get-Giacalone strategy to give the jury ringer something to work with in deliberations.

It was the best-kept secret in New York. Only Gotti, his brother Gene, Sammy, and the man who took the money from Sammy to Pape knew the story. The bagman was Bosko Radonjich, the new boss of a small gang of mostly Irish-American thugs known as the Westies because they were based on Manhattan's West Side.

Radonjich and Pape had met on a construction job years before. Radonjich moved into the Westies and Pape into a succession of odd jobs and periodic unemployment. Now forty-eight years old, Pape lived on Long Island with his wife, his two children, and his drinking problem. After reporting for jury duty and realizing he might land on the Gotti jury, he recalled that Radonjich's gang, the Westies, was a partner in West Side rackets with the Gambino family. He then began looking upon jury service not as a civic obligation but as a financial opportunity.

During Judge Nickerson's voir dire, Pape had lied several times when asked questions designed to eliminate jurors who might know people connected to Gotti or who had participated in legal cases that might affect their independence—as Pape had when he was a character witness for Radonjich in a deportation proceeding nearly ten years earlier.

The special lengths taken by Judge Nickerson to assure the jury's integrity were no match for one man's greed. The judge's decision to impanel the jury anonymously was meant to prevent defendants from contacting jurors; it did not imagine the opposite problem. Soon after the trial began with a ringer in the jury box, George Pape contacted Westies boss Bosko Radonjich, who contacted the de facto street boss of the Gambino family, Sammy Gravano.

Mortified by the half-page article on him in the *Daily News* a few months before, Sammy had not risked any more exposure by attending any part of the trial in Brooklyn. He got regular updates, however, from Gene Gotti, who was free on bail.

During an early update, while in a conference room at Gene's lawyer's office in Manhattan, Sammy told Gene the stunning news from Bosko Radonjich.

"Unbelievable that this fuckin' drops out of the sky like this," Gene said. "My fuckin' brother has nine lives."

"To get this goin', I just need an okay from John to tell Bosko to offer the guy money," Sammy replied.

The okay from John came two days later. "John likes it, so you do what you have to do," Gene told Sammy.

With his neck also on the line, Gene was equally delighted, but wary of letting anyone know, especially gabby Angelo, now also in the MCC. But the MCC did have that collect-calls-only phone for inmates that had gotten Willie Boy in trouble, and the joke in the family now was that someone could dial any seven random numbers and there was a good chance Angelo would answer.

"Don't tell nobody, especially Angelo," Gene warned.

Sammy contacted Radonjich and instructed him to give Pape one or two thousand dollars at a time. "When it gets to be a big number, call me and I'll reimburse you."

By the first day of jury deliberations, the reimbursement had reached sixty thousand. In the jury room, Pape said to his colleagues: "This man Gotti is innocent. They are all innocent and as far as I am concerned there is nothing left to discuss."

Several jurors thought otherwise and urged Pape to keep an open mind. He shook his head and said it was a waste of time to deliberate; obviously Giacalone had been out to get Gotti and the others but had failed to prove her case. For three days, the others deliberated almost as if Pape were not in the jury room. Most were leaning toward conviction.

At night, at the hotel where they were sequestered, Pape refused to mingle. He drank heavily, by himself.

As some jurors later recalled, some began to suspect that somehow the defendants had threatened Pape or his

family. This suspicion heightened the sense of danger that
some had felt in the stares of Gotti and his men from the
first day of trial and made them dwell on their own families' security. Over the last two days of deliberation, an
unspoken group paranoia took hold and the tide turned
the other way, creating a beach of reasonable doubt upon
which early beliefs in the strength of the government case
were gradually discarded. Not guilty.

Over the courtroom din, Judge Nickerson ordered everyone to stop clapping. He excused the jurors and announced that Gotti was free to go. Reporters rushed
toward him as Giacalone and Gleeson slipped silently
away through a rear door.

"Shame on them," Gotti said, wagging his finger. "I'd
like to see the verdict on them."

Gotti deflected the press mob by indicating that he
might say something outside the courthouse, but first he
had to clear up some paperwork releasing him from custody. He left the courtroom through a rear door and went
to the basement office of the U.S. Marshals Service. Anticipating this, *New York Post* reporter Philip Messing
staked out the office and got Gotti to himself.

"You didn't believe it from the beginning, did ya?"
Gotti said, jabbing a finger at Messing's chest.

A melee was under way outside the main courthouse
exit, as other defendants and their lawyers came out;
Gotti decided to avoid it; he was saying all he wanted to
Messing. A lawyer in the case went back upstairs and told
two Gambino soldiers that their boss would be leaving
through a garage-level exit on the opposite side of the
courthouse. Several marshals accompanied Gotti to the
exit, and Messing tagged along. "They'll be ready to
frame us again in two weeks," Gotti told him.

A gray Cadillac stopped beside the garage door, and
Gotti got inside—"Just watch, two weeks," he repeated—
and rode home to Queens, home of the New York Mets,
winner of the World Series a few months earlier. His first
stop was the V. G. Stylarama Hair Design Salon in Ozone
Park, across from the Bergin Hunt and Fish Club. Several
cronies spilled out and came over to greet him. A man on
the street yelled, "Queens has two world champions—the
Mets and John Gotti!"

After his trim, Gotti went into the Bergin for more

well-wishing. He then drove to his home in Howard Beach. Neighbors who believed he had ordered the murder of one of them—John Favara, the man who accidentally drove his car over little Frank Gotti—had tied yellow ribbons to trees. As Gotti left his car and walked toward his house, escorted by his son John, one neighbor called out, "Way to go, Mr. G!"

"Welcome home, honey," Vicky Gotti said, standing in the doorway. She was wearing a Minnie Mouse sweatshirt and holding the first of her three grandsons named Frank in her arms as her husband stepped into their home, which was beginning to pile up with flowers, gifts, balloons, and food baskets from captains, soldiers, and associates from across the volcano.

That night he celebrated with a five-hour dinner at his favorite restaurant in Queens, Altadonna's. That weekend, he would visit son Frank's grave, attend mass with Vicky, and pay his respects at a wake for Angelo Ruggiero's father; very much to his chagrin, Angelo remained jailed at the MCC.

In a few more days, Gotti would vacation in Florida without his wife; persuaded now more than ever by Salvatore Ruggiero's death that airplanes were not for him, he took the train and checked into a $730-a-day suite at the Marriott Harbour Beach Resort in Fort Lauderdale under the name Russo—a gag on the FBI, which had recently arrested a little old lady by that name, a federal courthouse clerk, for selling secrets to a family capo about the hierarchy case.

After lolling around the Marriott, he and his entourage—including son Junior, Jack D'Amico, Eddie Lino, Bobby Boriello, Joe Watts, and Carlo Vaccarezza—piled into Vaccarezza's sleek cigarette boat, the one with *Not Guilty* stenciled across its stern, and tore up and down the Atlantic shoreline, reveling in the in-joke left for boaters tossing in their wake.

Naturally, the verdict—the only not-guilty one in all the recent Cosa Nostra cases—fed the wildest blizzard yet of mythmaking publicity, for John Joseph Gotti Jr. did seem a genuine phenomenon, a modern-day Al Capone, an underworld "untouchable."

The mythmaking publicity and the nickname were predicated on a lie. All the ponderous stories soon to be written about him—that he was a modern-day Robin Hood, that his acquittal symbolized the nameless little guy's contempt for the faceless bureaucrats who ran his life—were constructed on a belief that Gotti had won his trial fair and square.

A headline writer gave the Dapper Don a new tabloid handle that was just as cute: Teflon Don. But if the headline writers had known what really had happened, maybe one would have been inspired to a more appropriate nickname. Such as Bogus Boss.

CHAPTER 11

• • • • • • • • • • • • •

Get Gotti

Gotti's victory stalled the federal steamroller. In the previous five years, in cities across the nation, the government had wounded or decimated the leadership of all twenty-three Cosa Nostra families. In New York, it had won a virtual life sentence against Bonanno boss Philip Rastelli and actual life sentences against three more bosses who had pillaged the city for decades in nearly the same way as Carlo—Carmine Persico of the Colombo family, Antonio Corallo of the Luchese family, and Anthony Salerno, a Chin Gigante stand-in, of the Genovese family.

Those four gangsters were great trophies, and if a gangster from central casting had not come along, any would have been an apt choice to illustrate a *Time* magazine cover story on the Cosa Nostra crackdown, as Gotti was when his trial began.

But Gotti had come along and made the cover a collector's item for gangsters. As the boss who got away, he also made the cover an instant office dartboard for agents and prosecutors—and by wagging a finger at Giacalone and Gleeson and taunting them while celebrating his victory, he made sure that agents and prosecutors would come after him with special gusto.

Just as there was the get-Giacalone defense, there would be a get-Gotti offense, and it began the day of the verdict.

Publicly, Gotti's enemies accepted defeat in professional stride. The personal contempt they felt was better left unsaid. Andy Maloney was particularly contemptuous, not only because he strongly suspected that Gotti had somehow breached the jury but also because he had met some substantial Cosa Nostra stalwarts in his day—and Gotti failed to match up.

As a young assistant U.S. attorney in Manhattan, Maloney had taken part in a grand jury investigation of Meyer Lansky, the financial wizard to the early Cosa Nostra bosses. Compared with Lansky, who helped engineer the development of Las Vegas and turned Cuba into a private criminal reserve, Gotti was a nobody.

"Gotti's just a punk, just a two-bit hijacker," Maloney had complained many times to a top aide, Lawrence Urgenson. "But the press is making him into a hero, a criminal mastermind!"

With the press in his office half an hour after the verdict, however, Maloney held his fire and toed the standard government line for such occasions: "The jury has spoken, we respect that, but in no way does the decision affect our determination to vigorously pursue those who terrorize our community."

Looking as though she'd been punched in the stomach, Giacalone was even more succinct: "A jury verdict is the end of a case."

Five years of effort had just come to naught. Asked how she felt, she icily replied: "My personal feelings are mine."

Privately, of course, Giacalone was devastated. Before the press conference, after exiting the courtroom, she had come into Maloney's office, fighting back tears. He quickly embraced her.

"You put your heart and soul into it," he said. "You did everything you could have done to win. It's not your fault."

Maloney waited until after the hubbub in his office had died down to tell Giacalone and Gleeson about the secret memo from Bruce Mouw quoting an informant as saying that somehow Gotti had reached someone on the jury.

Because a Gambino squad agent was a witness in the trial, Mouw had asked another FBI squad to investigate the informant's claim during the trial. That squad's agents got the okay from the chief judge of the Eastern District to obtain the identities of the anonymous jurors from the courthouse clerk and conduct background checks, an effort that led them to suspect two jurors, George Pape and one other man. Without more particular information from the informant, however, the agents were unable to go any further without risking a mistrial or exposing the informant.

Somewhere along the line, one of the participants in the fix—Gotti, his brother Gene, Sammy, or Bosko Radonjich—had said something to someone who should not been trusted. Of the four, the most unlikely loose lips belonged to Sammy.

Giacalone and Gleeson began to feel better as Maloney told them the story, but both also continued to wonder if they had failed as lawyers; perhaps if they had done a better job, some jurors would have refused to join Pape and would have held out for a hung jury—which would have meant a retrial.

"Look, you will be replaying this the rest of your lives," Maloney said as they relaxed in his office after the press left. "It'll never go away, but I'm telling you, Gotti was too cool during the trial, especially for the verdict. I don't care who they are, when the jury's out a week, defendants sweat."

Trying to cheer his troops some more, Maloney gave one of his assistants permission to buy a case of beer—at least they could toast the effort of a hard-fought battle.

"We may never prove it, but the case was fixed," Maloney was soon saying, as if he knew it to be a fact. "What happened in Nickerson's courtroom wasn't justice. It was fraud. We may not get Gotti for that, but we will get him. Mark my words."

In a few months, Maloney got the Justice Department to give Giacalone and Gleeson five-thousand-dollar bonuses for effort in the case. Giacalone's statement at the post-acquittal conference with the press—"my personal feelings are mine"—was her last public comment on the subject. In a few months more, despite her promotion to special prosecutions chief, she resigned and went to work for the local transit authority.

Gleeson, who had left his Wall Street decorum behind and stuck it to Bruce Cutler during a fiery moment in the trial—"he is not a lawyer either"—would stick around.

Bruce Mouw was driving across the Brooklyn Bridge with his car radio tuned to an all-news station when an announcer broke in with a bulletin about the Gotti acquittal:

In a stunning setback for the government, a federal jury in Brooklyn has just found organized crime boss John Gotti, the so-called Dapper Don, not guilty of all charges.

The normally reserved Gambino squad boss slammed the steering wheel of his car and cursed the announcer's voice. He had just left a meeting at FBI headquarters in Manhattan and was en route to a meeting at the Brooklyn courthouse with the Eastern District Strike Force lawyers on the Gambino hierarchy case against Armone, Gallo, Angelo, and others—a case that Gotti would have been in, had the strike force won its turf war with Giacalone years before.

The courthouse was a couple of minutes over the bridge; Mouw calculated that by the time he arrived, Gotti, his men, and their lawyers and supporters would be spilling into the streets and dancing to their cars—a celebration he did not care to see.

He made a mental note to telephone his apologies to Edward McDonald, the strike force boss, and instead of continuing on to the meeting, drove to the FBI's office in Queens, home of the Gambino squad. There, he went to his sixth-floor office and spoke with some of his agents.

"I heard about it on the Brooklyn Bridge," he said to one. "I was right by the damn courthouse, but I didn't stop. The last thing I wanted to do was cover a celebration by those jerks."

At that moment Mouw did not know that two of his agents, George Gabriel and Mark Roberts, had driven to Ozone Park to do just that—to cruise the streets around the Bergin Hunt and Fish Club and see who came to congratulate Gotti. Gabriel was also making good on the promise he had made, months earlier in court, to congratulate Gotti if he won.

Mouw entered his office, made his telephone calls, and began reviewing the squad's latest intelligence reports on Gotti. It was time to start a new case.

He had been investigating the Gambino family since 1979, when the bureau's New York bosses reorganized their organized-crime section into distinct squads—one for each of the city's five Cosa Nostra families—and Mouw was plucked out of a desk job in Washington to command one. Organizationally, the squads were like decinas and Mouw was like a capo.

It was a long way from his first job—sports reporter for his high school newspaper in Des Moines, Iowa. He was a bright, patriotic teen who worked in a print shop to help support his family, including his ailing, out-of-work father. He did so well in school that he won an appointment to the United States Naval Academy at Annapolis, then his commission.

While in the Navy, Mouw was involved in the highest-stakes cat-and-mouse game the world had ever known—a game beneath the oceans between the navies of the U.S. and the former Soviet Union. He was a navigator on a submarine with enough firepower to kill millions of people; tracking Soviet submarines beneath the seas, but never provoking a response that the world would regret, was a game requiring intelligence, patience, and nerves of steel.

After five years in the Navy and submarine patrol, the civilian engineering jobs that awaited Mouw seemed dull. He never thought of the FBI as an alternative until a bureau recruiter working from a list of recently discharged military personnel telephoned and invited him to apply.

In 1972, after spending his rookie year in St. Louis, Special Agent Mouw was posted to New York, where he spent two years investigating loan-sharking by the Genovese family. In those days, the FBI was just beginning to understand how the families were organized, thanks to an informer named Joseph Valachi—the first to reveal the existence of Cosa Nostra.

After four years in Washington, Mouw returned to New York in 1979 to take over the Gambino squad just as the FBI began making plans for a major campaign against Cosa Nostra. In 1981, after Ronald Reagan's election and after Congress gave the FBI more money and eased restrictions on electronic surveillance, the campaign moved into high gear.

With his background, Mouw was inclined to use electronic surveillance, and under him, the squad's first major undertaking was the assault on one Angelo Ruggiero, who had bragged that his home telephone was "safe." Mouw's first major electronic surveillance mission above the sea had yielded remarkable results.

But the Angelo tapes led to the demise of Paul and Bilotti and shot Gotti to power, and Gotti's legal victory now made the squad's triumph against Angelo, who hadn't even been brought to trial yet, look small.

Mouw was thinking about that when George Gabriel walked into his office; Gabriel was just back from Ozone Park, where he had made good on his promise to congratulate Gotti.

Cruising streets by the Bergin, Gabriel and Mark Roberts found Gotti shortly after he left the club and went for a walk with his brother Gene before driving home to Howard Beach; after the weekend off, Gene had to meet with his lawyers and begin preparing to go right back on trial—with Angelo, Carneglia, Mark Reiter, Eddie Lino, and others in the heroin case.

Given what had happened in court about one hour earlier, it is likely that among other topics the brothers were discussing the wisdom of having bought George Pape and wondering how the same thing or something similar might be accomplished in the heroin case.

From a block away, Gabriel got out of his FBI car and walked toward the brothers. The way the older, larger, smarter brother began staring at him suspiciously made Gabriel wonder if Gotti recognized him, or thought he was about to be arrested again, or was getting his dander up for Gene's benefit.

"You may not remember me, John," Gabriel smiled as he got within a few steps. "I'm George Gabriel, I work for Bruce Mouw."

"You mean, you're a fuckin' agent," Gene sneered.

"I was at your trial."

"Yeah, so?" John said, sneering too. "Everybody was."

"I told you if you got acquitted, like you said you would, I'd congratulate you and welcome you home. Welcome home."

"I got a lot of people congratulatin' me. I got a lot of nice people welcoming me home. Now if you'll excuse us, we're takin' a walk."

"Sure, John," Gabriel said, his smile fading. "Maybe I'll be seeing you around."

Gabriel walked back to the FBI car. After surveilling the well-wishers trooping into the Bergin some more, he and Roberts went to report to Mouw.

At age thirty, Gabriel was thirteen years younger than his boss. With his swarthy Greek American features, he was as New York–looking as Mouw was Des Moines. Growing up on Long Island, all he ever wanted to be was an FBI agent; he applied before he was even old enough, and then again after graduating from Hofstra University with an accounting degree.

His first assignment was in the bureau's suburban New York office in New Rochelle; there he learned how to hunt fugitives, surveil suspects, and investigate white-collar crimes. He also became a member of one of the FBI's several hostage-rescue and antiterrorist SWAT teams; outfitted in his commando regalia, the six-foot-four Gabriel would give a terrorist pause.

After five years, he sought a transfer to New York, to be closer to his and his new wife's families. He requested a job on a squad that investigated major drug-dealing crimes, but by the time his transfer was approved, the squad's positions were gone and he was temporarily assigned to the Gambino team.

In New Rochelle, Gabriel's only encounters with organized crime had been low-level and unproductive.

"This stuff doesn't look very exciting to me," he said to Mouw when they first met. "I'm here maybe three to six months, until something on the drug squad opens."

The remark had been made two years ago, early in 1985. Mouw put Gabriel to work on the Gambino hierarchy case—then involving Paul and Neil as well as Armone, Gallo, Angelo, and others. In December, Gabriel was away for SWAT training when the Sparks murders eliminated one defendant and suddenly made organized crime and the Gambino family an interesting assignment.

"I don't care about drugs anymore," he told Mouw upon his return. "I want to stay here."

Sixteen months later, late on the afternoon of John Gotti's acquittal, Bruce Mouw looked up from his intelligence files on the Gambino family and said to his young agent, after Gabriel reported on the trip to Ozone Park and his encounter with Gotti:

"How'd you like to be the case agent on Gotti?"

Gabriel was taken aback. All he'd ever wanted was to be an FBI agent, and now Mouw was offering him the biggest FBI case of the day.

"Fantastic, Bruce, fantastic."

"Good. It's yours."

The law enforcement establishment in New York comprised more parts than the FBI and the U.S. attorney for the Eastern District of New York. Just because Bruce Mouw had started a case and Andy Maloney had told crestfallen prosecutors in his office that someday they would get another shot at John Gotti did not mean that all the other law enforcement players in town had to sit back and let the FBI and the Eastern District have their way.

The New York City Police Department, for instance, had been investigating the Sparks murders for sixteen months. It had done a terrible job so far and had actually lost track of two of the witnesses who got good looks at two suspects—John Carneglia and Anthony Rampino—but if the NYPD ever did find solid evidence, the case normally would be prosecuted by the state district attorney for New York County, otherwise known as Manhattan.

Another piece of the pie was the New York State Organized Crime Task Force, whose agents had planted the listening device in the Bergin Hunt and Fish Club, before and after Sparks. Via the attorney general of New York, it could mount a prosecution in any county of the state, or through agreements with federal authorities, it could prosecute a case jointly with a federal attorney. The task force's still-secret Bergin tapes were not terribly incriminating, but they did contain several intriguing fragments of conversations that might, with further investigation, produce a case.

Then there was the U.S. attorney for the Southern District of New York; because the city and surrounding suburbs had such a large population, the region had two U.S. attorneys. The one in the Eastern District had jurisdiction in Long Island and part of the city—Brooklyn, Queens, Staten Island. The one in the Southern District had jurisdiction in the city's other two boroughs or counties—Manhattan and the Bronx—as well as several counties north of the city.

When the Fist came smashing down, Paul was a defendant on trial in a Southern District RICO case, the one in which he was accused of supervising the Roy DeMeo murder machine. Because Gambino crews under Gotti's direction plied the Bronx, Manhattan, and upstate, the Southern District already had jurisdiction for a RICO case against him, when it got evidence for one. But the murder of one of its defendants while on trial gave it a ready-made legal basis for also bringing a murder case—normally a state matter—if it got evidence against the prime suspect.

Because of all these overlapping jurisdictions, and the competitive and secret natures of their representatives, the city's law enforcement establishment was like a volcano too, as prone to conflicts and eruptions as Cosa Nostra was.

Naturally, because his office was defeated under suspicious circumstances, Andy Maloney believed that the Eastern District, working with the Gambino squad, was entitled to take the next prosecutorial crack at the now so-called Teflon Don. As surely as the sun would rise over Howard Beach, he was certain that Gotti would provide the opportunity. Gotti was not going to retire from crime. He was a boss, and bosses served for life.

Maloney figured his main rival in the get-Gotti competition was one subway stop away, across the East River in Manhattan, where Rudolph Giuliani, the U.S. attorney for the Southern District of New York, held considerable sway.

Giuliani, a media-conscious prosecutor planning to run for mayor, was much better known than Maloney. Giuliani had mounted a heavily publicized assault on insider trading on Wall Street and personally tried a major political corruption case. Under him, Southern District prosecutors had won the Commission case and several of the other big Cosa Nostra cases.

As the former third-highest-ranking official of the Justice Department, which he left to become U.S. attorney in Manhattan, Giuliani also had leverage in Washington, where jurisdictional disputes between the two New York City districts were resolved.

Maloney, on the other hand, was just beginning to build his reputation as a U. S. attorney. Up until two years earlier, he had labored effectively but quietly as a criminal defense lawyer. But he did know something about federal politics and about the Southern District—

two and a half decades earlier, when he was meeting people such as Meyer Lansky, Maloney was one of the Southern District's top young prosecutors.

Now camped in Brooklyn, he was galled by a presumption in the media and the legal profession that the ablest prosecutors in town worked for the Southern District—and that only someone such as take-charge Rudy Giuliani could take down Gotti. The public perception was that the U.S. attorney's office in Brooklyn was merely an annex of the U.S. attorney's office in Manhattan. When Maloney had been introduced to the media as the next U.S. attorney for the Eastern District, the city's police commissioner had identified the man Maloney was replacing as "Rudy's assistant."

As much as anyone, because of his own twelve years as an assistant U.S. attorney in the Southern District, Maloney knew that historically the district was a fountain of legal talent. Some of the nation's top judges, politicians, and lawyers had once been assistant U.S. attorneys in Manhattan. The assistant U.S. attorneys in the Eastern District were hardly unqualified, but the Brooklyn office of the Justice Department simply did not have the same glorious tradition as the Manhattan office.

Maloney did not want tradition to determine who got the next crack at Gotti. Two weeks after the verdict, he dropped a token into a subway turnstile and rode a train through a tunnel beneath the East River to Manhattan, exited at the first stop, and went to see Giuliani—the subject of so many glowing media profiles that Maloney had begun calling him, in not-so-gentle jest, "the world's greatest crime fighter."

In Giuliani's office Maloney was introduced to one of Giuliani's top assistants, Louis Freeh, the chief of his organized-crime unit and a future director of the FBI.

Maloney got straight to the point. "Gotti's power base is in the Eastern District, he beat the Eastern District in court, and as a matter of personal honor, I want the next Gotti case," he told Giuliani. "I want everyone else to back off."

As Maloney had expected, Giuliani looked down his Southern District nose. "That's fine, Andy, but you don't have anybody over there to try the case."

"That's bullshit and you know it," Maloney said. "I

have a lot of good lawyers, but just to let you know how strongly I feel, I am going to try this case personally."

"The state task force has already given us their tapes from the Bergin, they think there is a case there and want to work it with us," Giuliani replied, nodding toward Louis Freeh, who had just won a major case against a nationwide heroin ring run by the Sicilian branch of Cosa Nostra.

"I'll work with the task force. Give the tapes to me."

Giuliani hemmed and hawed some more, then said maybe, but only under certain conditions. He had, he told Maloney, already struck a deal with the Manhattan district attorney to jointly prosecute any case arising from the Sparks murders.

"I don't want those homicides," Maloney said, making it more difficult for Giuliani to say no. "I want a Gotti RICO case."

If he had not already been so well known and if he had not been planning to step down in a year to run for mayor, Giuliani would have resisted Maloney more and taken the jurisdiction issue to Washington, where he likely would have prevailed. But now he agreed to accommodate his determined counterpart across the river.

"Okay, you get the RICO, but we keep the murders."

"From what I hear about the NYPD on those homicides, all you need is some evidence," Maloney smiled, throwing a little rabbit punch at the world's greatest crime fighter and then taking a subway back to Brooklyn, which, after all, was the borough where John Gotti—and Sammy Gravano, for that matter—had grown into criminals.

The Gotti phenomenon only became more aggravating to the law enforcement establishment when—three months after his tainted victory—Gotti's muscle-bound son Junior, who had been accused of slugging an off-duty cop in a bar brawl a few months after his father slugged Romual Piecyk, was found not guilty.

The case echoed the Piecyk case. A waitress forgot what she saw, and a man injured in the brawl—the man the cop was trying to help—testified for the defense and said he never saw who slugged him and that the cop never identified himself as one.

In a profile that appeared before the trial opened, *Daily News* reporter David J. Krajicek described the trucking-company executive as a "baby bully," because Junior—sounding like dad—had threatened to "start choppin' off heads" if Krajicek and a photographer did not move their car from the street in front of the Gotti home.

The "baby bully" characterization provoked a bitter letter to the editor from Vicky Gotti: "After reading that bit of trash you passed off as journalism, I'm not surprised that people like Sinatra, Madonna and Diana Ross kick, punch and spit on you."

Husband John did not sign the letter, but he went to the courthouse to escort Junior through the media throng. "They gotta try to rig a case to get us," he crowed.

CHAPTER 12

• • • • • • • • • • • • • •

Nut Cases

In the spring of 1987, with his legal woes behind him, Gotti seemed about to get his wish—the one made while musing with his followers near the Bergin bug, shortly after Sparks: "If I can get a year run without being interrupted, get a year, I'm gonna put this thing together where they could never break it, never destroy it, even if we die." Crooked as it was, his acquittal in the Giacalone case had coated him with more Teflon than the headline writers knew; legally speaking, it amounted to an immunization for any crime he had committed on behalf of the family enterprise before the indictment in March 1985.

He had been in prison nearly half the time since. His law enforcement enemies would be starting from scratch; a new case would take time, and blunders by him. He would have at least a year's run—assuming that Chin Gigante was still unable, now that Gotti was back in circulation, to make him pay for Paul.

It had been almost a year since Frank DeCicco and the man mistaken for Gotti were blown up. To Gotti, whatever the car bombing was about, it seemed like water under the bridge now. Gotti still did not suspect Chin, although he would soon be given ample reason to change his mind.

As it happened, however, someone tried to beat Chin to the punch. Six weeks after the verdict in Brooklyn, as Gotti bounced out of the Bergin one sunny day, a man standing in the doorway of a florist shop across the street pulled a gun and fired a single shot at Gotti. The man wore two pairs of trousers, apparently so he could discard one and confuse potential witnesses. But his aim was bad, and so was his immediate future.

Gotti ducked back into the Bergin as the gunman fled on foot, an unusual mode of conveyance for a professional assassin. Several Gotti men gave chase; one, Bobby Boriello, a favored bodyguard, drew a pistol and brought the target down with a single shot to the buttocks—a remarkable shot, since he was two blocks away.

In view of many bystanders who later said they had seen nothing, the wounded man was put into the backseat of a black car that glided over from the Bergin a moment later. The man—presumably an assassin who could now be forced to tell who sent him—was taken to Staten Island and into the basement of a newsstand and candy shop whose real owner was a Gambino capo.

The name of the store—Paul's Sweet Shoppe—would have been nicely ironic if the attempted assassination had had anything to do with Sparks. But the more Gotti's men tortured Jeffrey Ciccone, the more he wailed that he had been sent by God—that Jesus had told him Gotti was the devil—and the more they began to believe that he was a lone crackpot.

Meanwhile, of course, back at the Bergin, Gotti could not shed any light when the police came to ask the ritual questions about a report of shots fired. "Shot? What shot? Who'd want to hurt a guy like me, except you?" he asked an NYPD detective.

Gotti did the same song and dance when George Gabriel, now in direct charge of making a new RICO case against him, came by later in the day. The shooting was an NYPD matter, but Gabriel intended to annoy Gotti with his presence whenever possible.

"John, my friend, I hear you had to do some duckin' today," Gabriel said, after finding Gotti outside the club.

"Nothin' happened, Georgie. We don't duck nobody. You're the ones who should be duckin', the way you treat people."

"You're right, John. But just make sure you stay indoors. We don't have the manpower to protect you from your enemies."

"I don't have no enemies. Everybody loves me."

While Gotti and Gabriel played with one another, Gotti's men on Staten Island became convinced that Jeffrey Ciccone was a Bible-quoting crackpot acting on his own. The main inquisitor was Joe Watts, backup shooter at Sparks and now big-spending member of Gotti's inner circle even though he would never be made because his father was not of Italian heritage.

Early in the evening, tired of bashing the hapless Ciccone around, Watts dispatched a messenger to Gotti. "The guy is a freakin' Jesus freak, nuts too," Watts said via the messenger. "He wasn't workin' for nobody. He's just a whack. What the fuck do we do with 'im?"

Gotti issued a two-word reply: "Kill 'im."

Watts, who had been in Paul's wing before siding with the Fist at Sammy's and DeCicco's behest, was eager to please. So he and some other men bound Ciccone's feet and hands; one produced an orange body bag, into which Ciccone, bawling and pleading, was stuffed. Another zippered the bag shut; aiming to please, Joe Watts fired six shots into Ciccone's head.

Watts and the other killers then left Paul's Sweet Shoppe, intending to return in a few hours, after they had arranged a disposal site, and remove the body. If another crime had not taken place that night, Ciccone's disposition likely would have remained another mystery on the Naked City's missing-persons roster.

While the killers were away, burglars broke into Paul's Sweet Shoppe. They avoided the basement but left the store's metal gates askew; a passerby noticed and called the police, who searched the basement and discovered the body.

The next day, the one witness in Ozone Park who was willing to say she saw a man fire a shot at Gotti gave a description that matched Ciccone's. Later, his blood also was matched to bloodstains found on the sidewalk where he was thrown into the black car.

"It looks like what we have here is a John Lennon–type situation," a top police official then announced, as the case headed toward the unsolved murder files. "It looks like some individual had a thing about John Gotti."

The individual whose thing about Gotti cost him his life was a sometime carpenter, thirty-eight years old, with a record of several minor drug arrests; he lived with two elderly aunts in Queens, one of whom later said he had "mental problems."

In a twist that was nicely ironic, apart from the fact that a man was dead, the victim turned out to be a distant relative of Sonny Ciccone—a Gambino capo who ran the rackets that were left at the city's once-grand shipping piers.

In a hurried visit to Gotti, Sonny Ciccone emphasized how distant the blood tie was. "He's some kind of bull-shit relative, a second or third cousin, or something. I haven't seen the fuck in years. He's a nut case, that's all."

"Forget about it," Gotti said boisterously. "The world's full of 'em. But good thing he was a lousy shot!"

By the perverse rules of his world, Gotti was entitled to administer his justice in the Ciccone case, which the police never solved. It was the same with a man who was only pretending to be a nut case—Chin Gigante.

For Chin, Gotti's return to the streets only meant that it was time to renew his secret war against Gotti and make him pay for breaking the Commission's rule that a boss cannot be killed without the approval of other Commission bosses.

His closet allies in the Gambino family, Jimmy Brown Failla and Danny Marino, were duly informed. The same scenario would be followed: After Gotti was dead, Chin would back Failla for boss; as the only boss (besides Gotti) not in jail, Chin did have the stature to convince the Gambino capos to see things his way and elect Failla—an old friend—to succeed Gotti.

Failla would then appoint Marino, another Chin friend, to be underboss. The close relationship that had existed between the Genovese and Gambino families before Sparks would be restored, and Gotti would be forgotten as the flash in the pan that he was.

To speed Gotti into history, Chin altered the equation he had formulated for the car bombing—Gotti and DeCicco for Paul and Bilotti—and decided that Gene Gotti would have to be killed too. With the two strongest Gotti brothers gone, the Bergin crew would not have the

stomach to muster a counterattack, especially with
Angelo in jail.

It all made sense, in Chin's mind. And it might have
gone as he imagined if Gotti had not, once again, caught
a lucky break. This time the break came even before the
plot was in place—and this time Gotti would finally realize that Chin was serious about Paul, and he and Chin
would make a shaky peace.

In light of the botched DeCicco bombing, the way the
second plot came undone made Chin's secret war seem
almost farcical. It came apart in the men's room of a
New Jersey restaurant. In the paranoia sweeping Cosa
Nostra, a men's room was about the only indoor place
where three Genovese family members felt safe to talk.

But FBI agents investigating the family's New Jersey
wing knew the bathroom was being used for secret talks
and had put a listening device there. In the fall of 1987,
the bug overheard the Genovese men making plans to kill
John and Gene Gotti. One of the three was the family's
chin-rubbing consigliere—strong proof that the men were
not just engaging in wishful thinking.

Much as the New Jersey–based agents might have preferred to let Chin's men go ahead with their plan, federal
policy requires agents who learn of such plots to alert the
targets that their lives are in danger. They turned the
chore over to their FBI counterparts across the Hudson
River in New York.

The next day, Bruce Mouw and George Gabriel traveled to the Bergin Hunt and Fish Club to inform Gotti.
But he had not arrived yet, and they went to his house in
nearby Howard Beach. It was two-thirty in the afternoon.

"I'll have to go get him," Vicky Gotti said after Mouw,
whom she recognized from his visit years before, apologized for troubling her. They detected annoyance in her
voice when she added, "He's still in bed."

"Nice hours," Mouw cracked to Gabriel, after Vicky
left them on the stoop.

"Such a hardworking boss," Gabriel chimed in.

The sight of two strangers standing on the stoop alone
excited a huge watchdog that lived in a pen abutting a
side door of the Gotti home. Charlie, a slobbering Nea-

politan mastiff, began barking wildly and trying to vault out of the pen.

"Jesus, after all these years of chasing John, I am going to get eaten by his dog," Mouw said, staring warily at Charlie.

"If that thing comes over that pen, I'm shootin' it," his new case agent said.

After an anxious moment, a groggy, unshaven Papa Schultz appeared in his bathrobe. "Shut the fuck up, Charlie," he said, and the dog quieted down.

"Good morning, John, uh, good afternoon," Mouw said.

"What's up, fellas?"

Mouw let his case agent do the talking.

"We're not here to bullshit you, John," Gabriel said. "We have solid information about a threat against you and Genie, a legitimate threat. This is not some wacko throwing a shot at ya. There's a plot to kill you both."

"There's a million plots, so what?"

"All we can say is that this one is for real."

"You make this shit up."

"No bullshit," Mouw broke in. "It's solid."

Gotti studied the agents, then sighed. "Okay, thanks fellas, but I'm sure it's no big deal."

The agents turned to leave, but Gabriel turned again and added, rubbing his chin mischievously: "By the way, John, it's coming from the Genovese family."

Gotti frowned. "There're my friends. Chin is my friend. Everybody's my friend. I don't have nothin' to worry about."

That night, Gotti held a emergency meeting with a man he'd just promoted to consigliere—Sammy Gravano. Seventy-seven-year-old Joe N. Gallo, under indictment in the hierarchy case, had decided he'd had enough and had asked permission to retire.

Sammy was a logical and deserving successor. He had shown loyalty by putting aside his misgivings and arranging Deebee's murder, had served capably as acting street boss and conducted the tie-ins while Gotti was in jail, and had then handled the George Pape situation—the reason Gotti was now free to pursue visions of grandeur.

"Me and you make a great team," Gotti had told Sammy.

"I am honored, John," Sammy had replied, now accustomed to the pace of events under Gotti and believing that although he was not taking over the same job, he was stepping into Frank DeCicco's shoes.

"Joe Piney will stay underboss. He might be going away for a hundred fuckin' years, but he wants to stay in that position, and I'm comfortable with it. If he does go, we'll make Frankie LoCascio actin' underboss. Okay with you?"

"I like Frankie. He don't have much to say sometimes, but he's a good guy. An old-timer like Piney."

"It's a good administration."

"What about Angelo?"

"I don't think Angelo's ever comin' home. He's got the two cases and you gotta believe he's gonna be fucked in one of 'em. You can't get to every fuckin' jury."

In their hastily arranged meeting about the FBI warning, Gotti told his new consigliere that he believed the warning was genuine. "I don't think the government is gonna lie about something like this. They must've got it on tape somewhere."

"I agree," Sammy replied. "If it was just some informant, they wouldn't have fuckin' bothered. But you know what I'm thinking now? Frankie DeCicco. Chin got Frankie."

"No, don't believe it. Not with a bomb. Chin wouldn't have used a bomb like that. Commission outlawed bombs years back."

"Always a first time. But so what do we do?"

"We can't make no moves with it being just the fuckin' FBI's word. But we gotta let Chin know that we know."

Gotti instructed Sammy to contact Chin's underboss and tell him about the agents' visit, but that Gotti didn't believe them. "Guarantee them that there will be no moves by us," he added.

Sammy did as ordered, and Chin's underboss soon reported to him that Chin himself was guaranteeing there would be no attempt on Gotti or his brother—and that if the FBI was not playing a trick, anybody who had been caught on tape was just joking.

"You know, Chin's just strokin' us," Sammy told Gotti.

"And we're strokin' him, but Chin ain't gonna try anything now. Knowin' we might is why he won't."

Down the road, Sammy would grow uneasy with some of Gotti's thinking, but he always regarded his reaction to the threat from Chin as a shining moment. By confronting Chin, and pretending to disbelieve, he put him on the defensive. With his hand tipped, the ex-boxer really would have to be crazy to try anything.

Gotti was a gambler on a hot streak. Nevertheless, he did increase his bodyguard contingent. He knew the odds were good that the FBI had just saved his life, but he could not count on the streak lasting forever.

The shaky peace between Gotti and Chin was tested almost immediately, but not because of anything either of them did. A man stewing in prison, Angelo Ruggiero, created the problem.

The problem occurred when Angelo attempted to settle an old score. The old score had nothing to do with Chin, but from where Chin sat, it certainly seemed like it. Before it all played out, Angelo would be confined to a doghouse from which he would never emerge, and Chin and Gotti would have their first meeting.

Angelo wasn't just stewing in the MCC; he was boiling. But it was his own fault. By losing his temper at the bail hearing in the hierarchy case and gesturing menacingly at a prosecutor, Angelo was responsible for the judge's decision to deny bail.

It cost him the chance to be by his old pal's side as Gotti celebrated the Giacalone verdict, and to whisper in his ear that he would be a better candidate for consigliere than Sammy. Since his old pal did not make prison visits, Angelo had essentially relegated himself to a sideline seat as the real dawn of the Gotti era broke over the volcano.

With so much time and anger on his hands, Angelo locked on to a slight from the past. After Angelo's indictment in the heroin case, a Luchese family capo had wondered aloud if Angelo would become an informer, to try and weasel out of trouble. Angelo heard about the remark and vowed revenge.

"The one thing no one can call me is a rat," Angelo had told Sammy.

"I would go to the source on that," Sammy had replied. "He might've been just foolin' or quoted wrong."

"You don't fool with my reputation! I've been in this life since I was a fuckin' kid!"

The capo in question was Anthony Casso—the same Casso who had orchestrated the DeCicco bombing for Chin. In the meantime, he had become the Luchese underboss, which, naturally, irritated Angelo all the more.

At the MCC, puffing on a Marlboro chain, Angelo poured out his bitterness about Casso in the presence of Michael Paradiso, a Bergin soldier awaiting trial on a hijacking case. "Mickey" Paradiso was a friend of Gotti's and Angelo's, and he became a made man about the same time.

One remark led to another and pretty soon—as he once had with Sammy in the Deebee situation—Angelo drew Paradiso into a plot to kill Casso. Angelo made up a motive, but crazily enough, it was right on the money: He told Paradiso that Gotti wanted Casso killed because he suspected Casso was behind DeCicco's murder.

Gotti did not suspect Casso, but it was perfectly plausible that he would. Paradiso quickly signed on; he even volunteered to hire the killer, who wound up adding another twist to the dark comedy of errors.

The attempt on Casso's life failed. He was shot, but not fatally. Worse, the assassin let Casso get a look at him; in a few weeks he was tracked down and captured by Casso's men. As he was being tortured, and shortly before he was shot dead, he admitted only what he knew—that Paradiso had hired him to kill Casso because Gotti thought Casso killed DeCicco. He didn't say anything about Angelo, but Angelo was Paradiso's capo, and the assignment had clearly come out of the MCC, where Angelo was.

A war pitting one family against two might have broken out right there if the new consigliere of the Gambino family had not established a working relationship with the new underboss of the Luchese family and had not earlier visited him in the hospital and wished him a speedy recovery.

The overtures had made Casso believe that Gotti and

Sammy had no idea he was behind the DeCicco bombing. And since he in fact was behind it, his immediate reaction was to try and make peace, even while beating a war drum.

He contacted Sammy and asked to meet, saying he wanted to give him and Gotti a chance to prove that Paradiso and Angelo, alone or together, had acted on their own.

"This's got to be about somethin' else," he said. "I never had no beef with Frankie DeCicco."

Sammy suggested that it was time for everyone to meet—Chin, Gotti, Casso's new boss, and the administrations of the three families—and clear the air. In the meantime, he told Casso: "I'll try to find out if Angelo's involved, but we can't go to war if Angelo went off half-cocked. I know John didn't have nothin' to do with it."

"I trust you, Sammy," Casso replied.

Everyone did meet—in what amounted to the first Commission meeting in several years; only three bosses attended, but it was a quorum. Chin, by sitting down with Gotti as an equal, finally recognized him as the Gambino boss—but it was in his interest to do so now; the plot in New Jersey had made it necessary for him to pretend he was not waging a secret war against Gotti.

In a bizarre conclusion to a bizarre situation, the whole meeting would be pretense. In addition to Chin pretending to be unaware of the New Jersey plot, Casso would pretend to be angry at being accused of killing DeCicco. For their part, Gotti and Sammy would pretend they didn't kill Paul. And new Luchese boss Vittorio Amuso, who knew what Casso had done, what Chin was up to, and what Gotti and Sammy had done, would pretend he didn't know the pretenders were pretending.

At the meeting, Gotti let his consigliere explain all they knew about the attempt on Casso, whose nickname was Gaspipe or, more often, just plain Gas.

After Sammy was done, Gotti spoke up. "I can tell you right now, Gas. Angelo will be busted. We're takin' his crew away."

"You should kill him," Gas quietly said, turning to his boss, Amuso. "Don't ya think, Vic?"

"Let's hear what John says," Amuso said.

"I can't do it," Gotti said. "Angelo denies it, and based

on what you told Sammy the shooter said, we got no proof. It's hard to kill Ange on suspicion after all these years. But we'll kill Mickey when he gets out. And, believe me, bustin' Angelo down is like killin' him. Almost."

Chin, who had gotten out of his pajamas for the meeting, did not say much about the Angelo-Paradiso situation; it was tough enough playing dumb about the New Jersey situation.

"Whatever was said, if it was said, was not authorized by me," Chin said. "We got enough problems with the FBI all over the place. We don't want to bring more problems on ourselves. Our families always have a good relationship."

"I agree with you, hundred percent," Gotti said. "We can't fight amongst ourselves. We fight the government!"

"Paul was fightin' the government when he was killed. He was standing up to two RICOs, like a man."

"I swear to you," Gotti said, "I'm as angry about that as you. We don't know who killed Paul. I've been tellin' Sammy and everyone else, the fuckin' cops might've killed Paul."

The first Commission meeting in years, and probably the most preposterous ever, ended with a round of handshakes and embraces and everyone promising to communicate better.

"We're all the same Cosa Nostra," Gotti told Chin.

Afterward, Gotti and Sammy whipped up some martinis, "How'd you like it when I told Chin the cops might've killed Paul?"

"Beautiful!" Sammy replied. "The look on Chin's face, he couldn't believe you were sayin' it!"

"What the fuck, it don't matter! But if I keep sayin' it, I might convince myself!"

The bigger joke, of course, was still on Gotti; while he now knew, because of an FBI bug in a New Jersey bathroom, that Chin had at least thought about killing him, he still did not know that he had already tried.

Gotti promoted brother Gene to replace Angelo, who slid into a deep funk, which darkened further as he, Gene, Carneglia, Mark Reiter, Eddie Lino, and others finally stood trial in the heroin case, the case that had started the Sparks ball rolling.

For Gene, promotion was not the sweet prize it once would have been. What good was it if he was headed off to prison for the rest of his life? Of that he was sure, and for many months lawyers for him, Carneglia, and Angelo had been discussing the possibility of pleading guilty in return for the prosecution's recommending to the judge in the case that they be sentenced respectively, to fourteen, sixteen, and eighteen years—great deals, since they faced about fifty if convicted.

Reiter and Lino intended to fight the cases, because they did not face as many serious charges and thought they might win.

Gene was forty-two years old; under policies that existed at the time he was indicted, he would qualify for parole after serving two-thirds of the fourteen years. That meant he would still have a life ahead of him when he was freed. Carneglia and Angelo, who were only a few years older, felt the same, especially Angelo after his Casso misadventure.

The only problem was John Gotti's earlier prohibition—prompted by Neil Dellacroce's son Armond's plea in the Giacalone case—against anyone taking a plea requiring them to admit that the Gambino family existed and that they were part of it.

Andy Maloney and Robert LaRusso, the prosecutor for the heroin trial, would have been happy to accept such pleas—and to save the expense and uncertainty of a long trial. But they would not negotiate the Gambino admission out of the proposed plea deals, and so Gotti ordered his men to trial.

With his strong suspicions about the jury in the Giacalone case, Maloney urged LaRusso to be especially alert for signs of jury tampering. "These people will try anything! They don't believe we have the right to put them on trial!"

Sure enough, after the trial began, an informant told the Gambino squad that two private eyes working for the defense were attempting to learn the names and addresses of the jurors; as in the Giacalone case, the jury was supposedly anonymous.

Then agents learned that a stockbroker from Brooklyn

had offered to give a new car to a juror excused from the panel for personal reasons—just to pick his brain about what his former colleagues were thinking.

Maloney ordered John Gleeson, the assistant prosecutor in the Giacalone case, to conduct a grand jury investigation with the FBI; as before, because the Gambino squad was involved in the prosecution, the bureau planned to assign non-Gambino agents to conduct background checks of the jurors.

Gleeson resisted the assignment. "Andy, with me in this, the other side's going to say this is just sour grapes. Maybe someone else would be better."

"I'm not worried about that. I'm worried that we can't use the squad that knows these jerks. But with you, at least we'll have someone involved who knows 'em who isn't involved in the case. I want you in on this, and so does the bureau."

Gleeson was a cautious person. In the absence of proof, he still did not fully share Maloney's suspicion that his own case had been fixed. And he continued to feel that way—even after he and agents from a white-collar-fraud squad found evidence that suggested the heroin defendants might have already bribed one juror and had also learned the identities of five more.

"They did it again!" Maloney exploded.

"Maybe. It looks like it, but it'd be tough to prove."

"This time, we're taking it to the judge."

Late in 1987, Gleeson and Maloney informed the trial judge, Mark Costantino—and after an unusual hearing attended by all the other judges in the Eastern District, Costantino found a high probability of jury tampering and declared a mistrial.

Maloney quickly announced plans for a new trial, but he knew that once again, in the public mind it looked as if the government was a ninety-pound weakling when it came to Gotti and the Gambino family.

Even as the case dissolved into a mistrial, however, the Eastern District Strike Force—the quasi-independent Cosa Nostra prosecutors in Maloney's office—won a victory in the hierarchy case, which had gone to trial almost at the same time.

Angelo had been "severed" from that trial so that he could be tried separately after the heroin case, but the

Strike Force won RICO convictions against two family stalwarts, underboss Joe Piney Armone and recently retired consigliere Joe N. Gallo.

The trial had not faintly resembled the Giacalone case, or the heroin case. Armone and Gallo had acted like gentlemen and had treated one of the female prosecutors in the case, Laura Ward, with respect. In return, Ward—the daughter of a judge in the Southern District—had compassion if not respect for them.

After the jury gave its verdict, Armone came over to her and protested his innocence about only one count of the multicount indictment, a count that alleged he and Gallo conspired to bribe a prison official on behalf of Gallo's son.

"Miss Ward," Joe Piney said, "I never bribed that guy."

"Joe, the evidence says you did."

"I know about evidence. It can be made to look one way or the other. I just want you to know."

Ward did not think she had just convicted an innocent man. Armone had not complained about any other count; only a finding of guilt in two was required for a RICO conviction, but she was struck by his lament.

"It was like, he was telling me they did everything else," she later said to John Gleeson, "but on this one, kind of as a badge, he was making a point that we were wrong."

"Maybe, but you can't worry about it, since the outcome's the same," Gleeson said. "But it shows the difference. Gotti would've never done that. Not in a million years."

After the guilty verdicts against Armone and Gallo, which came on December 23, 1987, United States district court judge Jack Weinstein released Gallo on bail, pending sentencing two months later, because Gallo was seventy-seven and the Gambino squad, through an informant, was saying he was no longer the consigliere; the bail meant that the old man would be able to spend one last holiday season with relatives.

The judge had another idea for the ex–Christmas tree thief, Joe Piney: The holdover from Lucky Luciano's time also would be granted bail pending his sentencing and allowed to spend the holidays with his wife and

daughter—but only if he made a statement publicly renouncing his life in crime.

The conviction, and the certainty of a lengthy sentence
condemning him to death behind bars, cracked Armone's
crusty shell. He mumbled that he would consider such a
penance.

Weinstein, who had a reputation for running an innova-
tive courtroom, told lawyers for both sides to draft an
agreeable statement and return to court the next day,
Christmas Eve.

Before Armone was carted back to the MCC for at
least one more night, the judge said the statement should
say something like " 'I hereby renounce and abjure any
connection I may have had with the Gambino crime family and resign any office I may have held in this or any
other crime organization.' "

The impending sound of cell doors clanging shut for
the rest of his life softened the heart but not the head of
Joe Piney. He sent Gotti a message asking for permission
to make the statement. The message was delivered by
Jack Giordano, a Manhattan capo who also was Armone's
nephew: "Piney doesn't think he's ever gonna get out
when he goes away, so he just wants this time with his
family. He doesn't think it matters what he says, it's just
legal bullshit."

Having ordered Gene, Angelo, and Carneglia to go to
trial rather than take a plea requiring such admissions,
Gotti was not about to let Armone, his underboss, make
the statement.

"I'm surprised by Piney!" Gotti shouted at Giordano.
"This is a Cosa Nostra! We don't make no official statements! He can't do it! You tell him that's an order! He's
my underboss, even if he's in fuckin' jail, until I say different!"

Giordano relayed that message to his uncle. Christmas
Eve morning, Armone went back to court and announced
through his lawyer that he had changed his mind and
would not make any renouncing statement.

Without comment on Joe Piney's choice, Weinstein
promptly ordered guards to return the sixty-nine-year-old
Armone to his MCC cage. Two months later, the judge
sentenced him to fifteen years in prison; seventy-seven-
year-old Gallo got ten, and would manage to cope with

prison very well, despite being almost the oldest prisoner in federal custody.

In 1992, however, Joe Piney would die of natural causes at the Federal Medical Center in Springfield, Missouri, a virtual nursing home for elderly prisoners. His family was not by his side, and by that time Gotti had stripped him of his title. He was just an old soldier who faded away.

CHAPTER 13

• • • • • • • • • • • • • •

Roach

Gotti was amazed by some of the gushing stories written about him after the Giacalone case. He was a Robin Hood, a folk hero, a man who stood up for the little guy and fought city hall with style and bravado. While amazing, the stories nonetheless nourished his ego; at the least, they were proof that he had been right to court the media before and during the trial.

The more he read, the more he believed in the value of a positive public image. Because he fully expected that someday, somewhere, for something, he would have to stand trial again, the way a jury might perceive him was more than an idle concern.

Many stories shaping the public image failed to associate Gotti with the violence, plundering, and treachery of his world. Remarkably, many people believed he was a fierce foe of drugs and drug dealing—despite all those around him—brothers, best friends, retainers, and nightlife pals—who dealt drugs and, in some cases, used them, although not in front of him because alcohol was the only drug he used.

The myth rose as the result of many factors. Laziness and incompetence on the part of some reporters were only two. In addition, the FBI memos saying Gotti was a secret drug dealer—memos written in the early 1980s, after agents met with their two informants in the Bergin crew, Willie Boy Johnson and Billy Battista—were never made public in the Giacalone case.

The biggest factor was that Gotti had never been charged with a drug crime; he had plausible deniability. Bruce Cutler had harped on this and used it to great advantage during his opening statement and closing argument.

Because Gotti was so concerned about his mainly positive image, Cutler—now more or less Gotti's press secretary—was always touting Gotti's supposed anti-drug posture.

"There is no single person in this city more opposed to drug use and drug trafficking than John Gotti," Cutler would tell the reporters who flocked to his office for Gotti profiles.

Most journalists never associated Gotti with stories going on under their noses—stories from the low and high ends of the heroin chain—that would strongly suggest otherwise and, in the case of the low end, would give up the first secrets about Sparks.

The low involved Anthony Rampino, one of the men who left the courthouse in Brooklyn as free as Gotti. He did not have any idea that juror George Pape had been bought, but Rampino rarely had ideas. He was an affably deadly gofer, as inclined to mop the bathroom at the Bergin as to linger in the shadows outside Sparks and kill Paul and Bilotti, so long as Gotti said so.

He latched on to Gotti in the late 1960s, when Gotti was a Bergin hijacking associate and he was a small-time thief, robber, and heroin dealer. By the early 1970s, Rampino, who was a year older, was introducing himself as "John's man"; he helped Gotti evade cops during the James McBratney murder investigation and was there when the cops finally got him.

Rampino continued to deal heroin, and he was caught and sent to prison for a few years. When he got out, the best future he had was Gotti, who paid him a few dollars to ferry messages and collect payments from loan-shark customers. With his sunken eyes and pockmarked face, the lanky, gawky Rampino was suited for the latter task. His nickname—Roach—was perfectly apt.

Over the years, his physical characteristics became even more cadaverlike as he developed a weakness for the heroin he sold on the side—three to five thousand dollars' worth a week—while working for Gotti. By the time he was indicted with Gotti in the Giacalone case, he had become an addict and ruined what little chance he had of ever becoming a made man.

Rampino's addiction was an embarrassment for Gotti, who would have responded the way Sammy did to such problems in his crew if Rampino had not been on trial with him. The small risk of a botched hit sending Rampino onto the witness stand against him was not worth the big consequences.

"You know, soon enough, we're gonna take care of all these problems like Roach," Gotti told Sammy after the acquittal.

The seven-month-long trial forced Rampino, who was free on bail, into temporary recovery. Judge Nickerson ordered him to give random and ultimately daily urine samples and required his attorney, David DePetris, to state under oath each day that his client was clearheaded and able to assist in his defense.

The trial ruined Rampino's part-time heroin business, but it was his moment in the gangster limelight. He became a favorite of reporters and sketch artists because he looked like such a goon. He liked the attention and was thrill to see himself quoted a few times. Once, however, he got carried away and offended Gotti's careful sense of public decorum.

Arriving for court with the other defendants who were out on bail, he saw a female photographer rushing forward to snap their picture. Like some oafish schoolboy, Roach Rampino made a face, grabbed his crotch, and began unzipping his fly. The resulting front-page photograph and cutline in the *New York Post* suggested that John Gotti and his friends were just crude louts.

"You fuckin' scumbag," Gotti railed at Rampino, after a copy of the newspaper was passed around the defense table during a break in the trial. "We're fightin' for our lives here. This ain't no game. Show some respect. Do it again, you're dead."

After the verdict, Rampino was not invited to the victory celebration in Florida. Unlike another man from Gotti's early days, Willie Boy—who was told that while he wouldn't be killed, he could no longer come to the Bergin—Rampino was not banished so much as de-emphasized.

Gotti ordered him to continue appearing at the Bergin each morning but gave him little to do except empty the garbage. Having lost his heroin customers, Roach was nearly broke.

"We've got plenty of time to take care of our problems," Gotti told Sammy, who would have taken immediate action—and, indeed, had taken recent action against a crew member of his, Michael DeBatt, who became Victim No. 13 after he also was stricken with the cocaine virus.

Rampino celebrated the verdict on his own. The resourceful Phil Messing of the *Post* found him at a bar tossing back shots of whisky with lemon and encouraged him to say a few words.

"I just want to tip my hat to the jurors," Rampino said, showing some fake respect. "I'm just glad they didn't convict us for our lifestyles," he added, showing he had absorbed a theme from Bruce Cutler's final argument.

When Messing showed Rampino a copy of the *Post* featuring a photograph of a smiling Gotti, John's man became reverential.

"Look at that face—does he look like a bad guy? He's got some charisma, eh? He's got a lot on the ball. He's got some IQ. He's self-educated."

Messing then wondered if Rampino had any future plans. The interviewee seemed dumbfounded by the question but finally answered: "Just say I'm a good-natured guy, and I'm gonna keep on doin' what I've been doin'."

True to his word, Rampino would soon be doin' what he was doin' before the trial—dealing, and using, heroin. By June 1987, three months later, he was shooting up eight times a day; most of his customers had gone elsewhere, so he wasn't making much money. But he was eking out a living for himself, his wife, and children—including a son stricken with cancer—by copping small amounts from street dealers for other junkies.

Despite the heavy use, Rampino managed to haul himself to the Bergin every day by 11 A.M. and to conceal his deterioration from Gotti, who was out and about the city most of the day, and frequently much of the night, reasserting his authority and basking in the limelight after ten months in prison.

Though he was functional, Rampino was always desperate, and so he quickly said yes when another low-achieving Gambino associate, Philip Paradiso, asked him to score heroin. Philip was the younger brother of the

Bergin soldier who got involved with Angelo in the cock-eyed scheme to kill Anthony Casso.

But Rampino didn't know that Michael Paradiso's future was now very dim; as far as he knew, Gotti intended to promote Mickey to captain once he got out of prison in a couple years. Given Mickey's presumed stature at the Bergin, Rampino figured it was okay to help younger brother Philip get some heroin.

"My brother told me I could trust you," Philip told Rampino at the outset of their first heroin-buying excursion to the Bronx.

"Me and your brother did more shit together," Rampino said, lying, but trying to impress the younger man.

Philip only wanted fifty dollars' worth, a mission that Rampino quickly accomplished before lamenting his current lot in life. "I used to be with Johnny every day. I wasn't fuckin' around then. I just started fuckin' around again."

Philip oozed sympathy, and Rampino warned him against the danger of an overdose before they parted company.

Three days later, Philip telephoned Rampino again. He said some Hispanic drug dealer he knew from when they were in prison together several years before wanted a "big package." If Roach could deliver, a decent commission awaited both.

Rampino was introduced to a Junior in Philip's car. Junior said he wanted not only a big package but a steady supplier.

Philip was eager to seal the deal. "I don't wanna lose him, and we can't bullshit," he told Rampino. "You got to let me know, right now."

"Of course, but yo, we don't get a package just like this."

The two men spoke for another hour; Rampino never suggested where he could obtain a wholesale-level "big package." He never sought much reassurance about the reliability of Junior, other than to say Junior seemed "like a nice guy."

"If he's a cop, I'm a faggot, you know what I mean?" Philip said. "I'll vouch for that all the way."

The exaggerated response flew by Rampino, who began rhapsodizing about a particularly potent "bundle" of morphine-based heroin that he had "cut" with more morphine.

"Now when I'm shooting it in, boom, I got hit with needles, needles and pins all in my fuckin' face and my back. I said, 'You, mother fuck, morphine.' I got flushed, my face felt like it was on fire. Pins and needles, 'cause that's the morphine. I says, 'Holy shit, I cut this mother fucker with morphine.' So I shot that for like about four or five days straight."

With a seemingly flush customer at hand, Rampino saw his chance to move back up the heroin chain and exit the dime-bag track of his post-trial life. Being a Bergin veteran, he knew who might have a big package; he contacted Mark Reiter, the dealer whom Gotti supposedly had banished from the Bergin in 1981. That was after some began wondering why Gotti let Reiter hang around—and after the FBI's secret informers said Gotti was backing the heroin deals of brother Gene, Angelo, and Carneglia.

The arrangements took four days, but Reiter offered Rampino a fairly big package—six ounces, big enough to earn a mandatory fifteen-to-twenty-five-to-life sentence in New York State if he were convicted of possessing it with intent to sell.

The heroin case was on its way to a mistrial, but Reiter, a codefendant on bail, was still dealing. Gotti had contemplated having Reiter killed, not because of the heroin, he told Sammy, but because he was "weak." But he backed off, just as he had with Rampino and for the same reason—because Reiter was on trial with Angelo, Gene, Carneglia, and Eddie Lino. The small risk of a botched hit wasn't worth the big consequences.

After meeting Reiter, Rampino met Junior again in Philip's car. Junior balked when Rampino said his source insisted that the purchase price, thirty thousand dollars, be paid in advance. He was afraid Rampino would take the money and run.

Anxious to do the deal and earn his cut in dollars and heroin, Rampino sputtered assurances, then added, "What can I do? Bring my wife and kids and let you hold on to the kids? My son's got cancer. On my son, you got nothing to worry about."

Junior hemmed and hawed, then relented. "All right.

Run it to your man that if everything is cool, you'll see a steady practice. Steady customer."

"You'll see," Rampino replied. "The first time is always the hardest. I ain't a greedy guy."

Later that night, June 25, 1987, Rampino and Junior met again on Sutton Place in Manhattan. With a last plea for trust, Junior handed over thirty thousand dollars in one-hundred-dollar bills. "Tony, please, you don't know, I'll be a dead man."

"And I'll be chopped up," Roach empathized.

Rampino went to First Avenue and Fifty-eighth Street, a short distance away, and met a man in the shadows. He then walked back and gave six ounces of heroin to Junior, who was really Detective Herbert Colon of the Brooklyn district attorney's office.

Rather than arrest Roach there on Sutton Place and spook whoever might be watching, two FBI agents working the sting of Anthony Rampino with the Brooklyn DA's detective squad waited until the next day. There was no need to hurry; the suspect wasn't going anywhere, and the case was open and shut. Every word that fell from Rampino's lips had been recorded by a listening device in the car of Philip Paradiso, who had set up Rampino to help himself out of his own pending drug case.

Now it would be Rampino's turn to try and help himself out—by setting up his man, John Gotti.

Agents George Hanna and Philip Scala arrested Rampino on a street in Ozone Park, near where he lived, early in the evening.

"Heroin?" Roach said to Hanna en route to the DA's office. "Don't know anything about it. Been home the last few days."

"You sold to an individual named Junior. Ring a bell? He was an undercover cop."

Rampino began stamping his feet against the floorboard of the federal car. "Lanky motherfucker!" he screamed, referring to Philip Paradiso. "I never should have trusted him! I knew I should have patted him down! Lanky motherfucker!"

At the DA's office, Rampino stamped and fumed some more—he was well aware he was looking at a potential life sentence—before he finally sat down and said to

Hanna, "If you can get me out of this, I can get you some big people."

Playing dumb, Hanna replied, "What do you mean?"

"You know exactly what I mean."

Rampino smirked and waited for Hanna to speak.

"Are we talking about John Gotti?"

"You know we're talkin' about John Gotti. You let me out of here, I'll wear a wire and get more than you'll ever get."

Hanna nodded dubiously, and Rampino threw a bigger card on the table. "I can I.D. everyone in the Castellano shooting. If you get me out on the street before eleven tomorrow morning, I'll get you more conversations than you can imagine."

More interested than he showed, Hanna contacted assistant U.S. attorney Charles Rose, one of U.S. attorney Andy Maloney's top aides in Brooklyn. Rose tried to talk Rampino into telling what he knew about Gotti right there, and joining the federal witness protection program—but Rampino kept saying he would not say anything unless he was released first.

"You're in a lot of trouble, Tony. You dealt hand to hand and it was taped. We got you dead to rights."

"I don't know about that," replied Rampino, suddenly coy and surprisingly confident. "I think I've got a great duress defense. I'm a heroin addict. I couldn't help myself."

"Your best bet is to cooperate. Get in the program."

"How you gonna hide this face?"

Around three in the morning, Rose and Hanna conferred. The suspect had tempted them, but his refusal to give more details about Sparks unless he was let go made them wary that he meant to flee, not cooperate. They decided to let him sleep on it, and Roach nodded off on a couch in the office of assistant district attorney Eric Krause.

In the morning, Rampino tried to pressure Hanna. He said if he was not at the Bergin by 11 A.M., men there would tell Gotti, who would know something was amiss. If Gotti didn't kill him, he would at least be careful about what he said in his presence, neutralizing the body wire Rampino would wear.

Hanna pretended not to hear. "What can you tell me about the Castellano homicide?"

"I can tell you the other shooters."

The reply momentarily startled Hanna; Rampino had just implicated himself.

"Other shooters?"

"You know exactly what I mean. I can tell you everyone involved in the murder."

"How many other shooters?"

Rampino remained silent but raised two fingers. He had been a backup shooter outside Sparks, the man stationed across the street in case the victims managed to flee. Probably because he was beginning to suffer the first pangs of heroin withdrawal and was desperate to enhance his importance, he made himself one of the three shooters who actually fired the fatal shots; Roach wasn't counting the fourth designated shooter, the one whose pistol jammed as he went to shoot Bilotti.

Hanna tried to elicit more, but Rampino decided he had played all the cards he dared and asked again to be released.

Rose and the other attorneys in charge of the case decided against it. Sometime after 11 A.M., the time he was supposed to show up at the Bergin, Rampino grew dour and edgy.

"I'm fucked now. Either way, John is going to kill me. If I get out on bail and he learns I was here, I'm dead. Or if I stay in jail, I'm dead. My life is over. I'm fucked."

That afternoon, agents took Roach to a hospital, where he was treated for heroin withdrawal and fear of death. Afterward, a judge ordered him held without bail, after another assistant district attorney, Eric Seidel, argued that the suspect was so fearful of John Gotti that he might run away and not show up for trial—if he wasn't murdered first.

A report of Rampino's statements was forwarded to Andy Maloney and Bruce Mouw. Three months into the reconvened reign of John Gotti, the truth of his takeover had begun to dribble out. Because they knew the Sparks murders were as much about heroin as about Paul's leadership and Gotti's ambition, Maloney and Mouw found a pleasantly perverse symmetry in a junkie like Roach Rampino causing the ball to start unraveling.

* * *

In retrospect, Anthony Rampino was fortunate not to have been released; John Gotti knew about his arrest within hours. Some denizen of Ozone Park saw Rampino being pulled off the street and put into a suspiciously police-looking car, and he immediately notified the Bergin.

Roach's attorney spent hours on the telephone, trying to learn which cops or agents had arrested his client. But he was stonewalled for nearly a day because Rampino, contemplating a deal, told Hanna he didn't want to speak to his lawyer, David DePetris. When the talks failed and the client finally called, enough time had passed, in Gotti's mind, to put a presumption of cooperation—and a death sentence—on Rampino's head.

"Roach will have to go," Gotti told Sammy two days later. "They had him almost a day before he called the lawyer. What does that tell ya? He has to fuckin' go, even if it's in jail."

"That ain't easy."

"He can bring it all down."

Once at Rikers Island, a jail for city and state pretrial detainees in the middle of the East River between Manhattan and Queens, Rampino considered his fate and chose to remain silent, at least for a while, about the Sparks murders. He also clammed up about his source for the heroin—Mark Reiter.

But Reiter, already on trial for heroin, was about to find himself in a brighter limelight—and his reflection would once again suggest that Gotti's anti-drug posture was bogus.

Reiter was orphaned as a boy and raised by adoptive Jewish parents. He was not sure of his heritage, but his early friends in Brooklyn happened to be Sammy and Gotti types, who dreamed of getting mobbed up and becoming made men. When he got older, he hired private investigators to trace his lineage and show that he really was Italian and thus qualified for induction.

His proof, however, was too dubious to overcome the bias against non-Italians—even to John Gotti, whose wife was half-Jewish. In time, like Angelo's late brother, Salvatore, Reiter made so much money dealing heroin that becoming made would have been too much bother, because under the rules he would have had to pretend that he was not a drug dealer.

With the restaurants and bars he owned, with his waterfront home, his yacht, and his fleet of luxury cars, pretense was not only undesirable but impossible.

Until Salvatore Ruggiero's private plane crashed during a heroin sortie to Florida, he was one of the biggest suppliers of heroin to Harlem, where the drug first became widely popular in the early 1960s. By 1982, when Salvatore died and Reiter filled his shoes, heroin addiction and its attendant miseries had laid waste to entire sections of the upper Manhattan neighborhood.

Salvatore's heroin was the reason Reiter had begun hanging around the Bergin in 1981, and when Salvatore's heroin became Angelo's and Gene's and John Carneglia's, Reiter was the one who helped them peddle it to major black wholesalers in Harlem and, eventually, Baltimore, Detroit, and Washington, D.C.

One of these wholesalers was James Jackson, a former street hustler and junkie who became a big-time dealer after he went to prison, kicked his habit, and came back to Harlem with contacts and newfound acumen. From 1982 to 1987, Jackson bought eight million dollars' worth of heroin from Reiter—a defendant on bail, awaiting trial in the heroin case almost the whole time—and turned it into seventeen million dollars in gross receipts.

Despite the cutthroat nature of their business, the five-foot-seven Jackson and the six-foot-four Reiter actually became personal friends—a "black and white Mutt and Jeff," according to one of the federal drug agents who began investigating them in 1984. Through their friendship, Jackson learned that Reiter was friends with John Gotti.

By 1985, after all of Salvatore's heroin had been shot into the veins of thousands of junkies, Reiter told Jackson he was having supply problems because Paul Castellano was giving Gotti a hard time about drug dealing, and so Italian dealers were lying low.

"But soon," he said, "I'll have more than I can handle."

A few weeks later, after the Sparks murders, Jackson saw a photo of Reiter with Gotti in a newspaper. He beeped his friend and said he was impressed.

"Man, when the man calls, I just be there," Reiter replied.

For the next two years, Jackson once again was able to get all the heroin he wanted from Mark Reiter. The bubble burst in 1987, when Jackson and several of his underlings were arrested; Jackson, who had squandered most of his money, folded like an accordion and agreed to cooperate—against his underlings and against Mark Reiter, who in the meantime had finally begun standing trial with the recently demoted Angelo and his replacement, Gene, as well as Carneglia.

Reiter, like another defendant, Eddie Lino, was not facing as many serious counts as they; he, like Lino, thought he had a good chance of winning.

Until he decided to make a deal, Jackson was housed on the same general-population floor of the MCC as Angelo, who had now been held without bail so long that he well knew what it meant when Jackson was taken off the floor without explanation and moved to a cellblock reserved for inmates whose lives were thought to be in jeopardy.

Angelo had also become a personal friend of Reiter's and had recently invited him to stand in for him at his daughter's wedding. He didn't wait until the next session of their heroin trial to alert Reiter to the unmistakable import of Jackson's sudden change in prison accommodations.

Though aware that calls on the MCC inmate telephone were periodically taped, Angelo gambled and called Reiter at home to tell him the news about a man they referred to as "the guy."

"This is not for me, pal, it's for you," he said. "The guy left the floor today. His friends just told me."

"Okay," Reiter replied. "Bye-bye."

With Jackson in the government tent, Reiter's confidence about his chances at trial evaporated. He jumped bail and fled to California. In three months, however, he was caught and taken back to New York—in time to see his old cronies get a mistrial. He was put on trial separately and quickly convicted, mainly because of the testimony of the star witness, James Jackson.

During legal arguments in the case, U.S. district court judge Richard Owen commented on the implication of

Jackson's testimony about Reiter's temporary dry spell in 1985: "The conclusion would be that Reiter was dry and Paul Castellano did not like dealing in heroin. And when Castellano died and Gotti took over, the spigot was turned on and the heroin flowed."

Showing more fortitude than Gotti granted, Mark Reiter refused to talk about the Teflon Don and heroin. He was then sentenced to life in prison, with no chance of parole.

CHAPTER 14

• • • • • • • • • • • • • •

Special Operations

While expecting his law enforcement enemies to come after him, Gotti saw little evidence of it during his first year as a boss without a Piecyk or a Giacalone hanging over his head. But RICO cases come a brick at a time, and his enemies had begun laying the foundation for another one against him only a couple of hours after he strutted free in Brooklyn. By the first anniversary of that day, something akin to a foundation would be in place.

The first step was Bruce Mouw and George Gabriel's opening of a Gotti case file on the afternoon of the verdict. The second came a few days later when Andy Maloney, the United States attorney in Brooklyn, traveled across the East River and struck a deal with Rudolph Giuliani, the United States attorney in Manhattan.

The deal was that while Giuliani would not try to persuade the Gambino squad to develop a RICO case with his office, rather than Maloney's, he reserved the right to develop—with the NYPD—a murder case against Gotti based solely on Sparks, and to co-prosecute it with his equally renowned counterpart at the local level, Manhattan district attorney Robert Morgenthau.

Having worked in both the Southern and the Eastern Districts, Maloney was steeped in the jurisdictional spats and rivalries that arise from office pride. He expected that down the line, somehow, the deal's terms would sour relations between the parties. He believed that the FBI and the Eastern District did not have to solve Sparks to make a RICO case against Gotti—but he was also sure the murders would become a point of contention.

How could they not? Inevitably, a major investigation of Gotti would yield information about the treachery and intrigue that had brought him to power. A simple sting of Anthony Rampino already had, not long after Maloney made his agreement with Giuliani. Somewhere, somehow, the cases would collide, and some law enforcement noses would fly out of joint.

Maloney also carried away something else from that meeting with Giuliani: a pledge from Giuliani to turn over all the evidence against Gotti that already had been collected by agents of the New York State Organized Crime Task Force during their probe of the Bergin Hunt and Fish Club in 1985 and 1986.

Understandably keen on seeing some results from his agents' work, the director of the task force, Ronald Goldstock, had taken his files to Giuliani in the hope of mounting a joint case with the superstar prosecutor and felling the superstar criminal. His men had earlier provided Giuliani's office some of the breakthrough evidence in the Commission case by planting a bug in the car of the man who preceded Vittorio Amuso as the Luchese family boss.

Giuliani had too many of his own cases in the pipeline to take much notice of the task force's Bergin tapes, and Goldstock, a deputy state attorney general pompous enough to covet Southern District cachet for its own sake, reluctantly agreed to let Giuliani send him across the East River to Brooklyn.

The involvement of Goldstock and the task force presented Maloney with a set of jurisdictional concerns and egos to match those had already existed in his own office, where until Diane Giacalone talked Maloney's predecessor into making an exception, Cosa Nostra cases were handled by the special unit known as the Eastern District Organized Crime Strike Force.

The strike force boss, Edward McDonald, answered directly to superiors at the Justice Department in Washington. His unit and others around the country had been organized years before, on the theory that the best way to take on Cosa Nostra was to create specialists within Justice whose mission would be the same no matter which political party was in the White House.

Consequently, the strike forces were stocked with civil-service appointees such as McDonald, rather than with political appointees such as Maloney and all other U.S. attorneys.

Maloney was opposed to the arrangement—on the theory that it is the FBI that normally makes an OC case, not the prosecutor—and in fact the strike force concept was falling out of favor even as McDonald's unit was putting Joseph Armone and Joe N. Gallo away.

Maloney wanted lawyers from his own criminal division staff to work with the Gambino squad and supervise the get-Gotti grand jury that would review the evidence and, if all went well, vote someday to indict Gotti.

But after Goldstock and the task force came onto the scene, Maloney decided to cover all the bases. He named two lawyers to work with the Gambino squad—Kevin O'Regan of his criminal division staff; Douglas Grover of McDonald's strike force—and appointed Barbara DiTata, a lawyer from Goldstock's office, as a special assistant U.S. attorney for the Gotti case.

At a meeting with McDonald, Goldstock, and the grand jury team, he also announced that he had told Giuliani that if they were fortunate enough to go to trial against Gotti, he would go into a courtroom for the first time in a while and try the case himself. That meant four lawyers would be at the government table—a crowd, typically.

Of course, as everyone recognized more than they could ever publicly admit, a Gotti case would be anything but typical.

The evidence that Goldstock's agents had collected formed the rough outline of a RICO case, and over the next year—while the Gambino squad began collecting its own evidence and stepped up surveillance of Gotti—Grover, O'Regan, and DiTata presented elements of their evidence to the grand jury.

Much of the state task force evidence was based on Gotti's conversations at the Bergin and on remarks he made while being secretly taped by an informer wearing a body wire. Some of the tapes were hard to hear, and many said a lot more about Gotti's personality than his criminality.

One excerpt suggested that he had ordered an assault on a union official he suspected of authorizing vandals to trash a Gambino-backed restaurant being built with nonunion labor—but without corroboration, it would be a tough crime to prove.

The most incriminating tapes dealt with his loan-sharking and gambling operations. Under RICO, even these comparatively minor crimes—Gotti had been overheard threatening a loan-shark customer and bragging about the gambling "stops" he controlled—made him vulnerable to a lengthy sentence, if the crimes were shown to be part of an illegal enterprise such as the Gambino family.

For that reason, in the spring of 1988, Ronald Goldstock told Maloney it was time to drop the hammer and ask the grand jury to indict Gotti. Maloney, however, thought Goldstock was more proud of the case than he ought to be and urged patience.

Their differences led to Goldstock's nose becoming the first in law enforcement to fly out of joint over Gotti.

"The evidence just isn't strong enough," Maloney said after Goldstock made an opening statement on behalf of indicting now.

"We've got him threatening to kill a loan-shark customer!" Goldstock replied. "We got him saying every gambling operation in Queens reports to him. And we know he's a loan shark and that he does run the operations. What more do you want?"

Maloney puffed on his pipe, looking less bothered than he really was by Goldstock's insistence.

"This jerk is a celebrity now. There's a real risk people won't want to convict him for this kind of stuff. We can't take another swing at this guy and miss. People might begin to think he really is invincible."

"We got a case and won't bring it! We look like the jerks!"

"I've listened to the tapes, Ron. Gotti is a big mouth; he exaggerates. We don't have any real smoking-gun conversation. A lot of the backup is circumstantial."

The wrangling lasted another hour, but Goldstock failed to move Maloney or McDonald, who felt the same as Maloney.

Finally, Goldstock said he might have no choice but to take his files and tapes to some other prosecutor's office. The conflict had gotten Maloney's own dander up.

"Fine," he said, calling Goldstock's bet. "Good luck and God bless."

By letting Ronald Goldstock go his angry way, Maloney was making his own bet—that the Gambino squad would come up with smoking-gun conversations and direct evidence of crimes more damning than loan-sharking and gambling.

For the past year, the squad had gathered intelligence about Gotti. A lot of information had come in from informants; the squad had a few, and was trying to develop more, but none had the same access that Willie Boy Johnson had once had.

Informants two and three times removed from the original source raised as many questions as they answered. That was the problem with the one who told the squad that Gotti had gotten a hook into the Giacalone jury—he didn't have enough information to help them do anything about it.

The squad needed to construct a picture of Gotti's daily life and habits, whom he met and where. Besides informants, this required extensive surveillance.

All agents are trained in surveillance techniques, but the real experts were on a squad specializing in deft and dangerous operations, such as breaking in somewhere and installing a bug. The "special operations" squad—referred to in the bureau as an "S.O. squad"—also was used when the bureau did not want a subject to know he was being followed.

When following a suspect in a car, almost always the case with Gotti, the S.O. squad worked in five-person teams. Each member had his or her own car, in which was kept a camera with different lenses and changes of clothes for disguises.

Their seemingly dull passenger cars had microphones built into the ceiling so they could talk to each other on a special channel without a handset. At night, with a switch inside the car, they could make it appear that one or the other of their headlights was broken.

After becoming boss, Gotti—with various men behind the wheel of his new black Mercedes—was involved in many wild highway encounters with news-media surveillants, who were always easy to spot and then to lose. But he never saw any agents, unless they wanted to be seen.

The S.O. squad avoided detection because the lead car of the five-car surveillance caravan was always changing. Anytime Gotti's car turned in a different direction, the "point" car closest behind kept going straight ahead. The second car then moved to the point while the first eventually doubled back to become the fifth. In this way, the squad could follow someone all day without any single car arousing particular suspicion.

Through informants and surveillance, the FBI established that Gotti was still a creature of habit. Only a couple of months into the case, any agent working on it could look at his watch and be reasonably sure where Gotti was.

If it was noon, he'd be home in Howard Beach, rolling out of bed. If it was two in the afternoon, he'd be at the Bergin in Ozone Park. By six, he'd be on his way to some restaurant—Altadonna in Queens, Tavola's in Brooklyn, or Taormina's in Manhattan. The last of these was owned by Gambino capo Joseph Corrao and was down the street from the Ravenite in Little Italy.

By ten in the evening, Gotti would be headed to Club A, a discotheque on the East Side of Manhattan that at the time was his favorite; it had been virtually taken over by Ernie Grillo, son-in-law of Neil and husband of Shannon Grillo, Gotti's longtime flame. Ernie and some associates were shaking down numerous East Side businesses and making a lot of money.

But Ernie was never going to be made, because that would mean that Gotti would be making moves on a made man's wife.

The informants and surveillance also helped identify the main members of Gotti's nightlife crew—Jack D'Amico, Joe Watts, Eddie Lino, and Bobby Boriello—and disclosed that Sammy Gravano was now consigliere and that, after Armone was convicted, Gotti had named Frank LoCascio acting underboss.

These were facts important to know, but late in 1987, the informants came through with especially significant news. They reported that Gotti intended to make the Ravenite—the lair of his departed mentor—his main headquarters. He would come there almost every day, just

John Gotti:
What me worry?
(PHOTO: *Daily News*)

Gotti is all smiles
after the jury acquits
him of ordering
the shooting of
union official
John O'Connor.
(PHOTO: *Daily News*)

Gotti smiles.
(PHOTO: *Daily News*)

Newly crowned
Gambino boss arrives
for an early court
appearance.
(PHOTO: *Daily News*)

The always present
cameras follow
Gotti to lunch dur-
ing his assault trial
in Manhattan.
(PHOTO: *Daily News*)

Gotti and body-guard/chauffer Joe Corrozzo joke with photogra-phers during happy days.
(PHOTO: *Daily News*)

Gotti followed by Gerald Shargel, Sammy Gravano's favorite lawyer when they were all on the same team.
(PHOTO: *Daily News*)

Gotti and lawyer-friend Bruce Cutler during happy days en route to acquittal at Manhattan assault trial.
(PHOTO: *Daily News*)

Gotti and capo Jackie D'Amico (*left*) at Madison Square Garden taking in the fights. (PHOTO: *Daily News*)

John A. (Junior) Gotti shields his father, and boss, from the elements. (PHOTO: *Daily News*)

Andrew Maloney, former West Point boxer and U.S. attorney who sent Gotti to jail for life. (PHOTO: *Daily News*)

The body of Paul Castellano outside Sparks Steak House.
(PHOTO: *Daily News*)

The death car of short-lived underboss Frank DeCicco.
(PHOTO: *Daily News*)

Carlo Vaccarrezza marches to John Gotti's tune.
(PHOTO: *Daily News*)

Brother Peter Gotti smiles and "adopted son" Lewis Kasman snarls at the camera
(PHOTO: *Daily News*)

Vincent (Chin) Gigante, crazy-like-a-fox Genovese boss and deadly enemy of John Gotti.
(PHOTO: *Daily News*)

Don Carlo Gambino, the family patriarch.
(PHOTO: *Daily News*)

Lisa Gastineau is sad that John Gotti is never getting out of jail.
(PHOTO: *Daily News*)

Tight-lipped Dapper Don before jury returns one of its verdicts. (PHOTO: *Daily News*)

A handcuffed Gotti under arrest on assault charges in 1989. (PHOTO: *Daily News*)

like Neil had, and would require each capo to report to him at least once a week.

The news astonished Bruce Mouw and his case agent, George Gabriel. The Ravenite was on a congested, narrow street in one of the city's most dense areas. Until late at night, because Little Italy and adjacent SoHo and Chinatown were all tourist centers, traffic was horrible and parking nearly nonexistent. It seemed the worst place for a bad idea: regular meetings between the boss and the capos, attendance mandatory.

Further surveillance of Gotti, however, indicated that the informants were right. In January 1988, Gotti began going to the Ravenite almost every weekday, arriving there between five and six in the evening. The S.O. squad also saw dozens of other men—many of whom they recognized but many they did not—entering and leaving the club over several days.

The men not recognized were described in the S.O. logs as "unsubs," for unidentified subjects—meaning that once they were identified, as they would inevitably be, the Ravenite meetings promised to open whole new veins of information about the breadth and depth of the Gambino family.

"Some secret society," Mouw said, when he informed Maloney. "I bet the old-timers love sittin' in traffic, just because they have to go down there and kiss his ass."

Mouw was excited because the investigative implications of Gotti's decision to make the Ravenite his headquarters were so immediately clear. He had been weighing the question of where to try and launch an eavesdropping attack on Gotti; now the choice was obvious.

This time Mouw intended to complement the eavesdropping with video surveillance of the sidewalk in front of the club. Visitors frequently loitered there, saying their good-byes and hellos, before entering or leaving the club and taking walk-talks around the block.

The video surveillance would help identify the "unsubs" and, if a case were indicted, help prosecutors establish the enterprise requirements of RICO. Defense lawyers would find it hard to argue to jurors that their clients were not members of the Gambino enterprise if they were shown on videotape hugging, kissing, and walk-talking.

The key question with the video was where to install the camera. The buildings directly across from the Raven-ite on Mulberry Street were not good options; many residents of Mulberry Street were as supportive of Gotti as they had been of Neil. Gotti had been a familiar figure on the street for nearly fifteen years; now that he was such a celebrity, many loved having him in their midst and would quickly let him know if they noticed something odd in the windows of the buildings across from the Ravenite.

Fortunately, telephoto lenses made it possible for Mouw and Gabriel to consider locations farther away, as long as they gave a view of the Ravenite entrance. After scouting locations, they settled on a high-rise apartment tower two and a half blocks north of the Ravenite—far enough out of the Little Italy milieu, but near enough for a telephoto lens.

The building was on the northeast corner of Mulberry and Houston, and one of its top-floor apartments, which was for rent, offered a view directly down Mulberry.

In February 1988, a federal judge in Brooklyn secretly authorized the squad to begin audio and video surveillance of Gotti and several others at the Ravenite after George Gabriel submitted an affidavit saying that through the informants and surveillance, the FBI had probable cause to believe that crimes were being committed there.

The "video plant" was quickly established. The next trick was getting a bug inside the Ravenite, which was on the ground floor of a plain four-story, brown-brick building.

The club, just two large rooms filled with cheap chairs and tables, had its own street-level door, but it also could be entered through a door in the hallway of the building's main entrance, which was used by tenants of the apartments on the upper floors. The tenants included the recently widowed Nettie Cirelli; her late husband, a soldier for Neil, had been the club's longtime caretaker.

When at the club, Gotti normally sat at a round table in the rear room, directly beneath two recently framed photographs—one of Neil and one of himself, a copy of the one that had appeared on the cover of the paperback edition of *Mob Star,* the book about his climb to power that had been published the year before.

It was a tight head shot, snapped when Gotti was outside a courthouse in Brooklyn and scowled into a photographer's lens, and thus now into the eyes of anyone who looked at it.

The goal was to place the Ravenite bug as close to Gotti's table as possible. Using informants' descriptions, Gabriel drew a diagram of the interior for the S.O. squad; in February 1988, S.O. agents descended on the club after Norman Dupont, its new caretaker and Nettie Cirelli's nephew, had closed for the night.

While others waited in the shadows on the street, keeping watch for passersby, two S.O. agents dressed all in black and wearing soft-soled shoes, walked into the tenants' hallway, picked the lock of the side door, and entered the club. Working quietly and feverishly, they ran wires, tapped into power sources, and installed a tiny transmitter that was never found—even though Gotti and his men were always looking for one.

By the time the agents left, agents at the "audio plant"—set up a few blocks away at the main New York office of the FBI—could turn the bug on or off from their desks.

Andy Maloney beamed when Mouw reported that the S.O. squad had placed an electronic ear in the Ravenite. "Fantastic!" he said. "The big mouth's going to talk himself right into jail!"

He agreed with Mouw that no other agency should be informed—not the state task force, or the Southern District, or the Manhattan district attorney, or NYPD. The more people who knew, the bigger the risk of a leak, deliberate or otherwise.

The optimism spawned by the successful installation of the Houston Street video camera and the Ravenite bug soon faded. The camera worked fine, but monitoring agents in the audio plant at FBI headquarters overheard only fragments of conversations and sometimes only the unintelligible noise of many men talking at once, coughing, laughing, and dragging chairs across the floor.

Gotti's arrival also always raised the decibel level in the club. It was just too many people talking too excitedly in too confined an area for the bug to capture coherent conversations. The regular hum of an electric motor in a soda machine against one wall compounded the problem.

It also became apparent that Gotti, having been burned by the Bergin bug, was being cautious. The few times it sounded as if he might be talking about something incriminating, his voice dropped to a barely audible whisper. Frequently, he exited the club and—joined by Sammy, LoCascio, or some capo—went for a walk-talk, trailed discreetly by two bodyguards.

Though frustrated by the problems with the bug, Mouw was delighted with the video. Every morning he reviewed the tape from the day before, and began compiling physical descriptions and other data on all the "unsubs" who made the required cameo appearances at the Ravenite.

"This is great," he told Gabriel. "John is introducing us to everyone in his family. We got guys coming in cars from New Jersey and Connecticut. We're gonna get to meet everybody."

Depending on whom the unsub arrived with, Mouw and Gabriel would know which of their files to pull, which informant to contact, or which law enforcement agency might be able to help. In this manner, they began identifying many previously unknown soldiers and associates in the family's twenty-three crews—as well as men from other families who occasionally dropped by.

"The secret society meeting in broad daylight!" Mouw exclaimed on another day. "The administration of the Gambino family strolling down Mulberry like tourists!"

The audiotapes were not as pleasing to review. But while they did not add up to anything on which a case could be made, they did offer occasional snippets of talk that were enough to satisfy the legal requirements for keeping the bug in place—and to open the window on Gotti's world a little further.

They showed, for instance, that he was still worried about the Sparks stories that heroin junkie Anthony Rampino might have told after his arrest. Though Roach had since decided to clam up and was in jail awaiting trial, Gotti still wanted to kill him.

"Yeah, I feel sad," he said, when someone asked if a contract on Roach was still in effect. "But that's what he gets for being dumb. He can carry away everybody."

On another day, Gotti was overheard using the words

"ice" and "hit" and "whack" while apparently discussing a series of homicides, including that of Robert DiBernardo, whose murder he had ordered from prison two years before. "You get that sort of respect with murder," was the only intact sentence to emerge from the jumble of whispered conversation.

At other times, the bug overheard fractured comments about construction jobs, waterfront shakedowns, union extortions and ghost payrolls, loan-sharking schemes and gambling percentages. Taken together, however, the comments only proved that the Ravenite was not an Elks hall.

"Gotta get a microphone on the street," Mouw told Gabriel, "or find out where they talk when they really want to talk."

In time, the squad placed a remotely operated microphone on Mulberry Street—inside an unoccupied van—but it proved ineffective and was abandoned. Meanwhile, S.O. agents also sneaked another bug into the Bergin Hunt and Fish Club.

But, in June 1988, soldiers at the Bergin found the bug installed there during the state task force's probe of Gotti; it was no longer operating but had been left behind when the state closed its investigation after Gotti's bail was revoked in the Giacalone case. The old bug's discovery prompted a furious search that turned up the newly installed FBI bug.

The discoveries at the Bergin heightened the paranoia at the Ravenite. Even whispered conversations ceased to be about anything important. And though the Ravenite bug was not found, Joe Watts installed a gadget that emitted so-called white noise that made whispers nearly impossible to decipher.

Confident that he had checkmated his enemies again, Gotti continued to waltz and prance along Mulberry Street, firmly in command of his world.

CHAPTER 15

• • • • • • • • • • • • • •

Yankee Doodle Don

When Gotti first told Sammy that he was thinking of making the Ravenite his headquarters—back before his bail was revoked in the Giacalone case—Sammy's reaction was to point out the obvious symbolism of Gotti's moving into Neil's old club. But at the time Sammy was a newly promoted caporegime, not a consigliere whose role it was to advise the boss on the soundness of decisions.

A turbulent year and a half later, the Ravenite move seemed very unsound, and Sammy advised Gotti that it was a mistake—and certainly a mistake to require the capos to meet him there at least once a week. It was too much visibility in a highly visible place. But Gotti did not agree, and he also did not agree when the aftermath of one of many new dramas in 1988 prompted Sammy to urge him to keep a lower public profile.

Gotti's refusal to take advice would not shake Sammy's confidence. Gotti had marched well to his own drummer several times before—in the Paul situation, for example, and with Chin. Sammy's concerns also would not diminish Gotti's faith in Sammy—in his ability to make money and make murder go smoothly.

Sammy first argued against the Ravenite plan at a meeting with Gotti and acting underboss Frank LoCascio at Taormina's in Little Italy, just down Mulberry from the Ravenite. It was owned by Joseph Corrao, known as Joe Butch, who had fallen into step with Gotti after Sparks; Gene Gotti, among others, had even urged his brother to make Joe Butch, not LoCascio, acting underboss.

"I know the idea of being in Neil's club feels good,

John, but we maybe oughta be more undercover," Sammy said.

"I've gone down there fifteen years! What's the big deal?"

"You're the boss now. You gotta be more careful."

"I could stay in bed like the Chin, and they'll still come after me!"

"Maybe, but what I was thinking, you could put Frankie in charge of the Bronx, let everybody up there answer to him. You and Genie stay out in Queens. Joe Butch will stay in Manhattan. I'll stay in Brooklyn. We'll get together when we gotta, in the middle of the night when the fuckin' agents are sleeping, in a graveyard or someplace."

"We don't have to run and hide! What're we afraid of? It ain't a crime to meet and get together. We're Italians. That's the way the Italian people are."

"The old-timers used to hide and sneak and stay in the neighborhoods," Sammy reminded Gotti. "Nobody who wasn't supposed to knew Toddo Aurello."

"Toddo was that way. But look at Neil, he was here on this street all his life. I'm not gonna be a back-door boss. It's better this way. Everybody sees the boss and the boss sees them. Keeps everybody happy."

"Times are different."

"I ain't Chin, and I ain't Paul, hidin' out in my house."

Sammy let it go. Gotti was obviously adamant. And soon after the Ravenite meetings began early in 1988, he also showed he was not inclined to stomach much complaining about the mandatory-attendance requirement.

Thomas DeBrizzi, a sixty-four-year-old soldier, was one of many who squawked about the illogic and inconvenience of weekly trips to the Ravenite. He ran a loan-sharking and gambling operation in Connecticut for Tommy Gambino, who in keeping with his country-squire image, controlled operations in the Nutmeg State—though it mattered nothing to him how much his crew made.

Unlike Tommy, DeBrizzi lived in Connecticut, which was two hours by car to Little Italy. He barely knew Gotti, and he had been in prison during Sparks—so he made the mistake of squawking too much, in the presence

of his capo, about the Ravenite meetings. Tommy told
Gotti about it, and it was all Gotti needed to hear.

DeBrizzi was found dead in his car's trunk at a shopping mall on February 5, 1988—shot by men in his own
crew anxious to know Gotti better. "A guy don't want to
come in, he's gone, that's all," Gotti told Sammy.

Gene Gotti also thought the Ravenite meetings were a
bad idea, and not just because his bail conditions in the
heroin case, which would go to trial a second time in
the spring of 1988, required him to stay away from other
criminals. It meant he was flirting with trouble each time
he, as the new caporegime of the Bergin crew, went to the
Ravenite.

"Why don't we just draw the fuckin' feds a picture?"
he complained to Sammy.

Gene thought the Ravenite policy was proof that
brother John's ego was over the top. But Gene, an outspoken type with anyone else, was tired of trying to get
a word in edgewise with him.

"That's your job, Sammy, you're the consigliere. He'd
never listen to me. He'd think I was jealous, but John, he
just wants to be the center of attention all the time."

"He loves bein' boss, that's for sure. You know how
Paul made people come to him in small groups. John
seems to like it when an audience comes."

"It's more than that. This guy, you oughta seen him
when his name started gettin' in the papers. Fuckin' loved
it. And when his face was on the tube? Forget about it. It
was like he was gettin' off for free."

Sammy had begun to see how such ego could cause
problems, but it was too late and too futile to worry about
it now. Recently, he and Gotti had been in a restaurant,
and Gotti had noticed that a young couple at the bar kept
staring in their direction.

"Look at the guy and the girl over there, lookin' at us,"
Gotti said solemnly. "They love me."

Sammy cringed, then realized that Gotti was serious. It
was easy to imagine that someone who'd been called
Robin Hood and a folk hero of "the little people" might
believe strangers admired him, but to hear him say they
loved him was so startling Sammy didn't know what to
say.

"They do. They love me. They can't stop lookin' over here."

"You're fuckin' nuts," Sammy smiled, then tried to change the subject. What he saw in the couple's stares was curiosity, maybe awe, but not love.

"I'm tellin' ya, they love me," Gotti protested, lifting a second martini, Boodles very dry.

Promotion to consigliere cemented Sammy's importance in the family, which had been obvious since Gotti named him an acting street boss and ordered him to tie in with the decinas while Gotti was in the MCC. Still, the title conferred a higher level of status on the onetime cupcake bandit of Bensonhurst.

What was especially sweet to Sammy was that the job almost always went to older men, such as Joe N. Gallo—men deemed wise and lawyerly, whose opinions were informed by long duty in the trenches. For many years, he had felt he was without peer in the trenches; but now it was more satisfying to contemplate that he, at age forty-three, was a member of the Gambino administration.

Though responsible now, with Gotti and Frank LoCascio, for responding to whatever conflicts arose in all crews, he stayed close to his roots. At Sammy's behest, Gotti had appointed one of Sammy's loyalists, Louis Vallario, to replace him as capo, but the former capo never gave up control. He was still in his moneymaking years, and he needed his Bensonhurst brigade.

Early in 1988, a drama that arose from Gotti's decision to name Louis Vallario as Sammy's successor demonstrated how close Sammy intended to stay to his crew and how important his moneymaking years were to him.

Of all people, Louis Milito should have known that. He was one of Sammy's early buddies in Bensonhurst, and he knew how Sammy responded when a crew member strayed out of line. He also was alongside in two of Sammy's early murders on behalf of Paul, who gave Milito his button based on Sammy's recommendation.

Milito also should have known that the ground beneath him was shaky enough without his loosening it more by complaining that he, not Vallario, should have replaced Sammy. Two years earlier, Milito had been exiled to a low profile on Staten Island—after Sammy and DeCicco learned he had guessed wrong about the future and begun a loan-shark book with Bilotti, which would not have been such a betrayal if he had not done it secretly.

Milito had spent the time since Sparks helping another of Sammy's men to control the fortunes of a large steel-erection company, which had to pay them and Sammy bribes if it wanted jobs free of union problems. Between that and his shylocking, Milito was doing well for someone in supposed exile.

The endgame began when Milito began venturing off Staten Island into Brooklyn, and into Tali's—Sammy's bar, restaurant, and clubhouse—when Sammy wasn't there, to express amazement that Vallario was now captain of the Aurello-Gravano crew.

Sammy heard of the noise Milito was making in about the time it takes to cross the Verrazano Narrows Bridge linking the boroughs, and he might have let it slide if Milito hadn't also begun doubting the quality of the new Gambino administration.

"He's bad-mouthin' me, he's bad-mouthin' you, he's bad-mouthin' Frankie, and I can't believe the guy, but he's bad-mouthing John too," Vallario reported to Sammy.

Beyond the obvious danger of such indiscretion, Milito also failed to appreciate what little consideration that he, a secret loan-sharking partner of Bilotti's, would get when Sammy reported to Gotti that Milito was mouthing off.

"We gave him a chance to stay on Staten Island, but he just can't live with it," Sammy reported to Gotti during a walk-talk at the Ravenite—as they unknowingly filled the frame of the recently installed Gambino squad camera on Houston Street.

"Do what you want," Gotti replied. "Get rid of 'im. Just talk to my brother Genie about it, and use Genie's people."

Milito's final miscalculation was believing Vallario, and that he was being restored to Sammy's good graces when Vallario telephoned a few days later and said Sammy wanted him to help "on a piece of work" at Vallario's clubhouse in Brooklyn.

When Milito arrived, Sammy, Gene Gotti, and one of Gene's lesser codefendants in the heroin case, Arnold

Squiteri, were sitting at a table, playing cards. Vallario was standing behind a counter, pretending to mix drinks; John Carneglia was relaxing on a couch, pretending an absence of malice.

Milito, Sammy's Victim No. 14, took a seat at the counter. Carneglia then walked into an adjoining room and came back out with a .38 silencer-equipped weapon hidden in his waistband. He put one shot into the back of Milito's head and then, after Milito slumped dying to the floor, one under his chin.

While Sammy, Gene, and Vallario cleaned up, Squiteri and Carneglia put the body, which was never found, into a car and drove off. They came back in a hour and all went to Tali's.

It was a Tuesday night, shape-up night for Sammy's crew; he had noticed lately that an agent, or a cop, was always around on Tuesday nights, conducting surveillance from a car parked up the block; now it appeared that whoever it was, was doing it again.

"It's good to let the fuckin' agents see us," Gene said, after Sammy mentioned it. "It'll be right there in the fuckin' government reports. How can we be in a hit if we're at Tali's?"

Gene didn't see the whole picture, however. The government man conducting surveillance that night outside Tali's was Kenny McCabe, an ex-detective who was now an investigator for the U.S. attorney in the Southern District. McCabe, who had spent nearly his entire career investigating gangsters, knew more about the Gambino family than Gene imagined.

He knew, for instance, that Gene Gotti had never been seen at Tali's in any other government surveillance. Seeing him there now, McCabe wrote in a report that something highly unusual must have occurred in the Gambino family on Tuesday, March 8, 1988.

Milito's murder required another demonstration of Sammy's ability to deceive grieving relatives; he had known Milito's wife and children for many years, and when they contacted him two days after Milito failed to come home, he professed ignorance while expressing sympathy.

"I haven't spoken to him," he told Milito's daughter Deena, a recent graduate of Hofstra University, after she said her dad—who telephoned her every morning while she was at college—had not kept a planned dinner date.

"He told me something came up and he couldn't make it, and I haven't heard from him since," she said.

"I'll search around," Sammy said. "Just give me a little time and I'll try to get in touch with him."

Sammy was even more comforting when after a few more days, Milito's wife, Linda, began to accept that the everyday peril of her husband's chosen life had claimed him. "I don't know what we'll do," she said. "Our house is all torn up because he was remodeling and now we have no money to pay the contractor."

"Whatever your needs, I'll take care of them."

Over the next few months, Sammy sent men from his construction companies to finish the remodeling of the Milito home. He also gave the survivors several thousand in cash, but it was only a pittance compared with the money he began making in the steel-erection business and—as he set about taking advantage of his consigliere status—other businesses.

Before Milito's murder, Sammy had pocketed a few thousand a month from the bribes that Milito and another soldier received for steering business to Atlas Gem Steel and keeping it free of union problems. Afterward, however, he formed a new company, S&G Construction, and sold the same services to Atlas Gem Steel in the form of a seemingly aboveboard consultancy contract that its owners were encouraged to buy.

Within weeks, he was pocketing seven thousand a week plus 3 percent of the value of each new job; within a year, he would pocket nearly a million dollars—a situation that would make it difficult for Sammy to deny to Gotti someday that the murder of Milito wasn't about more than bad-mouthing.

Unlike 1982, when he killed cocaine playboy Frank Fiala and banked most of the would-be gangster's $750,000 down payment on the Plaza Suite disco, he paid taxes on this windfall. With lawyer Jerry Shargel in his corner, he had wiggled free of the Fiala tax charges, but he assumed that now his IRS returns were automatically flagged.

Sammy loved thinking of himself as a millionaire, and he could only smile when his wife, Debra, scored big in

1988 too; after years of trying, she and her father picked the winning numbers in the state lottery and won $800,000.

"You always called me a sucker for playing the lottery," Debra said when she told Sammy the news. "Well, say hello to the sucker."

The Gravanos lived well but not extravagantly. They put a lot of money into remodeling their Staten Island home; with its Jacuzzi, marble floors, and expensive furnishings, it was more impressive on the inside than the outside. They also bought horses to go with the New Jersey farm they'd purchased after the Fiala murder, but they did not spend lavishly on personal items.

As he prospered, Sammy put a couple of extra thousand dollars into the five-to-ten-thousand-dollar tributes he routinely gave Gotti, but he plowed most of his money into his loan-shark book, which was worth over a million dollars already. At the outset he provided Gotti a paper accounting of his monthly income—to show that the amounts he was giving to Gotti were generous.

"I don't want to see paper no more," Gotti said after a while. "Paper makes me nervous."

Gotti was getting enough money that he didn't have to worry about the dimensions of Sammy's generosity. All told, he received about a hundred thousand a month from Sammy, the capos, and the deal Sammy set up for him with Louis DiBono's drywall firm. For Christmas, for his birthday, and sometimes just to demonstrate their loyalty, everyone was always enriching the pot.

But unlike rainy-day-minded Sammy, Gotti spent and gambled extravagantly. Unlike Sammy, he also was not filing any income tax returns, having decided to rely on some dubious advice from a half-baked tax lawyer that he did not have to—as long as he sent in a tax payment now and then.

By the spring of 1988, Sammy was the power behind the throne. As consigliere, he attended any meeting involving relations with another family. He was its main man in construction and unions. He was still its undisputed top gun too, the one Gotti relied on most when a piece of work was required.

One was deemed required in May, after John Gambino, a capo and distant relative of Carlo and Tommy came to

Gotti seeking revenge against a man who had killed a soldier in his crew during a fistfight in an apartment building hallway. The soldier died after one punch sent his head against a concrete wall.

The man who delivered the punch, Francesco Oliveri, was a downstairs neighbor who worked in a pasta factory and did not know what an avenging nest he had disturbed. The two men had feuded over petty issues involving their apartment building, cars, and parking spaces on their Queens street.

John Gambino had become one of Gotti's favorite capos—and he was yet another example of Gotti's hypocrisy about drugs. In the two and a half years since Sparks, Gambino had made a fortune dealing heroin. He had spent many years living in Sicily and was one of the family's main links to the old country—the transshipment source of his heroin supply.

Under Mafia rules in Sicily, Gambino could have taken his revenge without checking with Gotti, but in the U.S. even a revenge killing is supposed to be approved by the boss. (That was part of the reason why Gotti demoted Angelo when Angelo tried to kill Luchese underboss Anthony Casso without permission.)

Gambino didn't just ask for permission, he asked Gotti to help him carry it out. Gotti agreed, then left all details but one to Sammy: he wanted a soldier in a New Jersey crew that he was thinking of promoting, Robert Bisaccia, to do the shooting.

"You handle it, you supervise it, but let's see what Bobby can do," were Gotti's marching orders for Sammy's Victim No. 15. "He acts like he's got the *cajones;* let's see how big they are."

On May 2, 1988, agents at the Houston Street video plant saw Sammy, Gambino, and Bisaccia enter the Ravenite. As usual, however, agents in the audio plant at FBI headquarters did not detect any meaningful conversation among the three, and so the Gambino squad would have no reason to give Oliveri what Gotti had gotten a year before—a warning.

Bobby Bisaccia showed what he could do early the next day. While Sammy and three others waited in stolen cars parked on opposite sides of Oliveri's building,

Bisaccia shot Oliveri dead as the fifty-seven-year-old father of three started his car.

Bisaccia was back in one of the stolen cars and off the block before the first screams of neighbors pierced the chill spring air in the Queens neighborhood of Astoria. He, Sammy, and the others then ditched the stolen cars, switched to another vehicle parked a few blocks away, and sped safely off.

While now a fixture in Little Italy, Gotti also kept a high profile in Ozone Park. He usually held forth at the Bergin for a couple of hours each day before heading into Manhattan. The club and the community were important to him, a creature of habit.

As had been his habit for many years, he still sponsored the community's Fourth of July celebration. Because of his higher-than-ever profile, the festivities in 1988 drew many reporters and led to many headlines that made municipal officials look bad. The problem was that Gotti did not bother to get a permit to shoot off fireworks—the high point of the celebration—and the police did not make good on a promise to prevent him from doing so.

"We want the 'works!" a crowd of about two thousand people milling on the street outside the Bergin began chanting after the sun went down that day. "We want the 'works!"

The crowd became more excited when Gotti, dressed all in white, appeared in the Bergin doorway, smiling and waving like a movie star on Oscar night. The celebration had been under way since noon; he had provided two thousand pounds of food and hundreds of cases of soda; his men had erected carnival rides and strung patriotic bunting along 101st Avenue.

"This is just something we do for the neighborhood," Gotti had said during an earlier public bow coinciding with the arrival of television cameras.

In past years the party had always ended with a fireworks display, but this year the NYPD had announced it would enforce a law requiring fireworks' sponsors to get a city permit by which the sponsor agreed to observe various safety rules. The department appeared to mean business too, because earlier in the day, cops had come by and ordered the removal of two dumpsters from which Gotti's men planned to launch the fireworks.

The actual fireworks, however, remained inside the Bergin, and now the crowd was urging Gotti to defy the police.

Several dozen officers were on the street a block south of the club; one block north, several more sat in squad cars. But the police had badly estimated the size of the crowd that now formed between the cops on foot and the cops in cars.

"We want the 'works! We want the 'works!"

Moments after Gotti ducked into the Bergin, someone lit a bonfire in the street, around which the chanting crowd gathered. Gotti's weight-lifter son Junior then exited the Bergin, lugging a crate of fireworks. The youthful trucking-company president was followed by several other muscular young men; to the roar of the crowd, each began tossing cherry bombs into the fire. Some other confederates placed a row of metal canisters by the fire and began launching larger rockets and starbursts.

The crowd became more boisterous. It was mainly a crowd of teenagers—boys in tank tops and girls with pink lips and heavy eyeliner—but in the estimation of the police captain in charge they had been drinking something other than soda all day and seemed drunk enough to be both stupid and dangerous.

He ordered his men to stay put, as the fireworks burst over Ozone Park. Two fire trucks also arrived, but the firefighters wanted no part of a possible riot either and they soon left.

Gotti appeared again in the Bergin doorway and chuckled munificently at the frenzy before him. It took two hours to detonate the fireworks. The police made no arrests and issued no summonses, prompting the eldest Gotti brother, Peter, who had just gotten his button, to a satisfied taunt that the media made themselves look foolish: "All the police did was make themselves look foolish."

The remark was difficult to refute; the next day, official New York did not even attempt to remove the egg on its face. The fire commissioner, responsible for licensing, passed the buck to the police commissioner, responsible for enforcement, who would not even answer questions about why the cops failed to take action.

Editorial-page writers had a field day. In the *Daily News,* one opined that while it was unfortunate that so many in Ozone Park apparently admired that "All-American Yankee Doodle Dandy Don, John Gotti," what was worst was the police standing around like helpless children. "That's a pretty dangerous image to risk adopting. Even worse is the image it promotes: That the masters of organized crime are above the law, sneering as they put the city's law enforcement establishment where they believe it belongs—in paralysis and humiliation."

Meanwhile, on Staten Island, Sammy Gravano had hosted his first and last Fourth of July party. A barbecue for neighbors ballooned so out of hand that fifteen hundred people showed up, including—to Sammy's horror—a *Staten Island Advance* reporter.

"I ain't never doin' that again," he told Gotti. "You can't control it when you give away food and booze. I had to send out for more stuff. Everybody brought ten freeloaders."

As the flap over Gotti's party played out in the media, and though he was sure his words would fall on deaf ears, Sammy the consigliere felt compelled to advise Gotti to stay out of the news, especially when it made the authorities look bad.

"It don't help us if they think you're rubbin' our noses in their face," he said.

"I love ya, Sammy, but you fuckin' worry too much. I think this kind of stuff is good for us. It's good for our image."

"I'd slow it down a bit. Go a little more low profile."

"Next year, maybe we'll get the permit. Make the cops feel good. Make you feel good too!"

Unintentionally, the *Daily News* editorial conveyed an image and message that suited Gotti just fine. He was a Mafia boss, of course, but an "All-American Yankee Doodle" one—a "master" of organized crime, which was a fact of life, so a nice patriotic rogue like him might as well be in charge.

Many people in New York's neighborhoods embraced the image and the message—instinctively in many cases, but also in others because of the easy ride he so far had gotten in the media. But even people who thought he was bad for the public good thought he was something special.

The law's victories against Joe Piney, Joe N. Gallo, Roach Rampino, Mark Reiter, and other Gambino figures had gotten scant notice next to the remarkable run of dropped charges, mistrials, and acquittals involving John, Gene, and Junior Gotti—not to mention John's close friends Angelo and Carneglia.

Only a few days after the Fourth of July celebration, the image and the message got another big boost; for a second time, a mistrial was declared in the heroin case, which had quietly gone to trial again beneath the arc of the big story of the day, John Joseph Gotti Jr., the now so-called Teflon Don.

The mistrial was declared a couple of days after jurors sent a message to U.S. district court judge Joseph McLaughlin that they were hopelessly deadlocked— "hopelessly" being a suspicious sign to Andy Maloney and the trial prosecutor, Robert LaRusso. The judge ordered the jury to keep deliberating, but for naught.

This time, unlike the first heroin trial, it was too late for Maloney, John Gleeson, and the FBI to mount an investigation into whether the case was being fixed—a situation that they all now rued, given a clue that had emerged during the deliberations.

A juror was excused after federal marshals found cocaine hidden in a jogging outfit his girlfriend brought him to wear during deliberations. If a juror's girlfriend felt free to bring cocaine into the case, what else was going on?

Maloney came to believe that something else was going on when after deliberations resumed two jurors told Judge McLaughlin they suspected that FBI agents had tampered with the tape-recorded evidence.

"Too incredible to believe," Maloney told trial prosecutor LaRusso. "Somehow, they got to these people too."

Still, defense attorneys had planted the idea by showing that the FBI-prepared transcripts of tapes—including some of poor audio quality—had changed during the investigation as agents inserted words that became clearer through repeated listening. It happens all the time in eavesdropping cases, but the defense lawyers succeeded in taking the eyes of some jurors off the ball of evidence available on other tapes.

The lawyer who showed particular artistry, while defending John Carneglia, was the bearded wonder, Jerry Shargel, Sammy's savior in the Fiala tax case. He got into the Cosa Nostra game through Michael Coiro, an old friend and Gotti's former lawyer; Coiro was an original defendant in the heroin case, for helping Angelo hide his brother Salvatore's assets, but he was now set to go to trial separately—with Shargel as his lawyer.

"With Jerry, no matter how bad it looks, you always got a shot," Sammy had told Carneglia.

The mistrial provoked another significant event. Judge McLaughlin decided that it was no longer fair to keep former caporegime Angelo Ruggiero in jail without bail.

Angelo had been stewing and boiling at the MCC for twenty-five months while his main codefendants, Gene and Carneglia, remained free—free, as it happened, to murder Louie Milito.

At a hearing on the matter, Angelo's lawyer said his client was a good bail risk because he was a good father who cared for not only his own six children but two of his late brother Salvatore's as well.

LaRusso tried to persuade the judge that Angelo, who did not make any menacing gestures this time—was a poor bail risk. "He's got the greatest motive to flee with the evidence we have on him. If this defendant is released, he probably will not return—he will not return."

The statement would prove prophetic, but not in the way LaRusso intended. Free at last, Angelo fell ill before he had much chance to contemplate getting "in the wind" or working his way back into the good graces of the friend whose coattails he had grabbed onto long ago.

First came the diabetes and heart troubles that prompted a doctor's warning to stop smoking. Then, after he switched from Marlboros to a recessed-filter brand, came emphysema.

Depressed by his illnesses and the pressure of his legal woes—in addition to the heroin case, he was facing a separate trial in the hierarchy case, which had proceeded without him—Angelo actually obeyed the terms of his bail, which required pro forma contacts with court officials five times a week. He spent his days hanging around

his suburban house on Long Island, the one in middle-
class Cedarhurst that he'd remodeled with heroin cash
even as Gambino squad bugs documented the progress.

He was forbidden to contact anyone in the Gambino
family, but it depressed him further that his old Fulton-
Rockaway pal, Johnny Boy, never attempted a secret visit
or even sent a clandestine message.

Instead, several times over the next several months,
Gotti told Sammy that rather than take pity on Angelo, he
should kill him. Angelo's back-door plotting against the
Luchese underboss while in prison had almost caused a
war.

"He's caused us so much fuckin' trouble, and not just
us," Gotti said. "He don't deserve any passes."

Sammy marveled at the change of heart; the trouble
Angelo caused was once part of the motive for killing
Paul, and partly the reason that Gotti was now boss. What
was overlooked then couldn't be overlooked now? Then
there were the personal ties; Angelo was Gotti's oldest
friend, and his eldest son's godfather.

Each time Gotti worked up a murderous lather about
Angelo, Sammy and Frank LoCascio pointed out that
Angelo's health made the point moot. So did Gene, who
also went back to Brownsville with Angelo and could
blame him for at least part of his own troubles.

Finally, Angelo's doctors delivered the last bit of bad
news—lung cancer—and said he probably did not have
long to live. Still, Gotti did not visit or send a message,
and Gene grew particularly perturbed about it.

Gene was already perturbed at his brother because John
was still insisting that he stand trial rather than plead
guilty in the heroin case. The order deprived Gene of a
big sentence break on charges he felt he wasn't going to
beat—unless, somehow, he duplicated John's feat and
fixed a jury without the government knowing about it,
something he was desperately trying to do, but so far unsuccessfully.

"I told him the other day," Gene told Sammy. "I said,
'The guy Angelo is brokenhearted. He don't understand
why you're so hot still. This guy would've jumped in
front of a car for you. Ain't it time to let your beef go?' "

But Gene said his brother merely shrugged and asked
about the next order of business. The indifference amazed

even the stone-hearted Sammy. It seemed so utterly pointless. John Gotti would lose nothing by bestowing a little
absolution—insincere as it would be—upon a dying old
friend.

Gotti was not about absolution, as Sammy well knew.
In the two and a half years since he aligned with Gotti,
Sammy had murdered more than in all his twenty previ-
ous years in crime. But as always, victims were blank
slates, and murder was problem-solving. And now he was
Gotti's top problem-solver.

Once again, Gotti left it to Sammy to handle the details
when he decided that it was finally time to end the game
he was playing with one of his oldest associates, Willie
Boy Johnson, and make him pay for betraying him to the
FBI for all those years.

The game had begun three years earlier, when Willie
Boy was exposed as an informer and Gotti promised he
would be forgiven so long as he didn't take the stand
against him in the case.

Willie Boy kept his end of the bargain. Then, after the
trial, Gotti banned him from the Bergin but told him to go
on with his life without fear: "I'm gonna give you a pass
and I give you my word no one will bother you."

Willie Boy had never really believed Gotti, but he
wanted to, enough to deceive himself and his wife that
somehow his refusal to testify had washed the slate clean
and that he need not run and hide. He had never lived
anywhere but New York and did not want to force his
wife, to whom he was devoted, to leave the beautiful
home he had provided for her in one of Brooklyn's better
neighborhoods and join him in a life on the run.

He was caught between fear and hope, hate and love;
the son of a high-steel worker was still on his own high
wire, one false step from death, just like when he was
Source Wahoo.

In the minds of Willie Boy's former associates, it was
only a matter of time before he would be made to pay.
The FBI records turned over to Gotti's lawyers in the
Giacalone case showed that Willie Boy was the one who
led the police to Gotti when Gotti was on the lam in the
early 1970s. They showed that it was Willie Boy's information that helped the Gambino squad build a heroin-
dealing case against Angelo, Gene, and the rest.

It was what Willie Boy had not told the FBI that gave him a period of grace. "The rat will pay," Gotti had told Sammy after the Giacalone case. "But we'll let 'im get comfortable first. We can't make any mistakes. There's a lot he didn't talk about. He didn't talk about killin's he knows about."

The grace period ended on August 29, 1988, after Gotti got a message from Sammy's friends in the Colombo family, which was where Sammy had served his apprenticeship. Willie Boy had given information about Colombo men as well, and Alphonse Persico, son of the imprisoned boss, thought it time to lower the boom.

"What're you waitin' for?" an emissary from Persico said to Sammy. "This guy hurt a lot of people."

Sammy entrusted the murder of his Victim No. 16 to one of Gotti's nightlife crew, Eddie Lino, an ex-Bonanno associate who became a Gambino soldier after Sparks. Lino, also free on bail in the heroin case, sublet the contract to a cousin in the Bonanno family, which also had suffered Willie Boy's sting.

The cousin gave the actual work to three Bonanno gunmen, who caught Willie Boy at just past six o'clock in the morning, outside his home, as he left for the legitimate construction job he had taken.

The first shots took him to his knees; six more tore open the back of his head. The killers were gone before his wife ran out and cradled his body in her arms.

Later in the day, lawyer Richard Rehbock, who represented Willie Boy in the Giacalone case, commented on the murder for reporters, none of whom noted that Rehbock had gone on to win an assault case for Gotti's son Junior and that he was really in the Gotti camp more than the Willie Boy camp.

"He never expressed any fear [of Gotti]," Rehbock said of Willie Boy. "The only enemy that this man had in the world was the government."

CHAPTER 16

•••••••••••••

Brain Surgeons

The Gambino squad agents who traded turns monitoring the Ravenite bug in their audio plant at nearby FBI headquarters in lower Manhattan never overhead a whisper about Angelo Ruggiero or Willie Boy Johnson—from Gotti's lips or anyone else's. The discovery in June 1988 of two bugs at the Bergin—an old one left behind by the state task force, a new one freshly planted by the S.O. squad—made the Ravenite's visitors doubly conscious of laying an incriminating track on FBI audiotape.

On occasion, in some excited moment, a soldier or captain paying his mandatory respects to Gotti would speak loudly and distinctly enough to rise above the drone of the motor in the club's soda machine and the static of Joe Watts's white-noise machine.

But these words would amount to nothing—and eventually to demoralizing defeat for the get-Gotti offensive, which needed incriminating words to legally justify continued eavesdropping.

On the other hand, the FBI camera in the high-rise apartment two and a half blocks north of the Ravenite on Houston Street continued to record high-quality footage of anyone who entered and exited Gotti headquarters or went on a furtive walk-talk with him or Sammy Gravano or Frank LoCascio.

By the summer of 1988, the camera had helped the Gambino squad identify dozens of previously unknown gangsters. These included Bosko Radonjich, boss of the Manhattan gang known as the Westies—the name an NYPD detective had given to a group of extortionists and murderers on Manhattan's West Side that he had investigated almost a decade before.

One of Detective Joseph Coffey's findings was that the West Siders were actually a kind of farm team for the Gambino family, because of the two gangs' historical mutual interest in rackets on the Hudson River docks and at unionized West Side exhibition halls and sports-and-entertainment complexes such as the Jacob Javits Center and Madison Square Garden.

The alliance of gangs was unique—and later corroborated by many informants—because the West Siders were composed mainly of criminals of Irish descent. Historically, the city's Irish and Italian crooks had never gotten along; as the two biggest groups in New York's early immigrant universe, Irish and Italian people had engaged in fierce competition for jobs, respect, and power.

The businessman Paul Castellano was the first Mafia boss to strike a deal with the so-called Westies, a small army next to the Gambino family. To avoid conflict, Paul granted the Westies corruption rights in its backyard, so long as it gave him 10 percent of everything it earned, and 50 percent of joint schemes.

At the time, Paul assigned a future cross to bear, Roy DeMeo, to oversee it. After DeMeo was murdered because he led Paul into a RICO case, Danny Marino assumed the Westies watch; because Gotti had no idea that Marino was a closet ally of Chin, Marino remained in charge after Gotti took over.

Shortly after becoming boss, Gotti employed the Westies to deliver a harsh warning to a carpenters union official thought to have ordered the trashing of a Gambino-connected restaurant built with nonunion labor. The official, who was shot in the legs and buttocks, wasn't killed because he had taken bribes in the past and Gotti wanted to make sure someone corrupt remained in charge of the union.

During their investigation of the Bergin, state task force agents overheard a fractured conversation in which Gotti seemed to be ordering the attack on the official—but so far they had not found enough corroborating evidence to persuade a prosecutor to ask a grand jury to indict.

Although he used the Westies on that mission, Gotti didn't think much of the mainly Irish gang—until Bosko Radonjich, who wasn't Irish, became the boss and brought a gift to Gotti just in time for the Giacalone case: George Pape.

Radonjich was a Yugoslavian immigrant and contractor who filled a vacuum created when the Westies' leadership went to prison after a RICO case mounted by the NYPD, the FBI, the Manhattan district attorney and the Southern District.

Radonjich's appearance at the Ravenite would have made the bug's failures more frustrating if the Gambino squad had known he was involved in a plot to fix the Giacalone case and that he was at the Ravenite to tell Gotti that Pape—who got sixty thousand for taking a dive—had asked him to ask for Gotti's help in finding a job.

"I told Bosko it's crazy for me to get involved in that," Gotti later told Sammy. "He's gotta handle it. Sixty balloons ain't enough? I gotta get in bed with the guy too?"

"*Minchia,* fuckin' unbelievable."

"Dumb fuckin' potato head, or whatever the fuck he is."

Videotaping and identifying Radonjich was one of the small but regular achievements that made agents assigned to the audio and video plants feel like they were making progress, if only one little brick at a time.

The agents monitoring the plants worked when the gangsters met: normally Monday through Friday, from four or five in the afternoon until eight or nine in the evening, when the last of the gangsters—usually including Gotti—left the Ravenite for dinner, the nightclubs, or a card game at some social club.

Usually only two agents were required in each plant, one to operate the equipment, the other to maintain a log of who was being videotaped and recorded at what time on what day. Although other Gambino squad agents were rotated in to acquaint them with the faces and voices behind the names, two teams of agents spent the most time in the plants—young agents Mark Roberts and Greg Hagarty and veteran agents Frank Spero and Matty Tricorico.

The two teams took turns in each plant, which Bruce Mouw and George Gabriel also visited on occasion. In some cities, the sight of many different males entering and leaving the apartment where the video plant was lo-

cated might have caused indignation or alarm among the
building's managers and residents.

"This is New York," Mouw said one day, after Mark
Roberts said that the building doorman probably thought
the apartment was a clubhouse for a secret group of ho-
mosexual businessmen. "As long as you just go in like
you know where you're going, nobody's going to say
anything."

Roberts and the other agents followed Mouw's advice
and also made sure, now and then, to tip the doorman—
who never did more than think he knew what was going
on.

The anonymity of life typical of New York's big apartment complexes also assured that neighbors who lived in
apartments on the same floor never figured out what was
up either—or even bothered, after a friendly rebuff or
two, to try.

"Hi!" one of the neighbors said after knocking on the
FBI door one day. "I just moved in, I'm having a little
party, why don't you stop by and get to know people in
the building?"

"Thanks a lot," said Roberts, an earnest-looking agent
from the suburbs of Pittsburgh. "I really appreciate that,
but me and my roommate, we're just going to be here for
a little while and we're really busy. I'm going back to law
school."

Door-to-door solicitors who managed to slip past the
lobby-based doorman to work the hallways of the building were given a blunt send-off.

"Get outta here before I call the cops!" Roberts or one
of the other agents would yell, engulfed in a haze of cigar
smoke. Smoking cigars—which seemed vaguely appropriate to the work at hand—was part of the daily ritual at
the plant.

From their smoky perch, the video agents became acquainted with some of the trivial codes of conduct in the
Gambino family. They watched as Joseph Giordano, a
soldier who was a nephew of the imprisoned Joe Piney,
asserted his rank over an associate like Norman Dupont,
the Ravenite caretaker and nephew of the widow who
lived above the club, Nettie Cirelli.

Giordano usually brought several pizza pies when he
came to the Ravenite—but he always left them in his car

so that Dupont would have to come out and carry them back inside.

Familiarity bred contempt. Reviewing the tapes in his office, Bruce Mouw would marvel at the cast of gangsters who stood for hours outside the club, talking, kissing, embracing, jabbing fingers, smoking cigarettes, picking noses—fat ones, skinny ones, tall ones, and ones with ridiculous nicknames like Skinny Dom, Iggy, and Handsome Jack—all seeming so cartoonish and unimposing when caught in the camera's objective eye.

"What the hell could these guys be talking about?" Mouw wondered to Gabriel one day. "These brain surgeons? What do they talk about? The Yankees? Getting laid? Dinner?"

"The weather, I'd say," Gabriel said.

The occasional antics of the gangster brain surgeons at least gave the video agents a bit of comic relief from the tedious routine of fixed-location surveillance.

One night, the agents watched as several men accompanied a man in a wheelchair out of the club. The man in the chair had been previously identified as an ex-fireman and friend of acting underboss Frank LoCascio, who allowed him to come to the club to play cards. Outside, the men confronted a predicament; it was raining, and their disabled friend's car was down the block.

As the man gestured at the sky and pointed down the street, Mark Roberts said to fellow video agent Greg Hagarty, "Why don't they just get an umbrella?"

"Or have somebody bring the car up?" Hagarty replied.

Instead, one of the men went inside the club and came out with what looked like a black garbage bag. Another man cut holes in it and placed it over the disabled ex-fireman's head, and two more started pushing him quickly down the street toward his car.

If Roberts and Hagarty had not seen it with their own eyes, they would not have believed it. Roberts told Mouw, "And these guys call themselves wise guys!"

Another comic moment came late in the afternoon each day, when a man dressed like Robin Hood on some days and Tinkerbell on others, pranced effeminately up and down Mulberry Street, cadging change and attention.

"The Prince of Mulberry Street," as the agents called him, appeared from out of the camera's point of view and disappeared the same way, but his arrival always meant it was five o'clock.

The agents believed he lived nearby because he observed the same rule as other people who lived and worked near the club—he never paused on the sidewalk in front to cast a curious glance through the door, which was frequently open in warm weather.

The locals respected the club's privacy; only if they had been summoned to perform some errand—such as checking out the occupants of suspicious vehicles parked on the street—did they speak to the men outside. Sometimes tourists dared to dawdle while passing by, but a hard glance always speeded them along.

Except for Gotti's manicurist, women rarely went into the club—at least not during normal hours of operations. Norman Dupont exercised some of his associate's rank on neighborhood ladies by sneaking them in in the middle of the night.

During regular hours, LoCascio was usually the first member of the administration to arrive—when the club was quiet and the bug had the best chance of overhearing anything meaningful that might be said. But the gloomy-looking LoCascio rarely spoke unless asked a direct question, which usually elicited only a few words of reply. He just sat quietly at the table in the back room, beneath the photographs of Neil and Gotti, and played solitaire.

The agents thought LoCascio was a harmless caricature, and that his very harmlessness was why Gotti—who already had one strong leader in Sammy—had chosen him.

In the family LoCascio was respected; he had been a made man longer than any other still-active member. The agents did not know he had played a main role, with Sammy, in the tying-in ceremonies held while Gotti was in the MCC awaiting trial in the Giacalone case. They also did not know that the bespectacled, graying old gangster still got his hands dirty—and had helped dispose of Robert DiBernardo's body.

Still, LoCascio acted in ways that tended to confirm the agents' low opinion. For instance, he had chosen for a bodyguard a man who could not drive. Instead, LoCascio was always behind the wheel when he and the bodyguard, an oily, hunched-over hoodlum named Zef Mustafa, arrived at the Ravenite.

Once, the video plant agents saw LoCascio double-park by the club entrance and run in so fast that a bladder emergency seemed to be the reason. Then they saw Mustafa slide behind the wheel and attempt without success to maneuver the car into a parking space as other men on the sidewalk pointed and laughed.

"So that's why Frankie's always driving, because the other asshole can't even park a car!" Roberts yelled into his audio plant microphone, as LoCascio came out of the club, screaming and waving his arms until Mustafa got out and allowed him to finish the job.

On another day, George Gabriel was in the video plant when the acting underboss of the Gambino family came out of the club and gave a hard time to a beat cop taking down the license number of LoCascio's illegally parked car.

"Look at this piece of shit," Gabriel said to Roberts, as LoCascio began arguing with the cop, "giving this beat hump a beef over a fucking parking ticket."

When the cop kept writing, LoCascio, just like a punk kid on a corner in Bensonhurst, grabbed his crotch and thrust his hips forward—an old New York City fuck-you.

"Frankie!" Gabriel screamed two and a half blocks away. "Frankie, shut up and go inside. Fucking cheapskate! You're a fucking underboss, you fucking mutt!"

Consigliere Sammy Gravano, in his customary construction-foreman clothes, normally arrived between five-thirty and six o'clock and was usually accompanied by his handpicked captain, Lou Vallario, and his faithful brother-in-law, Eddie Garafola. To the watching agents, Sammy always seemed to be a man on a mission—he politely acknowledged the greetings of the men outside but marched straight in without ado.

The other important people in the family, the capos, were usually already there, or not far behind, because John Gotti liked it when everyone was there when he showed up, usually between six and six-thirty. Even if an S.O. team was not tailing Gotti on a particular day, the video plant agents always knew when he was about to arrive because, five minutes beforehand, the two bodyguards who trailed him on walk-talks around the block always came outside and stood almost at parade rest.

The man who considered himself the real prince of Mulberry Street had perfected the art of grand arrivals. After his black Mercedes glided to a stop, with him in the backseat, he waited until someone opened his door, then stood on the curb as each of the men outside shook his hand and kissed him on the cheek. Nobody stepped inside until he did.

The arrival of Gotti always raised the adrenaline level of the agent teams in both the video and the audio plants: Maybe today would be the day that during some pregnant lull in the club's noise level, he would utter an incriminating remark. The bug detected his voice just often enough to keep hope alive.

Once, the audio agents' ears perked up when they overheard Vincent Artuso—a soldier in LoCascio's old crew—begin talking to Gotti. Without proof, they accurately suspected that Artuso was one of the gunmen on the Sparks team.

This day, however, the agents soon learned that Artuso was there to discuss another matter, a scheduled appearance before a grand jury investigating drug trafficking. He was worried about the interrogation ability of the prosecutor who was to question him.

"I'll tell you the truth, John, I'm no dope, but I don't think I'm smart enough to bob and weave with him."

The agents cranked up the volume dials of their recording equipment to capture Gotti's reply; if he advised Artuso to lie, that was obstruction of justice, an indictable RICO crime.

Before his words became lost in a welter of others' words, Gotti sounded the same themes he once had for Sammy. "You don't have to bob and weave with him, Vinnie. If he asks you if you know certain people, you say, 'Yeah, I know him. From the neighborhood. It's all Italian. Italian people are like that. They all know each other.'"

On another occasion, the bug showed that Gotti expected his men and their retainers to keep him abreast of all legal matters that might affect him. But this time the bug failed to overhear Gotti at all; only the voice of a lawyer was detected.

"He won't hurt you," Gotti was told by the late Willie Boy Johnson's lawyer, Richard Rehbock, who was referring to someone involved in a different grand jury. "He won't hurt you. He won't say a word, I'm certain. Absolutely won't say a word."

The few times agents were able to overhear Gotti clearly, he was usually just berating or entertaining his audience. One night, they listened as he talked about a Neapolitan mastiff puppy he's just purchased to replace Charlie, the mountainous animal that had menaced Mouw and Gabriel when they went to Gotti's home in Howard Beach to warn him about the Genovese gangsters overheard in a New Jersey bathroom plotting to kill him.

Charlie had died, and, earlier that day, Gabriel and Mark Roberts had returned to Howard Beach—this time to tell him it should be obvious to him now that the FBI wasn't playing a trick before, because the Genovese men had just been indicted, and one of the charges was based on taped evidence that they had plotted to kill Gotti and his brother Gene. By now Gotti knew that the plot in New Jersey was real—but, thinking that Chin had been forced to bury the hatchet during the Commission meeting, he was continuing to pretend to believe Chin's claim that it was unauthorized.

The new mastiff reacted warmly when Roberts, waiting for Gotti to appear, approached its pen and petted it into sloppy submission.

"I ought to kill that fuckin' dog!" Gotti roared at the Ravenite. "My last dog would've fuckin' killed an agent for gettin' that close. He would've fuckin' tore his fucking head off in two seconds. This fuckin' mutt's dead, I swear."

For the bug to work best when Gotti was making innocuous remarks was grating. But over time, the agents began to notice that sometimes—even when the video camera had shown Gotti going into the club—the bug would not even detect his voice amid the jumble of words bouncing off the walls, the soda machine, and the white-noise machine.

"I can't hear John," Frank Spero, from the audio plant, would say to Roberts in the video plant. "Did he leave?"

"No, still there. Keep listening. He's gotta be there."

"I can't hear him. We hear everybody else, but not him. He can't be here."

"He's there, I'm tellin' ya, he's there!"

The Ravenite bug's periodic inability to detect even the sound of Gotti's voice added another layer of frustration to what was fast becoming a snakebit case.

By September 1988, it was recording so little of value that, given the expense and effort of monitoring, it could no longer be legally justified, and the squad pulled the plug. The electronic invasion of the Ravenite, once so promising, came to a sour end.

CHAPTER 17

••••••••••••••

Bust 'im Up

As well known as Gotti was in the fall of 1988, the peak of his celebrity was far off, and as much as Sammy, Gene, and others questioned the wisdom of his courting a high profile, the worst was yet to come. The law's inability to make a case against him and his love of the spotlight guaranteed it. As long as he remained free, walk-talking along Mulberry, it could not be otherwise.

The longer he was free, the bigger target and story he was. The more he pursued his grand ambition—to out-Carlo Carlo and build a Cosa Nostra legacy that could never be broken—the more he became a magnet for the ambitions of prosecutors, cops, lawyers, reporters, and television producers.

It was the same with gangsters. Just as the Gambino squad ended its audio surveillance of the Ravenite, a gangster trying to weasel out of trouble offered information that fortified the ambitions of others in the law enforcement world and handed the media's Gotti chroniclers a story to rival his still seemingly legitimate acquittal in the Giacalone case.

The gangster was James McElroy. Along with most of the core members of the Gambino farm team, the Irish-dominated gang known as the Westies, he had gone down for the count in the Southern District RICO case that led to Bosko Radonjich's becoming boss.

Like Anthony Rampino, McElroy was a violent, drug-addicted gofer; unlike Rampino, who gave up the first secrets of Sparks and flirted with the prospect of testifying against Gotti before deciding to succumb quietly to life behind bars, McElroy felt no ethnic pang of kinship for Gotti. Quite the contrary.

"I wouldn't never rat out an Irish guy, but the Italians, who gives a shit?" he told NYPD detective Joseph Buffalino as Buffalino escorted him from a federal prison to New York to sort out some lingering state charges.

"I have done some things with Johnny Gotti."

McElroy was puffing himself up, but he did have a few facts that rekindled the get-Gotti hopes of Ronald Goldstock, boss of the New York Organized Crime Task Force; since failing to persuade Andy Maloney of their prosecutorial value, Goldstock had been trying to get another prosecutor to file a case against Gotti based on the intriguing but inconclusive tapes that his agents recorded when they bugged the Bergin Hunt and Fish Club in 1985 and 1986.

McElroy's facts appeared to offer the corroboration that had prevented any prosecutor from bringing a case against Gotti based only on one of the most tantalizing excerpts from those tapes. He said he was at a wake in 1986 when a former Westies leader left a meeting with Gotti and said Gotti had enlisted the Westies to deliver a harsh warning to some union leader.

These facts fit other facts that Goldstock's agents and other investigators—including FBI agents who'd worked on the Southern District's Westies case and cops who worked on the Manhattan district attorney's detective squad—had found since the May 1986 shooting, in Manhattan, of John F. O'Connor.

The victim was the corrupt—and soon to be convicted—business agent of Local 608 of the United Brotherhood of Carpenters and Joiners, the largest local in the United States.

O'Connor was shot in the lobby of his union's office. He survived but was not interested in providing police a possible motive or helping them to find and identify his assailants. But Goldstock's agents thought they'd overheard Gotti providing the motive two months before, in February 1986, when the newly-flush-with-power Gambino boss was informed by underlings that O'Connor was behind the trashing by a goon squad of carpenters of a Gambino family-backed restaurant recently constructed by nonunion carpenters.

"We're gonna, gonna bust 'im up," Gotti replied in his sometimes repetitive way, or so it sounded on the tape.

FBI agents had also tailed several Westies to the wake

in question—the one for Frank DeCicco. In addition, later in the investigation of the Westies, a gang member who had agreed to cooperate secretly taped one of the four O'Connor shooters saying the "greaseballs" had given them the assignment.

"Oh, yeah, [it was] for the greaseballs, something they needed quick," the gunman said. "You know what happened? This guy O'Connor got a bunch of construction guys from his union. They went on the job and wrecked it. He was supposed to get kneecapped, but the bullets ended up high and one went in his asshole. He's got an extra asshole."

Taken one by one, each of these facts hardly made for a case against Gotti; in court, even his "bust-'im-up" remark could be made into idle words by a man famous for exaggerated speech. But Goldstock believed that McElroy's claim that the Westies leader told him the shooting was for Gotti, and McElroy's willingness to testify about it, tipped the case into prosecutable range.

Andy Maloney, among many others on the federal side of law enforcement, did not agree. Just as when he resisted Goldstock's attempt to talk him into a federal prosecution based on gambling and loan-sharking charges, Maloney feared that the O'Connor case was too weak and that a jury would want more than the beating of a corrupt union boss before it convicted Gotti.

But Goldstock did not need Maloney in the Eastern District or Rudy Giuliani's recent replacement in the Southern District, Otto Obermaier, to realize his ambition; the O'Connor shooting was a state crime in Manhattan, which gave jurisdiction to the elected Manhattan district attorney, Robert Morgenthau.

The sixty-eight-year-old Morgenthau was the Nelson Mandela of prosecutors—regal, grandfatherly, impossible to dislike, but also cagey, highly political, and, as the son of a former British ambassador and U.S. Treasury secretary, born to power.

"Morgy" often made decisions independent of his big brothers' interests in the two U.S. attorneys' offices; having himself been boss of the Southern District from 1961 to 1972—a tenure almost unequaled and almost unchallenged through three changes of the White House guard—he carried a big stick. He also had a history with the Mafia; in 1963, he talked a run-of-the-mill hoodlum, Joseph Valachi, into making a groundbreaking confession to a U.S. Senate committee.

With the usual reservations about imperfect evidence and going to trial with a scummy witness like McElroy, who once slit a man's throat for a hundred dollars in drug money, Morgenthau and the chief of his rackets division, Michael Cherkasky, came to agree with Goldstock. Neither would ever say their decision was affected by the accolades that a victory over Gotti would bring to their office, but his notoriety guaranteed that it indeed was.

Still, a prosecutor's moral code requires only belief in the defendant's guilt and the possibility of a conviction, not the beauty of the case. In addition, a provision in New York law dramatically raised the reward of convicting John Gotti of feloniously ordering the assault of John O'Connor.

In the 1970s, Gotti had been convicted of three felonies—two hijackings and attempted manslaughter. In New York (and many states), three-time losers can be deemed "predicate" felons—incorrigible career criminals who ought to be treated as such at their fourth felony conviction and locked up for a long time. So rather than the five-to-fifteen-year sentence a judge would give for an ordinary conviction for assault, Gotti was vulnerable to a twenty-five-years-to-life sentence.

It took a couple of months to work out a deal with McElroy; a state murder charge was dropped, his girlfriend got a pass on drug charges, and Morgenthau and Cherkasky agreed to write a letter on his behalf to the federal judge who had sentenced him to sixty years in the Westies case. Worse criminals have gotten more, but not in such a theoretically simple assault case.

In January 1989, for the third time in four years, Gotti was indicted, and a judge issued a warrant for his arrest. In the twilight hours of January 23, twenty-three NYPD detectives and state task force agents took up positions near the Ravenite and waited for Gotti to leave. Several were in uniform because they were afraid Gotti's bodyguards might think they were assassins if they confronted them while dressed in street clothes; under similar circumstances, a detective had been shot to death in Queens by jumpy gangsters in another family.

Accompanied by three bodyguards, Gotti left the Ravenite about seven o'clock and walked north on Mulberry. The arresting officers held off, thinking he was bound for his car; if they grabbed him there, they could search it and perhaps pick up an easy charge, if Gotti or the bodyguards had stashed an illegal weapon in it. But as Gotti continued on, farther than was normal for a walk-talk, they realized he sensed something was up and was leading them on an aimless walk.

Quite coincidentally, they confronted him just as he reached the adjacent neighborhood of SoHo and stepped onto the boardwalk of his Machiavellian dreams, Prince Street.

The suspect immediately fell into character.

"I'll lay you three to one I beat it," he said to Joseph Coffey, the Westies expert who had left the NYPD and joined the state task force, as Coffey and Detectives Joseph Buffalino and Frank Bayrodt announced the charges, slapped on handcuffs, and led him to a police car.

"I ain't goin' nowhere, why're you doin' this shit?"

"Forget it, jerkoff, get in the fucking car," Coffey said.

Booking at nearby Manhattan Criminal Court took some time. Gotti cooled his heels in a crowded holding pen behind the bail judge's court. A collection of two-bit drug dealers, thieves, and muggers—the detritus of the NYPD's other efforts that night—were startled to see him led into their midst and responded with a standing ovation.

Alerted by the bodyguards, Gotti's attorney Bruce Cutler raced to the courthouse. His immediate mission was to persuade the judge to release Gotti to his custody pending a formal bail hearing the next day. Tipped by police sources, the city's media raced to the courthouse too.

When his case was called, Gotti came into court with his practiced air of bemused confidence and feigned deference for the occasion's arch formality. Prosecutor Cherkasky urged the judge to treat Gotti like any other defendant and jail him overnight pending the bail hearing.

Adopting his own courtroom guise, Cutler tried to convey outrage and confidence at the same time. "If he was like every other defendant, they wouldn't have used one hundred policemen to arrest him!"

With so many reporters present, state supreme court justice George Roberts was not going to treat Gotti differently, even if inclined, so the suspect was led away to spend the night in the protective-custody "celebrity wing" of Rikers Island. The next morning, in a prison bus, he was driven to court with another infamous occupant of celebrity row—lawyer Joel Steinberg, soon to be a convicted of killing a child he fraudulently adopted.

Cherkasky did not expect the judge to hold Gotti without bail; as a defendant, Gotti had always shown for court, the main criterion, in state law, for fixing bail. But he argued for it anyway: Gotti was the head of a major criminal organization and had "enormous financial resources" enabling him to flee.

"He has never missed a court date," Cutler replied. "He gets to court before the building opens. He's always on time. He has never run away from a problem."

The two lawyers argued several more minutes, long enough for Cutler to strum all the canned notes of a song about John Gotti the loyal husband, devoted father, and doting grandfather who was unmercifully hounded twenty-four hours a day by agents and cops who never saw him commit a crime.

When he had finally had enough of this, the judge set bail that set Gotti back for about a week's worth of gambling—one hundred thousand dollars, or half of what he had spent the month before on a sumptuous Christmas party for a thousand gangsters and their wives, children, girlfriends, and lawyers.

While making his familiarly ritual exit of the courthouse, Gotti broke into a familiarly sly smile when asked whether the new case caused him any concern.

"Did I ever worry yet?"

The reporters clamored for more and he indulged them. "I have nothing to be worried about. They have nothing."

The shouted questions kept coming in a hail, striking all around, accumulating in nothing, until Gotti heard one he felt it would be productive to answer. It involved James McElroy, and his words tipped the tried-and-true strategy sure to be employed at trial: "This case is from the word of lowlifes."

The performance briefly sated the media beast and, for the most part, produced the desired result. The lead paragraph of one newspaper story actually began with Gotti's statement, in 1987 after the Giacalone case, that in no time at all, law enforcement would try to frame him again.

The story also included a quote from Bruce Cutler, who in his secondary role of outspoken press secretary for Gotti was becoming a particular annoyance to his former colleagues in law enforcement. "This is an absolute garbage case," he fumed. "It's an absolute farce and an absolute hoax with no merit. It's built upon two created informants John never met in his life. They sold John's name to buy their freedom."

That story and all the others barely noted that two others had been indicted with Gotti and accused of helping him enlist the Westies—Anthony "Tony Lee" Guerrieri and Angelo Ruggiero, Guerrieri's former capo, who was still alive but only barely.

Angelo was in a hospital a few blocks from the courthouse. The cancer in his lungs had spread throughout his body. When he had been an inmate at the MCC, awaiting trial in the heroin case and hatching plots behind Gotti's back, he weighed two hundred forty pounds, but now he was at one hundred fifty.

Because of his illness, his arraignment took place at the hospital. It was clear to lawyers on both sides that Angelo did not have much time left. Soon he would be severed from the case and, legally speaking, virtually forgotten.

Once again Gene and Sammy urged Gotti to bestow a little sympathy and visit Angelo, but once again, and for good, Gotti refused.

"Fuckin' guy oughta have his fuckin' tongue cut out," he said.

CHAPTER 18

. . . .

Gelosia

In hallway encounters with reporters during the pretrial hearings of the O'Connor case, Gotti expressed cheery disdain. But in truth he was very worried. The value of image building was going to be tested sooner than he had imagined, and he was as concerned about his words on tape as he was about the lowlife James McElroy.

"Who knows what the rat bum overheard or what he's gonna say?" he said to Sammy in one of his many tirades on the subject during the run-up to the trial, which would consume all of 1989. "I coulda said somethin', or nothin', I don't even remember."

Sammy felt awkward in these moments, unsure what to say; the O'Connor case had planted a poisonous seed. If Gotti were convicted and, as a three-time loser under the predicate-felon law, imprisoned for twenty-five years to life, Sammy was the most obvious candidate to replace him.

Publicly, even Jimmy Brown Failla and Danny Marino thought Sammy would be the logical choice, and LoCascio, who had little aspiration beyond tending his gambling and loan-sharking trade in the Bronx and hanging around the Ravenite playing solitaire and agreeing with Gotti, thought it publicly and privately.

"It's a bullshit case, John," Sammy would say, trying to escape the subject.

"And they're gonna give me same as life for this shit?"

Sammy thought the case was weak and that Gotti might win, especially if he would listen to his lawyers and not try to try the case himself. The lawyer Sammy admired most, the ubiquitous Jerry Shargel, had entered the case to defend Anthony Guerrieri, the Angelo soldier accused of helping Gotti enlist the Westies, and Sammy thought that improved Gotti's chances greatly, because in practical terms Shargel would be representing Gotti, too. He respected Bruce Cutler, but he thought Shargel—who had pulled many more rabbits out of the hat since extricating Sammy from the Fiala problem—was a master of criminal defense.

Still, in Gotti's presence, Sammy was reluctant to make a prediction about the O'Connor case, afraid that either way Gotti would misinterpret what he said. Over the past few months, Gotti had often made him feel this way—damned if he did, damned if he didn't.

It was never anything Gotti said to him directly, so Sammy continued to conduct his and the family businesses as if nothing had changed—performing superbly at both, he thought, and Gotti always said, especially when Sammy handed over another envelope stuffed with cash: "Like I always say, I wish I had five Sammys out there."

At first, as passed along by others, Gotti's words seemed harmless and understandable.

For instance, Sammy could understand Gotti's irritation at being informed by the Philadelphia borgata that it would rather exchange messages with the Gambino family through Sammy and not Sparks veteran Joe Watts.

"John was pissed when I told him that," Watts told Sammy, "but don't get him more pissed by tellin' him I told you. He said, 'Who the fuck is the boss? Me or Sammy?'"

"He knows I know who's boss. Everybody knows. I can't help they said that."

"He was just blowin' steam, bein' John."

"I go a long way back with those people. Paul sent me down there to do some things years ago. Me and Louie Milito."

"Ah, forget about it, he will."

"After Paul, we had a meetin' with those people at my brother-in-law's house. Me and John. Their one and two. Of course they're used to me!"

Sammy and Watts had been friends long before Watts began rising in stature, partly by always grabbing the check when he and Gotti were out nightclubbing. Sammy still regarded him as a friend and respected his ability and aptitude for murder, so he didn't say what he also was thinking: "Joe, you ain't even made and ain't ever goin' to be. How'd you or John think for a second that Philly would want to even sit down with you?"

Once the sword of the O'Connor case was raised, however, it was difficult not to receive Gotti's reported remarks with more unease. Such was the case with an innocuous and spontaneous trip to Atlantic City that Sammy—opting for a rare boys' night out—took with another old friend, Jack Giordano, and some others.

Giordano, a capo on the Lower East Side, was the brother of the soldier who—to the amusement of agents in the video plant—had asserted rank over associates at the Ravenite by making them carry his pizza pies inside. As a nephew of imprisoned underboss Joseph Armone, he also was the man Gotti used to tell Joe Piney that he could not publicly renounce Cosa Nostra just to be with his family for the Christmas holidays, and so instead he had to go straight to prison for life.

Giordano was a go-along, get-along type of man. He did not bear Gotti ill will for ordering his uncle to jail. His family nicknames were Handsome Jack and the redundant Good-looking Jack, and he was a slinky, silvery stereotype who had joined the crowd that accompanied Gotti at night—now to Upper East Side places more upscale than Club A, restaurants like the Four Seasons and nightclubs like Regine's and Tatou.

As a popular man and Armone's nephew, Giordano's name had been mentioned for the job Gotti gave LoCascio. The decision did not bother the easygoing Giordano; he was making enough money and knew that a promotion guaranteed greater FBI attention.

"I couldn't believe he was actin' this way," Handsome Jack told Sammy not long after the O'Connor indictment, "but Johnny gave me hell the other night."

"You? For what?"

"I shouldn't be sayin' this, but he was pissed as hell that I went down to Atlantic City with you."

"You've got to be kiddin'. For what?"

"I don't know, 'cept maybe he was *gelosia*," Giordano said, using the Italian word for "jealous." "You know, that you and I were there, and he wasn't."

"*Minchia!*"

"What he actually said was that we oughta told 'im, so

if he needed to reach us, he'd know where we were. But he made me feel like we were sneakin' behind his back."

Sammy calculated what suspicions Gotti might conjure, and one came quickly: The consigliere cavorting out of state with a man passed over for underboss. But it was a suspicion unrelated to reality, and that made it more unsettling.

"Can't fuckin' believe it! We were just hangin' out! We weren't havin' any secret meeting or anything."

"He knows it, the guy's just hard to figure sometimes."

"Doesn't he understand, I don't wanna be his equal? I don't wanna be out front like he is. I like where I'm at."

Giordano and others understood it completely. Sammy was not one for the limelight. He had quit talking about Gotti's decision to compel weekly appearances at the Ravenite, but he still thought life in Cosa Nostra meant being undercover and tried to conduct his affairs that way whenever possible.

As consigliere, he could not avoid the Ravenite shape-up, but he had stopped visiting the Bergin on Saturdays; it was an optional courtesy. But the showy Christmas party that Gotti threw just before he was indicted in the O'Connor case, the one that cost him two hundred thousand dollars, was not. Sammy cringed when he saw detectives outside the entrance, making no effort to conceal their cameras.

Sammy's penchant for secrecy—currently, and for the past two years, he had been conducting regular bribery business with Teamsters official Bobby Sasso at a motel in Brooklyn at three in the morning—and his even temperament made gangsters in other families who didn't like being around Gotti seek him out when their interests coincided or collided.

He always reported these requests for sitdowns to Gotti, who frequently gave him permission to conduct them without him. Gotti dominated any room he entered but was most effective in the type of sitdowns that Neil and Paul had once used him for—those requiring a show of malice. Sammy was no slouch in that regard, but with his experience in construction and unions, he was better equipped to iron out workaday problems of graft.

"Those people with that problem we spoke about told me they never win these sitdowns with Sammy," capo Joseph "Joe Butch" Corrao told Gotti one day. "They said they can bring seven or eight talkers to go up against 'im, but it don't ever matter."

"Sammy's the best," Gotti said. "That's why I send him."

Still, Gotti did not always send Sammy Gravano; it was one of those occasions, again involving Watts, that caused further unease for Sammy after Watts came to Tali's, Sammy's clubhouse and bar in Brooklyn, to tell him about a union-fixing mission that Gotti had assigned him.

"I don't want you to tell John I was here, but he sent me to these people, and they said, 'Where's Sammy? We're used to dealin' with Sammy.' I told John this and he went apeshit."

"If you send different people, it does confuse them."

"He said, 'What's this? Fuckin' Rome? All roads lead to Sammy?'"

"If he don't want me to take care of some things, all he has to do is tell me."

"He just didn't like hearing that, I guess. You know John. He likes everybody twenty-five steps behind."

"That's where I wanna be. You know it. I ain't never done nothin' to make him worry about me. I am as loyal as a fuckin' puppy. I'm the fuckin' consigliere and I'm out in the street with a gun doin' next-door neighbors if he tells me to."

"I know that. Everybody knows that. It's just John."

"He's got the glory, the power, all the broads he wants. I don't want that stuff. Not me. I'm an Avis guy, not a Hertz."

For all Gotti had, for all the ego stroking from his men, it was incredible to Sammy that Gotti could be jealous of him. But part of the problem was that, as the old Avis ad claimed, Sammy tried harder. He worked harder at being a gangster, and always had. Whereas Gotti rose on muscle and personality, Sammy rose on muscle and hard work. While Gotti spent many years in prison, Sammy was working; while Gotti gambled at racetracks, caroused in nightclubs, and held forth at the Bergin and the Ravenite, Sammy nurtured business, his and the family's.

At the time, the proof of this was in a pudding that only a few people in law enforcement knew about. Early in 1989, detectives from the Brooklyn district attorney's office mounted a double-barreled electronic assault against Sammy. They planted bugs in a construction trailer parked at a job site for one of Sammy's companies and in the storefront office of his main company, S&G Construction, on Stillwell Avenue in Bensonhurst—the same drab office in which the Fist rendezvoused before and after Sparks and where Robert "Deebee" DiBernardo was murdered.

Sammy visited both sites almost every day, especially the office because he had purchased a florist's shop next door and given it to his nineteen-year-old daughter, Karen. He wanted her next to him so she would not ever have to worry about a robbery. But he ended up regretting his paternal concern.

"That's one of the stupidest mistakes I've made," he said to his stand-in capo, Louis Vallario, after all the wise guys in Brooklyn began going out of their way to buy flowers there. "She's going to find out what I really am."

Karen already had a good idea, because in addition to the story about Sammy "the rising star" in the *Daily News,* Sammy's local newspaper on Staten Island had recently printed a story referring to him as a "man who has swiftly and mysteriously risen through the ranks of organized crime to become John Gotti's chief adviser."

Some law enforcement source told the reporter that Sammy resembled the actor Arnold Schwarzenegger, but that would be true only if comparing muscle strength per square inch.

But as in Sammy's and Gotti's youth, young people in New York, especially Brooklyn, did not need the newspapers to know when someone was connected. Such was the case with Jack Colucci, son of Victim No. 1 on Sammy's list. While he did not know that Sammy had killed his father, Colucci—who was trying to build up a small contracting business—knew enough that he realized Sammy was the man to go see when a company connected with another family tried to toss him off a job site in Coney Island.

"I helped the kid, how couldn't I?" Sammy told Vallario. "I've helped his mom out a lot too."

The two bugging operations against Sammy were in place for more than a year when a new district attorney, Charles Hynes, was elected and agents from Ronald

Goldstock's office had to assume responsibility for the monitoring because Sammy and a Teamsters foreman with an assault case pending in Brooklyn were overheard discussing the leverage that a ten-thousand-dollar contribution to Hynes's campaign might yield.

The contribution was never made, and most of the overheard discussions before and after Goldstock's agents took over never amounted to anything on which a prosecutor would want to try a case. Mainly, what the bugs and surveillance revealed was that Sammy was an exceptionally hardworking gangster.

Whether in the trailer or in his office, whether on the telephone or in meetings, Sammy was always discussing this or that job—construction, of course, but also painting, drywall, carpeting, restaurants, even some bagel shop in Staten Island that he had reluctantly taken over from a friend and deadbeat loan-shark customer and placed in the names of his and brother-in-law Eddie Garafola's wives.

On paper, Debra Gravano already owned 75 percent of the consulting company that Sammy founded after murdering Louis Milito, his former steel-erection partner, for bad-mouthing the administration. The consulting deal was urged by a tax lawyer of Sammy's, whose advice he carefully heeded; unlike Gotti, who was still not even bothering to file tax returns, Sammy was determined not to get tripped up on taxes again.

Usually in the afternoon, because his mornings were still given to brisk workouts at the gym and a leisurely health food breakfast, Sammy would meet with a vast array of contractors, union officials, and favor-seekers. But apart from periodic and vague talk about some loansharking deal or fixing his books to hide some ghost-employee deal, he never said anything—in more than forty-five hundred hours of tapes—that amounted to real trouble.

The discovery of bugs at the Bergin and the Ravenite, and his higher prominence in the family, had obviously heightened Sammy's already keen concern for loose talk inside a confined area. For critical conversations, he used streets as noisy as those around the Ravenite; if he was relaxing at Tali's, and weather was a problem and someone absolutely had to talk, he turned up the jukebox, the radio, and a forty-inch television, then used hand signals and eye movements to make big points.

Once in a while, however, the bugs in place against Sammy did reveal that when within his realm, he could sound a little like John Gotti.

"I think I'm going to end up whacking Eddie in the fuckin' head," he said one day, referring to his brother-in-law, after someone came to discuss some arrangement Garafola had made in Sammy's absence on one of Sammy's concrete-construction jobs in the Bronx. Some problem left unclear had developed, but Sammy was furious that Garafola had acted without him.

"I am the boss around here. I am the boss. I don't give a fuck about Eddie, or what he says about it, or what he did. I gotta know . . . I don't give a fuck what arrangements he makes; it's meaningless."

Although he had stood by in 1978 and let another brother-in-law, Nicholas Scibetta, be murdered, Sammy's threat was not meant or taken literally. He valued and trusted Garafola, and the bugs also showed that occasionally he lectured him about nuances of Gambino family interaction with law enforcement.

On one occasion, during a rare quiet moment at the trailer, Sammy told Garafola that the family sometimes permitted members to respond to law enforcement subpoenas and testify before grand juries, even though the oath that members took during initiation forbade any cooperation at all with official authority. But the oath had proved impractical; under law, grand juries may grant witness immunity and compel testimony under a threat of jail; the testimony cannot be used against them, unless they lie, but anyone who refuses to testify can be jailed.

It sounded worse that it was, Sammy added, because a smart person can finesse a grand jury appearance without jeopardizing anyone. Here was why and how:

"Common sense is seventy-five percent of the answers. Another ten to fifteen percent, you gotta dance and bob and weave. 'I didn't remember. I didn't think so, or to the best of my knowledge.' Okay? Let's say that's fifteen percent, so we're up to ninety. Ten percent, you out and out lie."

Sammy's grand jury lecture was given on March 17, 1989. At the time, he, John Gotti, and millionaire capo

Tommy Gambino had ample reason for thinking about such issues. The failure of FBI audio surveillance at the Ravenite had caused Andy Maloney, his Eastern District prosecutors, and the Gambino squad to resort to another tactic—the cudgel of the grand jury subpoena.

Maloney had impaneled a get-Gotti grand jury in the Eastern District almost a year earlier. Defense lawyers like to say that prosecutors can get grand juries to indict a ham sandwich, and if a sandwich had legs, they could. But Maloney had been patient in the grand jury, presenting excerpts from the task force tapes that Ronald Goldstock valued so highly, plus other lay-the-foundation material, but declining to ask the grand jury's twenty-three members to indict until the FBI got stronger evidence.

His hopes faded when the Gambino squad pulled the Ravenite plug, so he and strike force chief Edward McDonald resorted to a new tactic. They decided to put pressure on Gotti by using the grand jury's power to cloak people around him in immunity and force them to testify.

The law prohibited them from seeking immunity for the real targets of this legal squeeze play, Gotti, Sammy, and LoCascio—the Gambino administration. The law saw it as an unfair way to lead suspects into a perjury case; immunity was for people on a case's periphery—people less important than their information.

Trying to jump-start the stalled investigation, Maloney and McDonald first decided that Tommy Gambino was not as important as his information was. It was a risky call—Tommy was not only a capo but, as Carlo's son, a symbol of Cosa Nostra's long sway in New York—and Maloney and McDonald had to go to their superiors in Washington for approval. Their bosses agreed that the chance of building a case against Gotti was worth losing a chance to win a case against Tommy.

For Tommy, the pressure of having to testify or go to jail was a new experience; during the reigns of his father and his Uncle Paul, he lived a practically anonymous life, as far as the law was concerned, even though until Sparks the soft-spoken, well-mannered Tommy, who was married to the well-bred daughter of the Luchese family patriarch, was in line to replace Paul.

By that time, however, he had little lust for the job; he

saw the federal storm coming more clearly than most, and the millions he accumulated while working in the shadows of his powerful connections were enough consolation. After Sparks, he showed where his heart was by moving quickly to assure Gotti that he felt neither revenge or ambition.

Some remarks that Gotti made about Tommy in the wake of Sparks—within range of the state task force bug at the Bergin—were used to establish a legal basis for subpoenaing Tommy before the grand jury, not that a legal basis for a grand jury subpoena is ever very hard to establish.

In one conversation—the same one in which he talked about building a legacy that could never be broken—Gotti told George Remini, a soldier in Tommy's crew, that he would place only quality soldiers in that decina—not "hotheads" or "scumbags."

In an acknowledgment of Tommy's soft-boiled manner, Gotti also said it was better if Remini acted as the crew's capo in sitdowns requiring a little malice.

"Tommy don't know how to handle that. He's a sweetheart for everything else, but you would know how to handle it, Georgie."

Gotti also made it plain, however, that since Tommy had signaled his support so quickly after Sparks, he intended to treat him like an insider. "I told Tommy, 'Whatever we do, I want you to know, even if it's bad, off-color. I want you to know it from us. This way here, you're part of it.' "

Tommy went before the grand jury four times, the last just before Gotti was indicted in the O'Connor case. He seemed candid and relaxed when prosecutor Leonard Michaels asked him to talk about his childhood, his education, and his business empire. As Sammy had told Garafola, this kind of grand jury questioning was just commonsense stuff.

The empire was centered in the so-called garment center, on Manhattan's West Side, south of Westies territory; it was a grid of narrow streets and grim old buildings where much of the women's clothing in the United States was either made, bought, or sold.

With his even more low-key brothers, Joseph and Carlo Jr., Tommy controlled several trucking, leasing, and manufacturing firms employing seven hundred people and grossing more than thirty million dollars annually. With brother-in-law Robert Luchese, he had also invested twenty-five thousand into another company reporting ten million a year in receipts.

Tommy began to bob and weave when he testified that he had no idea why his companies—which were about 90 percent nonunion—were never victimized by union or Cosa Nostra shakedown artists, when such were historically part of the garment center whirl. He conceded that he had heard that other companies might have been victimized.

He began shifting in his seat, and blinking his eyes rapidly, when Michaels zeroed in on the taped conversation between Gotti and George Remini.

"I don't know what is in Mr. Gotti's head," Tommy said.

When Michaels asked about the Sparks shootings, Tommy even refused to refer to them as murders. "I know my uncle was found dead on the street. As far as I am concerned, it was an uncomfortable time in my life. I lost my uncle and that's it."

Retreating briefly—to the truth—he added that he never asked Gotti about the shooting.

"I know John Gotti is my friend. And he's a good man. That's all I know about John Gotti."

Michaels pressed on, and Tommy's answers began toppling onto one another like a falling house of cards. He remembered events that had occurred more than forty years before, but not a meeting he had with Gotti the night before his first grand jury appearance. He admitted that he visited Gotti on a regular basis at some social club, but he could not recall the club's name, what it looked like, where it was, or the names of fifteen or so other men he saw there regularly.

"Well, how did you know how to find the place?" Michaels asked.

"Well, just by instinct. I walked there and I know basically where it is. Diagonally across the street from the church."

"Well, if it is so dark at night that you couldn't see the front of it, how did you know you were there?"

"Because I know the relative position of it as I am walking."

By such circumlocution, Tommy got through his grand jury appearances without fainting, but his words would be used against him—and against the jealous Prince of Mulberry Street.

CHAPTER 19

• • • • • • • • • • • • •

Mack Attack

The O'Connor case and the newly aggressive Eastern District grand jury were not the only problems law enforcement would give Gotti in 1989. Early that year, a moribund investigation of the Sparks murders by the Southern District, the Manhattan district attorney and the NYPD was revived. This was the piece of Gotti hide that Rudolph Giuliani had reserved for himself and Manhattan DA Robert Morgenthau two years before, when he and Maloney met after the Giacalone case; normally, murder cases are tried in a state court, but a seldom-used provision of federal law made a murder committed to gain power in an illegal enterprise such as the Gambino family a crime against the United States.

Giuliani had since resigned to run for mayor of New York; without much direction from either the Southern District or the Manhattan district attorney's office, which was focusing on the O'Connor matter, the NYPD had bungled the Sparks investigation. Detectives who rarely bothered to compare notes had been rotated in and out of the assignment, and when speedy arrests did not occur, the police department lost interest.

The investigation was on its deathbed until Walter Mack, a former chief of the Southern District's organized-crime section, came on the scene. He had just finished a marathon RICO case against the remnants of the wicked Gambino crew led by Roy DeMeo, the capo whom Paul ordered Frank DeCicco to kill, in 1982, when it appeared that Mack's case might reach him. Even with DeMeo dead, however, the case did reach Paul, and he was standing trial for it when he was murdered.

Walter Mack plowed on without the lead defendant,

and over four years and two trials, won convictions against all but one of twenty-four defendants. To him, however, the murder of one of his defendants while on trial was part of the case, a piece of unfinished business, and so after DeMeo's men were put away for life, Mack focused his attention on Sparks, and only on Sparks, because Giuliani had promised Maloney that he would not try to persuade the Gambino squad to mount a more sweeping, RICO case with his office, rather than Maloney's.

The case against the DeMeo gang, which was credited with seventy-five murders and suspected in more than a hundred more, began when the former Marine Corps captain focused his attention on some seemingly low-level car thieves. But Mack kept turning over rocks, and the detectives and FBI agents who eventually joined a task force that put the crew out of business regarded him as a federal treasure.

What he found in his review of the NYPD's Sparks files was a mishmash of contradictory statements, undeveloped theories, and interviews with gaping holes. Leads had been left dangling, and witnesses who saw some of the gunmen had been allowed to leave the city without telling the NYPD where they had moved. Mack went to work; in weeks, Southern District grand jury subpoenas began landing on the doorsteps of Gambino soldiers, people deemed less important than the information they might have.

Tommy Gambino's performances in the Eastern District grand jury showed that while he may not have learned much about Sparks in his talks with Gotti, he did know how Gotti expected family members to handle themselves when he permitted them to testify: tell the truth about things that don't matter; fail to remember when the questions get close; lie where there is no choice.

Less than a month after Sammy Gravano articulated the main points of this policy for Eddie Garafola, Sammy was called upon by Gotti to discipline a soldier who signaled his intention to ignore it in an appearance before a suddenly newly aggressive Southern District grand jury. The balky soldier's defiance was partly self-interest, partly Walter Mack, whose reputation in the Gambino family, because of his relentless efforts in the DeMeo case, preceded him.

The soldier, Thomas Spinelli, had already testified once and was scheduled to testify again when he told others in his decina that he wasn't going to expose himself to a perjury charge by telling any more lies to Mack about things that Mack must already know. The rattled Spinelli knew only gossip about Sparks, but his crew leader, Jimmy Brown Failla, had been among those captains waiting inside Sparks that night for Paul and Tommy Bilotti, and that made everyone in his crew a potential target—and a source of pressure on Gotti.

While uninformed about Sparks, as well as Failla's secret alliance with Chin and Danny Marino, Spinelli knew a lot about Failla's role in the family's private-sanitation rackets—the subject of many previous investigations by different agencies. Spinelli was one of Failla's fixer bees, and the grand jury subpoena handcuffed him into the unenviable position of trying to guess what Mack already knew as Mack fired questions.

Spinelli's fellow soldiers immediately informed their capo of his decision to tell the truth and hope for the best. Failla immediately informed Gotti; he was still part of a Chin-directed plot against Gotti that was still technically alive. Since the show of pretense at the Commission meeting, Luchese underboss Anthony Casso, on behalf of Chin, had considered but shelved other plans for assassinating Gotti because the target was always in the company of so many people.

Until Casso made a move, Failla had to continue pretending to Gotti that he was loyal and tell him about such developments as a potential legal threat from Spinelli.

"Then he has to go," Gotti responded. "If he don't wanna play ball our way, he don't play."

Gotti gave the contract to Failla, but he doubted the old-timer's stomach and asked Sammy to make sure the job got done.

"You know Jimmy Brown and that crew," he told Sammy. "They take their time, but there ain't no time. The guy's gotta go."

The assignment eased some of the anxiety Sammy had felt lately. As long as Gotti still counted on him to carry out missions of this importance, his recent fits of *gelosia* seemed less ominous.

"I'll take care of it," Sammy said, dutiful as ever.

Sammy contacted a soldier in the Failla crew and in a few days they hatched a plan. As he had before, when Gotti sent him to Queens to administer the death penalty to a man who killed a made man in a fistfight, Sammy felt it was unseemly for a Cosa Nostra man of his position to be out in the street with a gun in his hand. But he and the Failla soldier did lure Spinelli to a factory in Brooklyn owned by another Gambino gangster's son. As Sammy waited outside, the soldier shot Spinelli behind the ear. Sammy then telephoned Joe Watts to come and take away the body, Victim No. 17 on Sammy's hit list.

"It's over," he told Gotti the next day, in a walk-talk at the Ravenite.

"Good, can't have no rats, or would-be rats. People gotta know that by now."

Two months later, Tommy Gambino was charged a comparatively small price for observing the policy that Spinelli did not. Tommy's bobbing, weaving, and prevarication in the Eastern District grand jury was ammunition for an obstruction of justice charge, or so Andy Maloney and strike force chief Edward McDonald decided. They got the grand jury to indict Tommy, who, after his arrest, was placed in handcuffs for the first time in his life.

Tommy's lawyers, including Michael Rosen, formerly an Uncle Paul lawyer for big trouble, immediately began crafting a trial defense that would rely on an appeal to Tommy's eventual jurors that the nice-looking gentleman before them was singled out for punishment only because of his infamous father and because he happened to know John Gotti, the real target of the case.

Rosen thought the defense was a winner and that the damage to Gotti would be slight, but Gotti was worried; the Teflon Don was beginning to feel besieged. The O'Connor case, with its virtual life penalty, was before him; and now he knew that the Eastern District and the FBI, and the Southern District and the NYPD, were behind him, coming at him with who-knew-what kind of cases.

"They're gonna keep comin' until they get something,

get a motherfuckin' scumbag rat to say what they want," he ranted to Sammy one day. "It's gonna cost me a fuckin' fortune to fight these motherfuckers off."

It did not help his mood when another troubled loner from Queens attempted to kill him, this time outside the Ravenite. This loner ended up better than Jeffrey Ciccone, who tried it outside the Bergin; he survived. Michael McCray's method also was different, and to Gotti's consternation, he also generated a lot of publicity for his motive: Gotti was not a neighborhood Robin Hood; he was a murderer who dealt drugs.

Three days after losing his job as a photo technician at a Queens hospital, McCray planted a homemade bomb in the Ravenite doorway. He hoped to ignite a fire that would trap Gotti inside, but the bomb was crudely made and did not detonate. Undeterred, McCray then mailed a letter to John Cardinal O'Connor, Catholic archbishop of New York, in which he claimed responsibility and demanded a summit with Gotti.

O'Connor turned the letter over to the police, who found McCray where he had demanded that the meeting take place—a national forest in Tennessee. The thirty-seven-year-old McCray, whose mother later described him as a crusading born-again Christian, was reading a Bible while sitting in his car, which contained several loaded weapons and hundreds of rounds of ammunition.

"Gotti is evil," he mumbled to the cops in Tennessee. "I want him because of the drugs and the murders."

McCray was returned to New York; he didn't seem dangerously mad, so a judge gave him three years' probation after he pleaded guilty to aggravated harassment and promised to leave town and avoid Gotti, who fell back on a familiar line when reporters staked out the Ravenite for comment: "Do I look worried?"

He did not, but the look was deceiving. He was becoming a prisoner of the image that he and the media—which by nature are inclined to build a newcomer up, and then, eventually, bring him down—had cooperatively crafted. He was forced to live up to his public's expectations, and so when the Genovese men in New Jersey who were accused of plotting to kill him were convicted, he tried to act like a politician who never got in the gutter with his enemies.

"I don't know anything about it, and it has nothing to do with me."

The New Jersey convictions did confirm what Gotti already believed—that Chin had been checkmated and there was no need to worry much. Chin, with time on his side, encouraged such confidence. He dispatched one of his captains, Liborio Bellomo, to meet with Gotti and Sammy and restate his earlier explanation that the men in New Jersey were renegades acting on their own.

After the opening pretenses were dispensed with, the Bellomo sitdown became more of a group lament about the government's continuing crackdown; in that context, they also discussed how the two families might better protect themselves against informers.

"They're comin' after us for the publicity," Gotti offered. "Look at fuckin' Giuliani with the Commission case. Wants to be the big shot now. Mayor."

"He used us to advance his position," Sammy said.

"It's gettin' so bad that when we make any new guys, we ought to make 'em undress so we know they ain't wired up," Bellomo said. "You know, have a ceremony in the nude."

Sammy felt that Bellomo was only half joking, and he felt like saying, "And if they get hard-ons, that would be another reason not to make 'em," but he held his tongue because informers were no laughing matter.

Gotti offered another solution, which reflected his renewed worry that, because of Mack's grand jury, heroin junkie Anthony Rampino was still a threat. He might change his mind and talk his way out of prison by telling what he knew about Sparks. "We just gotta be sure we don't make no drug users friends of ours. They're the quickest to rat."

Naturally, everyone agreed, but Gotti added an afterthought of high irony, considering that drug dealers in his circle had caused so many problems: "If the foundation of this thing gets fucked up, the whole thing collapses."

In the spring of 1989, Gotti decided that he needed some time away. Still afraid to fly, he and some of his closest cronies jumped in his black Mercedes and drove south; the destination was Fort Lauderdale, and the goal was just relaxing by the pool there and up the road at the condominium complex of the young garment district millionaire who called himself Gotti's adopted son, Lewis Kasman.

But local cops and agents tipped off by the NYPD and the Gambino squad tailed the group everywhere. After a couple of days Gotti had had enough. He drove back to New York, only to learn that FBI agents were now asking questions in the garment district about a phony garment accessories company that he and Jackie D'Amico had formed a couple of months before to paper themselves with an additional source of income from a seemingly real job.

It struck Sammy as odd that Gotti would worry about this, and not about his failure to file IRS returns, but Gotti said that he was still relying on the advice of a lawyer and former IRS agent who had advised him that if he sent an occasional estimated tax payment to the IRS, he need not worry much about actual returns.

In the past, Gotti had used a childhood friend's plumbing construction company for ghost employment, but on paper that job could not account for the upward thrust in his spending for the last couple of years. He needed something extra to reduce the peril of the IRS's asking how he could live so well on so little. The dummy company he chose was in the same building as a Lewis Kasman firm, which also provided the telephone.

Gotti, D'Amico, and others had occasionally used the Kasman company's building for meetings, but after concluding that the FBI had tailed them there, they stopped. Back at the Ravenite, they found no relief from prying eyes. The NYPD, unaware of the FBI video camera in a high-rise two blocks away, had begun its own still-photo surveillance on Mulberry; because it was virtually impossible to surveil Mulberry at street level without tipping off someone loyal to the Ravenite, the surveillants—hoping to annoy Gotti—were intentionally conspicuous. He was never sure who they were, NYPD or FBI, but he was nonetheless annoyed.

"Get your ass in here," he growled to an underling outside the club one day, "unless you want your fuckin' picture taken."

No one dared mention to him that it was his fault everyone was being exposed to photographs by congregating at the Ravenite; neither did anyone imagine that the authorities were amassing not only photographs but miles upon miles of videotape.

Gene Gotti was not seen on the videotapes very often; under his bail terms in the torturously prolonged, and still pending, heroin case, he was not supposed to consort with criminals. A few weeks after his brother returned from Florida, however, Gene dropped out of the picture altogether.

The heroin case, the root of Paul's fall and John Gotti's rise, had been in abeyance for almost a year—since the second mistrial and while Gene's lawyers argued in the appeals courts that it was unfair to put him and John Carneglia on trial for yet a third time. The fight was taken to the Supreme Court, where it was lost, and the trial began in April 1989.

With Angelo Ruggiero absent from the courtroom because he was too sick to stand trial, the Eastern District's prosecution team, headed by Robert LaRusso and FBI agent Billy Noon, pared the case down further by severing some defendants, such as Eddie Lino, for separate trials—much as they had done earlier with Michael Coiro, the lawyer who had helped hide heroin assets.

With the case tightly focused on Gene and Carneglia, even Jerry Shargel, in the courtroom again for Carneglia, was unable to do much, and finally Gene and Carneglia were found guilty—but only after one last attempt to fix the jury.

When no break as lucky as the one John Gotti got in the Giacalone case, when a man already on the jury announced he was for sale, Gene was left to try and devise something on his own—and he did. It was a remarkably intricate plan, which he didn't tell his brother about because it relied on one of John's sons-in-law, Carmine Agnello; he was afraid John might object. It also involved Eddie Lino, who agreed to help on the sly and risk the boss's wrath, because he felt a special bond with his former codefendants.

After employing private detectives to learn the names and addresses of the jurors, Gene discovered that one lived on the same street as Billy Noon, the FBI case agent, who sat at the prosecution table with LaRusso. He sent Lino to the juror's home, with orders to leave an anonymous note asking how the juror could pretend to be fair when everyone knew he was friendly with his FBI neighbor.

On the assumption that the juror would tell the judge in the case, the note was meant to provoke a hearing and the juror's disqualification. Although Lino left the note on the door of the wrong neighbor, it did, because that neighbor told his lawyer, who contacted the Eastern District.

In the meantime, Gene sent Carmine Agnello to the home of the first alternate juror in the case, who had been judged to be sympathetic, if not bribable; the alternate juror was both. And after the other juror was indeed excused from the case, on grounds that the note, even if left at the wrong house, might have poisoned his objectivity, the alternate took his place.

For twenty-five thousand dollars, however the alternate turned out to be a bad bargain. Rather than hold his ground in deliberations and simply refuse to vote for any verdict but an outright acquittal, he allowed his feet to turn to clay. He sent a note to the judge admitting nothing but saying that he was concerned about his and his family's safety and had to get off the jury because the wrong people knew where he lived.

The judge and the prosecution team did not know what had taken place, but they smelled something rotten. So the judge granted the clay-footed juror his wish, then ruled that the case would be decided by the eleven remaining jurors, who took only three hours to lower the boom on Gene and Carneglia and bring down the curtain on the longest federal prosecution in history.

To everyone's surprise, the judge let them remain free on bail, pending sentencing. But both had already decided they were not going to flee. Because the case began in 1983, it fell under federal sentencing rules that were not as punitive as rules that came into effect in 1985 and that John Gotti had confronted in the Giacalone case.

Whereas John faced the prospect of serving at least twenty-six years of a forty-year sentence, his brother and Carneglia would qualify for parole after ten years—and because they were only in their mid-forties, they saw light at the end of the tunnel, more light than in life as a fugitive.

"I can understand that," Sammy said, when John Gotti

said Gene and Carneglia were not going to flee. "When you run, you got so many things to think about—your wife, your kids, your friends, everything. You can't ever come back, and what are you gonna do anyway? Work in a hardware store?"

"They'll hit the parole board in ten years, and maybe get out in fourteen, fifteen. It ain't like what they're gonna do to me with this predicate-felon bullshit with this carpenter asshole," Gotti replied, referring to the O'Conner case.

A few weeks later, however, Gene and Carneglia got much stiffer sentences than they expected, thanks to the scrapyard czar, Carneglia.

After he and Gene were found guilty but released on bail to await sentencing, Carneglia had reverted to his Fulton-Rockaway days and promised a reporter that someday he would "piss on the grave" of the trial judge, John R. Bartels, an eighty-nine-year-old jurist who in the more boring parts of testimony had dozed off a few times.

Bartels was awake at the sentencing, though, and he gave Carneglia and Gene sentences requiring them to serve more than twenty years before they would have a chance to qualify for parole—and, in Carneglia's case, to carry out a badly timed vow.

The Bergin crew's original core was fast fading from the scene. Peter Gotti, John's older brother, was still around—and he became acting capo after Gene went down—but Gene, Carneglia, Angelo, Willie Boy, and Rampino were now in jail, dead, or dying.

But Gotti was not in a nostalgic mood when he told Sammy about saying good-bye to Gene the night before the surrender; he was agitated because Gene had told him about the attempt to fix the jury.

"I told him, 'You used Eddie and you used my son-in-law and you don't think you have to tell me.' He says, 'I didn't want to involve you.' Involve me. I'm the fucking boss and he don't want to involve me! He says, 'Well, maybe you wouldn't have let me do it, 'cause Carmine's your son-in-law.' Well, yeah, maybe, but I am the fuckin' boss!"

This was another one of those occasions when Sammy felt it best to say nothing, for fear that Gotti would misinterpret him.

"I don't mind them trying to fix a case. That's what we do, but I'm the boss. I'm gonna wring the neck of that no-good son-in-law of mine. Can't believe he didn't tell me!"

The trouble that tapes had caused his brother, the potentially dire consequences in the O'Connor case of his own "bust 'im up" remark on the state task force tapes, the unfolding pressure of the Eastern and Southern Districts—all these things made Gotti more cautious than ever about electronic or any other kind of surveillance.

Still, he was no chin-rubbing Gigante. It was impossible for him to remain in the background and demand that his men communicate with him by, what, smoothing their hair? He loved to talk; holding forth was his narcotic, a way to expel his anger, get inside his glory, revel in the glow of his power.

For a man who spoke as he sometimes did, in great rolling waves, in which he leapt from one subject to the next, quoted himself and others, and imagined conversations he intended to have, it was often difficult to understand him—or for him to edit remarks that might cause trouble on a wiretap.

Walk-talks were not his only defense against his verbal exuberance and the constant worry of surveillance. When the weather or his mood made walk-talks impractical or undesirable, he occasionally used the rear landing of a hallway that led to the apartments above the Ravenite. A door in the club opened onto the hallway, and he could loiter there without anyone outside the club seeing him.

More rarely and only with a few top-ranking men like Sammy, Frank LoCascio and Tommy Gambino, he had also begun to use an apartment two floors above the club. The tidy little apartment was the home of seventy-four-year-old Nettie Cirelli—the widow of Gambino soldier Mickey Cirelli, the club's caretaker for many years.

Whenever Gotti wanted to use the apartment, he would give Norman Dupont, Nettie's nephew and the club's new caretaker, a few dollars and Dupont would tell Nettie to go shopping. As a gangster's widow, Nettie knew better than to ask why; Dupont who was using the club for after-hours interludes with thrill-seeking girlfriends, knew better than to say why.

More than the hallway, the apartment violated Sammy's rule about speaking in confined areas, but Gotti said he had used it as far back as 1986 and if the FBI had had it bugged, he would already have been in prison for good. Even so, they usually turned on Nettie's stereo, which was tuned to an easy-listening station that favored love songs by Italian singers. In time, Sammy was able to relax there as much as Gotti; it was a relief to have such a comfortable and convenient hideaway.

The hallway and the apartment were the reasons why Gambino squad agents in the now closed audio plant sometimes argued with dubious agents in the video plant that Gotti could not be in the club; even amid the jumble of voices, they would have overheard some sound from his. But if they had not, the video agents must have been dozing on the job and failed to notice that Gotti had entered the club but then quickly left.

These arguments would end as soon as the video agents saw with their own eyes the proof that Gotti was inside, which was him walking outside. Then it would be their turn to question the alertness of their colleagues in the audio plant.

The video agents, however, knew they had the easier, and more entertaining, job. In addition to the car-parking follies of Frank LoCascio and his nondriving driver, Zef Mustafa, they on occasion were treated to the sight of many older men falling over themselves to greet a much younger man who frequently came to the Ravenite wearing his Walkman earphones.

The younger man was the boss's son Junior Gotti. Several months before, as his 1988 Christmas present, Junior—who was only twenty-four years old—was given his button and inducted into the borgata. Everyone but his father was against it, but of course his father was the only one who mattered.

Junior's trucking company, thanks to pop, was now fairly successful. He also had a little circle of followers active in car theft, construction, and extortion. With his brother-in-law Carmine Agnello—who survived a tongue-lashing about trying to fix cases without his father-in-law's knowledge—he owned a three-hundred-thousand-dollar house in the Poconos; he also was remodeling one of the same value on Long Island.

Sammy thought Junior's only qualification was that as far as anyone knew, he did not use drugs because he was a health-food and bodybuilding nut. Still, it was impossible to be candid about the boss's son in front of the boss.

To LoCascio, however, Sammy said that Gotti was actually doing a disservice to his son. "If anybody made a move against John, who do you think they'd take out? He ain't got the experience for a situation like that."

"Nobody's movin' against John. He's got nine lives anyway."

Unlike Sammy, who was encouraging his teenage son, Gerard, toward some kind of legitimate career, LoCascio was actively grooming his son, Salvatore, who was about Junior's age, to take command of his gambling and loan-sharking business in the Bronx.

Gotti didn't have to explain his decision to initiate his muscle-bound son, and he didn't much try. "He's ready, I was ready when I was his age. And I would've gotten it if fuckin' Carlo hadn't closed the books," he told Sammy and LoCascio.

After the O'Connor case came, and other pressure began to mount, Sammy began to believe that by inducting his son, Gotti was really thinking ahead—cementing his control of the family through his unquestionably loyal son, in case he had to go to prison. Viewed that way, the decision to make Junior, and to get him acquainted with the family's ways, was more self-serving than paternal.

"John really loves that Machiavellian bullshit," Sammy said to LoCascio. "Everything has two or three spins with him."

"That's why he's the boss."

The Walkman-wearing made man was still prone to juvenile barroom behavior, however; in June 1989, Junior and some of his Long Island nightclub crew attacked three men in a disco after one objected to a friend of Junior's ogling his wife. It was Junior's third barroom arrest in six years.

To his father's embarrassment, the media had fun with the story for a few days; but the ogled wife had actually suffered a serious injury when Junior or someone else slugged her too. Richard Rehbock—the lawyer who had moved so smoothly from the Willie Boy Johnson corner to the Gotti—had to be called in to try and make the case go away.

"It's embarrassing, but what can you do?" Gotti lamented to Sammy. "The kid's got a temper like you-know-who."

As it turned out, Rehbock did not have to do much, because in another echo of cases involving both Junior and his dad, the victims forgot who attacked them; although they had identified the assailants for the police the night of the incident, they were unable to identify photographs of them in subsequent meetings with prosecutors.

Gotti believed that the outcome was again proof that publicity had its benefits—now even if the publicity was bad.

"Like I've said before, people ain't stupid. They know who and what we are. They read the papers and you don't even have to think about threats. A little case like this folds up without any trouble."

In this instance, even Sammy had to agree that publicity was helpful: "Some stories are like jury tampering without the tampering."

"People read a story about a guy gettin' whacked," Gotti replied, "who knows how that's gonna help you down the line."

"Because of the fear. The fear gives the power. We lose the fear, we lose the power."

"That's it, Sammy. Now you got it."

"Except it didn't work in Genie's case."

"Not the third time, but it almost did. Gotta hand it to Genie. Government don't know how close he came to pullin' it off. Would've if the guy didn't panic. But it was them fuckin' tapes. Too much shit on those tapes. Tapes will kill you."

"But you can take it too far. With an innocent person, you gotta rely just on intimidation. Knock on the door, show your face, and back off. You hurt an innocent person and the public's gonna say enough. The public's dangerous when it says enough."

"Who'd we ever hurt who's innocent? Really hurt?"

"Nobody I can think of. Not us, but other mobs have."

"Some other mobs don't know what they're doing."

The outcome in Junior's case was about the only positive distraction for Gotti over the summer of 1989. He was named in an Eastern District civil racketeering suit aimed at breaking the Gambino hold in the sanitation industry. The Manhattan DA began mounting a similar civil action in the garment center. Even son-in-law Carmine Agnello was arrested—not for fixing cases but for dealing in stolen car parts.

Gotti's annual Fourth of July party was a relative flop too, because the NYPD flooded Ozone Park with so many cops that Gotti's men were able to fire off only a few harmless rockets.

The worst news, by far, came later that month, when Gotti picked up a copy of the *Daily News* and read that the underboss of the Philadelphia family, Philip Leonetti, had "rolled over" and begun talking to the FBI. It was a shocking story on many levels—Leonetti was the first underboss of a major family to turn informer—but the level that mattered most for Gotti was that in 1986, shortly after Sparks, he had met with Leonetti and in vague terms had acknowledged that he was involved.

The meeting was arranged by Sammy and took place in Eddie Garafola's home on Staten Island. Leonetti, the nephew of the Philadelphia boss, had come to meet Gotti—the new boss of a family that shared interests with his in Atlantic City.

Reading the *Daily News,* Gotti could not recall his precise words to Leonetti, but he did remember leaving a strong impression that it was a shoot-or-be-shot situation with Paul. But who knew what words Leonetti would recall? And if he was talking to the FBI, because he was trying to winnow down a recent forty-five-year RICO sentence, he would soon be talking to Walter Mack.

"Can you believe this?" Gotti railed at Sammy later in the day at the Ravenite. "A fuckin' underboss goes and rats."

"Whatever he says, he'll be wingin' it. But he's gotta give 'em somethin' for the sentence you know they're gonna give 'im."

"Motherfucking rats. We're surrounded by fuckin' rats."

CHAPTER 20

• • • • • • • • • • • • • •

Nettie's Place

More than he feared, Gotti was surrounded by informers. The prosecution wave that washed away Joseph Armone, Joe N. Gallo, Gene Gotti, and others, and caused even worse damage in the other borgatas, had eroded the Cosa Nostra foundation far more than he knew when he and Sammy exchanged hapless ideas about informers—"no drug dealers" and "nude ceremonies"—with a delegation from the Genovese family.

Over the past few years, harvesting the panic-induced spoils of their victories, FBI agents had lured more gangsters than ever before, from all the families, into the government tent. By 1989, some agents knew more about the workaday lives and businesses of some soldiers than the new bosses of those soldiers knew.

Because Gotti was the big trophy, the agents were especially keen on coaxing Gambino men into the fold—and after their audio surveillance at the Ravenite came to a sour end in 1988, Gambino squad agents became even more determined.

They looked for men who might need a favor, who might feel angry or slighted, who were popular and had access to the club—someone who was, ideally, a low-level, nonviolent criminal, a bookmaker or loan shark, close to his wife and children, a man afraid of jail.

Every informant's motivation is as different as the details of the arrangement he makes. Some get cash, some get favors, and some a wink and a nod about some crime the FBI, in the overall scheme of things, does not really care about. Most arrangements, however, are sealed by an FBI promise that it will never, ever reveal an informant's identity or force him to testify in a case.

The extra burden that Gambino squad agents had to overcome when they tried to develop informants was that of convincing the target that FBI promises meant anything. Willie Boy Johnson was promised he would never be surfaced, but he was and he was now dead. Agents could, and did, blame that on Diane Giacalone, who threw Willie Boy into her Gotti case over the FBI's objections. Agents could also rightly point out that Willie Boy had compounded the situation by lying to the FBI and committing crimes—such as murder—that unless he agreed to testify were difficult for her to overlook.

The explanation would make sense to someone ready to deal, someone either nonviolent or no longer violent, and so Gambino squad agents overcame their Willie Boy burden. Some informants had signed on soon after Gotti took over, but by the summer of 1989, at least nine men were meeting secretly with agents and providing information about him and the Gambino family. It was an unusually large informant pool, and it reflected the agents' intensified effort, the panic afoot, and the fact that John Gotti was resented and disliked more than his ego could conceive.

Most informants were "controlled" by one, or sometimes two agents. They were given code names, and only the control agents, and a supervisor, knew who they were. Any time an informant and an agent met, the agent was required to write a memo detailing the information he had received.

In the summer of 1989, the information that Gambino squad boss Bruce Mouw and Gotti case agent George Gabriel wanted most was where it was that Gotti felt safe to talk. The video surveillance had shown that on some days he never left the Ravenite for a walk-talk; that and the audio agents' failure to capture significant talk inside the club suggested that he used another location, but where? Both the S.O. squad and the Gambino squad had surveilled Gotti across New York and failed to discover an answer.

For a while, they suspected an office of Tommy Gambino's in the garment center, then one in Lewis Kasman's building, but he never used either enough to convince them that it was the place. Inevitably, all suspicions led back to the Ravenite, but where and how? As far back as

1986, just as Gotti was becoming boss, one of the early informants had insisted that Gotti had used an apartment above the Ravenite for an important meeting. Another even identified the apartment as the home of an old soldier in Neil Dellacroce's crew, Michael Cirelli.

But Cirelli had died, leaving only his widow, Nettie, behind. The rules governing surveillance applications are expansive, but a federal judge needed more than informants' gossip to grant the FBI permission to send a black-bag squad sneaking into the home of a seventy-four-year-old widow who was not suspected of any crime.

The informants did not mention the apartment again—not until three years later, after Tommy Gambino was arrested on obstruction of justice charges and "Source C" told his control agents that Tommy, after making bail, hightailed it to the Ravenite—and conferred with Gotti in Nettie Cirelli's apartment.

Suddenly the Eastern District's decision to pressure Gotti by pressuring Tommy Gambino seemed a better ploy than anyone had imagined. Mouw and Gabriel quickly checked the claim against logs made by video plant agents on the day in question—and there it was: a notation for the time that Gotti and Tommy were seen entering the club but none for when they left, meaning they must have used an exit that was not covered by the video camera.

There were only two possibilities—a rear fire escape for the apartments above the first floor, which was highly unlikely, and the Mulberry Street doorway that the tenants used, which strongly suggested that Gotti and Tommy had indeed used Nettie's place.

The informant was pressed for additional details, and soon Gabriel would summarize them in a secret FBI memo:

Source C also stated that JOHN GOTTI would continue to use the Cirelli apartment for very secretive criminal meetings when he has something very important to discuss with someone and does not want to be seen on the street with this individual. Source C further stated that these conversations would be concerning criminal matters, similar to those discussed inside the Ravenite Social Club or on the street in "walk-talks", but with a greater

need for secrecy. This secrecy includes conversations that
JOHN GOTTI conducts with another member of the
Gambino family that are not to be overheard by any other
members of the family.

The great need for secrecy was the one unbroken
thread of Gotti's life. At least since he was fourteen years
old and lied about the real reason a cement mixer fell on
his toes—and gave him his strutting walk, that bouncing
up before his damaged and missing toes hit the ground—
Gotti had a great need for secrecy. The need became more
crucial when he turned to a full-time life of crime, and
ever more complicated when he joined Cosa Nostra and
had to keep secrets from the police, from agents, from his
crew, from lawyers and jurors, from Paul, from Neil, and,
not least, from wife Vicky.

For someone who loved to gab, to reminisce, to needle
and cajole, and who was spontaneous and gregarious,
such a great need for secrecy was a yoke, and it was tire-
some carrying it around, especially when some matters,
such as Tommy's arrest, demanded urgent consideration.

He knew the case against Tommy was really a thinly
veiled assault on him, and it came in the wake of his indictment in the O'Connor case and the news about Walter
Mack's offensive in the Southern District. Events were
piling atop one another; the need for secrecy was great,
but so was the need to talk.

As he told Sammy, Gotti had used the apartment before, with no ill result; so he began to do so again, sending Norman Dupont upstairs with a hundred-dollar bill to
give to Nettie to go shopping—and not just for the
meeting with Tommy, but with others, such as his acting
underboss and consigliere, LoCascio and Sammy.

Soon, the existence and use of the apartment became
an open secret among the fifty or so men who shaped up
at the club three and sometimes four nights a week, and
soon more informants were corroborating Source C. At
about the same time, the informants began reporting that
Gotti was stepping out into the Ravenite hallway when he
wanted to talk privately; the informants said they had
seen it before, but more often now.

"Now we know why the audio plant guys couldn't pick
'im up sometimes," Mouw told Andy Maloney, as they

decided it was time to submit another application to the
federal judge who approved their earlier electronic surveillance applications. The number of informants, backed
up by the holes in the video logs, had pushed gossipy information into solid probable cause.

"Sooner or later, you know he's gonna talk himself into
a hole," said Maloney, jubilantly emerging from a depression brought on by the problems with the bug inside the
club.

Gotti's use of the hallway was a lot more careless than
his use of the apartment. It was much easier for the FBI
to bug the hallway than it was to break into the apartment
of an old lady who rarely went anywhere and who shared
the floor with neighbors. Furthermore, only the people
who went there with him knew for sure about the apartment; everyone in the club could see him using the hallway.

But, more and more throughout the summer of 1989,
the need for secrecy collided with the need to talk. The
defection to the FBI by Philadelphia underboss Philip
Leonetti was only one more of the collision points, and
Gotti knew Leonetti was going to be talking about the
biggest secret of all, Sparks. The more events pushed him
deeper into a corner, the more careless Gotti became—in
the worst and most obvious place, the Ravenite.

By October 1989, after Maloney's lawyers and the
Gambino squad amended their electronic surveillance application and got judicial approval to bug both the hallway and the apartment, Gotti was using both regularly.

The same S.O. team that had infiltrated the Ravenite
itself almost two years before had no problem with the
hallway, and the bug was up and running on October 15.
For many reasons, Nettie's place was not going to be so
easy.

"It's obvious we can't go in there at night, even if she's
a sound sleeper," Mouw said as he, Gabriel and members
of the S.O. team mulled over sneaky scenarios. "She
might have a heart attack."

"And you can't dress up like a Con Ed guy and go in
there during the day," Gabriel said, pointing out that in
New York utility workers tend to service the same neighborhoods and therefore an imposter might rouse suspicion.

All agreed that the best plan was to wait and hope Nettie took a trip somewhere; because they knew little about her, except that she seemed to stay in the neighborhood, they feared it might be a long wait. Still, her home was such a potential gold mine that it was best to be patient and seek ways to minimize detection risks for the S.O. squad; a failed mission would alert Gotti and save him from a chance to catch him being himself on FBI tapes.

In the meantime, a pen register—a device that authorities can put on a telephone without a court order because it merely lists the time of incoming and outgoing calls—was placed on her telephone so that agents might learn details about her daily routine. The deactivated bug inside the club was put back on; it might pick up a few words that would make words in the hallway make more sense.

Hoping to provoke more talking, the Maloney-Mouw team also decided to put Gotti in another legal squeeze. The obstruction of justice case filed against Tommy after his dissembling on behalf of Gotti in the grand jury months before gave them an ideal opportunity. Tommy's trial on those charges was set to begin in two weeks, and so George Gabriel was dispatched to the Ravenite to give Gotti a subpoena requiring him to testify at the trail.

"He's not here," reported Bobby Boriello, the soldier and Gotti bodyguard who in 1987 had fired the miraculous shot that slowed would-be assassin Jeffrey Ciccone down enough that he could be captured, tortured, and questioned before being executed.

"Tell him I'll stop by his house in the morning, then."

"Don't go too early. It just ruins the day for the rest of us when you wake him up too early."

The subpoena was really just part of a law enforcement ploy known as "tickling the wire." It was an attempt to make it appear that the Eastern District intended to ask Tommy's trial judge to give Gotti immunity, thereby forcing Gotti to either testify or go to jail, but its actual purpose was to get Gotti on tape. The team meant to withdraw the subpoena before the trial; for legal and strategic reasons, it did not want to risk complicating a future case by immunizing him in a comparatively unimportant case.

To enhance the ruse, agents also served trial subpoenas

on two other men at the same time—Joseph "Joe Butch" Corrao, a top capo, and George Remini, a soldier in Tommy's decina. The Corrao subpoena was another fake, but Remini—the man Gotti often used to relay messages to Tommy—would be squeezed all the way.

A stage built on trickery and deception was now in place, and at the Ravenite the subpoenas yielded the desired effect. They began prying open a window into Gotti's world of secrets and adding bricks to the RICO foundation.

They also provided a rare peak at a gangster's relationship with his lawyers and at how difficult it would be for any lawyer to represent a gangster like Gotti. Numerous times, Gotti expressed displeasure with his lawyers, Bruce Cutler and Jerry Shargel, whose job it was to save him in the O'Connor case—which, to make matters worse, was steaming toward a trial date in early 1990.

He seemed more displeased with Shargel and talked as though he felt responsible for saving Shargel's career— which had hit a slippery spot in 1985, thanks to Walter Mack, the prosecutor now trying to assemble a Southern District murder case against Gotti. In Mack's case against the extravagantly violent Roy DeMeo crew, he asked a judge to bar Shargel from representing a DeMeo soldier on grounds that Shargel was really "house counsel" for the DeMeo "enterprise" and unable to effectively represent a soldier whose legal interests conflicted with those of the enterprise.

After a hearing, in which a DeMeo turncoat testified he saw DeMeo give Shargel two hundred thousand dollars to defend other crew members and Shargel testified that he had destroyed office records that would have set the matter straight, the judge agreed and booted Shargel off the case.

It was at that point, Gotti said in a conversation that the reactivated bug in the clubhouse overheard, that Shargel came to him and asked for work.

"I tell you, when he got in trouble, Jerry, they brought him to my house. I said, 'Jerry, don't worry about it. Don't worry about it, all our friends will use you, and you're good. We all know you're good.' Boom! Two guys took him on right away."

Later, Gotti recalled how he had suspected Shargel of speaking to a *Daily News* columnist—not to help a client's case but to get publicity for himself—and how he had berated him for it.

"I told him, 'One day I'm gonna show you a better way than the elevator, out of your office!' He was doing this to have his name in the paper . . . 'Jerry Shargel, top criminal lawyer.' "

Despite his displeasure, which would grow as the cost of fighting off cases grew, Gotti stuck with his lawyers.

Along with Cutler, Shargel was called upon to fight the Eastern District subpoenas, and one of the first conversations taped by the hallway bug involved them. It occurred after Gotti arrived at the Ravenite and announced that to his dismay he had just learned that Cutler and Shargel had met with Tommy Gambino's lawyers and hatched a plan calling on Tommy to plead guilty and make Gotti's testimony unnecessary.

The lawyers' plan showed they did not know whom they were working for, Gotti fumed after calling Frank LoCascio, Jackie D'Amico, and Joe Watts into the hallway. He never allowed his men to plead guilty in an important case, even if it meant one less worry for him and probably only six months in prison for Tommy.

After Shargel told him about the lawyers' proposal, Gotti said he blew up and told him under "no circumstances" would he allow Tommy to plead guilty. It did not matter that in this case Shargel was representing Corrao and Remini, not Tommy; as always, there was only one client, the Gambino family, which was him. Of course, because of the hallway bug, it should have mattered; the no-plea policy amounted to obstruction of justice, an indictable RICO crime.

"Now you tell Tommy to fight it," Gotti agitatedly began, quoting himself talking to Shargel. "Break their fuckin' holes! And don't worry about us going to jail. Me number one! I like jail better than I like the streets. And do what I'm tellin' ya. And don't ever have these kind of meetings again."

Gotti's remarks about jail sounded more selfless than they were; if he refused to testify, he would be jailed only for the duration of Tommy's trial—likely only a few days.

Still, in another tirade for the same audience, Gotti

quoted himself giving a similar tongue-lashing to Cutler, his champion for the last five years, for failing to recognize that Joe Butch Corrao and "Fat Georgie" Remini would subject themselves to a contempt-of-court conviction, as long as Gotti wanted them to.

"Nobody is taking the stand! Tell them to go fight! You go in there and break their fuckin' heads. Don't worry about us. Go in there and fight. Get my cell ready; get Joe Butch's cell ready and get Fat Georgie's cell ready. Nobody is taking the stand!"

In two weeks the issue became moot. Remini was left on the hot seat, but the subpoenas of Gotti and Joe Butch Corrao were withdrawn as planned. In one tirade, noting that he was the one in the federal crosshairs, Gotti had even predicted this.

"You know, Bruce, the truth," he crowed when Cutler brought the news to the Ravenite. "Didn't I tell you they ain't gonna do the three of us?"

"Yes, you did."

Gotti's next prediction, about the outcome of Remini's case, was not as prescient. As Remini's time to refuse to testify grew near, Remini worried that the government intended to indict him and expose him to a lengthy sentence rather than just jail him for the duration of Tommy's trial. Gotti tried to soothe him.

"They're not gonna indict you," Gotti said as they huddled in the Ravenite hallway. "Impossible. Listen to me, listen to your friend, please. I've called every motherfuckin' step of the way . . . I call everything right. This is just a ploy."

Later, after Tommy's trial began in Brooklyn on November 28, 1989, Remini appeared with his lawyer, Jerry Shargel, and refused to testify. He was immediately taken to the MCC and jailed. After one day, he was released. But later on, after Tommy's jurors agreed with his lawyer, Michael Rosen, that Tommy was improperly targeted by a grand jury that really had John Gotti on its mind and acquitted him—Fat Georgie was indicted.

Gotti was not put in the same vise; with him it would have looked too unfair, too punitive, like trying too hard to get even. Besides, just a week before Remini's refusal to testify, an earlier decision to be patient about Nettie Cirelli had paid off, and the Maloney-Mouw team had new reason to hope they would soon have much bigger things in store for the so-called Teflon Don.

Ever since winning approval to bug the hallway and Nettie's apartment two floors up, Gambino squad agents had occasionally surveilled her—to learn where she went on errands and for how long. She never went far, nor for long.

George Gabriel had also been monitoring the pen register on her telephone, trying to determine what time she stopped making and receiving calls at night and presumably fell asleep. Usually she was on the phone every night, but usually no later than ten in the evening. To test this, Gabriel once dialed her number at midnight and hung up when she answered. Still, a nighttime break-in was deemed too dangerous, because of the effect that the sudden sight of strange men clad all in black might have on her if she woke up.

On November 19, however, the telephone in Nettie's place was silent all day. Knowing nothing for certain, but having a hunch, Gabriel became convinced that she had taken a trip, perhaps to visit relatives for the upcoming Thanksgiving holiday. He decided to recommend to the S.O. squad that it make its move that night. To his horror, he could not reach S.O. supervisor James Kallstrom.

The next morning he dialed Nettie's number, which rang on and on. More convinced now, he reached out for Kallstrom again, this time successfully.

"We've blown one chance, but I think we'll get another tonight," he said.

After Gabriel briefed him, Kallstrom agreed. That night, as other agents positioned themselves nearby—to provide cover and, if necessary, distractions—the S.O. squad's chief operative for surreptitious entry, John Kravec, and another agent entered the Ravenite building through the unlocked door that tenants of the upstairs apartments used. They walked up two flights of marble stairs, turned right and picked the lock of Apartment 10 in hardly any time at all.

Inside, on silent feet, they quickly determined that Nettie was indeed not home and then used their flashlights to determine the best place to position the bug. The apartment was small, and the most logical place for men who did not reside there to sit when they came to talk was the living room, which contained a couch and two chairs positioned around a coffee table. The bug went into the ceiling, directly above the table. It was perfect. Mission accomplished.

"If he goes in there and opens his mouth, we'll hear his lips moving," Mouw told Maloney the next day.

Nettie came home a few days later, and was unable to detect the few particles of dust in her immaculate apartment that had been disturbed. She had gone to California to visit relatives for Thanksgiving.

"I just felt it in my gut, that's all," Gabriel sheepishly said, when other agents applauded his fortuitous hunch.

With the stage now set with a second trapdoor, another fortuitous break occurred. Independently of the FBI, the NYPD cops now actively shaking the Sparks bushes for the Southern District decided to encourage someone in the media to revisit the Sparks story. Thousands had been in the vicinity of Sparks at the time, and it was hoped that the publicity might cause new witnesses to come forward. The cops decided to contact the nationally syndicated television show, *America's Most Wanted,* an inspired choice.

The show was popular in the law enforcement world because its nationwide spotlight had resulted in the capture of so many criminals. It also was a big ratings draw, and it could do more with the story than the local media, which had reported so many Sparks stories that it would be difficult for them to find a hook, a news peg, that would justify yet another story. In *America's* formula, the Sparks story was a ten: unsolved crimes, notorious gangsters, glamorous midtown Manhattan setting.

It would be no problem talking the show's producers into a Sparks story, with only the approaching four-year anniversary as a hook. It wasn't—and it was accomplished with breathtaking speed, thanks to a warehouse of already-shot video showing Gotti charming reporters outside courthouses and "Big Paul" Castellano and his friend and would-be underboss, Thomas Bilotti, dead on the street by Sparks. The show, which generated much secondary publicity and a large audience, aired on November 26.

Mouw and Gabriel had learned about the show a few days before and jumped for joy. The show was the functional equivalent of tickling the wire, and it would get Gotti's lips moving.

The very first words overheard on the hallway bug by newly inspired audio plant agents had presented everyone who listened to them a personally felt motive for inducing Gotti to reminisce about Sparks. The motive was that in this first dividend from the informants about the places where he felt it was safe to talk, Gotti implied he had a secret hook, a source somewhere in law enforcement.

The implication, given the well-documented history of Cosa Nostra infiltration and manipulation of law enforcement in New York, was entirely plausible—and acutely upsetting. What did Gotti already know about the NYPD, the FBI, and the Eastern and Southern Districts efforts against him?

The vague hint that Gotti had a hook came on November 1, before the business with the subpoenas, when the hallway bug overheard him talking as though he was now convinced that Philip Leonetti, the turncoat Philadelphia underboss, had given authorities what they needed to crack the Sparks case.

Gotti summoned Joe Butch Corrao and George Helbig, a Corrao associate, into the hallway and told Helbig to "find out" when the "pinch" for Sparks would come; the order implied that Helbig knew someone, or knew someone who knew someone, who could get such insider information.

After reviewing that tape, Bruce Mouw's suspicion was, dirty cop. The FBI had skeletons in its closet, but he knew that none of his agents would be selling out to Cosa Nostra. Besides, the FBI was not focusing on Sparks; Walter Mack and the Southern District grand jury were. Mack was above suspicion, but his investigators were from the NYPD, and many of its detectives had been raised on the same streets as the men in Cosa Nostra. Corruption born of childhood friendships was a familiar NYPD storyline.

Gotti's remarks also showed that while he was certain of a Sparks case, the hydra-headed offensive arrayed against him had him wondering if the case would be brought locally or federally.

"Why don't you just try to find out what the pinch is gonna be," he said to Helbig, ". . . the feds or state."

The apparent attempt to learn law enforcement secrets about the Sparks investigation amounted to more obstruction of justice, and by the time Gotti returned to the subject four weeks later, *America's Most Wanted* had just aired and named him not just the prime suspect but the man responsible.

This time the hallway bug was unable to distinguish about five minutes of whispering by Gotti, Joe Butch Corrao, and George Helbig. But Helbig apparently reported that it appeared that both state and federal prosecutors were planning Sparks cases, because Gotti summoned Jerry Shargel into the hallway to inquire, in Corrao's and Helbig's presence, if such a scenario were possible.

"Does that make sense they would do it at the same time? Do the same charge, two different places?"

"They've done it," Shargel replied. "They've done it, sure."

"Well, would it make sense with a guy like myself? I'm not saying me. Just a guy like myself. Make sense? Won't it look like overkill?"

Shargel reminded Gotti of a recent case in which a local politician had been accused of substantially the same crimes by both the Manhattan district attorney and the Southern District.

In his reply to Shargel, Gotti was as blustery as he was with his men, and he also went out of his way to protest his innocence—so far out of his way that it sounded as though he hoped eavesdroppers were listening.

"If I'm gonna get pinched, I'll break their fuckin' hole. When you're innocent, it's easy enough. I'll win on the merits. This case, I'm innocent. I ain't worried about it. But there's no overkill in these bum trials?"

"No, because in their mind, [it's] getting to you."

Gotti said Helbig had just told him that a federal murder case could be brought under civil rights laws, but Shargel said another federal law could be used.

"There's a statute called committing murder in furtherance of your position," the lawyer said, referring accurately to the law under which Walter Mack was indeed building a case.

"Furthering the position?"

Shargel's next four words created a pregnant pause: "Who was the guy?"

"Nobody," Gotti finally said, as Corrao and Helbig chuckled.

"Best way to put it," Corrao said.

"When did they come up with this?" Gotti asked. "Furtherance of your position, huh? That's nice."

Shargel did not have to be told why Gotti needed to know when the law was passed. "I'm not sure if it's December of 1985," he said, referring to the month Paul died. "I have to check."

Gotti told him to do so. "Not for myself. I'm just curious, that's all."

The law in question went into effect fourteen months before Sparks, and Gotti was told the distressing news on the following day, November 30, 1989—when, for the first time since the S.O. squad had visited Nettie's place nine days before, he went there.

Before climbing the stairs, followed by Sammy and LoCascio, he was told some other bad—but not unexpected—news. Earlier in the day, in federal court in Brooklyn, Michael Coiro, his lawyer during his Bergin hijacking days, was convicted of helping other clients, Angelo and Gene, to hide their heroin money.

Coiro was arrested at the same time that Angelo, Gene, and the rest were, in 1983, but he was eventually severed and tried separately—and the infamous Angelo tapes turned out to be as damaging to him as they were to everyone else.

"You're not our lawyer, you're one of us as far as we're concerned," Gene had said to Coiro, while agents listened.

"I know it, Gene, and I feel that way."

The case destroyed Coiro's career—at one time he was the man to see for a criminal problem in the state courts of Queens—and he fell into debt and became a heavy drinker, so heavy that his next-door neighbor, Lewis Kasman, told Gotti he was worried that Coiro had decided to drink himself to death. During the six years of pretrial wrangling, Coiro was represented for free by a lawyer whom he regarded almost like a son, Jerry

Shargel; Coiro had referred cases to Shargel when the younger lawyer was starting out.

When the time came to actually go to trial, Shargel was on trial in another case, and the judge in Coiro's refused to delay it to accommodate Shargel. Bruce Cutler took over for Shargel, and suddenly an echo of the Giacalone case was felt, if not heard, in the well of the courtroom in Brooklyn. Cutler's opponent was John Gleeson, Giacalone's former assistant, who still harbored a deeply felt grudge about Cutler's and Gotti's abuse of her; he also was beginning to share Maloney's belief—based on his knowledge of the attempts to fix the heroin case—that the case that shot Cutler to almost as much fame as Gotti had been fixed.

Lawyers always say they keep personal feelings out of their cases, but it had been personal between Gleeson and Cutler ever since Cutler called Giacalone a "slut" and Gleeson, in court, ridiculed Cutler—"he's not a lawyer."

Gleeson thought Cutler should really be in prison, not in such magazines as *GQ,* because he believed Cutler had suborned perjury in the Giacalone case—encouraged a defense witness to lie about the favors Giacalone offered him, such as drugs and her panties, when she was considering using him as a witness. After the case, Maloney had encouraged Gleeson to investigate Cutler's pretrial conversations with the witness, a bank robber and former Bergin hanger-on who did admit he lied on the stand. Later he denied the admission, and so even though he was eventually convicted of lying, it became impossible to build a perjury case against Cutler on the word of such a person.

Giacalone's former assistant had also conducted a grand jury investigation into the bogus acquittal itself, but all it led to was crow from Cutler, who was Gotti's press secretary as well as his lawyer.

"Sour grapes," he said, when the *Daily News* reported that the acquittal was being investigated. "The jury that acquitted John Gotti was a courageous, independent jury free of anything untoward. It doesn't surprise me [that] vindictive federal prosecutors who can't get what they want in court cry foul later on. That is their makeup."

Regardless of what he might have suspected, Cutler was able to summon such indignation without sheepish-

ness, because Gotti had been smart enough not to tell him
about the fix. And, later on, when Gleeson conducted yet
another tampering investigation into the first heroin case,
which led a judge to declare a mistrial, Cutler had been
equally indignant: "From what I understand the case is
going very well for the defendants, so I am not surprised
that the government is making these false allegations."

By 1989, Gleeson was no longer the inexperienced
prosecutor he had been in the Giacalone case. The reason
he was involved in many jury-fixing investigations was
that he was now chief of Maloney's special-prosecutions
unit; the now thirty-six-year-old lawyer had lost a case, to
Shargel, but that was about it.

Low-key but relentless, ambitious but happy with the
job he was in, he and the flamboyant Cutler were as different as Gotti and Sammy. And, as Sammy brought more
knowledge and more command of the details to a
sitdown, Gleeson brought more to a courtroom; in the rematch occasioned by Michael Coiro's trial, substance
overwhelmed style. Coiro was convicted after a two-week
trial.

It was hardly consolation, but at least the defeat did not
cost Coiro any money. Cutler, like Shargel, did not charge
him a fee. Even if Gotti had not encouraged Cutler to
show Coiro such consideration, Cutler had made so much
money defending Gotti he could easily afford it.

Immediately after the verdict, Gleeson asked U.S. district court judge Joseph McLaughlin to jail Coiro pending
sentencing. The judge refused, ruling that Coiro was not
likely to violate bail and flee. Gleeson then said that
while out on bail, Coiro should be prohibited from fre-
quenting certain places, such as the Ravenite Social Club,
but the judge instructed him to put the proposal in writing
and submit a motion the next day.

After everyone left, Cutler visited the judge's chambers
to make a special and fateful request: Would the judge allow him to escort his crestfallen client to the Ravenite so
Coiro could be comforted by a man who meant the world
to him, John Gotti?

Judge McLaughlin, who was as in the dark about the
Ravenite bugs as Cutler was, granted the request—and
Cutler escorted Coiro straight to the Ravenite and right
into more trouble.

While Cutler stayed downstairs, Coiro walked up to Nettie's apartment with Gotti, Sammy, and LoCascio; the audio plant agents monitoring the newly planted bug in her ceiling were already on their toes because the video agents had reported the arrival of the Gambino administration, and now Cutler and Coiro, all of which suggested that this might be one of those times when Gotti did not want lesser members of the family hearing him talk.

It was, and the agents grew ecstatic when the first sounds of Gotti and Sammy bantering about nothing of consequence came streaming across wires and into their headsets with almost compact-disc clarity.

It was so clean and the equipment was working so perfectly that one of the agents on duty, Mark Roberts, broke his concentration for a moment to whisper to another: "This is incredible, they're up there, completely relaxed, talking freely! Tremendous!"

Actually it was far more important for the agents to keep an eye on the equipment than an ear to the words being said. The words could always be analyzed, and would be, hundreds of times, but first they needed to make sure the equipment got the words—that new tapes were always ready, that the recording volume was always adjusted to the sound levels of the voices.

The chitchat stopped when Coiro entered the room. Over the years, part of his value to Gotti and of his success in Queens was that many times he had obtained law enforcement secrets from a corrupt source that he had never revealed, not to Gotti or anyone else.

Apart from a wondrous display of Gotti's endless need to affirm his wisdom, even in situations where it was the other person who needed affirmation, his words would make it clear that he was not satisfied with George Helbig's information; he wanted more, and so, after a few words of sympathy for Coiro, he turned to what was really on his mind—and drew Coiro into yet more obstruction of justice—and attempted bribery of some unidentified public official.

"First, you know, we're sorry," he said to Coiro.

"Thank you."

"I don't have to tell you how sorry we are."

"Oh, John."

"I knew you was guilty there. I didn't guess it. I knew

it. And I don't think you're gonna go away [to prison] before the [obligatory legal] appeal. So, you got a fuckin'
another year on the street, maybe. I think [the judge is]
gonna give you ten years. Maybe look for you to do about
three or four."

"I'll do it, John."

"Didn't I tell ya? I called the whole shot right down the
line."

Gotti then turned to his own problems and recalled for
Coiro how a "source" had told him to expect state and
federal cases on the same "pinch," and how Shargel had
explained it was possible.

"Feds, they got a new statute. Enhancing your position,
to commit murder to enhance your position. They're going at it tooth and nail, [to see] who's gonna try me first.
I think it's easier to beat a murder 'beef' by the state."

"No doubt about it," Coiro replied. "Federal court, you
get the kitchen sink."

While sure his information was accurate, Gotti told
Coiro he wanted him to corroborate it with his source and
to learn exactly when the cases would be filed.

"But what you gotta do is you gotta grab this guy.
Mike, we've been good to him in the past, we'll be good
to him in the future. I never once asked you who he is.
Did I ever ask you?"

"Never!"

"You know, Mike, again I'm, I feel lousy for pushing
your sins aside, your heartaches aside."

"Forget about it. It's over."

"Now let me ask ya a question, Mike. Can you see this
guy pronto?"

"Tomorrow."

"Mike, I'm not trying to be a wise guy. Don't have any
fuckin' drinks in between then and seeing me."

"No, come on, John. Will you stop?"

"I know, Mike. But you try to ease your pain with a
drink. I do, we all do."

"Believe me, it's done tomorrow."

Gotti and Coiro, with Sammy jumping in infrequently,
then talked about Coiro's conviction earlier in the day—
and how the case was a loser from the start because of
Angelo Ruggiero, now lying terminally ill in a hospital a
couple of miles away. Angelo had jeopardized so many

by being so careless and indiscreet in his home, Coiro said.

"You never heard me fuckin' jeopardize," Gotti said.

"You never did!" Coiro agreed.

Gotti then reminded Coiro that he never allowed people to talk indiscreetly when they visited him at home.

"Did I ever talk to ya in there?"

"Never!"

"As close as Angelo was, he was never in my fuckin' house talking. Nothin' to put us in fuckin' jail."

"That's the right way," Sammy interjected.

"Because you know why, Sammy?" asked Gotti, on the verge of providing audio agents with a particularly sweet moment of irony: "You gotta relax in your fuckin' house. The way we're relaxing right here."

Relaxed, Gotti fixated on Angelo. "That cocksucker, and I hate to talk about people that are dying. He ain't a rat. He ain't a mutt. But I gotta call him a cocksucker. A guy was telling me this morning, 'All your troubles came from two places, Willie Boy Johnson and Angelo's house.' Willie Boy Johnson and Angelo Ruggiero decided they wanted to be a big-shot operation. That's all our troubles."

After more lamenting, the conversation concluded with Coiro repeating his promise to contact his source and report to Gotti the next day; he said he would ask his neighbor and their mutual friend Lewis Kasman, to telephone Gotti and schedule a meeting somewhere—a remark that suggested to the FBI that Gotti relied on his "adopted son" for more than the sunny embrace of Kasman's Florida getaway.

There was no time to place additional bugs and wiretaps in homes and offices, and so Coiro's source remained a secret. In any case, Coiro and Gotti got a chance to talk privately only six days later, when Angelo Ruggiero died and they attended the wake.

Attached to a portable life-support system, Angelo—a one-hundred-and-thirty-pound shell of his former self—had left a Manhattan hospital just a couple of days before and gone to his home in Cedarhurst to die. Gotti had still refused to visit, or to send him a message, and he even considered boycotting the wake.

"He had to go and be a big shot and get us all in trouble," he complained to Sammy. "Oughta had his tongue cut out."

"Look, everybody knows how you feel," Sammy said, "but it's not gonna look right if you don't go to the wake."

So Gotti went to the wake, unaware that he had turned over the first few shovels of dirt for his own legal grave—by being as indiscreet as his old and dead Fulton-Rockaway pal.

CHAPTER 21

• • • • • • • • • • • • • •

Muck and Fuck

Tommy Gambino's win in the obstruction of justice case was only a small setback for the FBI–Eastern District team. The real goal all along was John Gotti, and because of his obstruction of justice conversations in the hallway and in Nettie Cirelli's apartment on November 30, the team was closer to its goal; soon it would be within reach. So much was going on in Gotti's secret life, he had such a need to talk, wires would not have to be tickled again.

The team was under no obligation to share the break-through conversations now in its possession, or its knowledge of the existence of newly installed trapdoors at the Ravenite, with other law enforcement agencies, and it did not—especially because it now appeared that Gotti had access to two corrupt sources in law enforcement.

While elated with the new tapes, the pursuers wanted more than an obstruction of justice case, which was about as sexy as the already rejected gambling and loan-sharking case. But Gotti's carelessness in the hallway—and his remark about feeling "relaxed" in Nettie's place—seemed to portend greater things.

For nearly two anxious weeks, however, the bugs picked up little more than Gotti commenting in the hall-way that a man who does not gamble "has no compassion." Then, on December 12, 1990, a week after Angelo Ruggiero's death, Gotti made a second visit to Nettie's place and began digging a much deeper hole.

This time, it was just him and Frank LoCascio—or, as Gotti said while the tape rolled in the audio plant a few blocks away, "my acting underboss Frankie." In and of it-self, the remark was a problem, because it tended to es-tablish LoCascio's membership in an illegal "criminal enterprise" as defined by the RICO law. Similarly, Gotti did himself no favors by calling himself "the boss"—or Sammy, by referring to him as "my consigliere."

The pulses of the audio plant agents quickened as these words streamed into their headsets, but Gotti gave them many reasons for feeling excited. He was clearly in a volatile mood—somber one moment, angry the next. In one of the angry moments, while explaining a boss's right and obligation to make the family's tough decisions, he came close to admitting that he killed Paul.

"Who's gonna challenge me? Who's gonna defy me? What are they gonna do? Take a shot? Like I did to the other guy? I'd welcome that. I'll kill their fuckin' mothers, their fathers."

By recalling for LoCascio how Paul had conducted business with the Genovese family, to the detriment of Gambino soldiers, Gotti even supplied at least a partial motive: "That's what made me hate, really, fuckin' Paul. He sold the borgata out for a construction company."

The hour-long conversation was really more of a monologue. Occasionally LoCascio provided some sympathetic interjection or some verbal connective issue for Gotti, who soared from one subject to another without much regard for transitions—or much reluctance to contradict earlier statements.

For instance, he was alternately upbeat and dour about his chances of surviving the troubles headed his way. "We're gonna be all right," he said at one point, referring to the upcoming O'Connor case—now due for trial in less than a month—and to the state task force tapes on which the case was partially built and which Cutler and Shargel, in pretrial motions, were trying to suppress on technical grounds. "We get rid of these fuckin' rat tapes, we're gonna be okay, Frank."

But at another point, he talked as though jail was inevitable: "I don't give two fucks about myself going to jail. Don't I know they ain't gonna rest until they put me in jail? So I fight it tooth and nail to the fuckin' end."

At the monologue's outset, Gotti said he was not one to talk behind another's back, then immediately became critical of his absentee consigliere, Sammy. He said Sammy was involved in too many companies and was so busy making money that he often overlooked the needs and interests of ordinary soldiers. It sounded like another attack of "*geloso*," because he also said he loved Sammy and did not doubt that Sammy was faithfully turning over a correctly respectful slice of illegal pies—a quarter million dollars every ten weeks now.

"I love him," he said, adding that he was even considering naming Sammy acting boss if he had to go to jail. "So obviously I gotta love the guy. I gotta think he's capable. [And] I know [if] I 'blast' him a little bit, he'll slow it down."

LoCascio let Gotti's remark about making Sammy acting boss fly by. He was happy in his current role, symbolic stand-in for the imprisoned and doomed-to-die-there Joseph Armone. Instead, thinking Gotti might want to blast, or reproach, Sammy now, LoCascio interjected, "You want me to go and get him?"

Gotti declined, emphatically. "No, no, no. No, no, no."

Instead, in different words, he repeated the same concerns about Sammy's dealmaking getting out of hand. But the more he spoke, the more it seemed that Gotti now, as before with Joe Watts and others, felt a need to remind people that he was the boss and Sammy Bull Gravano was not. "Am I lying?" he asked LoCascio. "Am I out of order here? Correct me! You're my fuckin' acting underboss, Frankie. Correct me, Frankie."

"I agree with ya."

"Yes, but am I wrong?"

"No, you're not wrong."

As he got deeper into the oration, Gotti became, for him, unusually introspective and self-deprecating. At times he seemed genuinely melancholy. Undoubtedly, the genuinely serious problems on his near horizon were the reason, but he also sounded like a man gradually coming under the emotionally liberating influence of a cocktail or two—and in the background the audio agents did occasionally hear what sounded like ice falling into a glass.

For instance, part of the reason Sammy was so active, Gotti said, was that he was filling a vacuum—one created by the boss's lesser experience in certain areas: "I don't know nothin' about building. I don't know anything . . . best I ever did was go on a few hijackings."

Gotti also said he found his newfound wealth remarkable, given that he started with nothing. "A fuckin' jerk like me. Never had nothing in my life." Still, wealth had not made him greedy: "That's not John Gotti. At least I hope that's not me. Maybe I see myself in a light that I'm not in, I don't know."

At the end of a lengthy passage in which to the delight of the agents he referred to many capos and various grubby problems in the crews, he said about his problems: "[They] break my fuckin' heart. Who the fuck wants to be here? We got nothin' but troubles. I got cases coming up. I got nothing but fuckin' trouble. I don't feel good."

One of the men, probably LoCascio, had turned on Nettie's stereo radio when they entered her apartment, but not so loud that words spoken directly beneath the bug in the ceiling were lost. The radio, however, could be heard in the background, and the music coming from it contributed to the melancholy aura in the room because, as always, it was tuned to an easy-listening station, whose playlist was heavy on Italian love songs.

"O, solo, mio," the agents could hear during brief pauses in Gotti's rumination, which in addition to being introspective and self-deprecating, was amusingly revisionist, given his weakness for gambling, nightclubbing, and women whose first name was not Vicky: "I'm sick, Frankie, and I ain't got no right to be sick. I'm not goin' partying. I'm not going to race[tracks], [or] popping girls. I'm not doing nothin' fuckin' selfish here."

No, of course not, LoCasico would interject, when it seemed appropriate and when Gotti's mood resulted in paranoid thoughts about the loyalty of the capos.

"What the fuck, am I nuts here? If I go to jail, they'd be happy. 'Minchia, we finally got rid of 'im.' Hah! I'm getting myself sick, Frank, sick."

"You gotta get it out," LoCascio soothed, encouraging his boss's ventilation.

"But one thing I ain't gonna be is two-faced. I'm gonna call 'em like I see 'em. That I gotta do 'til the day I die."

LoCascio's emotional support frequently moved Gotti out of self-deprecation and into more familiar self-justifying terrain, and so Gotti again reminded LoCascio of how wealthy he could be, if only he wanted, and what a trusting boss he was because he did not require his men

to prove with "paper" how much they made and, therefore, reveal for him the true level of their generosity. The
potential legal peril of making a paper record of percentages was the reason for Gotti's hatred of paper, a reason
a careful old loan shark like LoCascio plainly knew, even
as he indulged it.

"I would be a billionaire if I was looking to be a selfish
boss," Gotti said. "That's not me. You know I'm taking
care of the people. We don't need none of these papers.
We're too close for that shit. Ya see, I got that kind of
fuckin' trust in Cosa Nostra. We're where we belong.
We're in the positions we belong in, Frankie, and nobody
could change that."

From a law enforcement perspective, Gotti's mention,
in a single taped statement, of "boss" and "Cosa Nostra,"
was almost a prosecutorial home run. Still, it got better
Winding down, he provoked gasps in the audio plant by
swatting a few comparatively easy grounders toward his
pursuers. The man reporters called the biggest gangster
since Al Capone—who went to jail, and died there, only
because of tax charges—began talking about what he did
to keep the IRS at bay.

One strategy, he confided, was to control who was allowed to pick up, and hand to him, money from the family's enterprises. Sammy was allowed, of course; he was
the consigliere and beyond suspicion. Naturally, the new
Bergin acting capo, former city sanitation worker Peter
Gotti, was also allowed; the oldest Gotti brother was
never as important to John as their younger brother, the
moody and resentful Gene, but Gene was gone;
lumberjack-like Peter—the first of the Fulton-Rockaway
Boys—was now the last of them to run the Bergin crew.

"The only thing I make my brother, Pete, do," Gotti
told LoCascio, "is he picks up about ten thousand every
month, or every other month from Carl and brings it to
Sammy."

"Carl" was the Gambino family contact in a Cosa
Nostra–protected scam to evade state and federal taxes in
the gasoline industry by playing a sort of shell game with
dummy companies.

"Now, with the money that comes in," Gotti continued,
"that's my business if I want to distribute it, Frankie.
Someday I'll tell you what I take out, what I give out."

Gotti's offer led LoCascio to ask idly how much income Gotti showed on tax returns; Gotti did not admit he had not been filing tax returns but said he was making an effort to keep expenses in line with income—and that was why he had recently incorporated a phony garment center company, Scorpio Marketing, and was drawing a mythical vice president's salary from it.

"I just got on the fuckin' payroll. I'm trying to keep my ass out of fuckin' jail, no other fuckin' reason."

Between the garment center fakery and his longtime fake job with a childhood friend's plumbing construction company, Gotti said he was "showing" for "tax purposes" about eighty-five thousand dollars in annual income.

Because he was not filing returns, Gotti was not "showing" anything, so he was apparently unwilling to admit to LoCascio that he was relying on some dubious advice from a purported tax lawyer that he did not have to file so long as he occasionally mailed the IRS an estimated tax payment. He had done this, but only once in the last three years. The potential peril of that situation mooted the what-to-show issue, but Gotti had always been keen on the topic. The only time Neil Dellacroce went to prison for any serious time was when the IRS caught him spending more in a single weekend of craps at a casino in Puerto Rico than he had reported in income for the year.

"Eighty-five thousand, it's good for me, Frank," Gotti said.

"You don't want to spend more than that."

"My wife gets like thirty-three thousand. So, now it reads another thirty-three on top of it."

Gotti said he would increase what he showed, because the IRS—as it had with Neil—can build a case just by following people around and counting up how much they spend. In a final remark on the subject, he added another name to the list of people he put in jeopardy on December 12—which in the FBI and the Eastern District came to stand as the day a corner was turned on John Gotti.

"You want to know the truth?" Gotti confided. "If they followed us, Joe Watts has got the problem, not me! That fuck, he grabs two checks. Yours and the guy's under the table."

* * *

While the December 12 tape contained enough evidence to slap the handcuffs on Gotti, the Mouw-Maloney team bided its time. The target obviously felt relaxed in the apartment; he might go there again, turn over more dirt, and bury himself deeper.

Besides, the thousands upon thousands of words on the tape needed analyzing; Bruce Mouw and George Gabriel, aided by veteran agents Michael Balen and Carmine Russo, put on their headsets and happily went to work. The many obscure remarks on the tape needed deconstructing; the problems Gotti cited with his capos and crews needed checking with informants; the tax trail needed following; there was much work to do, and Gotti was not going anywhere.

For Gotti, the pressing threat was the O'Connor case and its potential life sentence. It was due to emerge from a yearlong swamp of pretrial motions and go to trail on January 8, 1990.

The big pretrial issue was the tapes made by the state task force at the Bergin in 1985 and 1986. Proving that at least one of his remarks on the December 12 tape—that he fought every case "tooth and nail"—was not self-serving chatter, Gotti had engaged his lawyers in a long and expensive attempt to get the tapes dismissed as evidence in the case.

Gotti attended some of the tedious hearings that resulted, knowing he would become the story of the day. During a break in one hearing, held a day after a mayoral primary election, many reporters approached and asked him to predict which candidate would win the upcoming general election—Rudolph Giuliani, the former Southern District U.S. attorney who was the Republican primary winner, or David Dinkins, the Democratic winner.

He declined a prediction but not the opportunity to charm the messengers. "I'm voting for you guys!"

"Do you like all this press attention? Are we a pain in the ass?"

"Nah. I've had bigger pains, let me tell ya. I know you're just doin' your job."

He moved on with his entourage, having left an impression that resulted in one reporter's writing of "another court appearance by the city's most popular reputed mob boss."

While Gotti declined to make an actual statement about the election, he did a few weeks later allow some of his men to hang four David Dinkins posters at the Ravenite. This said much more about his anger at the Southern District investigation of him, which began under Giuliani, than about his interest in the election or Dinkins, who would defeat Giuliani (and lose to him in a rematch four years later).

Meanwhile, the battle against the tapes continued to play out. Trying to suppress Gotti's critical "bust 'im up" remark—made three months before O'Connor was indeed busted up—Cutler and Shargel, assisted by another lawyer, appellate specialist John Pollok, attacked on numerous grounds. Although they lost round after round, they gleefully managed during one line of attack to paint state task force director Ronald Goldstock into an uncomfortable corner.

By law, Goldstock's agency was required to inform the judge who authorized the Bergin bugs that Gotti was a named target in previous judicial orders authorizing electronic surveillance. This was not done, even though Gotti had been named in many judicial orders related to the Gambino squad's taping and bugging of Angelo Ruggiero's telephone and house.

In a hearing, Goldstock was compelled to try and explain why. Under oath, he said he simply did not know Gotti had been named in the Angelo orders. He was then confronted with an affidavit from Eastern District Strike Force chief Edward McDonald, in which McDonald said he had told Goldstock that Gotti was named in the Angelo eavesdropping—and that he told him three weeks before Goldstock submitted an amended request to bug Gotti at the Bergin and again failed to notify the judge.

Goldstock said he did not remember McDonald's saying that, and in any case he would have forgotten it in three weeks' time. Such testimony raised dubious eyebrows in court and in the media; for such an acutely media-conscious man as Goldstock, who sometimes squandered tax dollars to pay public relations people to witness his press interviews, the dispute over his tapes' integrity was an embarrassing public disaster, far worse than his private failure to persuade Andy Maloney that a gambling and loan-sharking case was the best way to proceed against John Gotti.

Still, no one on Gotti's team, least of all him, held out much hope that the state court judge steering the case through the pretrial stages would rule in his favor and ban the tapes from evidence; Gotti believed that even if the judge eventually concluded that Goldstock was lying to cover up an oversight, he lacked the fortitude to risk Manhattan district attorney Robert Morgenthau's enmity by crippling Morgenthau's case essentially on technical grounds. Because Morgenthau was so influential in the state's judicial and political arenas, Gotti's view of the situation was entirely reasonable.

"Forget about it, these cocksuckers think I'm the fuckin' case of the century," is how he explained it to Sammy, who never was called up to Nettie's for the tongue-lashing that seemed so imminent on December 12.

Gotti's view of the battle over the tapes proved entirely accurate on December 13; the state judge ruled against him and virtually forgotten codefendant Anthony "Tony Lee" Guerrieri, and for Morgenthau and trial prosecutors Michael Cherkasky and Jeffrey Schlanger, and for Barbara DiTata, a lawyer representing Goldstock's office.

The January 8 trial date was reaffirmed, and now there was nothing between the Teflon Don and his third trial in four years. As expected as this was, and as much as it was his tooth-and-nail philosophy that kept lawyers' meters running, Gotti became highly annoyed at how much he was paying lawyers to try to keep him and others out of jail.

The proof of this came four days before the start of trial, when Gotti made another trip up to Nettie's, on January 4, 1990. With LoCascio and now Sammy in attendance, he began painting his lawyers into what would become an uncomfortable, embarrassing, and legally perilous corner.

The night before, video agents had seen Shargel entering the Ravenite, and audio agents had heard a fragment of conversation in the hallway indicating that he was there to discuss fees for himself and Cutler, and for appellate specialist John Pollok and another lawyer, who were to help them defend Gotti and Guerrieri at trial.

Whether on the next day Gotti accurately described the

fees did not matter; whatever they were, they were high and he was angry at his "rat" lawyers:

"They all want their money up front. You get four guys that want sixty-five, seventy-five thousand a piece, up front, you're talking about three hundred thousand in one month! Cocksuckers!"

Gotti then complained that because Joseph Armone and Joe N. Gallo were "brothers," he had recently paid a hundred and thirty-five thousand dollars to Pollok for unsuccessful appeals of their cases. Moreover, he had just paid about thirty thousand to Pollok for the printing of legal briefs and trial minutes.

"You can throw those in the fuckin' toilet," LoCascio said. "That's how much good they done."

Gotti was just warming up. He said he had doled out another twenty-five thousand dollars to Pollok for an unsuccessful appeal of John Carneglia's heroin case and that during the past year, he figured, he had paid another three hundred thousand to Shargel for cases against still other family members and associates. He said he had accused Shargel—technically, Tony Lee Guerrieri's lawyer in the O'Connor case—of "plucking" him and two of Shargel's other well-heeled clients, Sammy and Joe Butch Corrao.

Quoting himself speaking to Shargel, he said: "You're Tony Lee's lawyer, but you're plucking me. I'm paying for it. You got Sammy, you got one hand in his pocket. You got both your hands in Joe Butch's pockets. Where does it end? Gambino Crime Family? This is the Shargel, Cutler and Who-do-you-call-it? Crime Family."

"They wind up with the money," Sammy agreed.

"They're overpriced, overpaid, and underperformed," added LoCascio, who said the fees were especially galling because the lawyers lacked the "balls" to do what they really should do—which was "holler and holler" at judges and prosecutors.

Lawyers who do not holler was an old Gotti pet peeve, and he said he had just accused his of failing to holler because they feared that judges and prosecutors would investigate them.

"I told them yesterday, 'You don't want to do it, you cocksuckers, because you know and I know that they know you're taking money under the table. Every time

you take on a client, another one of us on, you're breaking the law.' "

On tape came the sound of men clearing their voices,
and the first voice to emerge with any clarity was again
Gotti's; he was still on the same subject, and about to issue an open invitation for someone in authority to investigate Bruce Cutler's accounts: "It's a bullshit agreement.
They don't fuck with you, and you don't go all out in
court. If they really want to break Bruce Cutler's balls,
what did he get paid off me? Three years ago, I paid tax
on thirty-six thousand. What could I have paid him?"

Sammy said that unspoken accords between defense
lawyers and the government probably existed and they
hurt the client: "We get the worst of it, every which way."

"It's no good, Sammy, but worse than that is this,"
Gotti said, by way of introducing a story about Shargel
complaining to him that he felt like a "high-priced errand
boy" when Gotti asked him, as he had Michael Coiro and
George Helbig, to find out when the big combined state-
federal "pinch" was coming.

"Bruce [is] worse yet," Gotti said, apparently now
bouncing to his little feet and mimicking the body language of his lawyers—the audio agents heard the other
members of the Gambino administration begin laughing.
"They got a routine, now, the two lawyers. 'Muck and
Fuck,' I call them. When I see Bruce, he says, 'Hi, Jerry
loves you, he's in your corner, hundred per cent.' When
I see Jerry, he says, 'Hi, Bruce loves you, he's in your
corner hundred percent.' "

"They must really like you!" Sammy guffawed.

"Sure, Sammy!" Gotti said. "What's not to like about
us?"

Someday, Gotti's Muck-and-Fuck routine would not
seem so funny. And the truth was, no matter how much
he ridiculed them behind their backs and complained
about how much they cost him, he did value them. Even
in his January 4 tirade, after his anger dissolved into hu-
mor, he told Sammy that if a lawyer won a case, "let the
guy [charge] whatever the fuck he wants."

Quoting himself in an imaginary speech to a lawyer
who has just agreed to defend him, Gotti said: "If you
win the case, I know I gotta do the right thing by you.

You win, [if] I promised you fifty [thousand], you get seventy-five. You get a fuckin' bonus, fifty percent, because we're here now."

The fees charged by Cutler, Shargel, and Pollok also were in line with what other criminal defense lawyers of their skill and experience commanded in New York. The Gambino family was not the most noble gravy train, but lawyers who represented Wall Street felons whose deals threw thousands out of work and savings-and-loan crooks who stole retirees' life savings charged even more.

Furthermore, by doing so much work for Cosa Nostra, Cutler and Shargel had diminished their market potential in white-collar gravy—particularly Cutler. By 1990, completing a metamorphosis that had begun in the Giacalone case, Cutler dressed, sounded, and almost looked like his principal client.

Cutler was now forty years old, eight years younger than Gotti. For many people, who remembered when Cutler was a leading prosecutor in the homicide bureau in the Brooklyn district attorney's office, and that he once applied for a job with the Eastern District Strike force, the metamorphosis was regrettable. It was okay to represent a gangster, but to revel in it was another thing.

But Cutler, twice divorced and childless, was flattered when physical comparisons between him and Gotti were made and pleased that his main job in life had become keeping Gotti out of jail.

"Today, the number one priority in my professional life is representing John," he told interviewers. "If someone says I look like him, I have no problem with that. My client is a very handsome man."

At the time, video agents were making a record of how much Cutler seemed to revel in his dual role of principal lawyer and press secretary for the city's most popular reputed mob boss. Many times, the camera two blocks north captured Cutler arriving at the Ravenite with nearly the same flourish as Gotti, and to nearly the same hoopla. He and the club regulars exchanged backslaps, handshakes, and cheek kisses.

"He loves being there!" Mouw said while reviewing one of these displays with Gabriel. "He's a junior wise guy."

"Wise guy! He thinks he's the consigliere, he's Tom

Haden," Gabriel replied, referring to Vito Corleone's consigliere in *The Godfather.*

Shargel, on the other hand, seemed more businesslike at the Ravenite—on the videotapes anyway. Although he actually did get a charge out of being in the company of Gotti, on videotape it looked like he just wanted to tell Gotti whatever the bad news of the day was and depart as soon as possible and get home to this wife, who was his college sweetheart, and his two children.

Even though they hated what his client stood for, Mouw and Gabriel, and even Gleeson, who was hard-nosed about mob lawyers, respected Shargel—whose keen courtroom ability, easy charm, and reluctance to at-tack prosecutors in the same Gotti-ish way as Culter helped carry him above his element.

Anytime either Cutler or Shargel—or any other lawyer—arrived at the Ravenite, the audio agents tele-phoned whichever Eastern District prosecutor assigned to the case happened to be on duty at the time. This was be-cause a tricky determination would need to be made if the lawyers turned up on the bugs: Was the conversation tak-ing place protected by attorney-client privilege or did its connection to the business of the Gambino family "enter-prise" obviate the privilege? If it fell under attorney-client, the recorders had to be turned off.

The same call needed to be made when Gotti began talking about his lawyers—was he talking about legal strategy, say, in the O'Connor case or about something re-lated to the enterprise?

On January 4, strike force prosecutor Laura Ward—who had joined the get-Gotti investigation after helping to put Armone and Gallo away—had to make the call, af-ter Gambino agent Frank Spero telephoned and said Gotti was upstairs in Nettie's place and beginning to talk about how much he paid his lawyers, on behalf of others.

"That's not strategy," she said. "That's enterprise."

It was a correct call. Gotti's comments about paying Cutler, Shargel, and Pollok to defend other family mem-bers was evidence of an enterprise; remarks about "under-the-table" payments were evidence of a possible enterprise crime. Similarly, one of Ward's colleagues, Le-onard Michaels, had made a correct call two months earlier when he kept the bugs operating as Gotti began talking about obstructing justice in the Tommy Gambino case.

As it turned out, Gotti also had much more than high-priced lawyers on his mind on January 4; other remarks he made that evening gave the FBI, for the first time in history, a fly-on-the-wall perch as a Cosa Nostra administration discussed one of its sustaining rituals: the making of new members.

Gotti sailed into this uncharted water by announcing he wanted to circulate the names of potential new soldiers to the other families—and, observing Cosa Nostra tradition, give them the opportunity to raise objections.

"I wanna throw a few names out, five or six," he said, adding this qualifying condition: "I want guys that done more than killing."

It became clear that the administration had discussed the topic only recently, and seriously, because Sammy produced a piece of paper on which a list of names had already been written. Sammy then began reading from the list, calling out the nominee's first name and sometimes which capo he was "with."

"The kid Richie."

"Right," Gotti replied.

"Tommy. With Frankie."

"Right."

"Tony from New Jersey."

"Right. Fat Tony."

"Johnny Rizzo. With Good-looking Jack."

"Yeah."

"Fat Dom. With Jackie Nose."

Because the video plant had been in operation for more than two years now, and agents had identified almost every habitúe of the Ravenite, the first names of these men about to join the so-called secret society were enough to identify them, especially when Sammy added their affiliation.

For the next half-hour, Gotti, Sammy, and LoCascio discussed the merits of the nominees, and the handicaps that had prevented other men recommended by the capos from making the list—which, in the case of a "Poncho," was age.

"I like the Richies, the Tommies," Gotti said, "they're young, twenty-thirty something, [but] these guys like

Poncho. [He's] sixty-one, sixty-two! Where the fuck are we going?"

The capos had nominated many more men than Gotti was willing to make—because some he did not know well, and thus trust—and so the "fuckin' hearts" of some "good guys" would be broken.

"This is not the time to make twenty guys," he said, adding that, so far as he knew, some of the nominees had never even been "used" in a murder and the capos ought not nominate a man who had not, as the expression went, "made his bones."

Near the meeting's end, Gotti instructed Sammy to show the list to bosses in the other four families and to explain it was "something that's been on the shelf" in the Gambino family lately "only because we're caught up pretty good" with other problems. "Tell them they can go to the bank on these people," he added.

Aside from its obvious and immediate prosecutorial value, the conversation showed that, for all his other faults and for all the times he did break Cosa Nostra rules, Gotti adhered to tradition and rules with enough frequency that, in his mind, he could rightly present himself to Sammy, to LoCascio, and to all, as an Old Guard, Neil-variety Cosa Nostra boss.

During one brief departure from the topic at hand, however, the discussion also showed that Gotti was still being hoodwinked by the most rule-obeying, tradition-observing, and patient Cosa Nostra boss left in New York, Chin Gigante.

Still biding his time, and waiting for Anthony Casso to devise a plan for killing Gotti without jeopardizing bystanders, Chin had recently sent Gotti a message about a development soon to occur in the O'Connor trial. The message cost Chin nothing, because Gotti would learn soon enough anyway, but it spoke of goodwill.

The message was that a Genovese captain, who lost his will after months of solitary confinement in prison, had "rolled over" and begun cooperating—and that the Manhattan district attorney's office intended to employ him in the O'Connor case as a witness on the "structure," or organization chart, of the Gambino family, where all orders—such as "bust 'im up"—flowed from the top.

The Genovese captain who lost his will was Vincent

Cafaro; his journey toward the witness stand began in 1985, when he ran into trouble and was jailed as a pretrial detainee at the MCC, which had just received the most infamous pretrial detainee of the time, John Gotti. This act alone increased his currency as a witness; as a capo, it only made sense that Cafaro—known as the Fish—would have had a few jailhouse chats with Gotti.

"The Fish is gonna testify against me," Gotti told Sammy and LoCascio. "He's gonna knock our fuckin' brains with the structure."

Still, Gotti did not consider Cafaro as threatening as his own "bust 'im up" remark on the task force tapes, or as James McElroy, the Westies' drug-addled killer who had lost his will even before solitary confinement and was ready to testify that the Westies boss had told him during Frank DiCicco's wake that Gotti had ordered a strong-arm attack on O'Connor.

About Cafaro, Gotti said that although there was always the chance a turncoat would make some outrageous claim, he never told the Fish anything important while both were dwelling in the MCC.

"I'd never let on to that motherfucker just once, I swear on my kids!" he said, while also predicting that the Fish would in any case, say anything to satisfy prosecutors. "What's he gonna do? He's not gonna get up and say I fucked him in the ass!"

The audio agents, and on the next day Mouw and Gabriel—and then, afterward, Maloney and his lawyers—were almost as thrilled by the January 4 tape as the December 12 one. No Cosa Nostra boss had ever been captured talking so openly, so obviously inculpatingly. But there was Gotti, his unmistakable voice unmistakably on tape, talking himself into a grave, as clearly as Nettie Cirelli saying good night to one of her relatives in California.

"Didn't I tell ya the big mouth would talk himself right into a hole?" Maloney could not resist bragging to Mouw.

There was one more highlight on the January 4 tape. Aside from its obvious "structure" value in a RICO prosecution, it showed how much Gotti, despite his *gelosio* and criticism, valued Sammy. It also signaled a rearrangement of the palace chairs in the Gambino family.

After LoCascio left Nettie's apartment and returned to

the club, Gotti told Sammy he was scheduling a captains-only meeting so he could announce how the family would be run if he lost the O'Connor trial and, as would likely happen with a "predicate" felon like him, was jailed without bail pending sentencing.

"I'm gonna tell them, 'I'm the [boss] 'till I say different,'" Gotti said, "'[but], soon as anything happens to me, I'm off the streets, Sammy is the acting boss.'"

Earlier, Gotti had revealed his intentions to LoCascio, but now Sammy was hearing it for the first time. Once again feeling damned if he did and damned if he didn't, Sammy said nothing and waited for Gotti to continue speaking.

Gotti said he would give Sammy any title he wanted, but whatever it was, it would mean "acting boss."

"So, I'm asking you, how do you feel? You wanna stay as consigliere? Or you want me to make you official underboss? Or acting boss? How do you feel? What makes you feel better? Think about it."

Sammy said he would, but did not think a title "made any difference."

Gotti said it did, because if Sammy remained consigliere, LoCascio, as acting underboss, would technically outrank him.

"I love Frankie, but I don't wanna [leave him in charge]," Gotti added. "There's nothing I wouldn't do for the guy. But I don't want [that]."

In the face of Sammy's reluctance to pick his own title, Gotti decided to pick one for him—one that would require some maneuvering. He said he would send a message to the imprisoned Joseph Armone and tell him that, nothing personal, but because he was never going to get out of prison, he would have to step down as underboss. Gotti, the man who had once railed against Paul for putting people in temporary situations, said he would then make Armone consigliere and LoCascio acting consigliere.

These moves cleared the way for Sammy becoming underboss, Gotti explained.

Finally, Sammy spoke: "It would be my pleasure."

CHAPTER 22

● ● ● ● ● ● ● ● ● ● ● ● ●

Teflon Don

The tent for another media circus—a John Gotti trial!—was thrown up outside the Manhattan Criminal Court building early on the morning of January 8, 1990. Television vans lined the street; blue police sawhorses carved a pathway to the courthouse. Vendors sold sundries to reporters, cops, elderly court buffs, gangster groupies, and the merely curious—all waiting for the Teflon Don to make his entrance in the bright frosty air.

Most everyone was familiar with the routine now, and most were good at it, especially Gotti, who arrived with his barrel chest thrust out, his cat-ate-the-canary grin, and a more pronounced blue tint to his carefully cut, widow-peaked gray hair.

"It's a beautiful day," he said, when asked if he had any comment. It was a beautiful bone, so why throw any more, when the yapping reporters were drowning each other out? Gotti bounced on inside like a man just admitted to heaven.

As is usually the case, the first day of the trial did not match its press buildup. No opening statements, no witnesses on the stand; instead, just the judge, Edward McLaughlin, tediously interviewing prospective jurors. Given the Gotti clan's history with juries, this was potentially the most vital part of the trial—but the reporters barely paid attention.

The focus was on Gotti—what kind of candy was he snacking on at the defense table? (Mint.) What did he smile about when Bruce Cutler poured him some water from the defense pitcher? (Cutler's hushed put-down of a prospective juror.) At whom did he wink in the spectator section? (Jack D'Amico.) Was his double-breasted suit olive-brown or just brown? (Olive-brown.)

It was impossible to construct a hard-news story on these details, however. Near day's end, the hard-news reporters, as opposed to the write-what-you-feel columnists and fashion writers, were desperately in search of a "headline"—something new to write or talk about in their newspapers and newscasts.

Just in time, McLaughlin provided one. He said that because he feared the media would hound them, he would sequester jurors in a hotel once they had been chosen. This was another judicial lie, of course; he was making them guests of the state for the trial's duration because prosecutor Michael Cherkasky, fearing that Gotti would hound the jurors, had filed legal papers citing the Gambino family's "notorious record" in that regard.

It was the first time in history that a state court jury in Manhattan would be sequestered during a trial—a pretty good headline. To protect jurors further, the judge ruled that the defense would be given only their last names—making it more difficult, but hardly impossible, for someone to learn where they lived with their loved ones when they were not guests of the state in some hotel room.

The judge also said it would take two weeks to find twelve jurors and four alternates who would be able to be fair about Gotti and his virtually invisible codefendant, Tony Lee Guerrieri. The press groaned and virtually forgot about the case until then.

Gotti, of course, could not forget. Day after day, he had to sit at the defense table and seem to be only a particularly well-dressed plumbing salesman and garment center entrepreneur as the judge called potential jurors into court and asked whether they could be impartial to Mr. Gotti and Mr. Guerrieri. To reduce the danger of succumbing to the monotony of this routine, Gotti again employed his defendant-decorum trick, which was to lay his right arm straight across the defense table, with his wrist cocked in and his fist hard against it, so that it was physically difficult and even painful to slip bored into a disrespectful slouch.

At the end of the day, he still could not forget—not about the O'Connor trial or all his other problems and se-

crets. And on January 17 these brought him back to
Nettie's place.

This conversation quickly revealed that another man
had been invited to enter the secret room; the guest was
Danny Marino, the keeper of his own big secret for the
last four years. He was on hand to discuss grand jury
matters involving the other closet ally of Chin's, Jimmy
Brown Failla. The matters involving Failla, who was being pressured to talk about Sparks, involved Gotti more
and were a nagging reminder that neither the Eastern District nor the Southern was granting Gotti any breathing
room just because he was on trial and facing a virtual life
sentence.

Marino reported that the day before, even as Failla was
dodging questions from Walter Mack in the Southern District grand jury room, FBI agents had visited his office
and attempted to serve him an Eastern District grand jury
subpoena.

"That's why he didn't come here tonight," Marino said.
"He thought that maybe they'd be waiting for him."

More than most, Failla knew how it important it was to
do the right thing by Gotti in a grand jury room; a couple
of months earlier, he had reported that one of his men,
Thomas Spinelli, was about to do the wrong thing—and
Spinelli had been quickly condemned by Gotti and executed by a Sammy firing squad.

Fortunately for Failla, although he knew of Chin's desire to kill Gotti for killing Paul, he did not know enough
about Sparks—other than Paul's dinner plans that
night—to have to worry much about his grand jury answers. Besides, he was a much older hand than Tommy
Gambino at grand jury dissembling.

Marino told Gotti that in the Southern District, Failla
was not asked anything he could not handle—but Gotti
wondered about a big specific.

"Philadelphia?" he said, a code for turncoat underbosses.

"Leonetti!" interjected Gotti's new underboss, Sammy.

"Yeah," Marino said.

"Piece of shit," Gotti said. "What the fuck does [Failla]
know about Leonetti?"

"He don't, he don't even know him."

Gotti told Marino he would meet with Failla so they

could talk in detail, then sent him on his way and turned to the next item on the agenda—a meeting with Joe Butch Corrao and George Helbig, the Corrao associate with a source in law enforcement.

Helbig was now known in Nettie's place as the "grim reaper," because his news was always bad; waiting for him to come up from the club, Gotti joked with Sammy about how much Helbig's bad news aggravated him. "This grim reaper, where is he, this fuckin' bum? If I knew we weren't gonna be here, if I knew we were gonna die tomorrow, I'd kill him tonight!"

Sammy had a good laugh, but the joke was on him; this time, Helbig had bad tidings for Sammy, or so it seemed after Corrao and Helbig knocked on the door and walked inside.

"What's up, brother G?" Gotti beamed at Helbig. "Good news?"

"I brought you bad news," Helbig, meek but candid, replied.

Helbig's bad news was that NYPD detectives attached to the Brooklyn district attorney's office had bugged Tali's, Sammy's bar and clubhouse in Bensonhurst, and the construction trailer where he met with union contacts and business associates. This news, of course, was only partially accurate; the trailer had indeed been bugged, but the first bug had been put in Sammy's regular office, the one where the Fist once convened—not Tali's.

Helbig's next bulletin was all wrong—and it provoked much panicky talk that gave the Eastern District eavesdroppers their first clues about Helbig's source.

Helbig said that Sammy had already been secretly indicted and the case would be prosecuted by Ronald Goldstock's state task force. The truth was that Sammy was never overheard saying enough to be indicted; the district attorney's NYPD investigators had merely turned the investigation over to the task force because on tape Sammy and another man had discussed a never-attempted scheme to make a small assault case against the other man evaporate by making a campaign contribution to Charlie Hynes, a candidate for Brooklyn district attorney who subsequently won.

The report from Helbig's source—partially accurate about bugs placed by the DA's police, inaccurate about a planned prosecution of Sammy—bolstered Bruce Mouw's earlier suspicion that the source was a dirty cop.

The wholly inaccurate part of the report, that Sammy had already talked his way into an indictment, put Sammy on the defensive. He told Gotti he never said anything of consequence in the trailer; as for Tali's, it was so noisy there and he took such additional precautions, he could not have been overheard, unless the police now had some new miracle technology available.

"I tell you, I don't talk, in Tali's; if they got this, they have to have equipment to shut off the whole joint just to hear us. And I don't see that. [But if they do], I surrender. I'll give up. They want me, they got me."

Gotti said such equipment might exist, and for that reason, no matter where they were, "We got to constantly whisper."

Joe Butch Corrao broke in to suggest that the case against Sammy might be based on "rats," not tapes, but Gotti did not think so.

"I think everybody in the city's got rats near them," he said. "But we ain't got 'em near us."

For FBI agents, that remarkably delusional boast was music to the ears, because it suggested that Gotti— clueless about Willie Boy Johnson for nearly twenty years—still had no idea that at least nine informers were talking about him. The Gotti ego was the only possible explanation; it would not allow him to believe that people would betray him or the Gambino administration.

"No, Sam, I don't think there's a rat. You ain't got no fuckin' rat."

Just before Helbig was to leave, Gotti asked him to contact the source again. "Tell him, give me a little more specifics so Sammy can prepare. How soon? Next week, next year?"

Sammy also piped up: "Try and ask him When, where, tapes, rats, anything?"

"Even if he's gotta get a few dollars, give him a few more," Gotti said, before waving Helbig out with a glib remark showing his relief that, for once, the grim news had involved someone else: "I can't say, 'Keep up the good work, Georgie!' "

Overall, the audio quality of the January 17 tape was good; in one short interlude, however, the men began whispering while coughing and clearing their throats. Still, a few whispers came through and they became the words by which Helbig's source began to be betrayed.

"He'd be the first cousin?" Gotti whispered.

"It's Pete," Sammy was barely heard to say.

"Pete," Helbig whispered. "You know him."

The words were not much to go on, but it was a start. They would not be immediately connected to a couple of let's-get-acquainted telephone calls that Bruce Mouw had received over the past several months from William Peist, a forty-three-year-old detective assigned to the NYPD intelligence division.

The division, considered a prestige assignment for only the most trusted cops, worked only on major cases and coordinated the NYPD's intelligence sharing with other law enforcement agencies. In Peist's job, it was important for him to develop relationships with key players in other agencies; so it seemed nothing out of the ordinary for him to telephone the FBI's Gambino squad boss.

As a former officer in the U.S. Navy's secret submarine wars with the former Soviet Union, however, Mouw was even more tight-lipped than the usual closemouthed FBI agent; he never trusted someone he did not know with anything worth knowing, and so his polite curtness with Peist—and his heightened alarm about the recent revelations on the hallway and apartment bugs—always resulted in short conversations.

At the time, Mouw knew hardly anything about Peist. But much was worth knowing. He was an affable, rotund cop who worked part-time as a pastry chef at the Waldorf-Astoria Hotel; his sixteen-year NYPD career was spotless. Many of those years had been spent in the public-morals division, but in 1987 he was assigned to the intelligence division—after losing his left leg below the knee in a violent accident on the Brooklyn Bridge three years before; his car had stalled, and after he got out to place flares and direct traffic, another car slammed into him.

The lost leg was why the affable detective began holding a secret grudge. After the accident, he sought to retire on full disability benefits that would have given him, tax-free, three-quarters of his annual salary for life. In hearings, the NYPD successfully fought his disability claim, arguing that since he had been driving relatives into Manhattan to go Christmas shopping, his disability was not job-related. Peist vehemently disagreed, and his lawyers argued that the moment an off-duty cop exited his car to place flares and direct traffic, he was on duty.

Peist thought the NYPD was cheating him. Its disability section was notoriously generous; many higher-ranking officers had won full disability on less-credible claims. In September 1989, however, the controversy lost its financial bottom line. In a separate personal-injury lawsuit against the other driver's insurance company—and against the city, for failing to keep the bridge safely lighted—Detective Peist was awarded $1.1 million. This meant that he no longer needed to worry about his disability pension, apart from its grudge value.

By that time, however, the new one-legged millionaire cop from Brooklyn had been sitting at a desk in the intelligence division for two years, occasionally tap-tapping into NYPD computers containing information about bugs, wiretaps, surveillance operations—but not indictments.

It took months to find out these other facts: Peist was married with four children; his wife had a cousin whose first name was Pete; Pete was a gambler whose last name was Mavis; his loan shark was George Helbig, known in some places as the "grim reaper."

The January 17 tape contained one other moment when Gotti's voice dropped to a whisper, but because the men had neglected to turn on Nettie's radio that night, the FBI's sensitive equipment picked up some more intriguing words. These involved the O'Connor trial, for which jury selection was now almost complete.

Talking to Sammy, Gotti said that the last name of one of the selected jurors was "Hoyle" or "Boyle" and "Irish, I guess." His next remark seemed to imply that because "Hoyle" or "Boyle" was a utility-company lineman, someone in the Irish-dominated Westies with contacts in utility unions might know him; Gotti also seemed to say it might not matter because the juror was already sequestered in some hotel somewhere.

"Maybe we can't reach him," Gotti said, "[but] we'll send word out to anybody who knows him."

Gotti's remarks presented the FBI–Eastern District

team with a dilemma: Was a real plot to tamper with the O'Connor trial jury afoot, or was he just engaging in wishful thinking? Assuming the plot was real, should the team tell Manhattan district attorney Robert Morgenthau and trial prosecutor Michael Cherkasky? If they did, and Cherkasky consequently asked the trial judge to question the Irish juror, would Gotti get suspicious and stop using the apartment, thus hurting the increasingly promising case?

It was Laura Ward's call to make, subject of course to Andy Maloney's approval. She was now the only staff lawyer working on the case; in recent weeks, the Eastern District Strike Force had finally gone the way of other strike forces around the country—out of favor and out of business. Edward McDonald and Leonard Michaels had left to enter private practice. Ward, a strike force lawyer for many years, had decided to stay and join a new con-solidated staff under Maloney.

Ward consulted a friend, John Gleeson, chief of Maloney's public-corruption unit. In a supervisors' meeting, Gleeson had been told about the Ravenite bugs a month earlier. Informally, he already suspected that something big was up; a day after his win over Cutler in the Michael Coiro trial, Gleeson was visited by Gambino squad agent Billy Noon, who made an unusual and urgent request: Would Gleeson forget about filing a motion ask-ing the judge in Coiro's case to bar Coiro from going to the Ravenite?

Gleeson's interpretation of Gotti's whispers was that even if they were evidence of a plot to tamper with the O'Connor jury, they were also vague and halfhearted, and therefore not serious enough to effect the potential harm to the Eastern District of disclosing them to the Manhat-tan district attorney.

"On that tape," he said to Ward, "George Helbig is tell-ing Gotti about two law enforcement bugs. We don't know who Helbig's source is, or where. Maybe it's in the Manhattan DA's office, who knows? Unless more turns up, I wouldn't tell anybody. Why, for this, risk our bugs?"

Ward's recommendation to Maloney reflected this ad-vice, and he accepted it, setting the scene for very sour grapes someday. The Manhattan district attorney's office stayed in the dark about Gotti's whispers—as much as the

Eastern District was still in the dark about Detective Peist, who was given a new, temporary, and completely coincidental assignment a few days later. The job: guarding sequestered jurors in the O'Connor case.

With, for the third time in four years, a group of New Yorkers now seated in judgment of John Gotti, the media circus at the O'Connor trial resumed on January 20. Gotti arrived in a good mood because, en route from Queens, he had passed a large banner that Lewis Kasman had arranged to have draped from a highway overpass: "Good Luck, John; Love, People of Ozone Park."

Just before opening statements, Judge McLaughlin handed the prosecution an important ruling: Jurors would be allowed to hear a secretly recorded jailhouse chat between a Westies informer and a Westies gunman, in which the gunman bragged that he was part of the team that busted up carpenters union official John O'Connor at Gotti's behest after O'Connor ordered a carpenter goon squad to vandalize a Gambino family-backed restaurant built with nonunion labor. The tape bolstered what another Westies turncoat, James McElroy, was expected to say on the stand.

In his opening, Cherkasky—a tall, thin man whose abilities, courtroom style, and trial record were similar to John Gleeson's—laid out the facts of the O'Connor assault, then pointed a bony finger toward Gotti: "Like all bullies, he could not allow a challenge to go unpunished."

Opening statements were Bruce Cutler's strong suit, and he did not disappoint spectators who remembered how he had once erased Giacalone's blackboard drawing of the Gambino chain of command and slam-dunked her indictment into a waste can. At one point, ridiculing Cherkasky's remark that the case was brought in the name of the "people" of New York State, Cutler stooped beside the prosecution table like he was peeking up some skirt and screamed: "Where are the 'people'? I don't see any 'people.'" Meanwhile, he added, somewhat incongruously, Gotti was a champion of some equally anonymous "little man."

His voice rising and falling, his arms pounding alternately a lectern, the prosecution table, even a Bible, Cutler rampaged around the courtroom—opening with a story about how disgraceful it was that the government spent millions to get Gotti while on the courthouse steps homeless men huddled in the cruel cold. In another echo of the Giacalone case, he said Gotti was the victim of a "modern-day witch-hunt" and "ambitious, career-minded" prosecutors, and that his chief accuser, McElroy, was a "soldier in the Robert Morgenthau family."

For anyone who really knew Gotti, some notes Cutler sounded were stupendously disingenuous—Gotti was a "devoted husband," a man "drug dealers ran away from"—but for most the performance was nearly flawless, and Gotti gave the out-of-breath conductor a familial handshake when Cutler sat back down.

The trial lasted only three weeks. The first witness out of the box was the Fish, Genovese turncoat Vincent Cafaro—who did not hammer Gotti with as much "structure" as Gotti had feared while speaking in Nettie's on January 17. Under the surgical knife of a Jerry Shargel cross-examination, Cafaro admitted he did not know whether Gotti "is or isn't" boss of the Gambino family.

Cafaro did say the Gambinos used the Westies as enforcers, but Shargel made it appear that prosecutors had coerced him onto the stand by tossing him into solitary confinement for nearly seventeen months after his and Gotti's paths crossed at the MCC in 1986.

At the defense table, until the fourth day of trial, Gotti exuded his usual public calm in the face of trouble. But then, on January 24, Cherkasky began unreeling some of the state task force tapes. Gotti had read transcripts of these, but this was the first time he had actually had to sit and listen to them in a courtroom, and the experience was embarrassing and upsetting.

After the trial was recessed for the day, he went to the Ravenite and unburdened himself to Sammy and LoCascio—while relaxing upstairs at Nettie's. It was the fifth time the bug caught him there—and, it turned out, the last.

Gotti said his only consolation was that most of the tapes were recorded before he succeeded Paul; somehow, the crudity on one particular tape—in which he threatened to shove someone's head "up his mother's cunt"—would have sounded more unseemly coming from a boss: "Only thing I can comfort myself with [is] . . . thank

God, this was 1985. If this tape [was] 1988, '89, I would've thrown myself off a fuckin' bridge for embarrassment."

In one of the rare times when he did not let his boss off the hook, LoCascio replied that he could understand Gotti might want to "shoot yourself," because he was the one who had always "preached" against indiscreet talk in enclosed places: "You've been preaching, preaching, and you're doing the same thing that you're preaching."

Sammy remained silent, but Gotti—to the incredulous delight of the audio agents—launched into a sermon about the need to watch what is said, and where, in "La Cosa Nostra."

"From now on, I'm telling you that if a guy just so mentions 'La,' I'm gonna strangle the cocksucker. You know what I mean? He don't have to say 'Cosa Nostra,' just 'La,' and he goes. I heard nine months of tapes of my life. I was actually sick and I don't wanna get sick. Not sick for me, sick for 'this thing of ours,' sick for how naive we were five years ago. I'm sick that we were so fucking naive. Me, number one!"

He cringed at the irony of one tape, where he was overheard admonishing the late Angelo Ruggiero to stop talking in enclosed settings. " 'Hey, you gotta do me a favor,' I tell him. 'Don't make nobody talk. This is how we get in trouble, we talk.' "

The audio agents were still gulping when Gotti next admitted his carelessness at the Bergin: "But I'm tellin' you, I'm sort of more guilty than any of you are simply because, I'm tellin' you, I know better."

In a final remark, which came in the middle of a long talk with Sammy about a soldier in a New Jersey family who was facing trouble and suspected of being "weak," Gotti again demonstrated his flair for contradiction and ignoring rules he had just imposed: "If you think a guy's a rat, or he's weak, you jeopardizing a whole borgata, a whole Cosa Nostra for this guy. *Minchia*!"

After January 24, Gotti never returned to Nettie's. Only later on did a reason for this emerge, and it demonstrated how law enforcement agencies conducting separate investigations of the same man at the same time can stumble into each other's paths disastrously.

When Jimmy Brown Failla was in the Southern District

grand jury a week before January 25, Walter Mack asked if he had met Gotti in "an apartment somewhere." Failla never had, but the question showed that the Southern District team had its own informers—and it strongly suggested to Gotti, when he finally found the time to speak directly to Failla about his testimony, that he ought to stay out of Nettie's.

Gotti did not have the same option with Judge McLaughlin's courtroom, where on January 29, he sat seemingly bemused as the people's star witness, James McElroy, took the stand. McElroy testified as expected: His former Westies boss had told him, at Frank DeCicco's wake, that Gotti ordered the O'Connor assault.

The testimony damaged Cutler's client, Gotti—not Shargel's client, Guerrieri—but Shargel conducted almost all the cross-examination because Gotti wanted it. A few times up to this point, Gotti had actually expressed annoyance with Cutler for, ironically, excessive hollering at the judge and the witnesses; he saw that it was annoying the jurors.

Under Shargel's dissection, McElroy became the addled thug he was. He blithely acknowledged that, why, yes, in fact, he had once slit a man's throat for one hundred dollars in drug money, and, oh, yes, in another case he had lied on the witness stand.

The damage from the task force tapes was harder to repair. During cross of a task force agent, Shargel adroitly insinuated that transcribing agents are inclined—when words on a tape are hard to hear—to pick the worst of meanings, and so transcripts can be unreliable. Still, transcripts are not evidence; it is what jurors hear that counts. On the key tape, it did sound as if Gotti did say, "We're gonna, gonna bust 'im up."

Near trial's end, the defense pulled a rabbit out of the hat—the victim himself, John O'Connor, a Jerry Vale look-alike who took the stand for the defense and said he had no idea who shot him or who might have ordered it. He did not come across as much of a victim—he was under indictment himself for labor racketeering (and would be convicted), and he pleaded the Fifth Amendment when asked questions about organized crime.

Cherkasky repaired some of the damage the victim had done to his case with a superb final argument. The defense's tactics, he said, showed "the loathsome desperation to besmirch anyone and everyone who threatens the dark power of John Gotti"—"an arrogant, egotistical, power-hungry" man "insulated from the dirty work that his minions do."

On behalf of the city's law enforcement community, which now felt a collective loathing for Cutler's incessant attacks on "government persecutors," Cherkasky pitched Cutler a high, hard one: Acknowledging that McElroy was a brutal "bellhead," he asked, "Do you think he has the intellectual capacity to lie so subtly and so consistently? He couldn't stand up to Jerry Shargel—maybe Bruce Cutler, but not Jerry Shargel."

Outside court, Gotti described Cherkasky's slight of Cutler to a group of reporters: "Did you hear him zing my lawyer? Bruce should hit him on the chin."

While hardly admissible, the remark was good evidence of how Gotti no doubt had responded to the slight of having a Gambino-backed restaurant trashed just after he became a boss.

In his final argument, Cutler hollered and hollered about what a "snake," "rat," "psychopathic killer," "lying bum," and general all-around "swill" McElroy was—and then finally, on February 5, 1990, the case went to the jury.

"The people like me," Gotti said, when asked about his chances. "At least I think they do."

Most onlookers expected a quick verdict of not guilty, but it did not happen—not for one, two, and then three days. To pass the time, Gotti and some cronies sat on hallway benches sipping espresso laced with anisette hidden in Canada Dry soda cans: the more he sipped, the more worried he became. In one edgy moment, he told a reporter that a line for "picking on me" existed and the reporter should go to the rear of it.

Because Gotti was no longer relaxing in the apartment and was holding only the most furtive conversations in the Ravenite hallway, and because Detective William Peist would never speak about his role in guarding the jurors, it is not known if Peist influenced the jury's deliberations. The jurors were never asked about any improper comments that the affable, one-legged millionaire detective with the secret grudge might have uttered about

Gotti; at the time of the verdict, he was not under suspicion.

What is known is that on their first vote, six jurors liked Gotti, one did not, and five were unsure. On the second day, the five who were not sure made up their minds and voted to convict, deadlocking the jury at six-six. On the next day, the five who were originally unsure changed their minds again and voted to acquit, after listening to the key tape again and reviewing a transcript of Dr. Shargel's lobotomy of McElroy.

That made it eleven-one for acquittal, and the lone holdout capitulated on the fourth day, February 9, 1990; the tarnishing of the Teflon Don would have to wait until some other day.

After the jury foreman said "not guilty" twelve times—once for each count in the indictment—Gotti clenched his right fist, punched the air, and bear-hugged his lawyers. Codefendant Tony Lee Guerrieri, along for the ride, got the same send-off.

"Yeah, Johnny!" some cliché in a sharkskin suit yelled.

Gotti rushed out of the courtroom to the circus outside; hundreds of people, drawn by radio bulletins that a verdict was in, formed a caught-up-in-the moment gauntlet as Gotti, escorted by Jack D'Amico, fought his way into a Cadillac at the curb.

"Way to go, Johnny!" shouted some homeless man, one of many Gotti had favored with twenty-dollar bills during luncheon-recess strolls to neighborhood snack shops.

Back in the courthouse, District Attorney Robert Morgenthau looked ill; big losses were hard for him to swallow. Still, he managed to sound dignified and above the fray: "I don't look behind verdicts. I think it was a fair trial. I think everybody recognizes that when you have a case heavily dependent on wiretaps subject to interpretation, and witnesses who may not be the cream of society, you have a case that can go either way."

Cutler, on the other hand, played another persecution card aimed at potential jurors in potential new cases: "This is our third case in four years, and I, unfortunately, always seem to have to get ready for another one. I hope

I don't have to. I hope I don't have to go to court again with John Gotti for anything other than a pleasant occasion."

As after the Giacalone case, yellow balloons appeared on 101st Avenue in Ozone Park, outside the Bergin, and in Howard Beach, in the yards of the Gotti home and others.

But Gotti did not go home first. He went to the Ravenite, Neil's lair, Gotti's lair, and after a few minutes, Mulberry Street was alive with fireworks ignited by neighborhood fans.

Gotti stepped out to take a bow. A smallish but powerfully built man with a faint smile was right alongside him, and thus the first photographs of Gotti and Sammy Bull Gravano together went into newspaper archives. Of course, the video agents also got archival material, including a tape showing Gotti inviting television reporters and a newspaper columnist into the club for a quickie tour of its humdrum interior—unremarkable and unrevealing, apart from the *Mob Star* portrait of Gotti, next to Neil's, above the conference table in the rear room.

"I can't stomach this anymore," Mouw said the next day, when he looked at the tape with Gabriel. "It sickens me, him celebrating, these reporters kissin' his ass."

That next day, in the media, the Gotti legend was taken to its highest elevation; the thin air caused much woozy analysis and commentary. One *Daily News* writer said Gotti should be the superintendent of schools, because he "would crack a few heads" and drugs would disappear from playgrounds. Several reporters built stories with comments from dial-a-quote psychologists, including one who loftily described Gotti as the "typical American frontier risk-taker."

The media's problem was that so much had already been said and written, fresh angles were elusive. The legend had already been explained numerous times: Gotti had tapped a civic vein of animosity for authority; he dwelled outside the law with style and bravado. The *New York Times*'s solution for this problem was to stir-fry the same hash under a mushy, classically *Times*ian headline:

GOTTI: DAPPER CELEBRITY
OR RUTHLESS MOB BOSS?

In the moment's excitement, the media also neglected an inevitable truth about civic attention span; as long as Gotti got away with dwelling outside the law, fine; as soon as he tripped up, well, forget about it. Next legend, please.

The most telling quote in the O'Connor coverage was buried in the quotation avalanche. It was spoken by Mouw's boss, Jules Bonavolonta, boss of the FBI's OC section in New York.

Asked to comment, Bonavolonta had ignored the question and spoken directly to Gotti: "He knows we haven't brought a case against him. And he also knows that when we do, he's finished. He can take all the bets he wants, but he's going to prison."

For an FBI official, it was a rare public display of verbal style and bravado—and there was an exceptionally strong reason for it. Back on December 12, in Gotti's second visit to Nettie's, the one in which he spoke monomaniacally about his problems and criticized Sammy behind his back, the Teflon Don also admitted he was a murderer. Not once, but twice—according to numerous headset sessions with the tape by the agents who specialized in decoding Gotti's words, Michael Balen and Carmine Russo.

The first victim he mentioned, while complaining to LoCascio that Sammy was too busy making money to care about the financial interests of ordinary soldiers, was Robert "Deebee" DiBernardo, the union fixer and original member of the Fist. DiBernardo was murdered in 1986, while Gotti was at the MCC awaiting trial in the Giacalone case; Angelo Ruggiero—who wanted to be underboss and felt Deebee was blocking his path—told Gotti that Deebee talked "subversive" behind his back.

Four years later, Gotti said to LoCascio: "When Deebee got whacked, they told me a story. I was in jail when I whacked him. I knew why it was being done. I done it anyway."

Later in the same conversation, Gotti admitted okaying the murder of Louis Milito, Sammy's ex-partner in the steel-erection business, after Sammy said Milito was refusing to stay low on Staten Island and was bad-mouthing the administration.

Gotti could have paused at many stops while sailing

down his memory lane of murder. That he chose these two, rather than, say, Paul or Bilotti, did not matter to Jules Bonavolonta or Mouw or Andy Maloney. Atop his other indiscretions on the apartment and hallway tapes—all his chatter about Cosa Nostra "structure," obstructing justice, tax evasion, bribery, and so on—the Deebee and Milito admissions had suddenly made the FBI–Eastern district RICO case look like a prosecutorial walk in the park.

Details needed assembling, but Gotti had talked his way into a clean case—and had taken Sammy and LoCascio along. The case did not need McElroy-like witnesses; with Gotti on tape killing Deebee and Milito in a Gambino enterprise context, it only needed proof that the victims were dead—an easy matter since their families had not seen or heard from them.

At the time, the case was actually better than Bonavolonta realized. On the same December 12 tape, but in a section yet to be decoded, Gotti had deposited evidence of another murder, one in the making. In the thin atmosphere of his invincibility legend, Gotti already was—legally speaking—a dead man.

CHAPTER 23

• • • • • • • • • • • •

Blondie

Several months of apparent calm preceded the now inevitable "big pinch." After a bit more indiscreet chatter in the hallway, the Ra   e bugs would fall silent, as would Gotti's corrupt sources. The get-Gotti campaign would be carried out from a distance that masked intentions and hid ironies.

For Gotti, life—and death—would go on. Someone new would come into his life, and someone old would go out—partly because the FBI, in the biggest irony, fell down on the job.

For those seeking to lower the curtain on Gotti's life and legend, the question became not when, but who— who would get the sweet and official glory? That issue complicated the march toward arrest and indictment, and it arose just as someone with a past with Gotti came into his future.

In the wake of the O'Connor verdict, Andy Maloney— though not as pointedly as Jules Bonavolonta—had also painted Gotti's victory as a momentary setback. After reviewing the hallway and apartment tapes, a soft-spoken but hard-edged prosecutor whom Maloney had chosen to be his new organized-crime chief held the same belief— privately, in the way of subordinates, but with extra relish.

After all, John Gleeson went back a long way with Gotti—back to the malodorous onset of the Gotti legend, the Giacalone case.

Gleeson, the special-prosecutions chief for the last few months, took over the newly created organized-crime job a few days before the O'Connor verdict turned up the media volume on Gotti. The job was created after the inde-

pendent Eastern District Strike Force was phased out and
Cosa Nostra cases came under Maloney's sole jurisdiction. Gleeson's new job, and the Ravenite tapes, meant
that he and Gotti were likely to arrive at a second cross-
roads someday—but by circumstance, not design.

A year before, Gleeson had accepted a partnership offer from his old Wall Street firm, Cravath Swaine and
Moore, but he delayed his return until some old business,
a case against an inner-city drug gang, was over. After
Gleeson won that, Maloney complicated his life by offering the special-prosecutions job, and Gleeson decided that
the opportunity of supervisory experience and more trial
work for the United States were worth it; he accepted
Maloney's offer and told Cravath thanks, but no.

Then, after Gleeson won the Michael Coiro case at the
same time the strike force was disbanding, Maloney came
calling again about the organized-crime post. Because it
now looked as though a Gotti prosecution would occur,
Maloney thought Gleeson the best candidate. Gleeson, after the Giacalone case, the Coiro case, and many jury-
tampering probes, knew more about Gotti and the
Gambino family than any other prosecutor in the Eastern
District.

"Whatever you want," Gleeson had told Maloney, "but
who will try the Gotti case?"

Maloney—who had earlier vowed to try the Gotti
case—had decided to limit his role to opening statement.
With his other duties, he would not be able to become as
familiar with the case as the lawyers who were on it every day.

"You'll do it," he told Gleeson. "I'll be at the table, I'll
give the opening, but you'll do the real work."

"Maybe I have too much baggage, because of what
happened in '87, with Diane. It'll look like I got a personal motive."

"Not to the jury, 'cause they won't know about it."

Gleeson told Maloney that the FBI might feel differently, and if it did, he would step aside—but only for a
lawyer in the new organized-crime unit that he was to
lead.

Over the next couple days, various FBI supervisors
told Gleeson that they favored experience over
appearances—and then the agents with the most to lose in

the Gotti case, Bruce Mouw and George Gabriel, visited him at the courthouse in Brooklyn. It was the first time Gleeson had met Gabriel.

"If I were U.S. attorney, I would not let me try this case," Gleeson said, "so if you have problems, I'll back out."

"You know more about these mopes than anybody," Mouw said. "We want you to try it."

While worried about the baggage he brought and offering to recuse himself, Gleeson was stirred by competing thoughts—a second chance with Gotti, the sweet potential of things coming full circle. And once Maloney and the FBI washed away his concern about appearances, he allowed these to float to the surface.

That night, walking home to Brooklyn Heights, Gleeson's mind whirred and a little bounce came into his step: "This is too good to be true. No way am I gonna be this lucky. Nobody gets a second chance. But we got one and it's a good one!"

Like his looming second chance with Gotti, Gleeson's path to the Eastern District was the product of circumstance, not design. Like Gotti, he was born in the Bronx, into a large family—seven children, of which he was the youngest. Unlike Gotti, his family left the city for the suburbs when he was a boy; he came of age in a town named after the mythological hall of heroes, Valhalla, in Westchester County, an area of well-tended lawns and manners north of the city.

Like his sisters and brothers—all teachers or professors—he was a studious and disciplined type who worked as a caddy for ten years to help pay his tuition at Georgetown University in Washington, D.C. He was an English major and met his future wife, Susan, there in 1975, his senior year.

After graduation, in his case, the only work available to egghead English majors was as a house painter. Susan, however, won a scholarship to study for her master's degree in nursing at the University of California in San Francisco, and the couple went there in the fall. Like Bruce Mouw had before he went to Annapolis, Gleeson thought he would be a sportswriter, but *San Francisco Examiner* editors laughed the inexperienced rookie out of their office. That same first week, *Time* magazine published a story on the San Andreas fault; the story contained an illustration depicting how much California real estate would fall into the ocean in the event of the big one, and it included the Gleeson efficiency in Daly City.

The couple returned to the nations' capital a week later, stopping ten blocks short of a Georgetown friend's apartment because their old Dodge Dart died; its engine literally fell from its rusted mounts to the street. Susan took a nursing job and Gleeson went back to being a house painter—for two years, while looking for a writing job that never came.

Finally, he entered the University of Virginia law school; after doing superbly, he clerked for a federal judge; in 1981, he joined Cravath Swaine and Moore—a den of Westchester County wealth and manners. After a few years of briefing issues for the firm's partners, he yearned for trial experience and began interviewing at both the Eastern and the Southern Districts.

At the Southern District, Gleeson made it into the office of the boss, Rudolph Giuliani, who was beginning to make a big name for himself with prosecutions against gangsters, politicians, and insider traders. During the hour-long interview, Giuliani bored in on Gleeson's opposition to the death penalty and attempted to shake it by piling increasingly egregious facts into an imaginary case. Gleeson did not shake; it was wrong for the government to kill people, when people who kill could be jailed for life.

"We'll check your references and call you," Giuliani said, but he never did either.

An interview with Raymond Dearie, then U.S. attorney in the Eastern District, was more wide-ranging—and Gleeson went to work there in February 1985, one month before a terminally ill Neil Dellacroce and John Gotti were indicted in the Giacalone case.

Like all new assistant U.S. attorneys, Gleeson was assigned to "general crimes"—run-of-the-mill bank frauds, insurance scams, and airport hijackings. But within a couple of months, a supervisor, David Kirby, came to him with a RICO case: "I know you came here because you didn't want to be an associate anymore, working for partners, but we got a case coming up and the person on it needs help, and you're the only person I got available."

"John who?" Gleeson asked Diane Giacalone, after they met.

While in law school, Gleeson had joked with relatives about a character in one of their favorite movies, *The Godfather.*

"When I graduate, I'm not gonna work for some stuffy firm, I'm gonna be like Tom Hagen," Gleeson would say, referring to the consigliere character played by actor Robert Duvall.

"You'll be the adopted Irish son," someone like his sister Winnie would reply.

John Gleeson as Tom Hagen was a running gag in the family because the notion of studious, clean-cut, and scrupulous John ever working on the other side of the law was so preposterous—and, after learning who Gotti was, Gleeson could not resist telephoning his sister and saying, "Hi, Tom Hagen here."

The gag wore thin as the Giacalone case wore on. At first, the men at the defense table, especially Gotti, did not appear unfriendly. During recesses, Gotti often teased the then thirty-five-year-old Gleeson—"after this is over, why don't you come work for us? You're a bright guy, we can use you."

"Thanks, but I like my job."

"We could pay more."

"I'm afraid," Gleeson teased back, "it would never be enough."

Several times, referring to disclosures about Willie Boy Johnson and to tapes played in court in which Angelo and Gene made unflattering remarks about Gotti and his gambling, Gotti thanked Gleeson for giving him "the truth" about "some of the guys I got around me."

The pleasantries decreased markedly as Gotti, Bruce Cutler, and the remainder of the defense team got deeper into their get-Giacalone strategy, and they disappeared altogether when the defense filed papers suggesting that Gleeson had used his wife—now a top nursing official in Manhattan—to get drugs for a witness.

By the time the verdict came, Gleeson thought the defendants and most of their lawyers were loathsome; and the memory of being in court—with Gotti, ungracious in victory, wagging a finger at the prosecution table and saying, "Shame on them, they should be investigated"—was all the more galling now that he was virtually sure the case had been fixed.

"Yes!" Gleeson thought as he walked home early in 1990; it did appear things were coming full circle. His excitement was soon tempered, however. A week after the O'Connor verdict, after a meeting of several top officials in the city's law enforcement establishment, Gleeson began to dread that he might lose the case—not to Gotti but to other prosecutors.

The meeting was called by Jules Bonavolonta, Mouw's boss; newly confident that Gotti was a goner because of the Ravenite tapes, he wanted every official and agency interested in Gotti to set aside ego and institutional pride and endorse a single RICO case against the Gambino administration.

Because such a case had been the Eastern District–FBI goal all along, Bonavolonta thought the Southern District, which was pursuing a case narrowly focused on Sparks, should yield to the Eastern; it was the consensus he sought when he invited Maloney, Gleeson, and counterparts in the Southern District and the Manhattan district attorney's office to the meeting.

To Maloney's anger and Gleeson's surprise, the threat to the consensus came not from their federal counterparts but from the local ones—which was especially galling because the locals, who liked to think of themselves as a kind of Cravath Swaine and Moore, had just lost a case against Gotti that in hindsight seemed a very dubious one to bring.

Representing the Southern District, Louis Freeh—a future FBI director who was then chief of organized crime under Rudolph Giuliani's successor, Otto Obermaier—said that there should be only one case and that Obermaier was not really encouraged by the Sparks proof that Walter Mack had so far gathered.

Michael Cherkasky, licking his O'Connor wounds, spoke next. "We took out shot, we lost," he said. "We thought we could win, we didn't."

His tone seemed to indicate that Cherkasky's boss—Robert Morgenthau, who was not at the meeting—had instructed him to forfeit a role in another Gotti case. But Cherkasky said that his immediate boss, Barbara Jones, Morgenthau's top assistant, would speak on that topic.

She said that a single federal RICO case was the way to go, and her office would be happy to join the effort, but that since the Sparks murders occurred in Manhattan, the case should be tried there, not in Brooklyn—where, incidentally, the Gambino family seemed able to tamper with whatever jury it wanted.

Jones's afterthought about Brooklyn juries struck Maloney and Gleeson as an insult, but they focused on the overall implication of her remarks: Robert Morgenthau wanted a second chance against Gotti too. Because he had worked for Morgenthau when "Morgy" was the the Southern District U.S. attorney, Maloney knew the potential effect of his old boss's desire for a second chance.

He knew that no other district attorney in the nation was accorded as much accommodation in Washington—and that Justice Department officials, to placate him, might very well decide to create a prosecution team consisting of both federal districts and the district attorney, and try the case in Manhattan.

Maloney had no interest in that, and after the meeting he told Gleeson that it was very possible that somewhere down the line they would be big-footed out of their second chance.

"Forget what Rudy Giuliani promised me when we started this thing three years ago, that he wouldn't interfere with us. Forget what Louis Freeh says. Forget Obermaier. Forget Mack. Morgy is the guy who matters now."

Walter Mack, who had preceded Freeh as chief of the Southern District organized-crime unit, was not invited to the meeting—and when he later learned that Freeh had said that Obermaier did not think much of his Sparks proof, he resigned in disgust and took a big job on Wall Street.

In the meantime, heading back to Brooklyn, Maloney ordered Gleeson to tie up all the threads of evidence and get the case ready to go as soon as possible. The more prepared they were, the better chance they had of winning Washington to their side.

Gleeson, assisted by Laura Ward and another new colleague from the organized-crime unit in the Eastern district, Patrick Cotter, rolled up his sleeves and went to work.

A few days after the fireworks at the Ravenite, John Gotti celebrated his O'Connor acquittal in the usual way—a vacation in Fort Lauderdale with some of the usual cronies: Jack D'Amico, Joe Watts, Carlo Vaccarezza, and Bobby Boriello. Sparks shooter Eddie Lino stayed home; in the last remnant of business from the heroin case, he was finally about to stand trial on charges that he bought some of Angelo's heroin.

The O'Connor celebrants checked in at their usual place, the Marriott Harbour Beach Resort, in a suite vacated by Vice President Dan Quayle—and preswept for bugs and wiretaps by experts hired by Lewis Kasman, who was becoming a kind of advance man as well as deputy press secretary.

Gotti was acutely mindful of other cases coming his way, but victory in the case posing the most immediate threat vented some of the pressure; the obvious shadows of surveilling agents and cops were not as bothersome as the year before, and he enjoyed himself—particularly when bouncing over Atlantic Ocean waves in Vaccarezza's speedboat, the one named *Not Guilty*.

At night the entourage sailed around town; in the men's room of one elegant joint, a well-spoken stranger asked D'Amico, Gotti's appointments secretary, to introduce him to Gotti.

"I'd like to meet him, just say hello, I've heard so much about him," said a man who introduced himself as Brian Mulroney; a man with Mulroney whispered in D'Amico's ear that Mulroney was the prime minister of Canada.

D'Amico was not sure if he was being put on, but he went to to Gotti, explained the request, and asked if it was okay.

"As long as he ain't got no fuckin' Mounties with him," a beaming Gotti replied.

It was a funny line, and everyone at the Gotti table had a great laugh about it after the man claiming to be Mulroney came over, chitchatted about nothing, and left—leaving everyone convinced that he was who he said he was.

A couple of months later, back in New York, it was Gotti who sent an emissary to arrange an introduction. While in Da Noi, Vaccarezza's Upper East Side restaurant, Gotti and probably most men in the room noticed a striking blonde, dressed all in white, seated at the bar.

Gotti was especially intrigued; the woman resembled Shannon Grillo, Neil's out-of-wedlock daughter. He had broken off with her, but not for lack of attraction; the affair just had nowhere to go, because he was never going to embarrass himself in a messy public divorce fight with Vicky.

The woman was Lisa Gastineau, a recent divorcée. Her maiden name was D'Amico, same as the appointments secretary's—to whom, he and she would soon learn, she was distantly related. She was born on the Lower East Side and had lived there in a working-class housing project until she was six and her family escaped first to the Bronx, then north of the city to Rockland County.

Despite the ethnic New York pedigree, Gastineau looked like a former prom queen from the University of Alabama; in fact, she was a nineteen-year-old sophomore at that school when, during summer vacation back in New York, she met her ex-husband, Mark. He was a football player, then in rookie camp for the New York Jets, eventually an All-Pro defensive end; his exuberance after sacking enemy quarterbacks gave rise to the term "sack dance."

The marriage, and his career, ended when he began chasing film starlets like Brigitte Nielsen. Since the divorce she had dated many prominent and wealthy men, but she told friends the only relationships that ever amounted to anything were with men who, like Gotti, were born under the sign of Scorpio.

The divorce's messiness threw a sympathetic spotlight on the astrology buff that she did not shun. She gave press interviews and appeared on many television talk shows.

She was in Da Noi, causing heads to turn while waiting for a friend, when Carlo Vaccarezza arrived with a message from Gotti, who in addition to everything else was vice president of a garment center firm known on paper as Scorpio Marketing.

"John would like to say hello to you, do you mind?"

asked Vaccarezza, a slim man with Roman-accented English, slicked-back hair, and the decorous manner of a Mediterranean Maître d'.

Gastineau knew Vaccarezza and who "John" was; a friend of hers was dating Vaccarezza, and she knew that the city's most popular reputed mob boss was a friend of his. She also knew Gotti was in Da Noi that night; she had noticed him noticing.

"Sure, Carlo, why not?"

Having eliminated the possibility of a quick rejection by sending a second in first, Gotti strolled to the bar. Gastineau later told friends that this first meeting between the mobster and his new moll was like a first kiss—sweet, tingling, a bit awkward. Tellingly, his break-the-ice lines were about her TV appearances, a subject on which he regarded himself an expert.

"I saw you on TV, and I seen you in here, and I just wanted to meet you and say hello."

"It's nice to meet you."

"I'll tell ya, television don't do you justice. You look a hundred percent better in person, a hundred percent."

"You look much better in person, too."

"Ah, with me, they usually jump me when I got troubles on my mind, you know what I'm saying?"

In the ensuing small talk, Gastineau let Gotti know she was in Da Noi to meet a man—Bo Dietl, a private detective who on her behalf investigated her ex-husband's closets during the divorce proceedings. But, she added, Bo Dietl was just a friend.

Gotti knew Dietl, and they exchanged greetings when Dietl arrived—after which Gotti retreated to his table and Dietl and Gastineau took theirs. Later, while Dietl was in the men's room, Vaccarezza gave Gastineau another message from Gotti.

"John would like to invite you to have a drink with him at Regine's. It would be best, you know, if you were alone."

Gastineau was not going to make it that easy. So she brought Dietl to Regine's—a popular nightclub with the aura of a French bordello, particularly in the upstairs room, where small velvety alcoves of plush chairs and sofas were arrayed around the dance floor. After a few drinks, Gotti turned the matter at hand over to his appointments secretary.

"John would like to take you to dinner and dancing, alone, someday," D'Amico whispered into his distant cousin's ear.

Gastineau handed D'Amico her telephone number and said it would be fine if Gotti telephoned. When the call came, however, D'Amico was on the line.

"The Rainbow Room. Ten o'clock. The reservation will be in your name. John will arrive a few minutes after you do."

D'Amico arranged all of Gotti's and Gastineau's dates over the next several months. She told friends that at first Gotti's refusal to telephone or to leave his name at a reservation desk made sense; a man as recognizable as he had to be careful. But the longer the routine went on, the less sense it made, because they frequently went to public places such as the Rainbow Room atop Rockefeller Center. People recognized him all the time.

She concluded that Gotti simply enjoyed the cloak-and-dagger aspect of the setup—as well as the rubbernecking that went on whenever he and the prettiest girl in class waltzed on the dance floor.

"You don't mind if I call you Blondie, do you?" he asked one night.

"People have called me that since I was a little girl."

"But I ain't no Dagwood!" he chuckled, gliding her across the floor with his 1950s-bred taste in dance steps and newspaper cartoons. "Some people call me Papa Schultz."

Gotti now knew that a young prosecutor he had enjoyed joking with in the early stages of the Giacalone case was now in charge of the Eastern District grand jury investigation; he learned when George Gabriel gave him a subpoena, signed by Gleeson, for voice and handwriting exemplars. As other agents sometimes did, Gabriel used prosecutors as foils when he delivered subpoenas to crooks; it made the transaction less personal.

"John Gleeson's running the grand jury now, John," Gabriel told Gotti. "He asked me to bring this, so you know I gotta."

The emergence of Gleeson introduced an element of

irony that clearly and immediately disturbed Gotti, because his response was even more vile and vehement than it usually was to bad news.

"That fuckin' faggot bastard! Motherfuckin', beady-eyed cocksucker! He's trying to get even, that's what this whole fuckin' thing is about!"

"I think it's more that that, John, but you'll think what you want, so I won't argue with ya."

In June 1990, Gotti summoned the capos to a meeting. The subpoena made him certain that the "big pinch" was near; as on the eve of the O'Connor trial, he wanted to state the law of succession, and it was the same now as then: "If I'm in the can, Sammy's in charge. I'm still boss, but Sammy's in charge."

For all the private doubt he once allowed LoCascio to see, he was defiant in front of his rank-and-file commanders. "It's a good thing I don't sweat when I'm in trouble, but we gotta stay strong! The fuckin' government's comin' at us every which way, but we stay strong and we fight!"

His ability to muster defiance was bolstered by the way the saga of the Angelo tapes had finally ended. In the last trial to stem from the tapes, Eddie Lino was found not guilty. The joy of this triumph was not so much the acquittal as how it came about: ten thousand in cash to a juror, a scheme arranged so adroitly by Sammy that prosecutors never even suspected enough to cry foul.

While the scheme revalidated the family's ability to reach jurors, its pipelines into law enforcement had dried up. Michael Coiro was now in prison. Millionaire detective William Peist had fallen under suspicion and was lying low. So Gotti did not know that a high-stakes bureaucratic fight was now raging in the government over exactly which way to come after him.

Just as Maloney had feared back in February after the O'Connor verdict, Robert Morgenthau was now actively campaigning for the next crack at Gotti—with a case based on the Sparks homicides and featuring his office and the Southern District, which had shed its earlier indifference and was now backing Morgy.

The federal districts had since exchanged glimpses of each other's evidence against Gotti, and Maloney and Gleeson thought the Southern District's Sparks evidence was weak; the strongest element was Philip Leonetti, the ex-underboss, telling Walter Mack's grand jury that in a meeting four years before, Gotti had admitted killing Paul.

"They bring a case based basically on Leonetti, they lose," Maloney said. "And what's it going to look like if we bring our case right after that? It's like O'Connor. Sour grapes."

In an ideal world, one free of clan rivalry and turf war, the ideal case against Gotti was an all-federal one joining the proof of both districts. Because the Eastern District would be bringing more to such a marriage, the Southern District should have yielded the lead role to it, and a local district attorney should have had nothing to say about it.

That was what Maloney believed. He was as competitive and territorial as the next ex–West Point boxing champion, but in this dispute he happened to have right and might on his side. The FBI–Eastern District case was more comprehensive, its proof was stronger, and it held the promise of poetic justice—the fall of John Gotti in the same courthouse where he rose.

But this was the real world, and in July, as the clock for determining who was to take the next crack at Gotti wound down, a meeting about these increasingly political issues was held at the Southern District. All the local players were there, as was a Washington player, Paul Coffey, chief of the Justice Department's organized-crime and racketeering section—where, ultimately, the decision would be made.

At the meeting's outset, Gleeson—now five months deep into marshaling the details of the case—was asked to give a summary. His even-keeled nature was one of his attributes, but in this room of heavyweights he was as nervous as a moot-court student.

"What kind of opening statement is this?" Morgenthau said, after Gleeson, to brace himself, began reading from his notes.

"I'm nervous, Mr. Morgenthau, I admit it. More nervous than I was when I gave my rebuttal in the '87 Gotti trial."

"Relax, you're among friends." Morgenthau winked. "For the most part."

The quip eased some of the tension in the room and re-

laxed Gleeson, who summarized for ninety minutes. The
Eastern District case was a racketeering and conspiracy
case, with an assortment of underlying "predicate acts,"
such as obstruction of justice and tax evasion, but its
theme was murder: "Gotti assumed power by murder, he
solidified power by murder, he exercised power by
murder—and we have him on tape talking about it."

Because the theme was murder, Gleeson said, the best
way to take prosecutorial advantage of the Southern District's evidence on Sparks was to fold it into the Eastern
District case. Gotti's tape-recorded words about the Robert DiBernardo and Louis Milito murders would bolster
Philip Leonetti's testimony about the murders of Paul and
Thomas Bilotti.

As cogent and sensible as Gleeson's summary was, it
did not sway anyone whose allegiance lay outside the
Eastern District, least of all the winking gray eminence,
Mr. Morgenthau.

"Well, that's fine, John, but in 1985 there was a double
murder here in Manhattan and we came to an agreement
with Rudy Giuliani that we would investigate and prosecute those murders with the Southern District. So we
want to do that, and you can bring your RICO case afterward."

That scenario—two cases, the Eastern District one
second—was what Maloney wanted most to avoid. "Bob,
you go first, you create legal problems for me, double-
jeopardy problems, not to mention how it's going to look
if you lose and we come in after you. The jury might
walk the guy and put us in jail."

"We've been working on this case for four years, with
Rudy and Walter Mack. I called Walter and even though
he resigned he's willing to come back and try the case."

"I know Rudy made a commitment to you, Bob; he
also made a commitment to me, that he would stand aside
and let us do the RICO case. But what's the situation
now? Everybody in this room knows the best way to get
this loudmouth is one case."

"Maybe so," Morgenthau said, "but if so, I think you'd
be better off with your case over here. We got a better
jury pool. Your bugs were here in Manhattan, just up the
street."

Maloney had warned him, but Gleeson could not believe his ears: the district attorney arguing on behalf of the Southern District taking over the Eastern District case, while Otto Obermaier, Giuliani's successor, sat quietly by—except to say that federal judges in Manhattan were also "better," meaning friendlier to the prosecution.

The blithe remark about Manhattan juries—a dig at the jury tampering in Brooklyn—was too much for Maloney to let pass.

"Bob, the Manhattan courthouse is one subway stop from the one in Brooklyn. Do you think the Gambino family could find its way over here too?"

"All I'm saying is, look at the record."

Trying to nudge Morgenthau into a corner, Paul Coffey, the Washington player, told Morgenthau that if he felt so strongly about prosecuting Sparks, the Justice Department would not object to his bringing a Sparks case on his own.

"It is our policy, in a murder case, to defer to local prosecutors whenever possible, you know that, Bob," he said.

But Morgenthau quickly said no, he did not want to bring a case on his own—an unspoken admission of his limited faith in the Sparks evidence, which under the different rules in state and federal courts, would travel much better in federal court.

The meeting ended with an agreement to disagree—and delay decision. Beforehand, Maloney asked that if Justice ruled that both districts could proceed separately, he get the courtesy of inducing his grand jury to indict first. In that event, he would omit the Sparks murders from his indictment.

"Castellano-Bilotti weakens my case. Gotti's on tape denying them. You can hear him joking, and we all know he's lying, but it gives the lawyers something to work with. So I don't want them, I don't need those murders. Just let me file my case first."

Once they were alone, walking to a subway entrance, Maloney told Gleeson to prepare a "prosecution memo"—a legal brief, in effect, for the bosses in Washington. "Do it quick, maybe we can still outflank these guys," he said.

They then took the No. 6 train to Brooklyn and got off at the first stop, a noisy, smelly underground station teeming with people following their own agendas—the real world.

One month before meeting Lisa Gastineau at Da Noi, Gotti waltzed with his wife, Vicky, in the Versailles Room of the Helmsley Palace Hotel in Manhattan; the occasion was an opulent wedding reception for their son Junior and Kim Albanese, daughter of a carpet installer from Valley Stream on Long Island.

The reception, featuring all the singers and entertainers that Gotti had employed for daughter Angela's wedding five years before, was planned and executed by Lewis Kasman.

"The champagne must be Cristal and the gin Boodles," Kasman insisted while working out the details of a fifty-thousand-dollar party for two hundred and fifty guests on April 22, 1990.

The guests included Sammy, LoCascio, the Gambino caporegimes, and important or favored soldiers—as well as the administrations of the city's other Cosa Nostra families, all except the Genovese family. Gotti, still unaware how deep Chin Gigante's grudge ran, lifted a glass of Cristal with each of the other administrations after the bride and groom departed—and chalked up the Genovese absence to Chin's aversion to surveillance and publicity.

Since Luchese underboss Anthony Casso did attend, Gotti had no reason to suspect that Casso was still planning to kill him for Chin—and had in fact rigged a bomb to a car that would be used in the assassination, once he decided when and where to carry out the attack with minimum chance of other loss of life.

"This fuckin' guy's always with a dozen guys," Casso told an emissary of Chin's. "You can't leave a car with a bomb outside his house either. Imagine if some little kid came by on a bike or somethin'."

To keep law enforcement and news media surveillance of the wedding to a minimum, Kasman hired a security force of twenty ex-cops, and snooping eyes and ears were pretty much kept at bay.

Consequently, the bride's pregnancy was not widely known until she gave birth two months later. Unlike his father, who did not marry Vicky until after their first child was born, Junior had elected to wed the mother of his child—if not right away, at least before the birth.

Of course, twenty-six-year-old Junior's life and balance sheet were a lot more secure than his father's had been at a comparable age. He owned two houses, a trucking company, several cars, and all the Walkmans and gymnasium equipment a weight-lifting made man would ever need.

A couple of weeks after Junior became a dad, in the summer of 1990, his dad gave him a uniquely Cosa Nostra gift—a promotion to caporegime. Once again, Sammy Gravano believed that Junior was too young for such responsibility and that Gotti was looking out for his interests as much as Junior's—shoring up his control in case he went to prison.

But once again the situation caused verbal paralysis. Sammy was now underboss and the designated "street boss" in the event of jail for Gotti. How would it look to Gotti if Sammy raised objections about Junior? What was Sammy afraid of? Or planning?

The paralysis was further assured by the manner in which Gotti implemented Junior's promotion.

"I've been thinkin' somethin'," he told Sammy and LoCascio at the Ravenite, "and I want you to tell me if you'd recommend we put Junior up to caporegime, and give 'im a crew with Bobby Boriello and a few other good guys."

"Yeah, he's ready, be a good thing," Sammy said.

"Junior's got *cajones,* John," LoCascio said.

Gotti told Sammy and LoCascio—neither was sure that he was part of the looming "big pinch"—to prepare Junior for the promotion ceremony; the ritual formality of what followed was highly comical to anyone not in Cosa Nostra—where "representante" was sometimes a synonym for "boss."

"Your representante is making you a caporegime," Sammy told Junior, after he and LoCascio pulled him aside at the Ravenite.

"I am honored," Junior said.

"Is there any reason why you cannot be a caporegime in this family?" LoCascio asked.

"None."

"We're gonna take you to your representante and introduce you to him," Sammy said.

The underboss, the acting consigliere, and the capo-to-be walked to where Gotti was, in the back room of the Ravenite, waiting with several other caporegimes.

"This is your new caporegime," Sammy said to Gotti, an acting captain at the time of Sparks.

"This is your representante," LoCascio said to Junior.

At that, the head of the clan and the newest officer of the clan embraced. Gotti turned, and with one arm around his chip off the block, waved at the others in the room and told Junior he was now an especially elite guardian of a glorious tradition.

The Gambino squad learned about Junior's elevation after the fact, from informers, because by the summer of 1990 all the bugs at the Ravenite were silent. Because Gotti had stopped using the apartment and because he had already said enough to make a case, the agents had suspended audio surveillance and now spent their time marshaling details for Gleeson and his chief assistants, Laura Ward and Patrick Cotter.

Before spring weather and a renewed sense of caution drove Gotti back onto Mulberry Street for walk-talks, however, the hallway bug did pick up a few useful conversations.

In one, Gotti provided an illegal-gambling thread to the case by losing his temper when a Queens-based soldier reported that independent-minded "Greeks" claiming to have a big "sponsor" had begun hosting a roulette-type game in a catering hall in Astoria—long the domain of the Bergin in nearby Ozone Park.

"We've got a game there for twenty years!" Gotti fumed. "Is this rat-fuckin' Greek's name Spiro?"

"That's right," said the soldier.

"You tell this punk, I, me, John Gotti will sever his motherfucking head off."

In another overheard hallway conversation, Gotti raised another obstruction of justice flag while at the same time driving Bruce Cutler further into an embarrassing corner.

Gotti told Cutler that he had learned that FBI agents were trying again to loosen the lips of imprisoned Anthony Rampino about Sparks. He predicted that agents would offer Roach immunity from prosecution and said Cutler should meet Rampino's lawyer and make sure an immunity deal was rejected.

"You wake him up," Gotti said to Cutler, referring to Rampino's attorney. "Open his eyes."

"I understand," Cutler replied.

Gotti then said he needed to use Cutler in another way. He said that because the boss of a Cosa Nostra family in Providence had recently been indicted, he now had to communicate with that family by sending messages to its lawyer.

"So I'm gonna send [the lawyer] a message, that if I ever wanna get a message to them, or from them, we'll do it through you."

"Okay," Cutler said, sounding an awful lot like Michael Coiro telling Gene and Angelo that he felt the same way they did, that he was one of them.

The significance of one of the last hallway conversations was not immediately apparent; agents also did not link the name of a man overheard in the conversation to threats Gotti had made on earlier tapes. Consequently, the man did not get an FBI warning that his life was in danger, and he would be murdered.

In Nettie's apartment, back on the watershed day of December 12, 1989, the day Gotti admitted approving the killings of Robert DiBernardo and Louis Milito, he also spoke of another man whose first name was Louis—but in such a way that agents initially thought he was still speaking about Louis Milito.

In many subsequent reviews of the tape, it became clear he was not—but it was too late for Louis DiBono, the soldier whose drywall construction business was used to funnel money to Gotti after Gotti became boss; by 1989, after letting himself and the business slide downhill into a mess of unpaid taxes and cocaine, DiBono had walked onto thin ice—particularly after his cocaine habit so clouded his judgment that he did not answer multiple Gotti demands for meetings at the Ravenite to discuss taxes that the company owed both the state and the federal governments.

Gotti was a silent partner but sill vulnerable to trouble if state or federal tax agents went after DiBono. IRS-paranoid Sammy was far more vulnerable; on paper, he was DiBono's legal partner and was coresponsible for the taxes, and so for almost a year Sammy urged Gotti to address the problem—but DiBono kept ignoring subpoenas from the Ravenite.

"Louie DiBono," Gotti said to LoCascio on December 12, "you know why he's dying? He's gonna die because he refused to come in when I called."

It was easier to see how the agents missed a second threat against DiBono on the apartment tapes. That time, on January 24, while telling Sammy that some unnamed "liason guy" who brought an informer into a Gambino crew ought to be killed, Gotti referred to the overweight DiBono by a nickname.

"He's gotta get whacked ... for the same reason that Jelly Belly's getting it. You wanna challenge the administration, we'll meet the challenge! And you're going, motherfucker!"

At the time, Gambino squad agents knew little of DiBono and nothing of his secret deals with Gotti and Sammy. By the time he stopped using cocaine and showed up at the Ravenite on March 28, 1990, they had not yet deciphered the two apartment tapes; they thought they were just overhearing more hallway conversation, not the words of a doomed man trying to appease his hangman.

"I'm in really good shape," DiBono told Gotti, referring to his cocaine problem, while saying he was back on the job and ready to make Gotti money from a housing project in the Bronx.

Earlier that day, DiBono continued, he had told a friend how much he admired Gotti. Quoting himself, he recalled, "I said, 'You know, I'll tell you, Joe, I love John, he's a good man. He's honest, he's straight as an arrow.' "

The obvious stroking failed to move Gotti, who raised the not-little issue of unpaid state and federal taxes.

"I'm paying all the bills!" DiBono promised.

"We don't need this fuckin' shit. I don't need it!"

"John, I'm working very hard. I'm in the office every day. I want you to know, you could reach me anytime. I'm on the ball."

In time, DiBono did make good on the taxes, but the penalty for his more serious crime—ignoring a Ravenite subpoena—was not lifted. He must have sensed that his apology and paying the taxes were no guarantee, because he never came back to the Ravenite; he moved out of his house and began avoiding all his usual places.

Sammy, despite his earlier emotions about how unseemly it was for a man of his position to be in the street with a gun in his hand, eagerly volunteered to do the work on DiBono. The tax situation was the second time DiBono had jeopardized Sammy. the first was in 1981, when Sammy caught DiBono cooking the books of their drywall company and threatened to kill him—provoking the telling sitdown with Paul in which Neil came to his defense.

Gotti wisely nixed Sammy's offer to kill DiBono. Sammy's name was on too much DiBono paper. Gotti gave the job to Bobby Boriello and two other men, including one he was thinking of making, if the man could demonstrate a stomach for bones.

Meanwhile, however, another job came up in August 1990, and Sammy put down Victim No. 18—a family-connected demolition contractor who was demolished by a team from Tali's after Lisa Gastineau's newest flame interrupted his sweet talking long enough to decide that the victim, fresh out of jail on a small case, was a threat—in the current environment.

Louis DiBono lasted until October 1990. He had managed to evade several Bobby Boriello–led missions and was becoming an annoying piece of unfinished business when an acquaintance in the construction business happened to mention to Sammy that he had seen DiBono, on a drywall job, at the World Trade Center in Manhattan. DiBono even gave the man his business card.

Sammy passed the tip and business card along to Gotti, which was enough to put Victim No. 19—his last—on Sammy's card. Louis DiBono was promptly shot dead in an underground World Trade Center garage by the Boriello squad on October 4.

Because two apartment tapes had not been accurately decoded, DiBono died without getting a FBI warning. In time, the murder would provoke a strange epiphany—and the agents and lawyers who listened to the tapes beforehand would not know whether to laugh or cry. Someone was killed, virtually inside their headsets, but at least they did have more dead-bang evidence against Gotti.

"The system failed," Mouw would later recall grimly.

CHAPTER 24

• • • • • • • • • • • • • •

The Big Pinch

The Louis DiBono murder brought the get-Gotti competition between Manhattan and Brooklyn to a rapid boil. Before a system failure caused another killing, the contestants realized it was time to declare a winner and bring an indictment. Late in October 1990, they set up a Washington summit that everyone agreed would be the last chance to make a best pitch.

In reality, the game was virtually over, and the news was bad for Brooklyn. Deputy attorney general George Terwilliger, the Justice Department underboss, had already decided that a single case would be brought, a RICO case combining the evidence of the Eastern and Southern Districts, and that it would be tried in Manhattan by a team of lawyers from both districts and the Manhattan district attorney's office.

The main issue left was who would be on the prosecution team. Terwilliger, representing Attorney General William Barr, did not want either local U.S. attorney, Andy Maloney or Otto Obermaier, involved in the trial; they feared the presence of bosses would elevate Gotti in the jury's mind and encourage a George Bush vs. John Gotti show-trial mentality in the media.

For lead trial prosecutor, Terwilliger favored former Marine Corps captain Walter Mack, a known factor in Cosa Nostra warfare, over onetime English major John Gleeson. Though in private practice now, Mack had agreed to return just for the Gotti case—after Morgenthau, not Obermaier, called and asked.

In practical and not-incidental media terms, Terwilliger's decisions and his choice for lead prosecutor meant that the Manhattan contingent was destined to get the thunder for getting Gotti. The FBI—after Jules Bonavolonta's initial attempt, back in February, to get the parties to agree on a single Eastern District case—pulled back from the bickering; bureaucratically the bureau had no official say, and in any case it was destined to share the thunder no matter which side prevailed.

Terwilliger arrived at his decisions after a briefing from Robert Muller, chief of the Justice Department criminal division, who actually leaned toward Brooklyn. But Terwillger told Muller that while the call was close, close calls should go to the Southern District. The difference: Robert Morgenthau.

Because Morgenthau's jurisdiction was limited to Manhattan, the only way to include him in the case was through the Southern District. In a close call, it was simply politically less painful to deprive Andy Maloney and John Gleeson of a second solo chance against Gotti than it was to deprive the nation's most respected former U.S. attorney and most prominent local prosecutor of an opportunity to avenge his office's loss in the O'Connor case.

If Maloney had known the decision was already made, he would have written his resignation letter before flying to Washington for the supposedly pivotal summit. But he believed the prosecution memo he told Gleeson to draft in July was such an effective presentation of the right and might of the Eastern District position that Washington would come down on his side.

The Southern District had written a memo too but failed to give Maloney—who had given Gleeson's memo to all interested parties—a courtesy copy. Still, a copy arrived in a brown-paper envelope one day—which Maloney took as evidence that someone in the Southern District was sympathetic to his position—and so he and Gleeson were primed to answer the points they expected Otto Obermaier, Maloney's opposite, and Morgenthau to raise.

Obermaier's and Morgenthau's points were the same as before. The "centerpiece" murders in the case—Paul's and Bilotti's—had occurred in Manhattan; the video and audio evidence was gathered in Manhattan; both the jury pool and the federal judges in Manhattan were "better."

Morgenthau added a new wrinkle. He said relations be-

tween the NYPD and the FBI would never be the same
because the FBI had cut the NYPD out of the information
loop on Sparks. This was a remarkably brazen complaint,
because if the FBI had shared its information, it likely
would have gone straight to Gotti, thanks to Detective
William Peist; while the evidence to arrest him was still
being gathered, he had been identified as a suspected trai-
tor and was being encouraged to retire.

"The morale at One Police Plaza is bad," Morgenthau
said. "It might help relations if they could play an important part in this case at the trial."

The purported display of concern for the wounded feelings of the NYPD brought an inner smile to Maloney,
who knew his former boss was really expressing his own
hurt at being cut out of the loop about the Ravenite bugs
until after the fact.

When his turn to speak came, Maloney came out
punching. "It's outrageous for my friends here to argue
that a major criminal cannot be tried in the Eastern District because of the jury pool. Do you know how far
the Eastern District is from the Southern? It's just over
the Brooklyn Bridge, one subway stop, and I think the
Gambinos can find their way over the Brooklyn Bridge.
It's not the other side of the moon."

Pointing first to Obermaier, then Morgenthau, he
added, with respectful bluntness: "I helped break Otto in,
and I worked for that guy ten years; I know they don't believe anything they're saying. They're actually laughing
at you, that you're buying this, and it comes from the
Manhattan tap water they drink."

Terwilliger smiled. Manhattan-Brooklyn disputes were
always amusing, if not easy. "The jury-pool issue does
concern me," he finally said.

"History will show they've had just as many problems
as we have. It's an insult to the eight million people who
live in my district to say, 'We're taking this case away
because we're afraid we can't find twelve honest people.' "

"All right, so each of you, tell me, what steps have you
planned to limit the possibility of jury tampering?"

Obermaier answered first. "Actually, I disagree with
Andy. Jury tampering just hasn't been that much of a

problem in our district. Frankly, we're not all that concerned. I don't think we'd do anything special."

Maloney's jaw dropped; the Eastern District had prepared many special plans, and he asked Gleeson to describe them.

This time, Gleeson was as calm as a moot-court judge. "We see it as a big problem," he began, "but the problem isn't the district; it's these defendants. It doesn't matter where they are on trial. So how do you attack that problem?"

Gleeson outlined his plan of attack: The prosecution would ask whichever Eastern District judge was assigned to the case to sequester the jury not just for deliberations but for the entire trial. It would seek a completely anonymous jury, not just the partially anonymous one of the O'Connor case.

To sway the judge, Gleeson said he would submit affidavits from informants that the Gambino family had a policy of always trying to tamper with juries—and that he would call witnesses who had firsthand knowledge of the policy, as it was applied in two of the three Gene Gotti trials (Gleeson did not yet know of the failed attempt in the third or about the Eddie Lino fix).

"I think our district's judges, because of recent history, are likely to agree with us," Gleeson said.

The man who no longer joked about Tom Hagen was not yet done. He said he was developing a minutely detailed questionnaire for the potential jurors. It reflected everything he had learned about the art and peril of juror screening during all his jury-tampering investigations, and he was confident it would expose predisposed sympathizers.

"Thank you, John," Terwilliger said.

The meeting drew to a close with a we'll-let-you-know-soon from Terwilliger. Maloney was disappointed, and as the Brooklyn and Manhattan contingents exited the marble hallways of Justice, en route to their separate taxis to the airport, Maloney fired a passing shot over Robert Morgenthau's bow during a brief aside with his Southern District counterpart, Obermaier.

"Otto, you and I will never be as good at these conferences as Bob because he's unencumbered by the truth."

Still unaware that Terwilliger came to the meeting with

his mind made up, Maloney and Gleeson shuttled back to Brooklyn and awaited word from Washington. Maloney's disappointment with the announced delay in the decision rubbed raw; he told chief assistant Mary Jo White that the right call was so obvious he would resign if Washington called it the other way.

"Then I will, too," said White, herself a Southern District alumna (and future U.S. attorney there).

Maloney and Gleeson also were unaware of the impact that Gleeson had made in the Washington meeting when he replied to Terwilliger's jury-tampering question. Next to the walk Obermaier took around the question, Gleeson's response was a grand slam—and it did lead to a come-from-behind victory for the Eastern District.

Maloney and Gleeson were never told, but after the meeting Terwilliger told his organized-crime chief, Robert Muller, that the Manhattan contingent was dangerously unconcerned about the jury-tampering issue; this was enough reason to change a close call and disappoint Mr. Morgenthau.

"Andy and John have thought this out, they have a plan, and they are right," Terwilliger said. "It's just as easy to try and fix a case over the bridge. Give it to Andy."

That the Southern District would lose because of Obermaier's weak argument on the issue that the Manhattan contingent had waved in the face of the Brooklyn contingent for nearly a year would have been especially satisfying to Maloney and Gleeson.

But Muller did not reveal that the decision had turned on a single issue when he called Maloney a few days later and said, "It's yours, Andy."

Muller said he still thought it would be good for harmony between districts if Maloney invited a Southern District lawyer to "second-seat" at the Eastern District prosecution table. Maloney said sure, knowing that the Southern District would (and did) decline a second-banana role in Brooklyn.

Just as the Ravenite bugs had built a stage for deception, a stage for poetic justice was now in place: the fall of John Gotti in the same courthouse where he had begun rising four years before.

Now it was time to assemble the last few pieces of the

case; theoretically, because of all the evidence on the Ravenite bugs, Maloney and Gleeson could have asked their grand jury to indict not just the administration of the Gambino family—Gotti, Sammy, and LoCascio—but virtually every Gambino capo, but they decided to include only one capo, Tommy Gambino. They wanted to keep the case short and simple; the others could be attacked later.

Once that decision was made, early in November, the Gambino squad devised a plan for arresting the suspects; Mouw and Gabriel wanted to arrest them at the same time, at the Ravenite, where a mandatory-attendance policy still held—and so the details of a Mulberry Street arrest plan were formalized.

At the last minute, however, the video agents reported some disturbing news: They had not seen Sammy Gravano in several days.

Other agents quickly consulted informants, who said they had not seen him in several days either.

"Could Sammy be in the wind?" Mouw asked Gabriel. "Where's a guy like Sammy go? He's probably been out of New York one or two times in his whole life, and then only over to Jersey."

"If he took off, did John tell him? Or did he panic? Maybe the prospect of heavy time is freakin' Sammy out."

"I don't know. But if we arrest Gotti without him, he might never come back."

Trying to confirm Sammy's absence, Gabriel and Gleeson came up with another ploy. Gleeson told Sammy's lawyer, Jerry Shargel, that he needed to serve Sammy with a subpoena requiring him to give the grand jury handwriting examples—and could Shargel produce his client?

"No problem, I'll contact him," Shargel said.

The next day, however, Shargel contacted Gleeson: "I am not sure I can produce him."

That was all Shargel had to say for Gleeson to know Sammy was indeed "in the wind."

"Then we just have to wait until we find the son of a bitch," Mouw said, after Gleeson relayed the news.

Trying to lure Sammy home, Gambino squad agents concocted stories about last-minute evidence problems with the case and planted them with informants, cops, and reporters. The resulting thrust of gossip at the Ravenite and stories in the media was that an indictment was now several months off.

Sammy was indeed worried about heavy jail time, but it was not his idea to run. Gotti, who fought the government tooth and nail, who always said a fugitive's life was pointless, had in a moment of uncertainty about the future ordered him to take off.

Gotti's uncertainty was the product of, of all things, an astonishing development involving Anthony "Gaspipe" Casso, the Luchese underboss who masterminded the DeCicco bombing but had failed to come up with a plan for killing Gotti. Fearing life sentences, both Casso and his boss, Vittorio Amuso, had gone into hiding to avoid an imminent RICO indictment.

"As long as you're out there, like Vic and Gas, maybe we can keep this thing together," Gotti said late in October, when the press was reporting vague stories about a meeting in Washington being the last step before a big indictment that likely would include Gotti, Sammy, and LoCascio, and maybe Tommy Gambino.

"I don't know if it'll work," Sammy replied. "It could go on so long. I know you ain't gonna get convicted, but if you do . . ."

"Yeah, I know, it's life plus a thousand years. But try it on for size. As long as one of us ain't in the can, people feel more secure. We'll set up a way to get messages back and forth."

"I could be away a long time."

"After I beat this case, you can come back; they won't want to fuck with us again."

Sammy took off, well aware that as a fugitive it was going to be much more difficult to keep in contact with Debra and his children than it would be as a prisoner. He ran without much enthusiasm, but he ran; to the end, he was following orders.

One of Sammy's friends from his teenage days in Bensonhurst, Louis Saccenti—now a trusted Tali's associate—went with him. The spontaneity of the decision to flee was apparent in their choice of hideout—a bungalow in the Pocono Mountains in Pennsylvania owned by Debra Gravano's parents.

After ten days, Sammy told Saccenti: "Are we fuckin' nuts? If the pinch is comin' down, and I'm not around, where are they gonna look?"

The Bensonhurst buddies then flew to Florida, Sammy under the name Frank James, the less colorful, more stoic outlaw brother of Jesse—a joke by Saccenti, who made the airplane reservations, aimed at lightening Sammy's mood.

There they stayed with acquaintances in the Fort Lauderdale area, where they flirted with the idea of trying to slip out of the country and into Brazil. They read somewhere that if they married Brazilian women, they could never be extradited to New York, under the terms of a treaty between the two countries.

The idea was as half-baked as the notion that a fugitive could effectively manage the Gambino family; it took three weeks and the murder of a close crony for Gotti to begin seeing clearly again. The victim was Eddie Lino, one of Gotti's nightclubbing pals and a drug dealer who had recently begun to use his own product. Lino was shot dead by highway assassins who pulled alongside his Mercedes in Brooklyn late in November.

The murder was proof that a fugitive could at least manage to orchestrate a hit. Gotti had no idea, but Lino was killed by gunmen working for Anthony Casso—who hadn't run very far, only to a girlfriend's house in rural New Jersey. Frustrated by the failure to find a way to kill Gotti without subjecting civilian passersby to risk, Chin had decided that killing men close to Gotti was the next best thing and directed Casso to take out Lino—a Sparks shooter—first.

Chin renewed his secret war at a time when he too was finally facing legal problems. He had been indicted in the same RICO case that had caused Casso and Amuso to flee—they and others were accused of taking part in a multifamily plot to rig the bidding on a big replacement-window job in city public housing projects.

The murder of Louis DiBono, an old Genovese acquaintance in the drywall construction business, triggered Chin's frustration. He left it to Casso to pick the killers, and Casso chose hit men with more reasons than made men for never talking about it; one was an off-duty

NYPD detective and the other was one of his ex-partners, now retired, at least from police work.

Naturally, without being told anything, Jimmy Brown Failla and Danny Marino suspected that Gigante and Casso were behind Lino's murder. But they never told Gotti, who thought Lino might have been shot by drug customers. Gotti knew only that it now made more sense to bring his troubleshooting underboss home.

Early on the evening of Monday, December 10, 1990, Gambino squad agent Billy Noon was monitoring the camera at the video plant when a short, bullish man came into view. Noon quickly telephoned Bruce Mouw: "Guess what? Sammy just showed up."

Mouw spread the word to his superiors and to Maloney and Gleeson. Sammy Gravano was back in town, and everyone agreed that it was finally time to make the big pinch.

Early in the afternoon of the next day, December 11, 1990, ten agents and three NYPD detectives took up positions near the Ravenite and waited for the Gambino administration. Another agent was posted outside Tommy Gambino's office in the garment center.

The subjects had not been under surveillance during the day; the slight risk of detection was not worth spooking them. It was better to let them continue to believe, as they now did, that the big pinch wasn't going to come until after the Christmas holidays. That way they would come to the Ravenite as usual.

LoCascio and his bodyguard showed at the Ravenite first, at about five o'clock. An hour later Sammy arrived, accompanied by his Tali's capo, Louis Vallario.

In keeping with past practice, Gotti should have arrived fifteen minutes later, but he did not. After thirty more minutes, the arrest team began feeling the pangs of adrenaline letdown. In the video plant command post, Mouw told agents: "If we take these guys without John, you know what Cutler will do. He'll call a press conference and make a big show of surrendering his oppressed client."

Fifteen more minutes passed. Finally, an agent saw Gotti's black Mercedes crawling up Mulberry with Jackie

D'Amico behind the wheel, and he alerted the command post.

"Wait 'til he and Jackie are inside, then go," Mouw said on the walkie-talkie network connecting the arrest team.

In a few minutes, after Gotti—wearing a camel-hair topcoat and a jaunty yellow scarf—walked inside, Gabriel led the team up to the door of the Ravenite. Some associates loitering outside recognized him but made no attempt to interfere as he walked inside, pistol in one hand, badge in the other.

"FBI! You know why we're here!" he yelled, once in the front room. "We're here for John, Sammy, and Frankie, and I want everyone to do us a favor and cooperate."

Smiling, Gotti bounced out of the rear room into the front, his arms extended in a handcuff-me gesture. Dressed in his usual construction-foreman garb, a grim Sammy was a few steps behind, trailed by a snarling Frank LoCascio.

"I knew you were coming tonight," Gotti said. "I knew."

"At least you and Frankie dressed up for it," Gabriel said, "but you forgot to tell Sammy."

"Fuck you, fuckin' agent," LoCascio said.

"Whoa, Frankie! Watch that mouth!"

"I knew, Georgie," Gotti repeated, trying to jerk Gabriel's chain. But Gotti did not know; deprived of reliable pipelines, he knew what reporters thought they knew, that the case was suddenly beset by evidence problems. The proof of this was that Gotti had not telephoned Lisa Gastineau beforehand to tell her he might be in prison on the following evening so they might have to cancel plans to attend a Frank Sinatra concert in New Jersey—very special plans because it was both Blondie's and Frank's birthday, her thirtieth, his seventy-fifth.

Sammy had warned Gotti against such public nights out with Gastineau; it was one thing to dance at the Rainbow Room, quite another to attend a media-saturated concert with twenty thousand people. But Gotti said two "beards"—or front men—would escort him and Blondie to big public events; he compared his situation to that of Donald Trump, the publicity-minded casino owner. The newspapers had just reported that Trump employed beards when he desired the company of his girlfriend, blond Southern-bred beauty queen Marla Maples, more than that of his wife.

"Carlo and Jackie are my beards," Gotti had explained. "Carlo's her date, Jackie's mine. We're like fuckin' Trump and that Georgia peach of his."

Twenty-nine beards witnessed the arrests at the club, but all they did was glare. As the suspects were hand-cuffed, Jackie D'Amico began walking toward the door; as a capo, he had certain leadership obligations—like telephoning Cutler and Shargel, so they could get to work on a bail application, and Blondie, so she'd know Papa Schultz was not willingly standing her up.

"You said you ain't here for me, so I'm saying good-bye now," he said to Gabriel.

"Relax, Jackie, I'll let you know when you can leave. We got to write a few names down here."

With that, the arrest team fanned out and began asking the others to state their names. As the occupants of the Ravenite complied, the agents made a special point of addressing them by their nicknames, to rattle their nerves and show how much they had learned about them.

Mouw arrived from the video plant and asked Ravenite caretaker Norman Dupont for permission to use the club pay telephone. He telephoned his office first, then Gleeson.

"John, I'm in the Ravenite, sitting right across from John Gotti and listening to George Gabriel read him his rights. It's a beautiful sight."

The news spread quickly through the local FBI hierarchy. William Doran, head of the New York criminal division, told Jim Fox, director of the New York office, as Fox hosted a Christmas party at the New York headquarters building. Fox immediately tapped his glass with a spoon and told his guests: "We just got a great Christmas present, we just arrested John Gotti."

By that time, Gotti, Sammy, and LoCascio were in separate FBI cars, en route to headquarters for processing. Gotti was with Gabriel. Once again, things were coming full circle; four years before, after the Giacalone verdict, Gabriel had kept a teasing promise made to Gotti during a break in the trial—if Gotti won, he would go to Ozone

Park to congratulate him; later that day, Mouw named Gabriel case agent for a new Gotti investigation.

"We got Tommy at his office earlier, he'll be joining us soon," Gabriel now said to Gotti.

"Tommy's a sweetheart, a gentleman, and you should not be messin' with his mind."

"We got you good, John—Paul's murder, Tommy Bilotti's, Milito's, Deebee's, some other stuff if that's not enough."

"Bullshit, I'm a legitimate guy, the only legitimate guy in the world,"

"And everybody else is illegitimate?"

"Nah, not everybody. Not you, I know you're a good guy, a little brainwashed, but a good guy for an agent. I know you're just doin' this for that faggot punk Gleeson."

"We got some pretty good taped conversations."

"You hear me in the club, it's braggadocio, it's bullshit, all nonsense."

Gabriel decided to jerk Gotti's chain: "You seem a little more serious in the hallway, John, and really serious in the apartment."

Gotti turned, faintly quizzical, then cleared his throat. "Ah, what do we talk about? It's just me and my friends."

Sammy rode to headquarters with the most veteran agents on the Gambino squad, Frank Spero and Matty Tricorico; they were soft-spoken, straight-shooter types, whom Sammy already knew and grudgingly respected because they had treated him respectfully the few times they had gone to his office with subpoenas or questions. Like Sammy, they lived on Staten Island.

The arrest put Sammy in a foul mood. A few days before, he was in Florida, ready to run to Brazil, and as half-baked as the idea was, here he now was, in handcuffs, staring at life in jail. Gotti had stared down virtually the same hole twice before and covered it over both times. Sammy never had; he had never spent more than two weeks in jail, and not since he was a kid held on a Brooklyn robbery warrant in, of all places, Tijuana, Mexico.

Riding with Spero and Tricorico, the normally disciplined underboss vowed to "kill anybody who puts me in jail." If they had wanted to, the agents could have interpreted this as a threat and caused Sammy more trouble, but instead they overlooked it and in soft, respectful tones pointed out that more than anything, John Gotti's mouth was putting Sammy Gravano in jail.

CHAPTER 25

• • • • • • • • • • • • • •

Total Separation

The war of wills between the law and lawlessness now moved onto its last battlefield—a formal plane of rules, procedures, and policies distilled from centuries of courtroom wars. Because one side now had the advantage and was closer to depriving the other of its freedom, the rules tilted toward the disadvantaged; but the rules applied to both sides, and an independent arbiter, a judge, was on hand to interpret and enforce them.

On this battlefield, fists became legal briefs; guns, pretrial motions. Disputes were resolved in rulings, not sitdowns. The battle would be fought until a winner emerged, and it would feature many surprise turns. Echoes of old conflicts would waft across the plain and reveal to both sides secrets about themselves.

At FBI headquarters, after the arrests of the administration and Tommy Gambino, a boisterous Gotti—coatless now but with the same jaunty yellow scarf framing his face—tried to lift his troops' spirits as agents fingerprinted and photographed them and vouchered their personal belongings.

"You're gonna love the food!" he shouted, referring to the meals that awaited them at the MCC, where they would be jailed at least until a bail hearing, and until trial if bail were denied. "We're gonna get in great shape!"

It was difficult to muster his troops. Sammy's anger had given way to a grim calm; LoCascio was profanely refusing to answer the most innocuous questions—name, age, address—for the "pedigree" forms that agents were obliged to complete. Tommy Gambino seemed sad and embarrassed to be involved in the seeming coming-apart of everything his father had held together for almost twenty years.

Gabriel "processed" Gotti, while the veteran agents, Spero and Tricorico, ran Sammy through the drill. Gotti was carrying eight thousand dollars in cash, which was vouchered by Gabriel. Sammy was carrying two thousand; he told the agents he regretted having that much on him because his wife Debra might need it.

"We'll take it to her, don't worry about it," said Spero, departing from procedure.

"It's on our way home," Tricorico added. "Just keep it between us."

The agents yet had no idea how murderous Sammy was, but over years of investigation and hours of listening to tapes, everyone on the Gambino squad had arrived at the same opinion: They would rather have sat down over a beer with him than with Gotti. This was out of curiosity, not compassion. Whereas Gotti seemed like smoke and mirrors, Sammy seemed real.

Around the time Lisa Gastineau was turning thirty and Frank Sinatra seventy-five, the four suspects were transported to the MCC, to await their bail hearing in the morning at the Brooklyn federal courthouse. Their overnight accommodation was a signal for what was likely to happen next; Tommy was held in a wing of the prison for new arrestees likely to make bail; the others in "total sep," or solitary separation—meaning the government was likely to seek to detain them without bail.

After the sun came up in Brooklyn, the signal proved true. John Gleeson, however, added a new wrinkle; rather than rely just on predictable reasons why Gotti, Sammy, and LoCascio were poor bail risks, he intended to play excerpts from the apartment tapes to show how dangerous they were if allowed freedom pending trial.

He asked the U.S. district court judge who drew the case off the Eastern District "wheel," or judge-assignment lottery, I. Leo Glasser, for a few days' delay to prepare for the hearing, and Glasser said okay, granted Tommy bail, and ordered the others to be held at the MCC.

Meanwhile, about a hundred reporters swarmed over Cutler, whose needle was stuck in the same old groove: His client was a persecuted man, and the new case was just more "Mafia madness by publicity-hungry prosecutors."

The swarm buzzed two flights upward to the U.S. attorney's office, where Maloney—now fortified by the indictment to publicly say what he believed—said: "Gotti is a murderer, not a folk hero."

When everyone came back to the courthouse a few days later, the defense turned suddenly publicity-shy and asked the judge to conduct the bail hearing in secret because the apartment tapes were likely to generate too many loud and negative headlines.

"Putting these conversations in the public domain in a case which has gained such wide media attention would have a significant potential to contaminate the jury pool," said Jerry Shargel, sounding completely reasonable on behalf of a client who had been trying to contaminate jury pools for the last several years.

After another few days of delay to weigh the matter, Judge Glasser sided with Shargel and ruled that the hearing would be held in secret, in a few days more, on December 21, 1990. For both sides, that day would prove to be a milestone.

A couple of hours before the hearing began, prosecutors Laura Ward and Patrick Cotter, accompanied by Gambino agents George Gabriel and Carmine Russo, went to the courtroom to verify that the machinery for playing the Ravenite excerpts was working properly.

Because his grasp of Cosa Nostraspeak was firmer, the Sicilian-born Russo was the agent most responsible for reviewing and transcribing tapes. He had immigrated to the United States when he was just a boy of seven, too young to know much about Cosa Nostra, but as a thirty-seven-year-old man, he considered it a blight on his heritage. He was an FBI liaison in Rome before joining the Gambino squad, and he also was a member of a team that demolished an international heroin cartel.

Gabriel put an excerpt from the December 12, 1989, tape into the tape player on the prosecution table, and he and the others put on headsets to sample the volume. The excerpt was the one that they knew featured Gotti's references to "Louis," meaning Louis Milito, and "Deebee," meaning Robert DiBernardo.

Maybe it was multiple ears hearing the words for the

first time, maybe it was that ears were more in tune because everyone now knew about the murder of Louis DiBono, but the words coming out of the tape player, into wires and then to speakers mounted around the courtroom provoked a strange epiphany: "Louis DiBono," Gotti said to LoCascio, "you know why he's dying? He's gonna die because he refused to come in when I called."

Until that moment, "Louis" and "DiBono" had been heard—by prosecutors and agents, during many headset sessions—as "Louie" and "Deebee," as one confusing reference to two murders mentioned earlier on the tape, not as a new reference to a third murder.

But now everyone heard "DiBono," not "Deebee." Seeing the dismay come into the faces of his colleagues, Gabriel rewound the tape, listened intently to it again, then saw that everyone else was as dumbfounded as he.

"Holy fuckin' shit," he said. "Another murder, it sounds like to me."

Gabriel played the tape a third time, with the same result.

Carmine Russo felt like falling to the floor, but his upper lip remained stiff. "I haven't been back to this tape in a while, but it's there, I missed it, I fucked up."

"I missed it too!" Gabriel said. "I can't believe it!"

As the agents melted down, so did the prosecutors. Their problem was that they had tended to rely on FBI transcripts, not their own ears. The reliance was understandable because many passages on the tapes—in which Gotti spoke in rolling waves, quoting himself, imagining conversations he might have—were difficult to follow.

"I've heard that tape a dozen times," Ward said.

"Me, too," Cotter said. "Maybe more."

"We better go upstairs and tell Gleeson," Russo said.

Gleeson was in his office, two flights above the courtroom, reviewing papers for the disqualification hearing.

"Forget about it," he said, after the dour entourage had briefed him and he went to the courtroom to listen for himself. "We'll just amend the indictment, no big deal; I listened to that tape myself, maybe a dozen times. I didn't hear 'DiBono' before."

"I can't believe I missed it, John," Russo said. "That guy might be alive."

As a foe of capital punishment, Gleeson was not a trivial person when it came to life and death. But system failure was something that happened now and then, in the gangster business or any other business. "Fuck it, Carmine, he might've been dead anyway. You can't blame yourself. We all missed it. This just shows that sometimes you hear things only when you know what to listen for. Then it's clear as a bell, like now."

With a fifth murder now in the case, the disqualification hearing got under way. Since Glasser had closed it to the public, the press did not hear the DiBono excerpt, or the sounds of hearts sinking and teeth grinding as the prosecutors began unreeling selected passages from the Ravenite tapes.

For the longest three hours of their lives, Gotti, Sammy, and LoCascio sat mostly stone-faced as the consequences of once relaxing in Nettie's place became abundantly and devastatingly clear. Each excerpt was chosen to illustrate an aspect of the case—murder, obstruction of justice, enterprise "structure," and so on; for the suspects, it was like watching bullets aimed at their heads leaving the gun.

Still, only once during this grim preview of the evidence did Gotti show emotion—and that was when he thought Patrick Cotter, while putting new bullets into the government tape player, was putting a hex on him.

As he introduced each excerpt, Cotter employed the fingers of his right hand to indicate which suspects' voices were to be heard. When it was just two, Gotti and LoCascio, he rolled his middle and ring fingers beneath his thumb—leaving his index and little fingers pointing at the suspects. This was unintentional, but some Old World Italians do use such a gesture when placing a hex or "evil eye"—a *malliocchia*—on an enemy.

"That faggot is putting the *malliocchia* on me!" Gotti fumed into Cutler's ear, particularly upset that a man of Irish blood would be so bold. "Who the fuck is he! The shithead! Motherfucking potato head cocksucker!"

At one point the excerpts became too much for Peter Gotti to endure. As a blood relative he had been allowed into the courtroom. He grimaced, squirmed in his seat, shook his head, and finally fled the room.

"No comment!" he snapped, when reporters in the hall-way bothered him for a quote.

Peter was now in a legal jam himself, having been indicted with Chin Gigante, Anthony Casso, and others in the multifamily scheme to rig bids in a big replacement-window job for the city's public housing projects. Before leaving the courtroom, he heard younger brother John complaining on tape to LoCascio that Peter would probably be convicted and jailed in the so-called windows case—only because Sammy had steered him into the conspiracy.

That remark by Gotti was one of many that landed at the defense table with special resonance. Peter was already in the conspiracy when Gotti dispatched Sammy to overcome a Genovese family beef about Peter's role, and Sammy had smoothed it over in a sitdown; former sanitation worker Peter would have made a bundle if a Genovese soldier had not "rolled over" and become an informer—a risk in almost any Cosa Nostra deal nowadays and hardly Sammy's fault.

The remark had been made on December 12, 1989, known in the FBI as the day a corner was turned on Gotti—and the day Gotti had monomaniacally unloaded his worries on LoCascio and complained about Sammy's excessive dealmaking. Now, Sammy heard Gotti malign him behind his back and rewrite the history of pivotal events. December 21, 1990, would become known as the day their relationship began to turn.

In one excerpt played as part of the "structure" evidence, Sammy heard Gotti complain that Sammy, then his consigliere, was really functioning as a caporegime, a moneymaker—but was using his influence as consigliere to reward himself and his soldiers.

"He's not a caporegime. He wants to be a caporegime, I'll take him down from consigliere and I'll make him a caporegime. He can have all the fun he wants to have. This is bullshit. These people are being taken away from him, Frankie.

"And I wanna know everything that every one of these guys are in. What businesses . . . I wanna know when and how they got in them. These are all businesses nobody had a fuckin' year ago . . . what do I do with the rest of the borgata? Throw 'em in the fuckin' street?"

Sammy could overlook those remarks. Gotti's *gelosio* about Sammy's abilities had begun to show months before the tape was made when, in only one example, he became angry when Joe Watts told him that some union fixers wanted to deal only with Sammy; to make his jealousy less unseemly, it was almost understandable to Sammy that Gotti would accuse him of greediness.

The irony, however, was distressing: Paul was jealous of Neil, now Gotti was jealous of Sammy; despite all, Paul felt he needed Neil as his underboss, and now Gotti felt the same about Sammy. Cosa Nostra had not progressed the least bit under its supposed savior from Queens; the glorious tradition was stuck in 1985, mired in the same duplicitous, self-serving muck.

Still, Sammy was prepared to forgive and hope for the best until the most damning excerpt from the December 12 tape—the one that the prosecution team had fully decoded only a hour or so earlier—began reverberating in the marble-and-mahogany courtroom like a gravedigger's backhoe.

It began with a Gotti lie about the first murder he ordered after becoming boss—that of Sammy's friend Robert DiBernardo, a finger of the Fist. Deebee was murdered, over Sammy's objections, after Angelo told Gotti, in jail awaiting trial in the Giacalone case, that Deebee had made "subversive" comments behind his back. At the time, Angelo owed Deebee money and considered him a rival for underboss.

"Deebee," Gotti said on tape to LoCascio. "Did he ever talk subversive to you?"

"Never."

"Never talked it to Angelo, and he never talked it to Joe Piney either. I took Sammy's word that he talked about me behind my back ... I was in jail when I whacked him. I knew why it was being done. I done it anyway. I allowed it to be done anyway."

Just as these remarks began to rub raw, more grating words came out of the courtroom speaker just behind Sammy.

Referring to both Louis Milito and Louis DiBono, Gotti said the only reason they were killed was that Sammy came to him and asked permission to get rid of business partners. "Every time we got a partner that don't agree with us, we kill him ... [the] boss kills him. He kills him. He okays it. Says it's all right, good."

Milito, a Paul loyalist, was killed because he questioned the new administration's judgment when he was already in hot water for opening a secret loan-shark book with the other side. DiBono was killed because he failed to answer a Gotti subpoena. DiBernardo was killed because Angelo either saw him as a threat to his own underboss ambitions or just wanted to beat Deebee out of a loan and had therefore concocted a subversive story.

But, in one thirty-second-long diatribe, Gotti had made all three seem solely Sammy's doing. At the defense table, Sammy, as always, was a block of granite; inside, he quaked. These remarks could not be forgiven; in his jealous ramblings Gotti had pinned three of the five murders now in the case on him, sentenced him—in all likelihood now—to a life behind bars.

Given the bloodletting on the excerpts, it did not surprise Sammy, or Gotti, LoCascio, and their lawyers, when Judge Glasser ordered them held for trial without bail. The suspects left the courtroom in the custody of federal marshals who were to take them back to the MCC, so it was difficult for them to talk privately.

Still, Sammy whispered to Gotti: "What the fuck was all the garbage on that December 12 tape about?"

"Just fuckin' words."

"Some fuckin' words."

"Forget about it, fuckin' nonsense. I get excited, I'm a jerkoff. That was just before the O'Connor bullshit."

"Yeah, but Deebee?"

Gotti nodded toward the federal marshals; Sammy fell quiet, accepted his handcuffs, got on the prison van, and rode silently back across the Brooklyn Bridge to the MCC with his boss and the nearly always silent Frank LoCascio.

In an official, punitive abuse of power, MCC bosses returned the three Gambino administration members to "total sep"—although none had broken MCC rules of engagement for guards and the guarded. Over the next two weeks, the heart of the Christmas–New Year's holidays and the fifth anniversary of the Sparks murders, each was confined to a lone cell twenty-three hours of the day and separated from the prison population during the one hour that he was allowed out to walk back and forth in a cellblock hallway.

Twice a week they were permitted visits with relatives or lawyers. The only relatives to visit Gotti were son Junior and brother Peter; Vicky Gotti remained at home, where her husband wanted her and where she liked to be. Sammy was visited by his wife, Debra, and his son and daughter, Gerard and Karen.

"I don't want you to come anymore," Sammy told Debra, after she and their children waited on line for ninety minutes to pass security checkpoints. "They treat you like animals. For what? To come see me? Maybe I am an animal. But this ain't worth your humiliation."

Those were the words of a man in depression. And, in total sep for the first time in his life, the tightly wound underboss did grow deeply depressed. It was just him, four concrete-block walls, and hours that took days to go by; at one point, after a visit from Jerry Shargel, he did get some reading material—a copy of the entire December 12 transcript, turned over to the defense by John Gleeson in accordance with pretrial evidence rules. The transcript contained much more Gotti monomania than was excerpted in the bail hearing, and Sammy thumbed the pages over and over.

With the hour-long conversation now before him, Sammy saw that the main theme was not murder but greed. Time and again Gotti accused Sammy of having "green eyes" and hoarding money and opportunity for himself.

"That's Sammy . . . every fucking time I turn around there's a new company poppin' up. Building. Consulting. Concrete . . . where the hell did all these new companies come from? Where did five new companies come from?"

In person, Gotti never complained about Sammy's wheeling and dealing—not before December 12, 1989, or after. The opposite was true; he always applauded Sammy's entrepreneurship, which at its height meant about two hundred forty thousand dollars to him every ten weeks. Yet, with LoCascio, Gotti made it seem like reining Sammy in was a constant struggle.

"I tell him a million times, 'Sammy, slow it down. Pull it in a fuckin' notch. You got concrete pouring. You got

Italian floors now. You got construction. You got drywall.
You got asbestos. You got rugs. What the fuck next?' "

As Sammy read, he noticed how many times LoCascio
offered to bring him upstairs to Nettie's so the boss could
rebuke him in person—and how each time Gotti refused.

"You want me to go get him?" LoCascio would say.

"No, no, no. No, no, no," Gotti would reply. "I'll see
him tomorrow, and I'm gonna tell him tomorrow."

Since tomorrow never came, jealousy became a less ac-
ceptable explanation for Gotti's accusations. Paranoia began to make more sense. As much as Sammy had always
stressed his comfort with his role, Gotti was afraid
Sammy wanted to be boss. That fear, Sammy decided, lay
behind Gotti's words. He was trying to get LoCascio to
agree with him, that Sammy would be a selfish boss; that
way, LoCascio could poison the Sammy well with the
caporegimes, carry Gotti's dirty water, and make it unlikely that they would start agitating for Sammy to become the boss if Gotti was jailed twenty-five to life while
Sammy was still free—a likely scenario back on December 12, 1989, eve of the O'Connor trial.

Gotti could never get LoCascio to agree with him,
however; instead, LoCascio told Gotti that he never knew
Sammy to be "in a deal without you in his mind." Sammy
believed that LoCascio's inability to read between the
lines of Gotti's remarks and say what the boss wanted
was the reason that Gotti ranted on for so long. In any
case, the conversation showed that no one could ever be
too effective an underboss under John Gotti.

Then, on page thirty of the transcript, all the man-made
muck came full circle: Gotti compared Sammy to Paul.

"[Paul] sold the borgata out for a fuckin' construction
company. And that's what [Sammy's] doing. I don't know
if you could see it, but that's what [Sammy's] doing now.
Three, four guys will wind up with every fuckin' thing.
And the rest of the borgata looks like waste."

Unless Sammy was restrained, Gotti added, the family
was headed down the same path as under Paul—a family
of factions, "a fuckin' army inside an army":

"You know what I'm saying, Frankie? I saw that shit
and I don't need that shit!"

At the end of one of these sessions with the transcript,

the dyslexic, chess-playing underboss would lie back on his cot and stare at the ceiling for hours.

After several complaints from Cutler and Shargel, MCC bosses took the suspects out of solitary confinement in January 1991 and relocated them to a less punitive but still high-security "administrative detention" wing. Privileges were limited, but at least the prisoners were housed two to a cell.

Only for symbolic purposes, Gotti and Sammy were put in the same cell; finally they could talk in private, and Gotti quickly tried to repair the damage. Instead, he opened a new wound.

"Sam I know you're upset. I don't blame ya. I'm upset at myself. Let's just forget I'm the boss now and settle this out. Man to man. For this, we're the same, equals."

"Green eyes, huh, John? You never complained. You never said nothin'. You were hackin' me about companies I don't even have. You accused me of sellin' out the borgata! Nobody's more loyal than me!"

"Sammy, Sammy, Sammy! I couldn't have believed that, could I? Made you underboss, didn't I?"

"Deebee. Deebee was your decision. I begged Angelo to call it off, but Angelo said you were steamed. Had to be done! Right away!"

"All I can tell ya is what Angelo told me, that Sammy says Deebee was subversive. Now we know Angelo was a liar."

"But three fuckin' years later, you talked like you still believed Angelo!"

"Sammy, it don't sound like it on that motherfuckin' tape, but I believe you. When I got word from that cop that you were a rat, I dismissed it. 'Impossible,' I said. I told . . ."

"Rat?" Sammy interjected, low and edgy. "What? Rat?"

Gotti frowned. Backpedaling from the December 12 tape, he had come upon another time when he talked behind Sammy's back.

"Relax, it was nothin'. Joe Butch came to me, said you were a rat and that's why you didn't get nailed with my brother Petey in that windows case. The grim reaper got it from you know who. But we know that jerkoff cop could be wrong, don't we?"

"Joe Butch calls me a rat and you don't tell me! I'm the fuckin' underboss! How could you do that to me?"

"I told Jimmy Brown, we agreed it was bullshit."

"As underboss, you owed me. That's Cosa Nostra, the life. We do a sitdown. Put me in the basement with pistols. If they prove it, kill me. If they don't, I kill them; it's my right. You took that away. Not telling me, you give credence to a fuckin' lie."

"Sammy, what do you want to do?"

"Soon as I get out, I'm gonna kill Joe Butch."

"See, that's why I didn't tell you."

"Bullshit. You're boss, you could've said, 'Sammy, do me a favor, give Joe Butch a pass.' I would've said, 'Sure'; maybe I would've whacked the cop, but then it's done. I would've had my credibility. But you make a punk out of me."

"Sammy! No one thinks you're a punk!"

"On the street, nobody could have said to me, 'John is a rat!' I would've killed him before he got the words out! The street was one-way with me. My mistake, I guess."

"Sammy, no mistake! I am your friend, you're my friend. I never doubted ya, and wasn't I right when I bullshitted it? I can't remember every little thing I don't think counts."

"I was your underboss!"

"Sammy, let's stop being girls. This happened, but it don't mean nothing. Now, we gotta fight hard to get outta here."

Shortly after the argument, Cutler and Shargel returned to court and proved to Judge Glasser that MCC bosses were breaking their own rules by holding Gotti and Sammy in total separation. Glasser ordered prison officials to play by the book, and Gotti and Sammy were transferred to general population.

With every available cell already occupied by at least one inmate, Gotti and Sammy were separated and assigned to different cells on the same floor—where, with his new pay-telephone privileges, Gotti began dialing Lisa Gastineau at Da Noi at half past nine in the evening a couple of times a week.

Persuading Glasser to order changes at the MCC was a

small legal victory for Cutler and Shargel—who, that very same day, began confronting a very big legal challenge.

Just as Gleeson used the apartment tapes to persuade Judge Glasser to detain the administration without bail, he now cited the hallway tapes in a motion asking Glasser to disqualify the administration's "house counsel" from taking part in the case. Cutler and Shargel (and to a much lesser degree, John Pollok) were too involved in the evidence—if not actually crimes—to properly defend their clients, especially against the charged obstruction of justice counts in the indictment.

The legal basis for disqualification was strong; the hallway chatter between Gotti and his two main lawyers made it impossible for them to stand before a jury and argue that Gotti did not order George Remini to take a contempt citation in the Tommy Gambino trial or that he did not conspire to encourage Anthony Rampino to take a contempt charge rather than answer questions about Sparks.

Still, because of the way it might be (and was) perceived in some corners of the public mind, the disqualification motion was a gutsy move. Denying Gotti and Sammy a basic liberty, the right to counsel of their choice, might look unfair; kicking Bruce Cutler out might look like revenge for the Giacalone case.

"I know what it'll look like to some people," Gleeson said to Ward and Cotter, as they mulled over their move. "Cutler kicks your butt in '87, so you kick him out now."

"And then what if the judge says no?" Cotter said. "What will it look like to people in the jury pool if the government lawyers tried to get the defense lawyers off the case, and the judge wouldn't allow it?"

"That we tried to run the lawyers out of town, just because it's Gotti and Bruce," said Ward.

The more time they spent with the transcripts, however, the more obvious the move became, no matter the perception. "The lawyers made themselves part of the evidence, part of what happened," Gleeson said, making his mind up. "If you don't want to be a fact witness, stay the hell out of the Ravenite."

"I agree," said Cotter. "Every single conflict a lawyer might have, this case has."

"And if we don't do it, and then win at trial, I will bet you, the big issue on appeal will be that the defendants were denied adequate counsel because of all the conflicts," added Ward, the federal judge's daughter.

Gotti and Sammy were stunned by the prosecution move; one of the apartment tapes—the one in which they lamented the supposed "gentleman's agreement" by which prosecutors overlooked the sins of defense lawyers, as long as the lawyers did not "holler" at them—seemed pretty silly now.

To keep Cutler and Shargel in their corner, Gotti and Sammy were willing to waive later claims that they did not receive adequate counsel because of lawyer conflicts. But what they wanted did not matter as much as the tapes, which contained more evidence than the obstruction of justice conversations.

Gotti's admission that he paid the lawyers to defend other members of the family was proof of an illegal RICO enterprise—the Gambino family. His remarks about using Cutler and Shargel to learn information about pending cases against himself and members of the enterprise provided more proof. Finally, Gotti's observation about "under-the-table" payments to Cutler constituted proof of a possible crime.

To hammer home these points, Gleeson knew which tape to quote first when oral arguments on the disqualification motion against Cutler, Shargel, and appellate specialist John Pollok were made in Judge Glasser's courtroom on February 22, 1991.

" 'Where does it end?' " he began, quoting Gotti complaining on the January 4, 1990, apartment tape, of hundreds of thousands of dollars in legal expenses. " 'Gambino Crime Family? This is the Shargel, Cutler, and Who-do-you-call-it? Crime Family.' "

Gleeson paused to let that evidentiary balloon float over the defense table, then added: "It's very rare, your honor, to have the name of the enterprise stated by the defendants. You don't often get tape recordings in which the enterprise alleged in the indictment is set forth for you by the defendant."

Gleeson added that Gotti's joking reference to the

"Shargel, Cutler, and Who-do-you-call-it? Crime Family" suggested "as forcefully as we could ever hope" that the lawyers played a crucial role in the enterprise and had to be disqualified.

The defense team tried to argue that voices and names of the lawyers could be "redacted" from tapes and transcripts and thus concealed from jurors, but Gleeson called the proposal "entirely unreasonable" because it would require hundreds of redactions.

"It would become ridiculous both as a matter of unfairness to us and confusing to the jury," Gleeson said, before pointing out that, inevitably, the jurors would realize that redactions were code for Cutler and Shargel. "Jurors have common sense. They are going to realize exactly what's going on."

Judge Glasser reserved decision, and Gotti and Sammy went back to the MCC; though now in separate cells on the eleventh floor, they were able to talk during recreation periods.

For Sammy, Gleeson's move was such an ominous sign that he began focusing on the prospect of never leaving prison again. He told Gotti they ought to develop an escape plan.

"We lose Jerry and Bruce, we lose," Sammy said. "I know nobody ever busts out of here, but we ought to put our heads together. Come up with something."

Gotti wasn't interested. In the last few weeks, the MCC had received hundreds of letters addressed to him, from people around the world—people writing the most folkheroish sentiment as well as others expressing needs for guidance, favors, inspiration, or a handwriting sample from the most infamous criminal of the day.

"Forget about it, Sammy. What you gonna do? Tie a sheet down eleven floors? Crazy, can't fuckin' do it."

"If we work at it, we'd come up with something. Maybe in a visit from somebody. Take a hostage. Go."

"I'll tell you what we're gonna do, if we lose this motherfucker. Sit tight and wait. The borgata's still ours. We'll still be earnin', so we'll appeal this, we'll appeal that. Reversible error. Bad judge. Improperly withheld exculpatory fuckin' evidence, or what the fuck. Supreme Court. All the way."

"That's just more money for the lawyers."

"You ain't listening. Five, six years of that, case looks a little tainted. So then we just buy our way out the front door. Anybody'll take the money, in the right situation."

"Who?"

"The fuckin' president, if we have to! We put five million under his blanket, get a pardon just like that."

Sammy looked to see if Gotti was kidding and saw that he was not—which disheartened him even more. Gotti was talking like nothing was different, like he was still on the outside building a legacy no one could ever break. But now to have such faith in his power was preposterous—and pathetic.

"And you're callin' me crazy, John?"

Sammy was aware that a former Teamsters boss, Jimmy Hoffa, was supposed to have bought a pardon by throwing his union's campaign support to Richard Nixon—but Gotti was no Hoffa.

"John, we're talkin' murder case. Mafia. Cosa Nostra. Fuckin' public wouldn't stand for it. Be an impeachment."

"Don't make a difference. You oughta see the mail I'm gettin'. We could do it. We could buy a president."

When Judge Glasser reserved decision on the disqualification motion, Cutler and Shargel took a calculated gamble. They asked him to delay issuing the decision until after he ruled on other dubious but standard motions, such as one to suppress the taped evidence. Arguments on these would take months.

It was a gamble because the government's motion seemed so strong, and the sooner Cutler and Shargel knew they were out, the sooner new lawyers could sign on, acquaint themselves with issues and clients, and prepare for trial. But Cutler and Shargel, with their clients' approval, bet that the longer they remained in the case, the harder it would be for Glasser to disqualify them; he was a scholarly, cantankerous judge, known for independence and occasionally hard-nosed rulings against the government.

He also ran a tight-ship courtroom. During oral arguments lawyers were given their due, but after he made a decision, they were expected to sit down and shut up. His tolerance for lawyers who pushed the judicial envelopes of patience and propriety was much lower than the judge's in the Giacalone case, the patrician Eugene Nickerson. Glasser was always prepared, too, and to help prepare for this case he had visited Nickerson's chambers for a judge-to-judge talk about the behavior of the main lawyer and defendant in the 1987 case, Cutler and Gotti. Glasser already knew of Shargel, a prized student when both were at Brooklyn Law School, and Sammy— because he had presided over the case in which Shargel won Sammy an acquittal on tax evasion.

In the current case, in one of his first rulings, Glasser had ordered Cutler and other lawyers, on both sides, to obey a federal court procedural rule prohibiting public statements that might affect a fair trial. Pushing the limits, Cutler—the John Gotti of the defense bar—had continued to holler in public about "government persecution."

By April 12, 1991, when everyone returned to court to argue news-media motions to lift the secrecy lid on the tapes cited in the disqualification motion, the Glasser-Cutler relationship was subject to sparks.

At one point in the hearing, the sixty-seven-year-old judge ruled that Cutler had gotten his due on some technical argument and told him to sit down, please.

"I'm not here like some potted plant!" Cutler erupted.

"Another outburst like that and I'll hold you in contempt!" Glasser shouted back.

The veins in Cutler's formidable neck throbbed, but Shargel flashed him a calm-down look. With the disqualification motion still pending, it was not time to agitate Glasser further.

Cutler immediately understood that he was not helping himself or his client and quickly regained his composure. With the perfect, and perfectly obvious, affect of a contrite man, he said he had come into court feeling bad because he had said good afternoon to his honor but got no response—so maybe that accounted for his terribly wrong, temperamental behavior.

"I don't want you to think I'm an ogre," he said to the judge. "I'll change. I don't want to do anything to hurt Mr. Gotti."

Some people, of course, did want to hurt Gotti badly, and the most lethal were Mr. Gigante and Mr. Casso. On

the very next day, April 13, they added another name to
the list of people who paid for Paul.

Unable to get Gotti when he was free and aware now
they might never get him because he might never leave
prison again, Chin and Casso relied on one of Casso's
capos to send another member of Gotti's inner circle—
Bobby Boriello, chief bodyguard in the post-Sparks era—
the way of Eddie Lino. Boriello was accurately believed
not be have been on hand for Sparks, but his former job
and current one—soldier in Junior Gotti's decina—was
enough symbolic value.

Because none of the usual law enforcement sources had
a clue about the motive for Boriello's murder, the media
were rife with wild speculation—the central theme of
which was that John Gotti had to have sanctioned the hit;
no one would have dared kill someone so close to him
without permission.

As with Chin's and Casso's other trophies—DeCicco in
1986 and Lino only five months before—Gotti remained
clueless now too.

"What the fuck this was about, I don't know," he told
Sammy at the MCC. "Maybe it was some personal beef,
like over a broad or something. I don't know any enemies
Bobby had."

Since committing the December 12 tape virtually to
memory, Sammy was unable to take anything Gotti said
at face value; Gotti lied so much that his truths sounded
like lies, and so Sammy believed that the most plausible
fact in the speculation about Boriello's murder was that
Gotti sanctioned the hit. Being in jail had not stopped
Gotti from sanctioning an earlier hit—Deebee's.

People who felt more loyalty for Gotti than Sammy
now did tried to rally public support for him. On July 4,
Lewis Kasman turned the annual fireworks show in
Ozone Park into a Gottifest. Spectators were given hats
and T-shirts appropriate to wear while giving a sound bite
to television reporters: "Thanks, John," cried the slogan
on the hats; "All Americans Have Equal Rights—Free
John Gotti!" screamed the T-shirts.

Neighborhood loyalists also arranged to give spectators
and TV cameras the most spectacular fireworks display
yet—a tribute to the absent fold hero's will and spirit. But
the plan, and the entire day, went awry when some fire-

works blew up, injuring three loyalists, one critically, and causing evening-news producers to dump the orchestrated sound bites for footage of bloody faces.

The ruined party was both metaphor and omen. On July 19, Glasser denied all defense motions attacking the Ravenite tapes. On July 26, in a scalding written opinion about their actions as lawyers, he dropped the gavel on the other big outstanding issue—and kicked Cutler and Shargel off the case.

In three trips, Gotti had gone to court with Cutler and not lost. In one trip with Shargel, Sammy had not lost. On the walls of the MCC cells the handwriting was getting clearer all the time.

CHAPTER 26

· · · · · · · · · · · · ·

Rollover

Judge Glasser's disqualification of Cutler and Shargel was almost a knockout punch for the two main defendants in the case. Now they would have to go into the battle of their lives without their security blankets. The decision enraged Gotti and drove Sammy to despair. With the trial near, the deck chairs on the *Titanic* of Cosa Nostra were sliding in different directions.

Glasser's ruling contained some slack: Cutler and Shargel could still participate in pretrial proceedings. With no jury present, their conflicts did not matter. However, when a pretrial hearing into the consequences of disqualification arose on August 7, Gotti ordered Cutler and Shargel to boycott it. He and Sammy, to show how oppressive Glasser's ruling was, would appear in court by themselves.

Gotti anticipated a large audience for this stunt because Glasser, in response to requests by several media lawyers, had decided to make public the previously secret excerpts cited in the disqualification motion; consequently, a new bout of Gotti fever had run wild in the media, particularly on television.

"Mr. Gotti?" Glasser asked, after entering the courtroom and seeing only LoCascio's lawyer, David Greenfield, at the defense table. "Do you know whether Mr. Cutler intends to be here this morning?"

Gotti rose, shot his cuffs, and turned toward Glasser. "He said you said he's not my lawyer anymore."

"At trial, Mr. Gotti. I didn't disqualify him from pretrial proceedings."

"Could you explain that to me?"

Glasser willed himself to stay patient; he could not be

as sharp with a defendant as he would have a lawyer who insolently asked for an explanation of arguments made clear in a written opinion. So he again explained to Gotti that Cutler and Shargel were "just not permitted to participate at trial."

Scowling, Gotti glanced at the media mob in the spectator section. "I thought the trial was on, your honor. If you put the TV on, you can see the trial."

Glasser ignored the sarcasm and asked Gotti if he had retained a new lawyer. But Gotti persisted on more explanation.

"Why can't I have my counsel, Bruce Cutler?"

"I made that clear in a decision, Mr. Gotti. I'm sure Mr. Cutler has explained it to you."

Gotti now turned toward the prosecution table and spoke in an angry, loud voice: "I think they should be disqualified! I'm not worried about their phony tapes or their phony transcripts!"

At the table, Andy Maloney and associates remained impassive as Gotti focused his dark eyes on the Maloney associate he blamed for his troubles, John Gleeson. He raised his right arm and cocked his thumb and forefinger like a pistol, which he aimed at Gleeson—that "Little Lord Fauntleroy," he said, adding, "He says he welcomes a good fight! He says he wants a fair trial! But he can't handle a good fight and he can't win a fair trial!"

"Thank you, Mr. Gotti," Glasser said, before turning to ask Sammy if he had retained a new lawyer. Sammy's heart was not in the stunt at hand, but Gotti had asked him to yank the judge's chain a little; going along, he wearily told the judge he had not had time to retain a lawyer.

"How much time do you think you will need?"

"I have no idea. It's pretty hard from the MCC. Jacoby and Meyers don't go there."

It was a pretty good quip and would inspire one reporter to track down a spokesman for Jacoby and Meyers, a legal automat, who said the company probably would not take the case because Sammy Bull Gravano was clearly in need of specialized counsel.

Glasser told the defendants he would give them two weeks to decide to invoke their "absolute right" to defend themselves or to retain lawyers. "And if you don't appear with your lawyers, I'll consider appointing counsel," he added.

"You can do whatever you want to do," Gotti barked. "It's your courtroom."

Having hollered at Glasser and Gleeson, and given the media his message of defiance in the face of persecution, Gotti sat down and shut up. In truth, he had already begun a search for Cutler's replacement—and for Shargel's, because, as always, he as boss would decide who defended codefendants such as Sammy, since any lawyer in any Gambino case actually represented him.

His first choice for Cutler was James LaRossa, a Shargel-type lawyer who was in fact one of Shargel's early mentors. His other strong credential, in Gotti's mind, was that he was once Paul's lawyer for Cosa Nostra–related problems.

"That'll look good," Gotti told Sammy. "The lawyer for the guy we supposedly whacked is representin' me. And I know Jimmy will do it. He's afraid I'd whack 'im if he don't."

"Who we gonna get for me?"

"I got candidates for that position, people are puttin' names up, but we gotta get this guy first, that's key."

But LaRossa told Gotti that the government would surely attempt to disqualify him too because he was a likely witness; LaRossa knew of Paul's efforts to secure copies of Angelo's heroin tapes, a key piece of prosecution evidence in two of the five murders charged in the case; at the time of Sparks, LaRossa also was defending Paul against Walter Mack–brought charges, and the last place Paul and Bilotti had gone before Sparks was LaRossa's office.

Unwilling to spend more money on what appeared to be another fruitless disqualification fight, Gotti gave up on LaRossa.

LaRossa was secretly relieved, but Paul's former lawyer did end up recommending the attorney that Gotti ultimately chose: Albert Krieger, a sixty-seven-year-old advocate with a booming voice, commanding presence, and Kojak-style shaved head. He was a past president of the National Association of Criminal Defense Lawyers and was regarded as one of the best defenders in the nation.

Krieger worked out of Miami, but he was a native of Brooklyn and had represented Joseph Bonanno, founder of that Cosa Nostra family; naturally Sammy did not tell Krieger that, long ago, he and Paul had discussed killing Bonanno because, upon retiring, the old Sicilian don had written a book about his secret life.

To represent Sammy, Gotti next chose Benjamin Brafman, a highly skilled former assistant district attorney in Manhattan now making his reputation on the other side of the street.

In a strategy session, Krieger and Brafman said that most of the government's evidence on two of the five murders—Paul's and Bilotti's—was highly circumstantial. The most threatening part of the evidence was Philip Leonetti's expected testimony about his post-Sparks meeting with Gotti, but the lawyers believed that the former Philadelphia underboss could be neutralized through cross-examination.

"Plus, you got me on tape saying we don't know who killed Paul, that we didn't kill Paul," Gotti quickly pointed out.

The evidence on the other three murders was a much tougher row to hoe, the lawyers replied, thanks to the tapes. The only defense was to argue that the tapes did not mean what the government said they did—to show jurors that the administration engaged in so much joshing, hyperbole, and idle rambling while relaxing in Nettie's place that the tapes were not reliable evidence.

Sammy Gravano did not say much during the meeting. He was more depressed than ever; the disqualification of Shargel had taken away what little faith he had that the case could be won. Now, it seemed useless to him to pretend the tapes did not mean what he knew they did.

The new lawyers made their first appearance in the case on August 28, when they sought, and received, more time to prepare for trial. This time, Cutler came to court and sat beside Gotti, but Kojak Krieger did the booming, commanding talking.

Sammy sat on the other side of Gotti, but before taking his seat, and while Gotti and Cutler were exchanging cheek kisses, he startled people at the prosecution table when he smiled and said, "Good morning, Mr. Maloney."

* * *

A new morning was about to dawn. In the quiet of his cell, away from Gotti, away from the life, Sammy had come to a decision that no one who knew him would have thought possible: He was going to turn, flip and roll over; he was going to join the other side; he was going to become what he had always hated most, a "rat."

He had been mulling it over since the bail hearing, when he first heard excerpts from December 12; he thought about it more after confronting Gotti and discovering that Gotti had withheld other secrets; he dwelled on it long and hard after Shargel was disqualified; and he made his decision after Gotti selected a lawyer for him and they all sat down to discuss strategy.

After that meeting, Sammy had come to his own epiphany, an acutely disturbing vision of how the case might end: Teflon Don, not guilty; Teflon Don's underboss, guilty. It was possible—the evidence on Sparks was light, and the jury might blame Sammy for the other three murders. On tape, Gotti had.

Sammy was now forty-six years old, young enough to start a new life, if he could make one. As consigliere and underboss, he had spent many hours with legal briefs and case documents; he knew all about "cooperation agreements"—the deals by which defendants charged with crimes agree to testify for the government to win sentence reductions for themselves.

He knew that if he went to trial and lost, Glasser would be required under new federal sentencing guidelines to jail him for life without a chance for parole. But he also knew the guidelines were part of another set of laws passed by Congress with Cosa Nostra in mind during the 1980s; to encourage cooperation, the guidelines offered an escape from prison rot.

If Sammy made a deal—pleaded guilty and agreed to testify against Gotti and whomever the government wanted—he faced a life sentence, but with a chance for parole. In reality, however, the guidelines offered a much better outcome. Prosecutors controlled the "cap" or maximum penalty by what they recommended to the judge; the record of Cosa Nostra cases showed that a twenty-five- or twenty-year cap was not an unreasonable expectation, even for someone with—Sammy was not exactly sure—eighteen or nineteen murders on his résumé.

In such a scenario as Sammy's, a judge would then have the authority, based on the defendant's cooperation and desire for redemption, to hand out an even lighter sentence. Consequently, Sammy could serve five or ten years and then be free.

The final outcome depended on how much "value" he brought to the deal, and Sammy the chess player knew that of all the pieces on the Cosa Nostra board, he had the most value; he was underboss of what the FBI called the most powerful organized-crime family in the country; he knew more than Gotti did about the other families in New York City. When it came to value, Philip Leonetti, the first underboss to flip, looked like a pawn next to Sammy.

Sammy also knew that if he cooperated, he would have to tell the truth about everything, turn over every rotten rock, shine a light down every dark hole and expose skeletons in his, Gotti's, and everyone else's closets. With eighteen or nineteen skeletons in his, he would be lugging an extreme amount of baggage to the witness stand. But the victims were criminals, and he was Sammy Gravano, a bishop of Cosa Nostra.

The glorious tradition, however, was now a sinkhole. Sammy was not going to drown for, or with, John Gotti; he was going to become the second underboss to flip— and the first ever to take the witness stand against his boss.

To go down that road, he had to send a more direct message to the government than a friendly "good morning" to Andy Maloney. He asked someone he trusted deeply, a person whose life would be in danger if anyone knew, to take a message to two Staten Island residents, Frank Spero and Matty Tricorico, the Gambino squad agents who had always treated him respectfully and had taken his two thousand dollars to his wife after he was arrested.

The message was that Sammy might want to plead guilty and cooperate, depending on the deal offered him.

Spero and Tricorico took the message to Mouw and Gabriel. The reactions of the four men ranged from amazed excitement to utter disbelief; all recognized the value of such a high-level defection but also the implausibility. It had never happened before, not in New York, so caution overrode all emotions.

"We gotta be careful," Mouw said. "John might be trying to lay a trap, make it look like we're fucking with the defense. Or maybe Sammy's volunteered to save Gotti's ass, to get up on the stand as our witness and say everything's his fault."

Mouw then contacted Gleeson, whose mind whirled with the same reactions and came to the same conclusion: the need for caution.

The vital next step was arranging a meeting with Sammy and evaluating whether his message was sincere or merely an opening gambit. Whatever, secrecy was a must. Gleeson could not go to the MCC for a meeting; if the message was real, but they could not come to a deal, Sammy would not be able to safely return to his cell. Similarly, Sammy could not be taken out of the MCC, even in the dark of night, for any reason that could not be explained. The MCC had too many eyes and ears, and he was on the same floor as Gotti.

The only way to minimize the danger was to create an opportunity for a meeting within the context of the pretrial proceedings—to somehow bring Sammy to the Brooklyn courthouse for some pretrial matter that would not raise suspicion.

Over two weeks, Gleeson and the four agents came up with a plan. It hinged on Gotti's tooth-and-nail policy; he had ordered defense lawyers to refuse to agree to pretrial "stipulations"—or acknowledgments—about any of the evidence in the case, even the most trivial details. So the prosecution team invented some trivial problem about the evidence and gave the lawyers subpoenas requiring the four defendants to come to the courthouse and give additional handwriting examples and "voiceprints."

At this point, another Gambino squad agent—Carmine Russo, the one who took the system failure in the Louis DiBono matter especially hard—was told about Sammy's overture. He had taken earlier voiceprints, and it was crucial that he take them now to make everything appear normal.

Risking his boss's goodwill, Gleeson did not tell Maloney about the overture, or the subpoena ruse. As chief of Maloney's organized-crime unit, he had the power to respond to overtures without running to the boss. Obviously, this was not just any overture, but Gleeson, like Mouw and the other agents, thought secrecy was paramount. If no agreement was made, the fewer the people who were aware that Sammy had tried to make a deal, the better.

The risk of a failed deal was death for the attempted dealmaker. Gleeson and the agents felt that at this point only they needed to know because only they would be deciding whether Sammy was sincere. They also were motivated by the bitter aftertaste of a deal from the past; the situation was different, but the last thing they wanted was a Willie Boy Johnson–type cloud over another John Gotti case.

Meanwhile, the defendants were given separate appointments for complying with the subpoenas for handwriting examples and voiceprints. Using the courier that Sammy had used, Gleeson sent a message to Sammy that if he wanted to talk, a chance to do so in secret would be created after his appointment at the courthouse.

Sammy was scheduled last, to establish the routine of the event in the other defendants' minds. Each defendant's attorney would accompany him to the appointment: the only trick left was to make Sammy's lawyer believe the session was over when it was really just beginning. So, after Russo recorded the last of Sammy's voiceprints on October 24, 1991, Sammy was taken to a holding cell in the basement of the courthouse.

Rather than visit with his client until a van came to take Sammy back to the MCC, a common practice, Benjamin Brafman left the courthouse. He had another appointment, and now so did Sammy.

Spero and Tricorico went to the basement holding cell, told the federal marshals guarding Sammy that the voiceprints had to redone and took him to Gleeson. Gabriel and Russo joined them; wanting Sammy to believe that the FBI saw his overture as a normal event, the boss of the Gambino squad decided to stay away.

It was the biggest sitdown of Sammy's life, and after the initial awkwardness subsided it became clear he had been thinking about what he wanted to say for a long time.

At the outset, however, Gleeson needed to hear Sammy

say he was agreeing to meet without his lawyer present. "Unless you waive the right, I can't talk to you without your lawyer here."

"I think Ben Brafman is a good guy, but if he knew I was here, it'd get back to John and I'd be in a little trouble," Sammy said, with a tight of-course smile. "Even in MCC."

"Okay, we all know why we're here. What's on your mind?"

Sammy had decided to eliminate his anger at Gotti as one of the things on his mind; instead, he cast his overture as purely a matter of self-interest coinciding with a loss of faith.

"I'm not here because I'm mad at John Gotti," he began. "In fact, if John beats this case, I'd be very happy. I'm here to try and help Sammy Gravano."

That opening statement rang an alarm in Gleeson's mind, but he and the agents kept quiet as Sammy kept on talking.

"I'm tired of the life. I'm looking to get out. I got a lot of information. If John's the biggest mobster in the country, then I'm the second. He picked me, I was his right hand for everything. I can give it all up, and I would."

"Do you know what a cooperation agreement entails? You have to give up everything, or the deal's no good."

"I know. I'm ready. You guys have more loyalty than we ever did. I sold myself a bill of goods a long time ago, but at least now I can sell it back, do something for myself, maybe get with my family again someday. Cosa Nostra is dyin'. We got guys who sell drugs, guys who do drugs. We got all these fuckin' rules and all we ever do is break them."

Gleeson was beginning to believe that Sammy was sincere, that this was no ploy, and so he asked what amounted to a test question. If Sammy dodged it, his sincerity was questionable.

"Before we go any further, we have to know something. Tell me, is our indictment on the money? Do we have it right? Did we wrongly charge anything or anyone?"

"Yeah, you did."

Gleeson felt a knot tying in his stomach. "What was that?"

"Deebee. You got Deebee wrong. I killed him, but I didn't want to. It was Angelo's idea, and John ordered it."

"But you did it."

"On John's order."

Feeling the knot untie, Gleeson tossed out another test: "How many murders have you committed?"

"A lot. I only pulled the trigger once. But I know it don't make no difference. So, eighteen, nineteen. Scumbags. Cheaters. Dopeheads. People who broke our rules, like I'm doin' here."

"What about Paul?"

"I was there. John was there. We were in a car together."

Now a vision came into Gleeson's mind—a picture of Sammy Gravano on the stand, an accomplice witness, shoring up the weakest part of the Eastern District case, Sparks.

"You were there with him?"

"We were in a car on the street. I was the backup, in case the shooters missed Paul and Tommy."

"Wasn't that kind of reckless? What if somebody saw you?"

"Nobody knew John then. Nobody knew me, not until John made me and everybody known to you. I always thought Cosa Nostra meant being undercover."

Now convinced that Sammy was for real, Gleeson steered the talk toward the bottom line—the sentence Sammy might receive if he cooperated. Gleeson spoke in hypothetical terms because a deal could not be finalized until a lawyer was appointed to advise Sammy. Although hypothetical, his bottom line was clear: his first offer to Sammy would be his last: a twenty-year maximum.

Sammy was surprised; he had intended to seek a smaller "cap" and expected Gleeson to start with a bigger one—but twenty years was the best he thought he would ever get. If he held up his end of the deal, twenty really meant five or ten.

"I've gotta think about it," he said.

Gleeson decided to offer Sammy a large incentive because as an organized-crime unit chief he was looking beyond the current case. Sammy opened the door to an entire family, maybe others.

"Your value to us goes beyond this case," Gleeson said.

"I'm not lookin' to be a witness for the rest of my life."

"Other cases have to be part of the deal."

"Like I said, I gotta think."

"How much time do you need?"

"Two weeks. I need to get my life in order. There's some things I have to work out with my family."

"We can give you that, but I want to get the ball rolling. We have to get you a new lawyer. there's a procedure for it, in situations like this. I can't pick the lawyer for you."

The procedure involved a judge appointing Sammy a lawyer, if Sammy told the judge he did not know a lawyer he could trust. And so Sammy agreed with Gleeson's suggestion that Judge Glasser be invited to join the sitdown. In a few minutes, Glasser arrived and after some procedural talk, Glasser said he would appoint Sammy a new lawyer in a couple of days.

The deal's official terms remained up in the air, but the die was cast. Sammy went back to the MCC, but there really was no turning back; he had rolled all the way over.

Three days later, on October 27, 1991, on the MCC wing known as Eleven-North, Gotti celebrated his fifty-first birthday. Some inmates brought gifts of food and candy. At one point he went to the collect-only inmate telephone to place a call; farther down the hallway, a door leading to a wing known as Eleven-South briefly swung open and he saw Sammy on another telephone.

The man who always said he could smell a "rat" the way a dog smells a man who's afraid gave a cheerful little wave, and Sammy waved back.

Over the next week, during visits at the MCC, Sammy worked things out with his family. The most difficult part was telling them that he was about to become the most infamous informer in the history of "the life." His wife, niece of a Bonanno family soldier who spent half of his life in prison, understood more than most wives how guilty Sammy felt.

"I know I always said you can never betray your friends," Sammy told her and his children, Karen and

Gerard. "People are going to throw that in your face and call me a rat. But I made mistakes in my life and now I have to put them behind."

To deflect some of the fallout, Sammy suggested that Debra announce to their friends that she and he had been separated for some time, that the marriage was on the rocks and as far as she was concerned her husband was out of her life.

While Sammy worked things out with Debra and his children, Gleeson worked them out with his boss. He waited a week to tell Maloney about Sammy, waited until he had completed a memo spelling out the benefits and proposed terms of a cooperation deal.

"Read this before you fire me," Gleeson said, after walking into Maloney's office on November 1.

Reading the memo, Maloney became excited and annoyed all at the same time.

"Why didn't you tell me about this?"

"I didn't tell anyone else. Bruce didn't either, so nobody above him knows. We made a pact. Everything had to be routine."

"I'm not sure I like the twenty-year cap. I would've gone for more, like life."

"Sammy is a clever guy. He'd thought out what he was going to say, and I am certain he knew he could have held us up for less. I figured, cut the crap and bring the guy in fast. We're going to trial in two months. We got a lot of debriefing to do."

"Eighteen, nineteen murders, I bet you do."

"That doesn't surprise me. We got about six hours of tapes from the apartment, and all they talk about is murder. Andy, this guy is going to give us the whole family."

Gleeson then asked Maloney for permission to invite Laura Ward, Patrick Cotter, and another young lawyer recently added to the trial team, James Orenstein, to join them to talk about the ramifications of Sammy Gravano joining the team.

"Okay, call them—and John, this was good work, but next time, let me know. I am the U.S. attorney. You can trust me."

Gleeson's trial partners also were not pleased that he had withheld the news from them, and Gleeson agreed that it would have been like Diane Giacalone telling him, in 1985, "John, I didn't tell you, but Gene Gotti has come over to our side."

Everyone got over the wounds as Gleeson reported that the Gambino squad was devising a plan to pull Sammy out of the MCC on November 8 and that a message had been sent to him designating that as the day and he had agreed.

"There's a possible downside to this," Cotter said. "If we go ahead, we give the other side a defense. Before, all they could do was cross-examine a tape recorder. Now they got someone to point a finger at."

"Yeah, but to point a finger, that requires them to admit that there is a Cosa Nostra," Ward said. "John doesn't do that."

"There's no way we can't use Sammy," Gleeson said. "He gives the case depth. He makes Sparks. At the end of this case, all we will have to do is tell the jury: 'You can convict on the tapes, you can convict on Gravano's testimony—but together, the conclusion to this case is inescapable.' "

"I think John has thought this out pretty well," Maloney said. "Let's get Gravano out and get him ready for trial."

A little after midnight on November 8, Mouw and Gabriel went to the MCC and told the night-shift duty officer they had a court order, signed by Glasser, authorizing the release of an inmate to their custody for transfer to another federal prison. The court order was real, but the prison part was phony.

The officer asked to see the court order, whose cover sheet contained the names of all four defendants in the case; the first name was Gotti's, the lead defendant. He only glanced at the second page, which specified Sammy as the inmate to be transferred.

"Holy shit, you're here to pick up a big guy, huh?"

"Yeah, a pretty big guy," Gabriel replied.

The officer said he had to make a call, and went to a phone several feet away. It was hard to overhear what he said into the phone, but Gabriel thought he heard the words "John Gotti."

"I have a feeling this guy is ordering the wrong person," Gabriel told Mouw.

Panicking, they quickly confronted him. "Did you just

call up and order someone to get the person for us?" Gabriel asked.

"Yeah, that's what you wanted, ain't it?"

"Who'd you ask for?"

"The big guy, John Gotti."

"Holy Christ! Call again! Rescind it! We want Gravano!"

The order was rescinded, just as guards on Eleven-North began walking toward the cell where Gotti was asleep.

Sammy, meanwhile, was awake and anxious. He began to relax after he was escorted out of his cell and to a reception area where Frank Spero and Matty Tricorico now waited.

"Howya doin', guys?" he said as Spero and Tricorico greeted him and led him to a convoy of FBI cars waiting outside. He waved hello to Mouw and Gabriel, and with Spero and Tricorico, got into a car driven by Carmine Russo—the agent who blamed himself for Sammy's No. 19—and started his new life.

Fifteen minutes later, in another chain-pull, a prison guard woke Gotti and told him that Sammy must have jumped ship because he had just left the MCC in the custody of FBI agents.

"I don't believe it! You're lyin'. They're just puttin' him in another joint. Bustin' his balls."

Confirmation would come soon enough. That afternoon Sammy would sign a letter addressed to Benjamin Brafman. It was a short, curt letter, hand-delivered by FBI agents and impossible to misinterpret.

"I have decided to retain new counsel. Your services are no longer required and you are discharged immediately."

By the time Brafman was notified, Sammy had already begun selling his bill of goods back. He had arrived at some secret destination about 4:00 A.M., and talked with Mouw and Gabriel for two hours while awaiting the arrival of Maloney, Gleeson, and his new Glasser-appointed lawyer.

Having already placed Gotti and himself outside Sparks in his first government sitdown, he now identified the entire ten-member hit team—Angelo, Rampino, Lino, Carneglia, Watts, among others—and the role of each. He recalled the layers of motive, the founding of the Fist, and Gotti's takeover once Paul was dead.

"I was at the meeting where the capos talked about who would be boss," he said. "I had a gun, everyone knew what was goin' on, but no one admitted knowin'."

Mouw's and Gabriel's astonishment at the spigot Sammy had turned on grew as he turned to his other murders and recited the ones that came more immediately to mind.

"It's gonna take a while to remember all this. You guys are trained to remember. I trained myself to forget."

Finally, after about two hours, Sammy said he was tired.

"Before we stop, I gotta ask one thing," Mouw said. "After John's trial in '87, we got some surveillance that seemed to show people congratulating you for something. Did you have anything to do with that jury?"

"Sure I did!" Sammy replied pridefully. "I fixed it! I was in charge of a guy on the jury. Did a good job, didn't I?"

"How'd you do it?"

It hardly mattered now, but Sammy said: "C'mon. I gotta hold somethin' back. Let me sign the deal first. And then I'll tell you about another case I fixed. Eddie Lino's."

Maloney, Gleeson, and Sammy's new lawyer, William Cunningham, arrived at about 6:00 A.M. While Cunningham conferred with his client, Mouw briefed Maloney and Gleeson.

"John, the first thing you might want to know is, Sammy fixed your case with Diane; the fix was in."

"Son of a bitch. All that effort . . ."

"I told you!" Maloney interjected. "I knew it! The guy was just too cool when the jury came back."

The rest of the day was spent trying to hammer out the details of Sammy's cooperation deal. The entourage then moved on to the FBI's training complex at a military base in Quantico, Virginia.

For two days, Sammy and Cunningham tried to get Gleeson to come down on the twenty-year-cap proposal.

"You tell them we are not going down," Maloney said. "Tell Sammy he can get back on the MCC bus. No way."

At one point Sammy halted negotiations and asked to

read what newspapers in New York were reporting about his defection. Agents in New York faxed copies of several stories, one of which stuck in Sammy's craw.

Quoting "underworld" sources, the *New York Post* said Sammy was a degenerate, murdering thug addled by years of steroid use.

"They're making me into a McElroy, I never killed nobody for a hundred dollars of coke. These guys that talk to reporters, they're half-rats. They don't got the balls to do what I'm doin'. Go all the way!"

In New York, the news of Sammy's defection struck many with the force of a shadow on a chest X-ray. Joe Butch Corrao, Danny Marino, Jimmy Brown Fialla, Joe Watts, and many others concluded, accurately, that the news was as bad for them as for Gotti. Crooked millionaire cop William Peist now knew the game was up, as did George Pape, the ringer on the Giacalone jury, who took to the bottle more and waited for agents to come arrest him for lying during voir dire about his friendship with Westies boss Bosko Radonjich, who fled to Yugoslavia.

Sammy's deal, with a twenty-year cap, was finally signed on November 13. He agreed to tell all and to testify in whatever cases the government wanted over the next two years; if Sammy lived up to the deal, Gleeson agreed to write Sammy's sentencing judge a letter saying how cooperative he had been—the key to five or ten years in prison instead of twenty.

After the signing, Maloney asked Sammy, "You think John would ever come in and take a plea, save us a trial?"

"John? First off, you ain't gonna give him a twenty-year cap. But John? Never. He cares too much what people think. He's spent his whole life makin' people think he is Cosa Nostra. And maybe he is, what's left. John's old-fashioned. He's a die-hard."

Over the next several weeks, Sammy unwound the threads of his criminal life, in day after day of debriefings by the agents and members of the prosecution team.

As always in such situation, former enemies began building strong bonds. Sammy enjoyed being around intelligent, dedicated people who treated him as a member of the team. During the off-hours he played chess and boxed with a couple of especially large agents brought in to give him a good workout—and in one bout, such a working-over that further bouts were postponed until after the trial, for fear of scarring the star witness.

As always too, the person in transition became reflective and mournful. One day, Gleeson and Sammy discussed their mutual fondness for *The Godfather* movie, the first one in 1972.

"I saw that movie when I was twenty-seven," Sammy said, "a kid with Shorty Spero. I walked out feeling so good. That was my life. My life was honor and respect. Now, years go by, and the only thing I can love about my life is the movie. There's no honor, there's no respect. Everything is a double cross."

On another day, New York FBI boss Jim Fox came to Quantico to meet the big catch, and they had a long talk in which Sammy was similarly mournful but also upbeat about his future.

"Far as I remember, all I wanted was Cosa Nostra. It began when these goons tried to shake my old man down and the big shot in the neighborhood put a stop to it. In Bensonhurst, that was it, becomin' a made guy. It's all we kids ever talked about.

"I never saw the other side of it until I was in, and then it's too late and you just do your work. At one time, we were strong, but then you guys came with these sentences and these RICOs and you made us weak. You undermined the code. You made guys think about themselves. You're gonna see more rollovers."

During a pause, Sammy commented on a small gold pin, shaped like an apple, in a lapel of Fox's suit jacket.

"This is something the director of the FBI gives out when an agent makes an outstanding case," Fox said. "An agent does a good job, he or she gets a gold apple."

"Like a star on your report card."

"That's it, Sammy," Fox replied, removing the lapel pin. "You're doing something good, you're making us an outstanding case, I want you to have it."

Like everyone else, Fox came to believe that Sammy would be a solid witness and that he made it unnecessary to call Philip Leonetti to the stand. Sammy spoke in the gruff, clipped argot of a criminal, but he was smart and quick; he listened well and, before answering a question, corrected built-in errors; he regretted and mourned his past, but he was not ashamed—all of which meant it was not going to be easy for defense lawyers to bait and rattle him. Sammy's attitude now was, he was good at the life, when he was in the life.

Everyone now felt the case was airtight. Things really had come full circle; the case was going to be as easy as erasing a blackboard, or slam-dunking an indictment into a waste can.

CHAPTER 27

• • • • • • • • • • • • • •

Poetic Justice

The media billed Gotti's fourth trial in six years as the gangster case of the century. The buildup, however breathless, was difficult to dispute. No one like Sammy had ever taken the witness stand against Al Capone, or any other mafioso, and while other gangsters since Capone had ruled longer than Gotti and wielded greater power more wisely, none had achieved such notoriety.

The trial dominated most front pages and newscasts in New York for nearly three months. Several local reporters doubled as commentators for radio and television stations in Rome, Naples, London, Hong Kong, Sydney, Auckland, and other cities where the Dapper/Teflon Don had become more than an idle curiosity.

The trial's mood swung wildly from dark to light, from real to surreal, one day to the next. It began with demonstrations and ended in a riot; in between, people threatened to blow up the courthouse and kill the judge. It included hysterical outbursts by mothers, cameo appearances by movie stars, and, more so as it wore on, a highly agitated and not very charming lead defendant.

Of the original defendants, Sammy was not the only one no longer at the defense table; Tommy Gambino was gone too. In the law enforcement Cosa Nostra free-for-all, the Manhattan district attorney's office and New York state troopers had mounted a new racketeering case against the country squire's garment center empire; to give the locals a clearer shot, Maloney had agreed to sever Tommy from the Gotti case and try him later.

Maloney accommodated Robert Morgenthau and Michael Cherkasky to help improve relations, which were worse than before because Manhattan now believed that

Brooklyn was partially to blame for its loss in the O'Connor case. The district attorney and his deputy now knew that the apartment bug had overheard Gotti talking about a "Hoyle" or "Boyle," an Irish juror that some Westie might know—and talk that Laura Ward and John Gleeson had evaluated as vague, wishful thinking was now evaluated, one subway stop away, as evidence, especially by Morgenthau.

"This would've made a difference," the don of prosecutors loudly complained to Maloney, his underling of many years before. "Whether Peist got to a juror is another question. But if we knew about that tape you had, we could've used it to show the jury the connection between Gotti and the Westies."

"Bob, what can I say? My guys were protecting their case."

The trial began on January 21, 1992. Most reporters were drawn to what Gotti and Lewis Kasman wanted—a demonstration outside the courthouse, featuring pickets with "We Love You, John" placards, and a sound truck that slowly circled the block with its loudspeaker declaring, "Gotti's Number One!" Gotti son-in-law Carmine Agnello, who had tried to help fix his Uncle Gene's third heroin trial, provided the sound truck.

Given the hole he was in, Gotti seemed sanguine over the first few days of jury screening, even after Judge Glasser ruled that the jury would be sequestered for the duration of the trial. This was a first in Brooklyn federal court history, as sequestration in the O'Connor case was a first in Manhattan state court history—and, as usual, the media were falsely cited as the reason. Gotti's main hope now was that when deliberations began, jurors would be too afraid to convict or too affected by some combination of old and new favorable publicity to send him away forever.

Outside the courtroom, during breaks, Kasman and several Gotti acolytes worked the hallways with the aplomb of tobacco-industry lobbyists. They now had two messages for sale—the handy persecution one, of course, but also Sammy the Rat.

Kasman wanted to make sure reporters kept mentioning how Gotti was on trial without his first choice of counsel: "It's unfair because Bruce has won three cases for John. If your wife is having a baby, wouldn't you want to go back to the doctor who successfully delivered the other three?"

The assistant press secretary was cocksure about his ability to manipulate the media—so much so that he couldn't stop himself from boasting about it in a way that exposed the cynicism beneath. He had already gotten one newspaper to run a story about how Gotti, while in the MCC, had read another story about a young cerebral palsy victim whose puppy was stolen and had promptly ordered Kasman to buy the victim, a little boy, another dog.

"Please, Lewis, get hold of the family; we'll buy them five dogs if they want," Gotti was reported to have said, according to Kasman, who was quoted as describing Gotti as "very emotional" about the little boy's loss.

"I set that up," Kasman explained. "Pretty good, huh?"

After a valuable urn used in religious services was stolen from a church, Kasman had also gotten several television stations to run stories saying that Gotti wanted the thieves to return it.

"John saw me on TV at the MCC talking about that, and he couldn't believe it!" Kasman recalled. "He said, 'Lewis, you were so convincing. I started believing I actually said that.'"

The lobbyists also included Peter Gotti, Jackie D'Amico, and Carlo Vaccarezza. Peter praised the ability of his brother's new lawyer, Albert Krieger, but he also pined for Cutler, and for good reason: Cutler had just won him an acquittal in the windows case. He did say, however, that with no-nonsense Glasser on the bench, Cutler might not have stayed in the case for long anyway.

"Even if that guy on the bench didn't disqualify Bruce, he would've contempted him the first or second day."

The most engaging lobbyists were the Lisa Gastineau beards, Vaccarezza and D'Amico. They were charming and funny, and always quote-ready—as long as the instigating question was not overtly hostile or invasive. Gastineau herself never came to the trial and had stopped writing letters to Gotti in prison, once she met another man born under the sign of Scorpio.

"John's a man's man," Vaccarezza said in his languid

maître d' style. "Loyal, true. He's only on trial because
the government hates it that people love him."

"A John only comes along once in a life," added the
salt-and-peppery D'Amico, now a caporegime. "They
broke the mold with John; he's original."

One of the authors of this book interrupted that testi-
monial to ask D'Amico what made Gotti such an original.

"John had two things going for him. He was loved and
feared. He's the only person I've seen with both. You call
it charisma. He has that, but love and fear was what
counted. People don't cross a man they love and fear."

"Sammy apparently has," the writer pointed out.

"Well, because of the situation that happened. But
Sammy only ever had one thing going for him. Fear. People were afraid to warn John about Sammy."

Over the last four years, D'Amico had spent more time
with Gotti than Vicky Gotti had. His boss had made him
an officer of Scorpio Marketing to give him a phony salary, and he remained loyal and true; the fact that Gotti
had called him an unimaginative "cripple" on an apartment tape was just John being John.

D'Amico and Sammy had never been close, and now
the hallway gave him the opportunity to gleefully
Sammy-bash. Sammy, he said, made "Charles Manson
look like an altar boy." He warned reporters against buying the sales job the government would surely mount on
Sammy: "They're gonna try and make him look like a
priest. By the time he gets on the stand, they'll have made
him into a monk."

The lobbying group included another capo, a capo's
son, and Frank DeCicco's uncle. It did not include Gotti's
son, Junior, but it did include LoCascio's son, Salvatore,
now an acting capo.

Gotti did not want Junior at the courthouse. Junior was
so volatile, he might bench-press a reporter and undermine the publicity operation. Salvatore LoCascio was
enough of a hothead; "Tory" had thrown a fit on opening
day when he was momentarily denied admittance to the
courtroom: "What is this, Nazi Germany? They don't let
the family in? This is my father. What do they think
we're going to do, shoot 'em in the courtroom?"

Gotti's sanguine demeanor began to fade midway
through jury screening, after the *Daily News* broke two

big stories. The first disclosed that the 1987 case had been fixed; the second was a preview of Sammy's expected testimony about Sparks, including the fact that Gotti was at the scene, in a black car with Sammy.

The jury story exposed the Teflon Don myth just when Gotti needed myth most; the Sparks story brought Sammy into the case earlier than expected and showed that he was shining a light down every black hole. Both stories, widely reported by other media, did undermine the publicity operation. For their possible effect on jury screening, they also annoyed Judge Glasser.

In between the *Daily News* stories, thousands of flyers also with the potential to influence jury screening began appearing on trees, Stop signs, and light poles around the city. The flyers featured a photograph of Sammy's face, atop the body of a rat, and these words:

EPITOME OF A RAT WHO LIES:
SAMMY "THE LIAR" GRAVANO

In court, at the first opportunity, an edgy Judge Glasser told Gotti he was concerned about the flyers and efforts to "poison" jurors: "It might be a good idea, if you can do anything about it, to put an end to it."

"I don't do these things with this flyer baloney!" Gotti snapped indignantly.

Summoning his own indignation, LoCascio asked Glasser why he was allowing the press to run amok, but Gotti cut off a reply.

"Forget about it, Frankie, he don't care about that!"

Gotti wagged his right index finger at the prosecution table again and said the government knew he was not responsible for the flyers because it monitored his calls and mail at the MCC—and, by the way: "I get good mail! People out there, they like me!"

Gotti's anger deepened as the jury screening dragged on, and many tongue-tied, obviously frightened people made it plain that they would rather fall into a rattlesnake pit than be on a Gotti jury. At one point Glasser summoned the lead lawyers into chambers to discuss the potential jurors' fears, and Gotti wound up alone in a conference room with a pool reporter, Gabriel, and some federal guards. The reporter asked Gotti what he thought about Cutler's disqualification on conflict-of-interest grounds.

"Conflict?" Gotti began, pointing to Gleeson's empty chair. "He's the one with a conflict! He's had one for eight years! You know how they say I'm Bruce's only client the last eight years? Well, I'm Gleeson's only case. This guy, you know what he says when he wakes up in the morning, rolls over, and looks at his wife? He says, 'Hiya, John.' This guy learned to talk listening to my voice! I'd like to have a bug on him for three hours!"

Three days later, on February 6, 1992, Gotti gave a preview of the personality that would be on display once the trial began. It emerged after Glasser said he might move the trial to another city if the ex parte noise in the case did not abate.

"I am giving very serious thought to moving the trial to another venue if this kind of media coverage and poisoning of the jury pool continues," the judge said just before retiring to his chambers with Maloney and Krieger; Gleeson and his trial partners remained behind, in a room with another pool reporter, Gabriel, Gotti, LoCascio, other defense lawyers, and the federal guards.

"Where is [Glasser] going to move it?" Gotti said to LoCascio, but for Gleeson's benefit. "Stuttgart, West Germany? Is that supposed to be a threat? Frankie, get down on your knees and beg him not to move it, that faggot!"

Gleeson, Ward, Cotter, and Orenstein began laughing out loud, partly so the pool reporter would not be able to hear Gotti and write another distracting story, partly because Stuttgart seemed such a baffling place to pop into Gotti's mind. But they didn't know that of the now thousands of letters Gotti had received at the MCC in the last year, one was from a man in Stuttgart, who offered to contribute cash to Gotti's commissary account.

Hearing the laughter, Gotti redirected his venom toward the prosecution table, whose overworked male occupants had not been to their barbers lately. "When's the last time those punks washed their hair? Those faggots!"

The room fell silent, and Gotti's and Gleeson's eyes locked for a long moment. Still staring at Gleeson, Gotti nudged the shoulder of a defense lawyer who remained in the room and said, referring to Glasser: "Tell this punk, is that supposed to be a threat? Let him go ahead and move it. If Bruce Cutler was here, he would've told him off in a minute."

The charming public mask that Gotti had worn in previous trials now lay on the floor; because Sammy's defection was the reason, not even Bruce Cutler could have stopped the mask from falling. At the time, Cutler was in Chicago, trying to get that city's underboss off the hook, and so he was not even on hand as a lobbyist when the trial—after an anonymous jury was finally selected and sequestered—got down to brass tacks on February 12, 1992.

As planned all along, Andy Maloney big-footed Gleeson and gave the prosecution's opening argument himself. Gleeson and his trial partners had done all the heavy lifting in the case and would continue to do so, but Maloney had decided in March 1987, when he smelled a fix, that this moment would be his if a second chance came, and here it was.

With gray suit and tie of patriotic colors, the still trim former West Pointer was a model of federal rectitude— apart from one personally satisfying moment when, Gotti-like, he cocked his forefinger and thumb into an imaginary pistol, pointed at Gotti, and made like he was pulling the trigger as he said:

"This is a case of a Mafia boss brought down by his own words, his own right arm and, in the course of it, bringing down his whole family."

Opening for Gotti, Albert Krieger honed in on the obvious target, Sammy, booming at the twelve jurors and six alternates: "Mr. Gravano is a little man full of evil, connivance, manipulation and vanity who has tried to clean his slate by admitting to nineteen murders! ... There are only eighteen of you up here! We don't have enough chairs to put all the victims in!"

Krieger added that the tapes jurors were to hear proved only that Gotti was prone to bad grammar and profane language. "John Gotti wishes he went to college, that he was a member of the Union League and that he could say three words without cursing. He received his education on the streets, from the people he grew up with. He learned to speak what they speak."

Krieger got a handshake from Gotti when he sat down,

but not the backslap Cutler would have gotten. That typ-
ified their public demeanor for the rest of the trial—
friendly but formal, respectful but distant. Krieger would
labor hard to save Gotti, but he was not a missionary like
Cutler was.

As Gleeson and company began introducing the government's evidence, the slopes of the hole Gotti was in
grew more slippery by the day. At the defense table, Gotti
tried to show either indifference or contempt. The latter
reaction was usually packaged with profanity or an insult-
ing gesture directed at witnesses or the government lawyers.

Thus, when a freshly barbered Gleeson put Gabriel on
the stand to narrate the Ravenite videotapes, Gotti sat
with his back to the screen brought in for the premiere
and rarely glanced at the proof of the damage his
mandatory-attendance policy had caused.

But when Gleeson summoned another agent, Lewis
Schiliro, to interpret some of the Cosa Nostraspeak on the
audiotapes, Gotti waved dismissively and called Schiliro
a "fuckin' scumbag"; and when Gleeson put relatives of
Robert DiBernardo, Louis Milito, and Louis DiBono on
the stand to try and put a human face on departed loved
ones, Gotti blew sarcastic kisses at the prosecution table;
one of Gleeson's partners, James Orenstein, kept a scorecard of each remark and gesture, so Gleeson—focused on
questioning of witnesses—would later know what seemed
to upset Gotti most.

It was a scorecard no defendant ought to have helped
compile in front of a jury, and after Gotti began to act out
with greater frequency, Gleeson complained to Glasser in
a sidebar conference that some jurors might be thinking
that Gotti's unruly behavior was really a message for
them, not prosecutors.

"We are used to it," Gleeson said. "Our skin is thick.
We don't really care. We think they are jerks." But to a
juror, he added, the behavior "can only be perceived as
intimidation."

Glasser issued the first of several warnings to Gotti and
asked Krieger to control him. Krieger would try, but to no
avail. He was a stranger to the inner circle; he had no past
with Gotti, or any particular present, beyond his responsibilities as a lawyer. As a lawyer, he comported himself

in the usual way, joshing with adversaries during recesses—something Gotti had done in 1987, but not now.

During one recess, while chatting up lobbyists in the front spectator row, Gotti saw that Krieger was on the government side of the courtroom, talking with Maloney. "Krieger, over here!" he said beneath a tight grimace.

Seeing Gotti's summons, Krieger poked fun at his situation, unenviable except for his near half-million-dollar fee. "Andy," he whispered before walking over to Gotti, "if you keep talking like that, I am going to wind up in the trunk of a Cadillac."

Krieger was joking, but on many days an aura of danger, a sense of imminent violence, did hover over the trial. The menace emanating from the words and gestures of the lead defendant was a major factor, but so were the abundant federal marshals positioned around the courtroom.

Then there were the bomb threats, three of them, which led to the evacuation of the entire courthouse and the sight of bomb-sniffing dogs poking their noses here and there in the courtroom. At one point, in a sidebar, Judge Glasser revealed that his life had been threatened by several different anonymous callers and that he was under heavy guard.

On other days, however, a completely different aura hovered over the trial—a light, day-at-the-circus kind of mood. Carlo Vaccarezza was responsible for many of these days; he arranged for a parade of minor and major celebrities to troop one by one into court to sit with the Gotti lobbyists and say a few nice words about Gotti to the media.

The celebrity cheerleaders included heavyweight boxer Renaldo Snipes, civil rights leader Roy Innis, singer Jay Black and actors John Amos, Al Lewis, Mickey Rourke, and Anthony Quinn—but the testimonials did not always go as Vaccarezza had hoped.

For instance, while speaking with print reporters, Mickey Rourke—who had sought and received a meeting with Gotti while researching a film role—said what Vaccarezza wanted him to say about what a classy man Gotti was and how he was concerned about whether Gotti was getting a fair trial.

Outside the courthouse, however, when television reporters pounced on him, Rourke clammed up, fled across a park, and got into a car that sped away. He ducked most questions about why he was there, how he knew Gotti, and how he regarded him.

Rourke's camera shyness irked Vaccarezza, who came back into the courthouse to tell the hallway lobbyists what happened. "What a jerk," he told D'Amico. "He didn't say anything nice. He froze. Despite all the time John spent with him. He's not a man."

Anthony Quinn, who had socialized with Gotti at Da Noi years before, caused the biggest fuss, inside and outside court. At the lunch break, he walked toward the well of the courtroom to shake Gotti's hand, but federal marshals stopped him short; Gotti was in custody, and even a handshake was against rules.

"Hello, John," Quinn said, hunching his shoulders in a what-else-can-I-do? way. "Sorry, John."

"See," Gotti replied, holding his right thumb and forefinger close together, "we're this close to Russia here."

Outside court, Quinn said the trial was "the best drama going on in America right now. This is the greatest theater you can possibly see." The heart of the drama was "the friend who betrays a friend. I'm not here to sit in judgment of Mr. Gotti but in judgment of a friend who betrays a friend. Friendship is a sacred thing. When I was growing up in East Los Angeles, the worst thing was to be a snitch."

Quinn said he had appeared in thirty "gangster pictures" and that "the boys" liked him because he knew how to portray them. He neglected to mention that he was currently under consideration for another film project, a starring role in which he would portray a real-life gangster, Paul Castellano.

Back in court, Maloney joshed Krieger: "Albert, tomorrow the good guys are going to bring in Clint Eastwood."

On the afternoon of March 2, 1992, after six weeks of scene-setting, the dramatic high point of the play, the moment everyone in the audience anticipated most, finally came.

"The government calls Salvatore Gravano," Gleeson said.

An expectant hush fell over the courtroom; John Gotti and almost everyone else began staring at a door next to the jury box, the entrance to court for witnesses in custody.

It was the most pregnant of moments—two hundred and forty seconds of tension-building silence; backstage, in a room off Glasser's chambers, the star was taking his sweet time getting ready. Sammy, for a change, was sweating bullets.

He felt almost like he had in 1977, when the important men of his world called him downstairs to the basement den for the ceremony by which they replenished and re-affirmed themselves and sustained their peculiar tradition.

"Okay, Bo, let's go," he finally said to one of his guards.

A tight end–size guard escorted the five-foot-five ex-underboss—dressed, in another change, in suit and tie—into the courtroom. The witness's heart was pounding, but his head was up, and his eyes were inventorying everything in the courtroom except the defense table—where Gotti, wry grin in place, still stared.

When Sammy offered no return stare, Gotti broke away, caught the eyes of reporters in the spectator section, and mouthed the words, "They dressed him up!"

Sammy kept his eyes straight ahead as he answered Gleeson's first few preliminary questions; beyond Gleeson, however, it was impossible for him not to notice Peter Gotti, D'Amico, Vaccarezza, and other lobbyists bunched together in the spectator section; as a likely witness about Scorpio Marketing, Lewis Kasman was forced to remain in the hallway.

Hoping to rattle Sammy, the Gotti contingent had arranged to have a special guest, a young man Sammy regarded almost as a son, Joseph D'Angelo, sit with them in court. In the 1970s, D'Angelo's father and Sammy were best friends; when the father was murdered, in Tali's, Sammy gathered the son under his wing with money and attention. But that was then: now the son had come to court to give Sammy the *malliocchia*.

Earlier in the day, Frank Spero and Matty Tricorico—aware of the connection—had seen D'Angelo in court and reported it to Gleeson and Maloney, who asked for a sidebar and complained to Glasser.

"After his father died," Gleeson said, "my understanding is the son became very close to Gravano, and I noticed that now for Gravano's testimony, he's there in the first row."

"Your honor," added Maloney, "he is there for one reason, to intimidate and try to make Mr. Gravano clam up."

Glasser ordered D'Angelo into the second row, where he was as Sammy began testifying. But he was almost as short as Sammy, and it was difficult for him to make eye contact because of the bulky frames of federal agents lining the well of the courtroom.

To make sure Sammy saw him, D'Angelo decided to make a showy exit from the courtroom. He rose slowly, took his time shuffling down the second row to the aisle, then paused there for a brief moment—all the while staring at Sammy. The stunt was right out of the movie *The Godfather,* in which Michael Corleone arranged for a long-lost relative to watch a turncoat's testimony before a congressional committee.

On the stand, Sammy tensed and his eyes followed D'Angelo out. Moments later, D'Angelo reentered, and this time Sammy lost his concentration. He stumbled over a simple Gleeson question and asked to hear it again; he had been coached that this was the way to handle a momentary lapse, and this would be the only time he needed to recall it.

"I was the underboss of the Gambino organized crime family," he said, after Gleeson quickly steered him toward the matter at hand. "John was the boss, I was the underboss."

In a series of short, matter-of-fact answers, he explained how he began in Bensonhurst and ended up in federal custody—and how, along the way, he was involved in nineteen murders, because murder was a way of life in Cosa Nostra.

Gleeson led Sammy right up to the most pivotal murders—"We had Sparks sandwiched in," Sammy began—before Glasser called it a day and adjourned court.

Backstage again, Maloney, Gleeson, Mouw, and Gabriel patted Sammy on the back, but he only wanted to talk about D'Angelo.

"Did you see that fuckin' kid? I helped him out his whole fuckin' life. Three years ago, he came to me beggin' for work. Now he comes in here and tries to rattle me. Get up, walk out, come back. What's this, a movie? Fuck 'im, and fuck them!"

Philip Leonetti had been brought to New York and was ready to testify if Sammy failed on the witness stand, but now Maloney pulled Gleeson aside: "We won't be needing Leonetti; Sammy will handle whatever they throw at him."

Doing what he could to make Sammy feel important and like part of the team, Gleeson telephoned New York FBI boss Jim Fox, who had handed Sammy his golden-apple lapel pin only a few weeks before, and asked him to watch the rest of Sammy's testimony.

"When you're out the door, even hours afterward, the guy's still feeling good, so if you have time, as often as you could make it over here, I think it'd be helpful," Gleeson said.

On the second day, Fox was there as Sammy gave a minute-by-minute, shot-by-shot account of Sparks. That morning, and the night before, Gotti lobbyists had lambasted Sammy in the media, and that was all he wanted to talk about when Fox huddled with him during the luncheon recess.

"Every fuckin' one of those guys is a rat, but they don't have the balls to do it out in the open. They're rattin' on me to the newspapers and the TV people and they're lyin'. At least I'm up-front about it, and I'm tellin' the fuckin' truth."

As Sammy took the stand on the third day, he finally engaged Gotti in a long staredown. His face betrayed no trace of anger, guilt, or any other emotion except indifference. Gotti's had that thin smile of his, that wry smirk. Neither man blinked, and Sammy did not turn away until Gleeson began asking questions.

Moments later, a sixty-eight-year-old woman yanked open a rear door of the courtroom before guards were able to stop her and screamed at Sammy: "Murderer! I want to spit in his face!"

She was hustled away, but her niece stayed behind to

tell reporters that the woman believed Sammy had killed her two sons and that she "just lost it" when she peeked through a small window in the courtroom door and saw Sammy on the stand.

Sammy had not killed her sons, and although all denied it, someone in the Gotti group was no doubt behind her outburst.

More confident than ever, Sammy was not affected, by her or by the few other victims' mothers and relatives who came to watch him; following a brief recess, he returned to the stand and calmly fielded a series of questions about his nineteen murders.

"Sometimes I was a shooter," he summarized at one point. "Sometimes I was a backup shooter; sometimes I set the guy up; sometimes I just talked about it. When you go on a piece of work it doesn't matter what position you're in. You're all out there. You're all liable to get charged the same. It doesn't make any difference."

He said he told the truth about the murders because under his cooperation agreement, "It would be in my best interest not to get caught in a lie."

At the defense table Gotti motioned reporters to look at him, then tapped his chest, rolled his eyes, jerked his head toward Sammy, and pressed his hands together, like an altar boy.

With that, Sammy's direct examination came to end. It was now time for Krieger and Anthony Cardinale—a protégé of F. Lee Bailey's who came into the case at the last minute to represent LoCascio—to take their whacks at the star witness.

Through five days of relentless cross-examination, Sammy held his ground firmly. The hardest part was when Krieger boxed him into a corner and forced him to acknowledge that in Bensonhurst he would now be known as a "rat."

Sammy also was embarrassed when spectators laughed at his explanation for how his life of crime began.

"When I was a kid, I was involved in gangs, dropped out of school in the eighth grade. It didn't seem wrong; the whole lifestyle didn't seem wrong."

"In effect," Krieger mockingly responded, "the devil made me do it?"

"The devil didn't make me do it. I did it on my own. But the lifestyle helped."

But Sammy got spectators to laugh at Krieger, after Krieger asked what future Sammy would have faced if he had not decided to cooperate. "You would've faced a life sentence at Marion Federal Prison, where inmates are locked up in cages twenty-three hours a day and get one shower a week. Isn't that correct?"

"I believe it's two times a week."

It was one of Sammy's few biting rejoiners. For almost his entire time on the stand, he demonstrated great discipline and handled everything else that Krieger and Cardinale threw at him. He listened to questions and corrected built-in errors. One time, his patience under a blistering attack by Krieger elicited a wink from a woman juror, boosting his confidence ever more.

Laura Ward's father, a Southern District judge, had seen part of the direct examination, and returned to see some of the cross. "Sammy," he told his daughter, "is the best witness I have ever seen, and that goes for FBI agents. He's under control, he doesn't ramble, he should give them lessons."

Before and after court, Sammy's teammates kept him company. Before Sammy was taken to a witness-security unit at the MCC each night, Gleeson visited, only to say good night; trial protocol at this point did not permit them to discuss testimony, and Gleeson was as much a stickler for rules as his witness was.

One morning, Maloney brought Fox's organized-crime chief—Jules Bonavolonta, a former Special Forces captain in Vietnam—into the room where Sammy waited for court to begin.

"Sammy, this is Jules Bonavolonta, Bruce Mouw's boss. He's probably the only guy who's killed more people than you have. He was in 'Nam.'

On the third day of cross-examination, after Krieger began a series of questions about the December 12 tape, then asked for a sidebar, Sammy's eyes sought Gotti's for another staredown. This time Gotti did not smirk; if looks could kill, both men would have dropped dead in the courtroom.

When Krieger resumed and asked another question

about the tape, Sammy broke his reply into controlled, pointed parts.

"I didn't know. What took place. On December 12. Until I read these transcripts. And heard the tape."

Krieger tried to question Sammy about his brief flirtation with steroids, but Glasser ruled that the issue was immaterial. While Krieger unsuccessfully appealed the ruling in a sidebar, Gotti abruptly stood, waved at Sammy, mouthed the word "junkie" to reporters and plunged an imaginary syringe into his left arm.

Later on, however, near the end of nine remarkable days on the stand during which the retired underboss observed his forty-seventh birthday, Sammy plunged a tersely figurative dagger into Gotti that memorably summed up their five years atop the volcano: "I was a good, loyal soldier. John barked and I bit."

At the end of the ninth day, which like the last few began with a friendly "good morning" from jurors as he entered court to resume testifying, Sammy said good-bye to his new friends.

After one more night at the MCC, he would be taken to another witness-security unit in some other prison in another state, where he would be held until the next of many Gambino family cases now in the pipeline came to trial (such as the "severed" case of Tommy Gambino, who was found guilty and sentenced to five years in prison).

He was proud of his performance and determined to live up to his cooperation agreement, serve his five or ten years, and try to rebuild a life with Debra and his children. He had one final insight for John Gleeson:

"I know John Gotti. I read the guy like a newspaper. And I'm tellin' ya, he's accepted the fact that he's losing."

Essentially, the trial was over. Some mop-up work, the tax charges, remained, but all the heavy nails were in the coffin.

"The jury is ready to vote now," Pat Cotter told Gleeson. "Let's get this sucker wrapped up."

"I agree, but we can't count on anything. John's message to the jury is, 'I'm guilty, so what? You got to acquit me anyway.' We can't do much about that style of defense; that scares me."

Fittingly, the endgame featured one last celebrity visitor, Bruce Cutler. He arrived from Chicago, where he had just won a partial victory for that city's underboss, a couple of days after Sammy departed the stand. He watched the trial from a seat in the Gotti support section, but during recesses he went into the well of the courtroom and sat beside his role model.

A special prosecutor, appointed by Judge Glasser after the disqualification ruling, was now weighing whether Cutler should be held in criminal contempt of court for violating Glasser's order against out-of-court statements tending to jeopardize a fair trial. But if Cutler was in for a dime, he was in for a dollar, and so he kept on talking.

During one break, he ventured into the hallway to complain to reporters after Glasser refused to allow the defense to play a Ravenite excerpt in which Gotti blamed his problems on Gleeson. "They hate me ... prosecutors," Gotti said in the excerpt, after learning about some new subpoena. "If this is fuckin' Gleeson again, this fuckin' rat motherfucker again ..."

"The excerpt goes to John's state of mind," Cutler argued to his press jury. "John was thinking, 'This guy Gleeson's got a vendetta against me. He won't rest until I'm in jail.'"

Mostly, however, Cutler was in court to cheerlead, but it sounded more like whistling past the graveyard. "John's optimism is contagious," he said during another break, "you can feel it filling the courtroom."

Later that day, Gotti's unruly behavior while the jury was in the courtroom finally went beyond Judge Glasser's tolerance. The climactic moment came as Gleeson questioned a childhood friend of Gotti's, Anthony Gurino, whose plumbing company provided one of Gotti's phony income streams. As Gleeson bored in on Gurino, Gotti threw his arms up in disgust and swore loudly enough for Glasser to hear.

Glasser ordered the jury out, then stood and faced Gotti.

"Mr. Gotti, this is addressed to you. If you want to continue to remain at this trial and at that table, I am going to direct you to remain at that table without making comments which can be heard in the courtroom, without gestures which are designed to comment on the character of the U.S. attorneys, or the questions which are being asked of the witnesses. If you can't refrain from doing that, I will have you removed from the courtroom. You will watch this trial on a television screen downstairs. I am not going to tell you that again."

"That's your prerogative," Gotti barked back, standing now and gesturing at the prosecution table. "They don't need me to make gestures to describe them, that's for sure."

"Mr. Gotti, I don't want to engage in any debate about this with you."

"Neither do I."

"I am just putting you on notice."

"Neither do I," Gotti said again, insisting on, and getting, the last word. "I'm not here for a paycheck!"

He was not there to put up much of a defense either. On that same day, March 24, the prosecution rested its case. A day later, the defense rested, after calling one witness—the tax lawyer who had dubiously advised Gotti that he did not have to file income tax returns and who was destroyed by Gleeson on cross-examination.

None of the other crimes cited in the indictment—five murders, conspiracy to murder, bribery, loan-sharking, operating an illegal gambling game, obstruction of justice—were addressed by the defense, except on cross-examination.

The one-two punch of the tapes and Sammy had indeed made the case virtually indefensible, just as Gleeson had predicted when Sammy rolled over; the only defense was the one Gleeson had mused about with Cotter—the "I'm-guilty-so-what?" defense.

Gotti had been planting the seeds of that defense for the last five years, and while he may have endangered the harvest during trial with his unruly behavior, some shoots might have survived, and it did not matter whether jurors liked their taste, or were afraid to touch them; the payoff would be the same.

Still, given the hole the tapes and Sammy had put him in, it was shaky defense. During final arguments, Albert Krieger and LoCascio's lawyer, Anthony Cardinale, desperately sought to bolster it.

In his argument, Krieger called Sammy a "sick serial killer" and a "master of deception" who had only one product to sell—"John Gotti's head on a silver platter"—and said he sold it by making up a story that put Gotti in the middle of the Sparks plot.

Cardinale, on the other hand, went straight at Gleeson—because Gotti ordered him to. "What colors and shapes this prosecution is this overriding, overpowering desire and effort on Mr. Gleeson's part to get John Gotti at any cost, to do whatever it takes to win."

That was just the opening salvo of an intensely personal attack. Gotti enjoyed it so much he did not notice that several jurors were squirming uncomfortably; judging from a letter that one of them anonymously sent Andy Maloney later, they were squirming because they had come to admire Gleeson and believe in the integrity of the prosecution team.

In his final argument, which took a day, Gleeson called the evidence "suffocating." Alternating between soft-spoken outrage and gentle sarcasm, he dryly noted that the government did not make a sick, serial killer an underboss; John Gotti did.

"We'd love to bring you witnesses with absolutely impeccable credentials, of unquestionable honestly and integrity," he added, pointing at the defense table. "The problem is, they don't know any such people."

He reminded the jury that the apartment tapes contained only six hours of conversation. "It probably seems like more because the conversations are so dense with criminal activity. We caught six hours and it's absolute mayhem. Who they've murdered, who they're going to murder, why they have to murder."

Maloney also gave a summation, a much briefer one in which he told jurors that if they believed Gotti headed a "murderous and treacherous crime family, you would be less than human if you didn't feel some personal concern."

The remark brought Krieger, Cardinale, and a third defense lawyer, John Mitchell, screaming to their feet and demanding a mistrial. "This was a purposeful effort to throw a hand grenade into deliberations," Mitchell said after Glasser called for a sidebar. "It's not summation but an attempt to influence and prejudice."

As Maloney walked past the defense table on his way to the sidebar, Gotti muttered, "fuckin' bum"—but Maloney ignored it and told Glasser he was merely underscoring the obvious, that if the jury accepted the evidence "they'd be less than human if they didn't have some fear."

After all, back when the trial began, Glasser had injected fear into the equation by telling jurors that in the history of the Eastern District no one had even suffered personal harm as a result of jury service.

Even so, while denying a mistrial, Glasser did tell jurors to ignore Maloney's remark, and the furor dissipated as quickly as it had begun. It was time for the jury to deliberate.

For a RICO case, the jury did not deliberate long—fourteen hours over one and a half days. At one o'clock in the afternoon of April 2, 1992, the forewoman sent a note to Glasser that a verdict had been reached.

The jury's speed surprised all and touched off mad dashes to the courtroom; Glasser was known as a judge who did not waste any time once the jury sent its note, and thirteen minutes after the note arrived, Gotti was brought into the courtroom. The defense lawyers arrived from adjourned lunches a minute later, and they looked far gloomier than he—as if they were still denying what he had accepted, that the speedy verdict spelled doom for the "I'm-guilty-so-what?" defense.

Most of the prosecution team arrived in another minute, all but Pat Cotter, who was racing over from a nearby restaurant. At the eighteen-minute mark, with the spectator section still only about half full and Cotter rushing in and flinging his overcoat to an agent, Glasser ordered his courtroom clerk, Louise Schaillat, to call in the jury.

The fall of John Gotti was coming much faster than the rise, and at nineteen minutes past the hour, Schaillat stood and asked the anonymous jury forewoman the first of several questions: With regard to the first charge in the indictment, the one involving the murder of Paul Castellano, had the jury found whether the government had "proven" or "not proven" the charge?

"Proven," the forewoman replied.

Gotti winced, then smiled, then winked at his retinue in the spectator section, then smiled again as the forewoman kept saying "proven" about every count regarding him and all but a minor one regarding LoCascio.

During the rendering of the LoCascio verdicts, his son Tory screamed "Injustice!" but Gotti looked over and motioned for him to remain quiet.

Gotti turned to Krieger and, sounding as though he had resolved months earlier how he would comport himself in this situation, said, "We'll be all right, don't worry, we got the appeal, we'll continue to fight."

At the prosecution table, Maloney whispered into Gleeson's ear, "Magnificent, John, magnificent. You did a superb job."

"Thanks, Andy," Gleeson said, allowing himself the slightest of smiles. "We wouldn't be here if it weren't for you."

In the spectator section, Mouw and Gabriel shook hands and winked at other Gambino agents spread around the courtroom.

Moving right along, Glasser thanked the jurors, dismissed them, and said he would sentence Gotti in two months. Gotti stood, shook hands with his lawyers, kissed Krieger's wife, Irene, waved good-bye to his supporters, and ambled on out a rear door with his dour-looking acting consigliere and their guards.

Downstairs in the courthouse lobby, Jackie D'Amico dragged glumly on a Marlboro and said Gotti was a "class act" to the end. "When you're born round, you don't come out square."

Meanwhile, twenty feet away, Jim Fox was in the middle of a media knot. "The Teflon is gone," he said, throwing out a quote that his spokesman, Joseph Valiquette, had suggested during their hurried ride to the courthouse. "The Don is covered with Velcro."

Fox, Mouw, Gabriel, and the Gambino squad agents then went upstairs to Maloney's office to congratulate him, Gleeson, and the other prosecutors. Gleeson was on the telephone, saying to Diane Giacalone that what goes around comes around. Someone suggested they also telephone Sammy, and guards of the prison where he was brought him to the warden's office.

"Thanks, Sammy," Fox told him, "you did a great thing."

"I know. I know the mob don't say so. They say I'm

the biggest rat of all, but I don't give a shit anymore. That life's over, the life's dead. Fuckin' bury it."

On June 23, except for Sammy, the trial's main participants returned to the courthouse for sentencing. Because of the federal sentencing guidelines, which handcuffed Glasser into giving Gotti and LoCascio multiple life terms in prison without any chance of parole, the only potential drama was what Gotti would say when Glasser gave him the obligatory chance to speak.

But Gotti said nothing. He stood with his arms folded and smiled his usual smile. Instead, LoCascio assumed the role of designated speaker: "I am guilty of being a good friend of John Gotti. If there were more men like John Gotti on this earth, we would have a better country."

Gotti also let others do his talking—about one thousand people, mainly from Ozone Park and Howard Beach, who arrived in chartered buses outside the courthouse just as Gotti bounced on his little feet out of the courtroom without so much as a wink or a nod to anyone in the duly assembled press corps. In the end, the media had done him no good.

Outside, the crowd marched toward the courthouse entrance and began chanting, "Free John Gotti!" Several hotheads in the crowd, egged on by members of Junior Gotti's crew shouting into bullhorns, began rocking a police car and, before long, three cars lay on their roofs and a riot was on.

Inside, as the crowd surged forward and began fighting with an outmanned squad of cops, federal guards barred the courthouse doors and stood back from a floor-to-ceiling wall of glass at the front entrance. Standing in the lobby, watching the riot unfold with Mouw and Fox, Gabriel said sarcastically, "John always told me he would go quietly if we ever got him. That John, he's a man, a man's man."

The NYPD rushed over another hundred cops to beat back the demonstrators. Several cops were injured and given first aid in the lobby, near where the FBI men stood. "John would have the world believe this was a spontaneous demonstration," Fox said, shaking his head. "Pathetic."

By this time, Gotti was already back at the MCC. Unlike LoCascio, he would not spend the night there; when it came to Gotti, federal prison officials wasted no time in implementing the sentence. In a few hours more, guards took him out of his cell, placed him in shackles, and drove him to an airport. There, the man with a well-known fear of flying was turned over to other guards and put on a government plane bound for Marion, Illinois—home of the most punitive prison in the federal system, one that Amnesty International calls inhumane.

Before the sun rose again, he was in solitary confinement, where he would remain, twenty-three hours a day, every day—until at some future point in time prison officials decided that he was a beaten man and could play by regular prison rules.

A day later, back in Howard Beach, John Joseph Gotti Sr., the father he never respected, would die of old age—but four months later Junior Gotti's wife would give birth to a boy, who was promptly named John.

"What's my reaction to the birth?" Bruce Cutler said when a reporter called for comment, not long before Cutler was charged with criminal contempt of court for violating Judge Glasser's prohibition against out-of-court statements that tended to prejudice a fair trial.

"My reaction is that the world is a better place with another John Gotti "

Epilogue

These days, one of John Gotti's pleasures in life is to be able to sit in a chair. He has no chair in his six-by-eight-foot cell at the United States Penitentiary in Marion, Illinois—the most restrictive prison in the federal system when he arrived in 1992. All he has is a radio, a twelve-inch black-and-white TV, single cot, a basin, and a toilet.

But five times a month, when he is allowed visitors, Gotti gets to sit in a chair in the inmate visiting room, on one side of a partition separating him from well-wishers. At other times, in his cell, he makes a chair out of his mattress—by folding it into a L shape and propping the short side against a wall. It beats lying on his back all day.

He is confined to his cell twenty-two to twenty-three hours a day. Prison officials refuse to say when he will qualify for a less onerous regimen or be housed in a regular maximum-security prison, where he could fraternize with other inmates. Most Marion inmates under life sentences are transferred out after thirty months, but by October 1995—more than three years after he got there—Gotti still had not made it out of the worst of three levels of confinement.

Prison officials will not say why, or whether they plan to send him to an even harsher federal prison in Colorado that has opened in the meantime. Gotti's lawyers are loathe to talk about his still being in the most restrictive level of confinement at Marion—for fear of prolonging the situation. But it is a good bet that Gotti has not proved himself to be the model prisoner yet. The problem would not be behavior—it is virtually impossible to misbehave at Marion; it would be his attitude. The institution abhors a defiant attitude.

His lawyers do say he still gets up to a hundred letters a week, many from crackpots but also many from strangers wishing him well and asking how to confront crises in their own lives. Once in a while, he will ask his lawyers to write someone back for him—maybe a lady whose aunt has cancer.

Mainly, he reads, watches and listens to talk shows, and does push-ups, usually one thousand a day. His legal appeals have been exhausted. The only hope is bribing a president.

In addition to his five monthly visiting periods, he is allowed to make two fifteen-minute collect phone calls. His visitors include Bruce Cutler and another lawyer who became close to the Gotti clan during the second federal trial, Anthony Cardinale, as well as personal-family members, especially his son Junior.

Gotti is still the boss of the Gambino family, the FBI says, and Junior is his acting boss—a situation that Sammy Gravano had imagined would happen someday, back when Gotti—knowing a "big pinch" was coming—promoted Junior to capo.

The FBI says that Junior, now thirty-one years old and no longer wearing his Walkman earphones, is somehow able to decipher his father's wishes when they talk at Marion—even though the visits are monitored by prison guards. Junior allegedly uses his Uncle Peter and Jack D'Amico to spread the word to the capos trying to ride out the thunderstorm of cases brought on by Sammy's co-operation.

Here's how it went for other characters in this story:

George Pape, the corrupt juror who helped Gotti to the top of the volcano, was convicted of bribery and served two years in prison. Pape's bagman, Westies boss Bosko Radonjich, was last seen in the country formerly known as Yugoslavia.

Joe Butch Corrao, who broke a Gotti rule against making any admissions and pleaded guilty to bribing NYPD detective William Peist, was sentenced to seventy months in prison. He won't get out of prison until two days after Christmas in 1998.

Peist, who pleaded guilty to taking Gambino graft for

four years, is scheduled for release two days before Christmas, 1999.

Jimmy Brown Failla and Danny Marino, closet allies of Chin Gigante, also broke Gotti's rule against admissions and pleaded guilty to conspiring to kill Tommy Spinelli, the Failla soldier they were afraid was wilting in the face of Walter Mack grand jury heat. They will not leave prison until the year 2000, assuming that they live.

Failla is seventy-five and suffering a variety of ailments. For his own well-being, Marino was put in segregated confinement after his alliance with Chin was revealed by Anthony Casso, the Luchese underboss, who "did a Sammy" and became a cooperating witness to try to save himself from a life behind bars. In another example of what hard times Cosa Nostra fell upon, Casso's acting boss did a Sammy too.

The unmade man who was Paul's pal, Sammy's pal, and then Gotti's pal, Joe Watts, rejected the seven-year deal that Failla and Marino took and was to go trial in early 1996 for helping to murder Paul, Bilotti, and Spinelli. He was never officially implicated in the murder of the emotionally disturbed man who fired a shot at Gotti outside the Bergin.

Casso, who car-bombed Frank DeCicco to smithereens but could never get Gotti alone, was scheduled to testify against the man who anointed him to do the work, Chin Gigante. After more than half a decade of delays, however, it was still doubtful in early 1996 whether the ex-boxer was going to have to stand trial in the case that was finally brought against him.

Tommy Gambino—who was indicted with Gotti and LoCascio, then severed for a separate trial—was found guilty, but of lesser charges resulting in a comparatively benign five-year sentence, which he began serving in January 1996.

His former codefendant, LoCascio, was serving his life sentence in another federal prison in the Midwest, a less onerous one in Terre Haute, Indiana.

Drug-dealing caporegime John Gambino and Bobby Bisaccia, the New Jersey hood who became a capo after he helped carry out the murder of a man who accidentally killed a John Gambino crew member during a fistfight, both got long prison stretches for conspiring to kill

Francesco Oliveri. Gambino pleaded guilty; Bisaccia was convicted at trial.

Sparks enabler and retired consigliere Joe N. Gallo was showing great staying power for someone eighty-three years old. He was released from prison in June 1995, after "maxing out."

Would-be adopted son and assistant press secretary Lewis Kasman went to prison, too. He had dissembled when called into the Eastern District grand jury and was indicted for perjury. He pleaded guilty, served six months, and was released in July 1995.

Carlo Vaccarezza, like his upscale restaurant, Da Noi, went south very fast. With more FBI agents than customers in the restaurant on some days, Vaccarezza threw in the towel and left for Miami, where he reentered the restaurant business.

Another friend of Gotti's, Lisa Gastineau, was managing a boutique and modeling on the side. "I have great affection for him," was all she wanted to say when contacted. "I was really disappointed to learn he was never coming home."

On the other hand, John Gleeson—the young prosecutor when the Gotti saga began, the sage one when it ended—was nominated for a federal judgeship by President Bill Clinton, and he took the oath on October 24, 1994, the third anniversary of his dramatic face-to-face with Sammy, the first underboss to testify against his boss in a court of law.

Former midshipman Bruce Mouw won the Justice Department's highest award for employee achievement—for getting Gotti and for a decade's worth of other accomplishments as Gambino squad boss.

Mouw and case agent George Gabriel joined assistant U.S. attorney Laura Ward to build RICO cases against what little was left of the legacy Gotti wanted to build and then moved on to new assignments. Andy Maloney, after a changing of the White House guard, went back to private practice with a top Manhattan law firm.

Patrick Cotter, the *malliocchia* in John Gotti's mind, was in private practice in Chicago after teaching for a year in Ireland, where all the students wanted to hear about was the Teflon Don. James Orenstein was working organized-crime cases, focusing on Sammy's first mob affiliation, the Colombo family.

Robert Morgenthau was still district attorney of Manhattan and the most influential local prosecutor in the country. Walter Mack, after a couple of years of working on Wall Street, returned to government to be the chief of the NYPD's anti-corruption unit. He later clashed with a new police commissioner and went back to Wall Street again.

Albert Krieger, the last-minute stand-in for Bruce Cutler, resumed the practice of defense law in Miami, where he was still considered one of the greatest defenders in the land. His colleague at the second federal trial, Anthony Cardinale, got a break when Judge Glasser retracted a threat to put him in jail for excessively unruly objections to the judge's rulings.

The first important lawyer in John Gotti's life, Michael Coiro, was convicted again, this time for lying in the Eastern District grand jury about his one visit to Nettie's place, and he won't get out of prison until 1997.

The most prominent lawyer in Gotti's life, Bruce Cutler, was convicted of criminal contempt of court for violating Judge Glasser's order against out-of-court prejudicial statements. He was sentenced to three months' home detention.

However, a grand jury investigating Cutler and another key lawyer in Gotti's life, Jerry Shargel, for funny business on tax returns and obstruction of justice went out of business without returning an indictment.

On Staten Island, Sammy's son Gerard, who dropped his pants and mooned reporters when he was arrested for assault after some silly traffic brouhaha, was graduated from high school, won a dismissal of his case, and left New York with his sister, Karen, and his mother, Debra—who sold the home that her husband's criminality had bought. Officially, Debra and Sammy arrived at an amicable divorce settlement, but they may be reunited someday soon in a place where no one knows their names, or their true history.

On September 26, 1994, in the same courtroom where Sammy had pointed a damning finger at Gotti eighteen months before, a last piece of business from *U.S. v. Gotti, et al.* was wrapped up.

Sammy, who had gone on to testify in several other trials, was brought before Judge I. Leo Glasser to learn what his RICO sentence would be. Before sentencing, John Gleeson and others praised him as the most important cooperating witness against Cosa Nostra in U.S. history.

With many of the ninety law enforcement officials who had attested in letters to his value and truthfulness on hand for the sentencing hearing, Glasser declared Sammy a changed man and gave him a penalty of five years in prison.

Because he had been in prison since late 1990, the sentence meant that he would be free to start a new life soon after he turned fifty in March 1995, which is what happened. It was almost the best-case scenario that Sammy had hoped for when he made his biggest chess move.

"I hope they won't be disappointed," said Glasser, referring to Sammy's new law enforcement friends.

"They won't be, your honor."